Redirecting Ethnic Singularity

Critical Studies in Italian America

Nancy C. Carnevale and Laura E. Ruberto, *series editors*

This series publishes works on the history and culture of Italian Americans by emerging as well as established scholars in fields such as anthropology, cultural studies, folklore, history, and media studies. While focusing on the United States, it also includes comparative studies with other areas of the Italian diaspora. The books in this series engage with broader questions of identity pertinent to the fields of ethnic studies, gender studies, and migration studies, among others.

Series Board

Marcella Bencivenni

Simone Cinotto

Thomas J. Ferraro

Edvige Giunta

Joseph Sciorra

Pasquale Verdicchio

Redirecting Ethnic Singularity

Italian Americans and Greek Americans in Conversation

Yiorgos Anagnostou, Yiorgos Kalogeras, and Theodora Patrona, Editors

FORDHAM UNIVERSITY PRESS
NEW YORK 2022

Copyright © 2022 Fordham University Press

All rights reserved. No part of this publication may be reproduced, stored in a retrieval system, or transmitted in any form or by any means—electronic, mechanical, photocopy, recording, or any other—except for brief quotations in printed reviews, without the prior permission of the publisher.

Fordham University Press has no responsibility for the persistence or accuracy of URLs for external or third-party Internet websites referred to in this publication and does not guarantee that any content on such websites is, or will remain, accurate or appropriate.

Fordham University Press also publishes its books in a variety of electronic formats. Some content that appears in print may not be available in electronic books.

Visit us online at www.fordhampress.com.

Library of Congress Cataloging-in-Publication Data available online at https://catalog.loc.gov.

Printed in the United States of America

24 23 22   5 4 3 2 1

First edition

CONTENTS

Preface: Una faccia, una razza / μια φάτσα μια ράτσα:
More to It Than Meets the Eye   vii
FRED L. GARDAPHÉ

Introduction: Italian Americans and Greek Americans
in Conversation   1
YIORGOS ANAGNOSTOU, YIORGOS KALOGERAS,
AND THEODORA PATRONA

Part I. Constructing, Historicizing, and Contesting Identities

"Dirty Dagoes" Respond: A Transnational History of a
Racial Slur   23
ANDONIS PIPEROGLOU

A Greek American Vice President? The View from the
Italian American Community   46
STEFANO LUCONI

Mediterranean Americans to Themselves   72
JIM COCOLA

Part II. Identity Construction in Two Ethnic Communities

Style and Real Estate: The Architecture of Faith among
Greek and Italian Immigrants, 1870–1925   105
KOSTIS KOURELIS

Ethnic Language Education: A Comparative Study of Greek
Americans and Italian Americans in New York City 141
ANGELYN BALODIMAS-BARTOLOMEI AND FEVRONIA K. SOUMAKIS

Part III. Ethnic and Gender Identities in Literature and Music

Identity, Family, and Cultural Heritage: Narrative Polymorphy
in *Let Me Explain You* and *Catina's Haircut* 185
ELEFTHERIA ARAPOGLOU

Ethnic Investigations of the American Crime Scene:
Comparing Domenic Stansberry and George Pelecanos 210
FRANCESCA DE LUCIA

Imaginative Living in Mediterranean New England 238
PANAYOTIS LEAGUE

Part IV. Ethnic Identities and Visual Culture

An Ethnic Can't Be Like Other People? The Construction of
Greek Americans and Italian Americans in *Kojak* 271
SOSTENE MASSIMO ZANGARI

Irrevocable or Irreversible? Authenticating Identities in
Italian and Greek Immigration Documentaries 298
YIORGOS KALOGERAS

American(ish) Rebels: Class, Gender, and Ethnicity in
Moonstruck and *My Big Fat Greek Wedding* 323
MICHAIL C. MARKODIMITRAKIS

Afterword: Beyond Methodological Singularity 351
DONNA R. GABACCIA

Acknowledgments 365
List of Contributors 367
Index 373

PREFACE: UNA FACCIA, UNA RAZZA / μια φάτσα μιά ράτσα: MORE TO IT THAN MEETS THE EYE

Fred L. Gardaphé

"One face, one race." I can't tell you how many times I've heard this expression when it came to comparing Italian Americans to Greek Americans. I first recognized the significance of this phrase when George Kanelos was introduced to me as simply "Greek." That was his nickname, and it joined the roll call of our neighborhood friends who, in childhood, found ways of uniting ourselves through our differences by baptizing each other with the new names of our own making. Now, Greek taught us there really wasn't much difference in our ancestral backgrounds. Why, didn't he celebrate Easter, like us Catholics? Even if it was a week or two after ours. His mother cooked lamb for that day's meal, just like ours. His moussaka was like our eggplant parmesan; his father's ouzo could have been Nonno's anisette. Greek danced in our circles and fought to protect us when threatened. Yes, there was more to the connection than simply a face; cultural and religious affinities transcended bodies, turning strangers into friends for life.

This connection was broadened and deepened through my studies of Greek and Roman cultures in high school, and through those studies I learned to see how cultures touch and shape each other. Through my studies of Latin and ancient Greek, I came to better understand my native English language and to see how much of what I had taken for granted in my daily speech had already been shaped by the pasts of these two cultures. I learned of Magna Grecia, which much later, in 2005, became the focus of an entire conference of the then American Italian Historical Association (now known as the Italian American Studies Association). There I learned from the many papers presented that Italy had become the place to which

Greeks feeling the pressures of war and political unrest would migrate, the same way that contemporary Africans flee to Italy. Those migrating Greeks formed colonies in places such as Tarentum in Puglia; Sybaris, Terina, and Croton in Calabria and Basilicata; Naxos and Catania in Sicily; in Campania, where Napoli comes to us from the Greek name Neapolis, "new city." This sharing of cultures and languages continued over the centuries through the traditional studies of ancient cultures and the evolution of the Christian religion.

Without those studies, the public covers of these cultures become stereotypes, often all that most people know; they become possible realities, when all they mean to do is make the storytelling easier than it should be. Stereotypes, so useful in telling stories but dangerous in writing history, mask those hybrid identities built from class aspirations and social mobility enabled by whiteness, creating cultural anxieties that often lead to social conflicts. While there might be a shared genetic heritage between Greeks and Italians greater than that overused phrase *"una faccia, una razza"* suggests, there is more than genetics at work in the dynamics of their cultural interaction, as you will see in reading this volume. *Redirecting Ethnic Singularity: Italian Americans and Greek Americans in Conversation* represents the first academic attempt to bring these two US ethnic groups into dialogue on the pages of a single volume. As such, it points to a bright future in comparative studies of American ethnicities.

Yiorgos Anagnostou, Yiorgos Kalogeras, and Theodora D. Patrona have dedicated much of their professional careers exploring the impact of Greek immigrant culture in the development of US culture, and the fruits of their labors have led them to this collection of essays, which compare these two Mediterranean-based cultures. I first encountered these scholars at conferences organized by the Society for the Study of Multi-Ethnic Studies: Europe and the Americas (MESEA) and the John D. Calandra Italian American Institute. Kalogeras gave lectures at the Calandra Institute and Queens College when he was a visiting professor, supported by the Onassis Foundation. Each of them has proven to be a formidable presence in the study of Greek American culture and pioneers in the process of comparative studies of Greek and Italian Americans.

This publication is a milestone in the evolution of comparative ethnic studies in US culture in revealing the knowledge that can be created when borders are crossed and contact zones explored. I was surprised at how much I learned from reading each of the essays. Yes, it takes time to have the means to shape an environment through real estate, but when that time and the resources became available to each immigrant group, they first took what was there, adapted to it, and then made it their own by rehabilitating old structures and using new architectural designs to make their spaces reflect their ancestral cultures. Through social organizations like the *kinoitis* and the *società del mutuo soccorso*, they began to take care of the needs that weren't met by the existing social support structures already in place when they arrived, creating spaces of solidarity where they could maintain their differences while they tried to fit into what was expected of the American citizen. From their earliest jobs they built financial foundations that enabled future generations to take advantage of educational opportunities that enabled them the social mobility they sought. Schooling, which began as private for the Greeks and public for the Italians, became a key in fostering that mobility, and through this volume we come to understand how each group achieved the same result through different ways.

Along the way to Americanization, each group dealt with discrimination and prejudice that often appeared in derogatory language and epithets such as "dago," a transnational slur that had to be overcome. As each group began to work outside and inside the political systems in place they came to participate in a democracy that had its roots in Greece and a republic that had its roots in Italy. Together they have joined other immigrants from the Mediterranean region, but just how useful can that category be in the attempt to better understand the historical and political implications of their status as ethnic Americans?

In this volume you will find studies of poets, journalists, novelists, filmmakers, actors, television stars, bodybuilders, wrestlers, and politicians that reveal similarities to and differences from other Americans in the same professions, as each individual engages social realities through the lenses of his and her unique ethnic perspective on the fundamentals of American life: the family and the individual, the group among other groups, the artists among the philistines. You will see that we have come a long way from Michael Novak's popularization of the term "PIGS," those Poles, Italians, Greeks, and Slavs who failed to disappear in the great melting pot metaphor. But where are they all headed? The answers to this and many other questions can be found in these pages. Through concepts such as "paraethnicity" and "polymorphy" these scholars attempt to forge new ways of understanding the importance and prevalence of understanding the need to maintain ethnic identities into the twenty-first century (often labeled as "postethnic,") and how they've changed over time. As Yiorgos Kalogeras suggests in his contribution, a postethnic identity depends on locating a usable past upon which to build approaches toward the future. We need to recognize that which has been sloughed off and that which remains in order for us to continue to use ethnicity as a means of locating similarities and differences as we build viable identities that will be useful as we contemplate the future.

Reading these essays at this point in my life and career as an ethnic scholar and a scholar of ethnic cultures has changed the way I look back at my upbringing in a working-class suburb of Chicago, where I worked for Johnny the Greek in his Italian beef sandwich stand; where my brother Michael worked as a busboy in his godfather Louie's Golden Horns restaurant; where tough guys like Gus Alex held court at Tom's Steak House, where Paul Karas served breakfast and lunch in his tiny diner across the street from my grandfather's pawnshop; where Jimmy and George ran the Confectionery, an after-school hangout for local teenagers. There was Terry, who once stood on a bucket to wash the dishes at the snack bar of Portes's Drug Store and grew up to own Ki's Restaurant, one of my favorite hangouts when I return to the Chicago area. All of these men formed a long line of public personae who looked and seemed to act like the Italians in my neighborhood, but who I was to find out later were actually Greek. These essays have also added to my better understanding of the role that Greek women, whom we hardly saw in public, played in their culture and ours, and for that I thank these able editors for putting together this unique collection of essays.

Redirecting Ethnic Singularity

INTRODUCTION

Italian Americans and Greek Americans in Conversation

Yiorgos Anagnostou, Yiorgos Kalogeras, and Theodora Patrona

This volume contributes to US ethnic and immigration studies by bringing into conversation scholars working in the fields of Italian American and Greek American studies in the United States, Europe, and Australia. The work moves beyond the "single group approach"—an approach that privileges the study of ethnic singularity—to explore instead two ethnic groups in relation to each other, primarily in the broader context of the United States and secondarily in Greece, in Italy, and in one specific case Australia.[1] The chapters bring into focus transcultural interfaces and inquire comparatively about similarities and differences in cultural representations associated with these two groups.[2]

This conversation is necessary for several reasons, one certainly in relation to a powerful academic discourse that often tends to undervalue the study of European Americans. Seen as tenuously holding onto surface identities and largely assimilated into "whiteness," Italian Americans and Greek

Americans have been marginalized by a significant sector of the US academy. Italian American and Greek American studies have certainly been effective, the former more so than the latter, in bringing into focus the vibrant cultural production of their respective ethnic groups. Indeed, one might speak about a proliferation of research on food, community history, diaspora affiliations, transnational connections, literature, and popular culture, among other topics. Since the 1960s, scholars have begun responding to the devaluation of their subject matter by establishing in their publications its academic and public value. They bring to the fore the arts, cultural expressivities, and histories of these two groups, demonstrating how Italian American and Greek American ethnicities keep shaping American society and their respective historical homelands.

Our book contributes to these developments from a particular angle, namely transcultural and comparative scholarship. The volume reflects our interest in promoting the understanding of Italian Americans and Greek Americans through the study of their interactions and juxtapositions. This is rarely practiced in the scholarship of European Americans.[3] Initiating a broader conversation that moves beyond seeing ethnicity as singularity, the chapters come closer to ethnographic, popular culture, and historical realities.

Immigrants and individuals connected with hyphenated identities do not live insular lives, nor do they negotiate solely in relation with "American culture."[4] Instead, they interact, collaborate, clash, and affiliate with each other in various modes and degrees.[5] How do the groups' experiences both converge and diverge in matters of music, sensory memory, and affect? What do we know about the fields of their interactions? In what manner does popular culture represent all this? The transcultural and comparative angle of this volume illuminates new and unexpected facets of Greek and Italian ethnicity in the United States.

The book explores Greek and Italian US encounters and coexistence, both at the level of ethnography and political discourse—a musical gathering, for instance, and national electoral politics—as well as of media representation. The analysis of the transcultural encounters in various chapters takes cues from concepts such as contact zones, focusing on social dynamic processes involving negotiation, conflict, cooperation, solidarity, and cultural exchanges that have marked these encounters. We identify differences, similarities, and intersections across the historical experiences of these groups. We map specific encounters and comparisons to find out what they tell us about American society as a transcultural terrain.

Greek Americans and Italian Americans have certainly been classified under the same rubric as "white ethnics," but also as "probationary whites," in Matthew Frye Jacobson's ironic term.[6] The concept of kinship implied in the chapters focuses on personal relations and the practices that maintain them rather than on group membership with its attendant othering of nongroup entities; it champions boundary crossing over boundary maintenance. Our contributors emphasize the seemingly natural but ultimately unstable logic of whiteness, probing the classification of Greek Americans and Italian Americans into joint racial categories and identifying the cultural and political specificities that nuance the historical negotiation of these groups with whiteness.

Embracing the Comparative Approach

We embrace the comparative approach in this work as a method to explore ethnicity relationally: how the practices of one ethnic group illuminate the practices of the other. Both groups have built robust religious and educational institutions. In what ways are their adaptations and cultural expressions similar, and in what ways are they different in specific contexts? How do we account for the similarities and differences? While the two groups have been classified in relatively similar situated ethnoracial otherness, their historical experiences also differ markedly. For instance, the negative association of Italian Americans as enemy aliens and criminals—during World War II and through the Mafia discourse respectively—differentiates them from the US Greek experience. There is also the issue of regional variations within each group. Ethnic groups encountered different social dynamics on the East Coast and the West Coast, and in turn they negotiated their place in society differently. The chapters register regional historical realities in addition to national ones. They explore how Italian American and Greek American authors and cultural producers have represented their ethnicities in literature, film, and documentary. They also ask how the two groups have been represented on television. All in all, in what ways did Italian American and Greek American histories, experiences, self-representations, and representations by others converge or diverge?

Our volume contributes to the fields of transcultural and comparative studies. The book is multidisciplinary. It features scholarship from the perspectives of architecture, ethnomusicology, education, history, cultural and literary studies, and film studies, as well as whiteness studies. It examines the production of ethnicity in the context of American political culture as well as popular culture, both visual and "lowbrow" crime fiction. It includes analysis of literature. It involves comparative work on religious architecture, transoceanic circulation of racialized categories, translocal interconnections in the formation of pan-Mediterranean identities, and the making of the immigrant past in documentaries from Italian and Greek filmmakers. This volume is the first of its kind in initiating a multidisciplinary transcultural and comparative study across European Americans.

Comparisons, Encounters, Identities

Comparison is a vested practice. A scholar's selection of the entities to compare and the aim of bringing them in relation to each other result from particular interests. The juxtaposition of two groups of people, for instance, may serve the purpose of understanding the Self via the study of the Other or understanding each other. Both endeavors value communication across cultures. Comparison may also be driven by the desire to fashion grand theories about humanity, a product of both academic paradigms—evolutionism, structuralism—vying for institutional power, and personal vision. Both epistemological and political interests are at play in the examples given here. There is no such thing as neutral comparison. Any claim to its practice, therefore, requires the explicit recognition of the motivations that drive it.

Our interest in connecting Italian Americans and Greek Americans speaks to several interrelated institutional and epistemological exigencies. Our project is a response to the largely unheeded call to move beyond the "single group" approach in the study of European Americans. The rationale for this move is that cross-cultural analysis can yield new insights about immigration and ethnicity in the United States that otherwise might remain invisible. In moving toward this direction, we foreground the importance of Italian American and Greek American studies—two relatively undervalued fields of study—for contemporary conversations about immigrant integration, transatlantic circulations, cultural preservation, the making of whiteness, representations of ethnicity in US popular culture, tactical political solidarities, and the forging of intercultural bonds.

The comparative approach concerns itself with similarities as well as dissimilarities. In its exploration of difference, our project makes the case further for rethinking a host of academic assumptions that have had a major effect in the marginalization of the two academic fields under discussion. It is not rare for one to hear members of dissertation committees speaking—formally or informally—about early twentieth-century immigrants from southeastern Europe as a uniform phenomenon: poverty-stricken illiterate, patriarchal peasants, deeply immersed in religious beliefs and superstition. It is common also for one to read about the superficial ethnic affiliations of contemporary "white ethnics" and their eventual decline or even apocalyptic loss. Greek Americans and Italian Americans are assumed as already known, unworthy of further research. The denial of their value in the academic marketplace discourages junior scholars from engaging these topics. Our project sets itself against this epistemological bias, seeking to curve conceptual spaces such as "transnational Mediterranean" and "US Southeastern Europeans" to promote new knowledge about these subject matters. In this manner we contribute to the empowering of Italian American and Greek American studies.

What is the reasoning for selecting these two particular peoples for the comparative exercise? Our departure point is a recurrent commonality. We build on the sociological fact that both groups have been classified similarly in various historical periods by powerful social discourses. Both were seen as "racially in-between" people in the era of early twentieth-century mass migration; they were the probationary whites, not "fully white," not "fully nonwhite." They were put in the same category as "white ethnics" in the context of ethnic and racial competition for material and symbolic resources as well as the struggle for public cultural visibility in the tumultuous 1970s.

And both are now rendered as "symbolic ethnics," with thin and readily disposable ethnic affiliations. Throughout the twentieth century, US Italians and Greeks encountered and grappled with assigned normative classifications. How did they negotiate this constitutive historical experience?

This route to comparison raises the issue of self-representation. It opens up the terrain to examine comparatively how two groups subjected to similar external representations worked out issues of survival, dignity, making a home, integration, mobility, status, and cultural reproduction. What cultural resources did they activate in their respective negotiations? What set of cultural resources was selected over another? What were the implications of these processes to each group? How did they contribute specifically to a particular trajectory of cultural change? What was retained (or modified) for contemporary purposes? Our comparative endeavor aims to generate insights about these topics that we would not have been able to identify had we stayed with the study of a single group.

We approach Italian and Greek transnational communities as internally differentiated. We view immigration and ethnicity as a dynamic social process whose comparison contributes to our understanding, of "how similarly or differently it is experienced in different locations and by different populations by gender, national origin, age," and other sociological variables.[7] We carefully attend to how and who resisted, manipulated, or even contributed to the making of these groups. Understanding how agency was mobilized, by whom, and for what purpose is of central importance in this endeavor.

US Italians and Greeks exhibit significant historical and social differences. Their respective demographics, both in the past and the present, are of a scale that is incomparable. The massive influx of Italian migration took place between 1870 and 1920 with 4.1 million people entering the country, ranking Italians as the second largest group of Europeans in the United States after the Germans.[8] A significantly smaller group, 450,000 Greeks entered the United States in the period of mass migration (1890–1924),[9] with the numbers on the increase again in the period between 1946 and 1982, reaching 211,000.[10] More recently, the 2010 census shows that 17.6 million identified themselves as Italian Americans and 1.3 million as Greek Americans.[11] While the 2020 census data are still being processed, Robert Oppedisano estimates an increase in the number of people who identified themselves as

Italian Americans; this increase between the 2010 and the 2020 census, according to Oppedisano, results from a need of people to "maintain their cultural identity."[12]

An additional variable is how their respective religious affiliations shaped the social organization of their communities and the visual communication of their identities via religious architecture. On the political front, the fact that their historical homelands allied with opposing camps during World War II deeply affected their place in the United States and their aspirations to national belonging. Let us also take into account those historical moments in which Greece and Italy figured differently in the American national imagination, affecting the perception, status, and cultural production of their diaspora populations in the United States.

The comparative angle foregrounds the manner in which these differences played out in the respective ethnic negotiations in specific sociohistorical moments. How did each group handle adversity? How did it capitalize on favorable conditions? Under what circumstances did they forge alliances and intercultural communities? In what way did authors, political elites, and ordinary citizens negotiate difference, and to what end? This volume casts light on how US Greeks and Italians navigated historically situated difference and similarity.

Italian Americans and Greek Americans shared structural similarities. A host of common problems shaped their immigrant and later ethnic lives: survival as economically and socially vulnerable groups; protection (importance of kin and regional relations; residential clustering); confrontation of negative stereotypes; suburbanization and the issue of cultural reproduction (education, family); self-representation; and social and economic empowerment. Usually scholars discuss these issues under the rubrics of adaptation, cultural preservation, and cultural politics. Comparison sheds light on how similarly situated groups negotiate their predicament. It asks how different histories and cultural positioning (beliefs, attitudes, cultural capital) lead to different or similar solutions to a common problem.

Notions of similarity, however, should be treaded cautiously. Italian and Greek immigrants in the early twentieth century were for the most part impoverished peasants migrating from agricultural areas of their respective countries. In the case of the Greeks, migration had a starting point in the

Middle East as well, an ever-expanding diaspora. On the other hand, there was a clear divide between the Italians who arrived in the United States from the north and those who arrived from southern Italy, the Mezzogiorno. It will be therefore erroneous if their shared "peasant" status is treated as a measure of sameness. We know that Greek and southern Italian peasants were positioned differently in relation to the market economy, and in turn they placed themselves differently in relation to US capitalist modernity. Knowledge about the workings of the market furnished cultural capital that guided the entrepreneurial orientation of Greek immigrants in the niche economy of small businesses at the time. Italian and Greek immigrants possessed different sets of beliefs and aspirations regarding the importance of education in social mobility and the connection between education and family cohesion. Belonging to the similar socioeconomic category "peasant," then, is not evidence of a fundamental sameness. If comparison is to avoid erroneous analogies, it must historicize the entities that it brings next to each other.

What histories, cultural, and political processes have connected Greek Americans and Italian Americans? To begin with, why were they both part of the early twentieth-century mass migration to the United States? How did policies of their respective states and regional economies bring them together on the same ship headed for Ellis Island? Or later, in the tumultuous 1960s and 1970s, in what way did the civil rights movement and its aftermath shape US Italian and Greek political interconnections? What brings them together today in musical gatherings in the contemporary United States, and how does this coexistence challenge conventional notions of ethnic identity? In what way did Italian and Greek authors capitalize on the American genre of crime fiction to place their respective ethnicities in popular culture? In what manner do second-generation Italians and Greeks negotiate historically specific ethnic patriarchies? Close attention to the context in which texts are produced, human mobility materialized, cultural expressions animated, and cultural categories generated is of paramount importance for meaningful comparisons.

Contributors to this volume practice the mode of what Bruce Lincoln endorses as "weak comparisons." Unlike comparative projects aspiring to reveal universal truths or general patterns, weak comparisons work on a different scale, at the level of the particular. They set in motion "inquiries that are modest in scope, but intensive in scrutiny, treating a small number of examples in depth and detail, setting each in its full and proper context."[13] In this approach, the necessary task of the comparativist entails careful reflection about the processes producing commonalities or differences, the contexts in which they are deployed, and the specific human agents who cultivate and deploy them for specific purpose. This volume mobilizes this comparative endeavor not only to illuminate anew the histories and cultures of Italian Americans and Greek Americans but also to start opening new analytical routes toward the understanding of southeastern or Mediterranean European Americans.

The Sections and the Chapters

For the editors of this volume, a series of fundamental questions is addressed by the contributors: How did each group negotiate externally imposed categories? What cultural resources did they activate? Why were particular resources and not others chosen? What were the strategies of negotiation? What were the implications of these processes for each group? How did they contribute specifically to a particular trajectory of cultural change? What was resisted from the old culture? What was retained or modified for contemporary purposes, bearing on the question of usable pasts?

At the most basic level, this volume explores historically specific strategies of self-representation and agency in the context of externally imposed representations. In what way did dominant representations of each group change through time, and why? How did each group, and specifically who within each group—elites, ordinary people, women, politicized immigrants, leaders—negotiate its place in the United States at specific historical moments? Finally, in what way does each comparative project in the volume contribute new insights about southern European ethnicities in general in the United States?

PART I: CONSTRUCTING, HISTORICIZING, AND CONTESTING IDENTITIES

The three chapters in Part I bring attention to how we can think relationally, transnationally, and comparatively about the parallels and especially the interdependences of the Greek and Italian American and Australian situations. Italian and Greek Americans and Australians found themselves as objects of US and Australian racialized categories. The chapters illustrate the analytical value of simultaneously practicing comparative transnational and transcultural approaches in investigating intersections between racial classifications, class, nation, and migrant histories in the making of new migrant identities. The formation of a white consciousness among Italian Americans involved solidarity across southeastern European American populations in the backlash against affirmative action policies set to redress racial injustices. Furthermore, one of the chapters contributes to the comparative project by illustrating that ethnicity functioned differently as a determinant in political behavior between Italian Americans and Greek Americans.

Andonis Piperoglou explores the transnational history of the racial slur "dago" and its meanings in early twentieth-century United States and Australia as a starting point to investigate the process of Italian Australian and Greek Australian identity formation. This transnational comparativism illuminates the racialized contours of this identity formation, and particularly the way whiteness discourse, which circulated between the United States and Australia, contributed to the racialized amalgamation of Italian and Greek migrants. The histories of these groups, he argues, cannot be seen independently from dominant racial classifications, like "dago," that mediated their making. Piperoglou practices "cautious comparativism," seeking neither absolute uniqueness nor regular uniformities but instead historically situated commonalities and differences as they were expressed and negotiated in public speech and popular representations. His attention to migrant responses to the racial slur "dago" ventures into a transcultural analysis of the ways in which Greek Australians and Italian Australians articulated common purpose and experience based on their distinct, yet overlapping, histories, claiming joint inclusion into whiteness. Piperoglou's work illustrates the analytical value of simultaneously practicing comparative transnational and transcultural approaches in investigating intersections between racial classifications, class, nation, and migrant histories in the making of new migrant identities.

Stefano Luconi brings Greek American and Italian American studies in conversation around a pivotal historical moment in the making of Italian American "whiteness." He explores Italian American voting patterns in the 1968 presidential elections in connection to Richard Nixon's decision to favor a Greek American over an Italian American as his vice presidential nominee. The analytical move to place the political behavior of a particular ethnic group in relation to a political figure from another "white ethnic" group enables Luconi to highlight a key mode in the racial politics at the time. The formation of a white consciousness among Italian Americans involved solidarity across southeastern European Americans in the backlash against affirmative action policies set to redress racial injustices. Luconi further contributes to the comparative project by illustrating that ethnicity functioned differently as a determinant in political behavior between Italian Americans and Greek Americans. This finding probes further research to explain this difference.

Jim Cocola discusses a wide range of literary and filmic depictions in which Greek and Italian Americans have regarded one another and closely juxtaposes the treatments of Italian Americans by Elia Kazan and evocations of Greece by Gregory Corso. His examples from American and Australian spheres show that the expressive cultures of the Mediterranean diaspora have been marked by ambivalences, competing affiliations and disaffiliations, and contending exclusions and inclusions vis-à-vis whiteness. Cocola observes that whether asserting dubious claims to, exercising attendant privileges of, or resisting interpellations into whiteness, the writers and filmmakers he discusses have never fully transcended their regional and ancestral origins; nor have they fully assimilated into national identities. He proposes the concept of paraethnicity to understand the process of taking into account adjacent populations in the process of consolidating these identities, or, by contrast, disavowing them. Greek American representations of Italian Americans and Italian American representations of Greek Americans and of Greece retain particular distinctions, and even more granular local manifestations, but they also deserve to be read in a broader key as Mediterranean American self-representations.

PART II: DEPLOYING IDENTITY CONSTRUCTION STRATEGIES IN
TWO ETHNIC COMMUNITIES

The two chapters in Part II examine their case studies deeply to explore important dimensions of social, material, and heritage production. The authors corroborate the view of how architecture and education are foundational to identity construction. Overall, this section focuses on identity formation through language and architecture at the intersection of local, national, and transnational processes.

Angelyn Balodimas-Bartolomei and Fevronia Soumakis undertake a comparative history of Italian American and Greek American educational institutions in New York City to examine the role of cultural background, class, religion, and settlement patterns in shaping the organization and politics of each group regarding language retention via ethnic education throughout the twentieth century. Their comparative inquiry identifies how differences in the socioeconomic experiences upon the arrival of these groups early in the twentieth century, as well as the place of their respective religions in the city's ethnoreligious milieu, decisively resulted in two distinct educational trajectories. Whereas Greek Americans privileged an ethnoreligious orientation in ethnic education, Italian Americans adopted a cosmopolitan approach to Italian language. The historical comparison in these chapters projects differences and similarities in ethnic strategies for cultural reproduction. Anchored in a particular urban context, discussing the particulars of community activism, and taking into account transnational lineages, this study clarifies identity formation through language at the intersection of local, national, and transnational processes.

Kostis Kourelis situates the agency of Italian and Greek immigrants in the period from 1870 to 1925 to express identity via monumental religious architecture in connection to the structures of their respective religious institutions as well as ethnic and national histories. The analysis casts a global cultural, historical, and religious net to explain regional and national differences between US Greek and Italian architectural styles and arrangements in the internal spaces of worship. This broad net is crucial for historicizing comparison as a transnational project. One cannot explain, for example, the canonical Greek Orthodox style in the United States—a generic pan-European "round-arch-style"—independently from the formation of Greek national identity and its formation in connection with Western Europe. What is more, this visual expression of identity needs to take into account the intercultural religious dynamics between Byzantine Christianity and Islam. Similarly, one cannot understand the particularities of Italian immigrant visual signatures—the Renaissance and the Baroque—in the eclectic US religious landscape without considering their ethnic negotiations with universal Catholicism as well as the transcultural histories of Catholic and Protestant architectural styles. In his painstaking transnational and transcultural charting of routes of styles and histories of institutions, Kourelis offers a paradigmatic approach for historicizing comparison. His attention to institutional structures as a key variable in mediating, even determining, local expressions of identity via religious styles strengthens his comparative insights. Various degrees of local agency between early Italian and Greek immigrants cannot be explained outside the webs of institutional power and the transnational histories of each group.

PART III: EXPRESSING ETHNIC AND GENDER IDENTITIES IN
LITERATURE AND MUSIC

The authors in Part III compare and describe identity making in literature and music to probe the power of kinship within the family but also beyond it. They identify relational ethnic identities, acknowledge the regional specificity of ethnicity, and reckon with gendered dimensions. Their examination of music and literature uncovers how identities in performance and identities in fictive narration animate selective memories of ethnic pasts, as well as individual reflections in connection to group identity.

Eleftheria Arapoglou applies a transcultural approach as a mode of comparative inquiry. Her close reading of the narrative structure of two novels, Annie Liontas's *Let Me Explain You* (2016) and Paola Corso's *Catina's Haircut: A Novel in Stories* (2010), demonstrates the value of exploring in each work how particular narrative voices engage in dialogue across generational differences, across differences in gender and sexuality, and across the pre-immigrant past and the American present. This "dialogic transculturalism" contributes to the mapping of ever-evolving subjectivities in relation to family and communities as well as the particularities in the enactments of individual identity. This reading foregrounds intraethnic plurality, unravels techniques for belonging, and identifies strategies of resistance women employ to counter immigrant patriarchy. Arapoglou also employs the transcultural reading across the two novels as a comparative tool. Bringing *Let Me Explain You* and *Catina's Haircut* in conversation pinpoints a literary space in which characters enact shared concerns and voice different experiences across the gendered landscape of Italian American and Greek American subjectivities.

How do American authors of Italian and Greek background inflect the genre of the hard-boiled detective novel with ethnic elements, and what insights about ethnicity does this inflection reveal? Francesca de Lucia examines this question via a close reading of a pair of novels by two established writers, Domenic Stansberry and George Pelecanos. Her comparative inquiry identifies commonalities and differences on several levels. Within Italian American writing, she brings to the fore contrasts between West Coast and East Coast Italian American writers. Across the writings of Stansberry and Pelecanos, she points to the importance that these two writers assign to the local urban context and discusses the particular racial dynamics that shape the protagonists' engagement with ethnicity and views toward racial Others. She also ventures in cross-genre comparisons, stressing how "ethnic" hard-boiled fiction differs from the immigrant novel. This set of comparisons reflects the differences in the historical experience of the two groups, intergenerational tensions and affinities, ambivalence in the ethnic identification of the second generation, and interracial solidarities, as well as conflicts. Bringing the two authors in conversation, de Lucia charts interethnic and interregional diversity within "white ethnicity," alerting scholars about the importance of analyzing subjectivity in its particular social and racial contexts, including everyday interactions.

Panayiotis League discusses how an everyday gathering of a few musicians and dance educators provides the occasion to consider how these individuals compare their intercultural connections with and disconnections from their Italian New England and Asia Minor Greek heritages and "mainstream" categories of ethnicity and national identity. This localized cross-cultural encounter takes place within a cultural space that the participants share, namely their affective and interpretive engagement with Asia Minor Greek music and dance. League practices a "concept-based" analysis that focuses on everyday sociality as the means to explore the collaborative and emergent cross-cultural intersubjective understanding among the participants. His dialogic microethnography moves away from generalized comparisons of ethnic identities. The interest instead is in uncovering how individuals attach meanings to particular cultural aspects of their regional heritages, and how they consciously curate their imaginative living in connection to selective cultural identifications. Emphasizing complexity and nuance in negotiating multiple heritages at the level of the individual, dialogic microethnography enables the critical scrutiny of narratives of collective "white ethnic" identity that either reify ethnicity or render it thin and easily disposable. League recognizes the limits of conversation as a site of knowledge production. Microethnography nevertheless offers a valuable tool to recognize the place of cultural heritage in individual lives and a starting point to raise poignant questions about how to connect particularized exchanges with broader discourses of belonging.

PART IV: ETHNIC IDENTITIES AND VISUAL CULTURE

Part IV focuses on the representation of ethnic identity in visual culture with attention to the lens of postethnicity: the struggle to uphold US identity, the performance of ethnic identity in private and public, the breaking away from popular stereotypes, and the intricacies of Greek and Italian ethnic and racial politics.

Sostene Massimo Zangari's chapter brings to the fore the all-powerful role of television in the reshaping of Italian American and Greek American identity. Zangari sheds light on the impact of the CBS series *Kojak* (1973–78) on the rise of these two white ethnic groups as new American cultural heroes. This comparative approach discusses the media projections of the eponymous Greek American policeman Kojak, played by Telly Savalas, and his Italian American colleagues, while emphasizing the reestablishment of a new connection between the ethnic hero and the mainstream viewer. Through a critical examination of the overall changing sociocultural and political framework of the 1970s, Zangari specifies how the series repudiates numerous ethnic stereotypes of the past by highlighting the centrality of family bonds and middle-class values. The Greek American hero represents these middle-class values and the balance between family loyalty and the avoidance of tribalism. On the other hand, the Italian American characters, though typically steeped in corruption, crime, and the Mafia, are often led to criminal acts by their need to protect family harmony. The author concludes by identifying the legendary figure of the ethnic cop, depicted in *Kojak*, as the embodiment of a reborn version of the American Dream, a hard worker smoothly assimilated with his "humble" origins in the European South.

The visual culture of immigration offers a fruitful site for comparing how the immigrant past is narrated in the present. Yiorgos Kalogeras draws from a pair of Italian American documentaries and another pair of Greek American ones to explain the differences and commonalities in their telling of histories of immigration. The measure for his comparison, however, is not ethnicity. It is the intended primary audience of the documentaries. Italian and Greek documentaries whose primary intended audience is the US public, including "American ethnics," share this commonality: they represent the Americanization of the immigrants as a teleological trajectory toward fulfillment and cultural closure. They produce celebratory accounts and unveil a fixed notion of identity. In contrast, Italian and Greek documentaries whose primary intended audiences lies in Italy and Greece recognize immigrant history as a multifaceted process defined not merely by success but also experiences of loss, cultural mixing, interethnic coalitions, and open-ended identities. They refrain from a linear narrative of completion to acknowledge instead ambiguity and complexity in identity formation. Kalogeras organizes his discussion around the concept of post-ethnicity, which he explores to illuminate the reasons for the bifurcation between celebratory idealization and stark historical constructions of the immigrant past.

According to Michail C. Markodimitrakis, the representation of the ethnic American subject in popular culture, especially film and television, often reinforces the relationship between stereotypes and lived experience. For Italian American and Greek American characters on screen, the portrayal of their journey to assimilation into the "melting pot" of American society without abolishing their ethnic cultures is often connected to class aspirations and social mobility; the process of belonging also includes performances of the ethnic subject's gender roles in public and private spaces. Occupying a different economic status compared to their ancestors, younger generations of Italian and Greek Americans, as portrayed in popular culture, negotiate their status as American citizens through cultural anxieties related to their own "pursuit of happiness," one of the primary, constitutive principles of the American Dream. The author compares *My Big Fat Greek Wedding* (2002) and *Moonstruck* (1987) as two filmic examples that display the complexities of immigrants and ethnic Americans in the process of striving to belong to the society they live in. The protagonists perform the meaning of being American at home and in public. The Portokalos and Castorini families redefine themselves as part of the American society, while also retaining their distinct cultural identities. Markodimitrakis focuses on the performance of the key filmic characters in public and private, bringing attention to ethnic belonging as a function of gender and class. He then shifts attention to how the two female protagonists engage in the pursuit of happiness; their goal is realized through segmented assimilation to the dominant white middle-class culture. In other words, the author compares how the two characters let go of their ethnic identities in favor of a more commodified, liberal form of womanhood.

NOTES

1. Conzen, "The Invention of Ethnicity."
2. There is a fascinating discussion and comparison between Italian American and Jewish American experiences in Moss, *Creating the New Right Ethnic in 1970s America*.
3. The bibliography on the discussion between the cultural representations of the two groups is rather scarce. One of the earliest of the few comparative works on Italian American and Greek American literature is Helen Geracimos Chapin, from 1977: "If You Seek Justice, Put a Gift on the Scale" (https://bit.ly/3B5jDgt), an article comparing the works of Nelson Algren, Pietro Di Donato, and Harry Mark Petrakis. Chapin has also examined ethnic female writing in "Struggle, Sorrow, and Joy: Women in White Ethnic American Literature" (https://bit.ly/3FrilPA). For a comparative analysis on Greek American and Italian American representations on cinema, see Kalogeras, "Entering through the Golden Door." See also Patrona, *Return Narratives*.

4. An interesting exploration of mixed Italian American and Greek American heritage can be found at https://bit.ly/3iwMBi3. Additionally, a joint analysis of both migrations can be found at https://bit.ly/3a4pSVM.

5. The coexistence between Italian and Greek immigrants has been noted in Kallia Papadaki's award-winning Greek novel *Dendrites* (Athens: Polis, 2015). Another recent novel of return, Perry Giuseppe Rizopoulos's *Wheat Songs: A Greek American Journey* (Brookline, MA: Cherry Orchard Books, 2018), explores memory and belonging through the author of mixed Greek/Italian and American heritage who, through his grandfather's narrations, returns to the Greece of World War II. On the other hand, Maria Lombardo's novel *A Camp without Walls* (Newton Center, MA: Italy Enterprises, 2001) unravels her Italian father's experience in Greece as a soldier and later partisan during World War II.

6. Jacobson, *Whiteness*.
7. Brettell, "Anthropology," 657.
8. Luconi, "Italian Americans," 1248.
9. Patrona, "Greek Americans," 1001.
10. Frangos, "The Greeks."
11. Luconi, "Italian Americans," 1247; Patrona, "Greek Americans," 1000.
12. https://bit.ly/3msSL45.
13. Lincoln, *Apples*, 11.

Bibliography

Brettell, Caroline B. "Anthropology, Migration, and Comparative Consciousness, New Literary History." *Comparison* 40, no. 3, (Summer 2009): 649–71.

Conzen, Kathleen Neils, David A. Gerber, Ewa Morawska, George E. Pozzetta, and Rudolph J. Vecoli. "The Invention of Ethnicity: A Perspective from the USA." *Journal of American Ethnic History* 12, no. 1 (Fall 1992): 3–41.

Frangos, Steve. "The Greeks of the Western Hemisphere: Much to Read and Much to Explore." *The National Herald*. https://bit.ly/3AbM23h.

Jacobson, Matthew Frye. *Whiteness of a Different Color: European Immigrants and the Alchemy of Race*. Cambridge, MA: Harvard University Press, 1988.

Kalogeras, Yiorgos. "Entering through the Golden Door: Cinematic Representations of a Mythical Moment." *Journal of Mediterranean Studies* 21, no. 2 (2012): 77–99.

Lincoln, Bruce. *Apples and Oranges: Explorations In, On, and With Comparison*. Chicago: University of Chicago Press, 2018.

Lloyd, G. E. R. "Introduction: Methods, Problems, Prospects." In *Ancient Greece and China Compared*, edited by G. E. R. Lloyd and Jingyi Jenny Zhao, 1–27. Cambridge: Cambridge University Press, 2018.
Luconi, Stefano. "Italian Americans." In *Multicultural America: A Multimedia Encyclopedia*, edited by Carlos E. Cortes, 1247–50. Los Angeles: Sage, 2013.
Moss, Richard. *Creating the New Right Ethnic in 1970s America: The Intersection of Anger and Nostalgia*. Madison, NJ: Fairleigh Dickinson University Press, 2017.
Patrona, Theodora. "Greek Americans." In Cortes, *Multicultural America*, 1000–1003.
———. *Return Narratives: Ethnic Literature in Late Twentieth Century Greek American and Italian American Literature*. Madison, NJ: Fairleigh Dickinson University Press, 2017.

PART I

Constructing, Historicizing, and Contesting Identities

"Dirty Dagoes" Respond

A Transnational History of a Racial Slur

Andonis Piperoglou

In 1905, *The Sunday Sun*, a Sydney-based newspaper, printed an article that provided an account of the origins of the term "dago." The correspondent noted that the Italian-language Australian newspaper *L'Italo-Australiano* had recently stated that it was "largely the custom of the Britisher and Yankee to dump all Italians, Spaniards, Portuguese, Greeks, Levantines, and even Turks, under the generic appellation of 'Dago,'" and that the term was understood to be "one of opprobrium" by Italians who had settled in Australia. Convinced that the use of the term was not offensive, the author noted that the "etymology of the word is so simple that no one seems to know it." After providing a sweeping historical overview of the maritime endeavors of Portuguese sailors, it was added that "one of the most common of [Portuguese] Christian names . . . was, and is, 'Diego' (James) and this was easily corrupted into Dago."[1] "As a matter of fact," the correspondent concluded, "there is nothing derogatory in the name, any more than there is in 'John Bull' or 'Uncle Sam.'"[2]

In 1912, the *Goulburn Evening Penny Post* printed a letter to the editor that provided an alternative explanation to the origin and meaning of the term. After noting that a Greek migrant was recently referred to as a "dago," the author, who was presumably not Greek owing to the signature "A. de L. H.," thought it necessary to inform the newspaper's readers that "the word is often misapplied." "It was originally employed in the United States," A. de L. H. added,

> by manual labourers to their Spanish fellow-workmen, as a national nickname, just as we use Jack and Mac and Pat, being, as it is, a pronunciation of the name Diego, or James. Then, as Italian immigrants were, with the Spaniards, indiscriminately classed as foreigners, the same name was given, by extension, to them. Next, the term became one of contempt—no unusual sequence—and then, because the newcomers did, or were supposed to, work for lower wages, it was turned into one of abuse and hatred. . . . But to apply the term to a Greek is to use an entire misnomer, whether he be labourer or shopkeeper, or of any other avocation. He is of a totally different race—and a grand one, too, if we consider his history—of different characteristics of different temperament.[3]

Each article aptly conveys what historian Matthew Frye Jacobson notes as "the seemingly natural but finally unstable logic of race."[4] Debate over the term "dago" appears to be a matter for conflicting racial classification: in the first article the word "dago" is assumed to be a simple, generic, and harmless label for a wide assortment of people from the Mediterranean region, and the question of its derivation is simply tied to the mispronunciation of the name *Diego*. But in the second article, a more mobile historical origin is articulated that takes into account the intersecting dynamics of immigration, race, and labor in the United States while also singling out which groups of people to whom the "nick-name"—which morphed into an insult of "abuse and hatred"—could and could not be applied. Italians, as "foreigners" who supposedly worked for "lower wages" in the racial operations of labor in the United States, could be pigeonholed as dagos, yet applying the term to Greeks, whatever their occupation, was presented as a fundamental misuse of the word because of the perceived grandeur of their civilizational heritage. Indeed, the differentiation of Greek migrant "characteristics" and "temperament" from other migrant groups from the Mediterranean region seemed to imply biological continuity between ancient Greeks and modern Greeks and consequently challenged the notion that Greeks were a degenerate race.[5]

Despite the contestation over its meaning, each article clearly illuminates that dago was derogatorily and prejudicially applied to people from the Mediterranean region. Put simply, "dago" was a racial slur—an insult that positioned Italian and Greek migrants as alike within the operations of popular racial speech. Each article further reveals, however, that "dago" had a transnational circulation that contributed to the amalgamation of Italians and Greeks within the dominant constructions of racial taxonomies. Used as a marker for Italian and Greek migrant communities that lived and worked in the United States and Australia, "dago" was a racial slur that crossed borders and challenged the constructed categorization of people into fixed racial binaries.[6] In this sense, the meaning and use of "dago" exposes a particular contestability within the transnational "project of whiteness."[7] Its adoption by both "the Britisher and Yankee" signified that its mobility was tied to larger historical dynamics in two settler colonial societies, the United States and Australia, that prided themselves as "white men's countries."[8]

I am interested here in teasing out the transnational circulation of the racial slur "dago." Historical flashpoints in Australia and the United States show that the use of the slur in public speech contributed to the complex ways that Italian and Greek migrants were jointly amalgamated into a singular precarious racial group that did not neatly fit within the binary racial logic of whiteness. Positioned as a racial anomaly, for example, "the dago," as *The Northern Herald* noted in 1917, "might be a bit white, and again might be a bit black."[9] Prejudicial connotations of the slur were routinely contested, and its circulation influenced the self-representations of Italian and Greek migrants. The history of how "dago" traveled echoes the work of David Roediger by acknowledging that "messiness" was a "central characteristic of racial order" in which so-called new immigrants like Italians and Greeks were placed and placed themselves.[10] By transnationalizing the slur's circulation in

Australia and embracing what Ania Loomba frames as "cautious comparativism," we can learn how the word "dago" was not only an imposed racial category but also sometimes an embraced, although frequently refuted, identity that freely traveled across the Pacific.[11]

The Dago in the Historiography of Italian and Greek Migration

Australian historians Marylin Lake and Henry Reynolds argue that the project of whiteness was "at once transnational in its inspiration and identifications but nationalist in its methods and goals."[12] Yet, despite the transnational turn in historical whiteness studies, histories of Italian and Greek migration to the United States and Australia have usually been told as self-contained national stories.[13] Some historical studies, to be sure, have identified parallel developments in race and immigration restriction in the United States and Australia, yet specific analysis of the slur "dago" is sparse.[14] In 1963, for example, Charles Price noted in *Southern Europeans in Australia* that the term "dago" was used "quite indiscriminately to embrace any migrant from the Mediterranean." Its arrival into Australian English vernacular, he suggests, probably took place during "the gold-rush period when many persons left the diggings in California to try their luck in Victoria and New South Wales."[15] William Douglas, in his later analysis of Italian migration to northern Queensland, further notes that labor recruiters in Australia "would not introduce the 'Dago' [labor force]" because it was "looked upon with such dislike in many of the cities of the Southern States of the American Union."[16] Despite Price's and Douglas's assessments, however, analysis of the transnational circulation of "dago," along with examination on its origin, use, and meaning, has been only fleetingly addressed within histories of Italian and Greek immigration and histories of migration more generally.[17]

A recent notable exception, however, is the work of Stefano Luconi. In his localized analysis on race and Italians, Luconi confirms that "dago" originated in the United States as a racial slur but that its precise etymology is uncertain. It may have resulted, he claims, from "incorrect pronunciation of a few expressions with negative implications."[18] Affirming the etymological link to the Spanish first name *Diego*, such a derivation might point to the failure of people in the United States to distinguish between Italians and Spaniards; Luconi also suggests that the word could be a variation of the word "devil." He further adds, however, that the phrase might be linked to the saying "paid as the 'day goes,'" signifying that Italian migrants, who were often hired as unskilled day workers, held lower positions within the hierarchies of industrial labor.[19] This possible derivation of the slur is also recognized by Ilaria Serra, who, in her analysis of the imagery of Italian migration, stresses that whatever its etymology, the word expressed "contempt and hate" particularly in the operations of labor.[20] Thus, the term was also connected with the exploitative operations of class that often intersected with how migrant groups experienced racialization. Although the precise arrival of the term into the Australian vernacular is difficult to locate with absolute historical accuracy, Italians and Greeks jointly experienced yet separately responded to the invented, pervasive and parallel dynamics of race, labor, and immigration in the United States and Australia.[21] For, as Roediger argues, large numbers of non–Anglo-Saxons who arrived into the United States would have been taught their racial place through the proliferation of loaded slurs that were promiscuously applied when their arrival and working practices intersected with the economic dynamics of race, labor, and nation-building.[22]

According to historians of race and migration, the conception of racial division within whiteness was common in the United States and Australia for much of the early twentieth century. For example, Jacobson describes southern and eastern Europeans migrants and their children as "probationally" white, while Thomas Guglielmo distinguishes between nation-race and color-race categories.[23] Roediger, however, prefers the term "in-between" to describe the instability of the racial categorizations within whiteness and their diverse manifestations across different times and places.[24] In order to analyze how these competing white racial ideologies were created and reproduced throughout the United States and Australia, historians have analyzed labor relations, literature, residential patterns, popular culture, intellectual discourse, judicial rulings, census categories, material cultural, migrant self-understandings, and forms of media such as radio and film.[25]

To date, however, historians have not investigated how the transnational circulation of racial slurs like "dago" have functioned in the identifications of "provisional or probationary" white-racial populations like Greeks and Italians who settled in the United States and Australia during the late nineteenth and early twentieth centuries.[26] I hope to remedy this here.

Dirty Dago Deluge

In December 1890, *Popular Science Monthly*, a quarterly magazine that disseminated scientific knowledge to the educated layman in the United States, published an article by lawyer and public commentator Appleton Morgan. Titled "What Shall We Do with the Dago?" the article provides an early example of how people from the Mediterranean region were racially understood within the operations of industry and the criminal system in the United States. After declaring that "'dagoes' as they are nicknamed" was "a corruption" of the Spanish word "hidalgos," which "came to be sneeringly applied to a foreigner of Latin Europe," Morgan revealed particular concern for the living standards of Italians who were working on the railroads in the nineteenth century. "The 'dagoes' collected . . . bones and boiled them for their soup! What terrors have jails and prisons for such human beings?" He added, "What have they to lose by pilfering, assaulting, robbing, and murdering?"[27] Clearly "dago" carried racially disdainful meaning. The association that the "foreigner of Latin Europe" was able to survive on very meager resources, was prone to stealing and killing, and was unable to be rehabilitated through the criminal justice system strongly asserted such people were a less than ideal human type. Indeed, the negative inversion of Morgan's early projection would become indicative of how moral, aesthetic, and cultural values were fundamental to classifying and describing the dago.

In Australia such connotations were also expressed and, at times, the slur was lengthened to "dago deluge" or "dirty dago." As *Truth*, a Sydney-based newspaper, noted in 1904, because "the Dago was a European" who was more welcome "than the Jap and Chow and other scum of Asia, there was at one time little notice taken of his steady but constant arrival." Yet, it was professed that "the Dago was a menace almost as much to be feared as the very worst of the Asiatics themselves" because they were "a big competitor in the labor market." "White miners," the newspaper concluded,

> are getting tired of seeing their places filled by unskilled, cheap labor from the shores of the Mediterranean. They are tired of walking from mine to mine asking in vain for a job, whilst the dirty Dago walk on in front of him and finds a place without asking.... They do not settle upon the land, neither do they develop any of our resources. They simply undercut the workman in wages, and save and hoard their scanty earning with the one set purpose of returning to their native land as comparatively rich men.[28]

In this instance, where "dago" laborers are associated with nonwhite Asian populations that supposedly undermined the ability of Anglo-British workers to obtain a sufficient wage, the slur is especially meaningful. As Erika Lee writes, in terms of immigration restriction new migrants were closely racialized along the "Chinese immigrant model," and metaphors of an invasive menace were applied to both groups, though through differing modes of expression.[29] Furthermore, the observation that "the dago" was solely interested in returning to his homeland with accumulated wealth and was someone who did not wish to toil "upon the land" was a serious criticism within Australian settler discourse. It implied that "the dago" in Australia was understood within the intersection of race and nation to be a measly sojourner, uninterested in permanently residing and contributing to the economic growth of the settler colonial nation. In this sense the slur was a racialized term that operated within the same racial ordering that insulted Asian peoples while also contributing to the colonialist image of Australia as an undeveloped land that was ripe for the conversion of raw materials into commodified products that would, in turn, boost the country's nation-building agenda.

"Dago" also circulated in visual culture. In 1911, Sydney's *Truth* noted that "both fish and fruit trades are practically 'cornered' by Dagoes; the former by Dagoes of Greek, and the latter of Italian nationality ... one has only to follow the frequent prosecutions of both kinds of Dago breed, for keeping filthy premises and other offences against the public welfare."[30] A caricature titled "Choice Pairs" (Figure 1) accompanied the text. It depicted an Italian fruiter wearing a vest and rolled up shirt sleeves and a poster that read "fruita cleened for da kostumma." With his black curly hair and exaggerated moustache and eyebrows, the fruiter cunningly avoids the gaze of the viewer as he projects his saliva on a pear. Below the caricature, a detail of two fruit flies speaking to each other was added with a speech bubble that noted, "the dagos spitting us out all right."[31] Some years later, during World War I, Brisbane's *Truth* caricatured a restaurateur in a similar vein, albeit with a particularly Greek overtone. Titled "The Dago's Dilemma," the image (Figure 2) portrayed a food proprietor, who serves the popular Australian meal of steak and oysters, as being frustrated because patriotic Australians have boycotted his business due to the Greek king Constantine's neutralist but essentially pro-German attitude during the war.[32] Wearing a buttoned suit and bow tie, the figure looks respectable yet angry. He holds one palm out, as if he is about to serve a customer, while his other hand tightly grips a knife. Similar to the misspelled text in the caricature of the Italian fruiter, an accompanying poem stipulates in broken English that "the Dago is saying" that the Greek king's wartime position has "killa da biz" and that he wishes to "cutta his throat."

Read as a cultural metacommentary, each cartoon and the accompanying texts work in tandem to capture a visually effective but generic image of Italian and Greek shopkeepers as figures of suspicion, derision, and dirtiness. Each "Dago breed" is represented as unwelcome foreign intruders whose working practices did not fit within the fair and reasonable industrial conditions for which the Australian labor movement had advocated. Such visual imagery contributed to the commonly held view that, willing literally to expectorate on products or resort to violence when wronged, Italians and Greeks were amoral businesspeople who practiced beastly habits unfit for Australian society. Moreover, the misspelled English in each image accentuated the generic features of the representations. The misspelling of simple English words (like "da" for "the") gives the impression that despite their different origins, Italian and Greeks mispronounced the lingua franca of their host society in a similar fashion.

If we further juxtapose the images, however, we can see that the generic visual representation of "dago" was also amenable to accentuating cultural specificity. In the Greek caricature, for example, the national politics of the homeland along with regional particularism is clearly discernible. Not only did King Constantine's wartime sentiment give rise to how a Greek restaurateur was pictured and treated, but the threat of violence in the image also points to Britain's imperial obsession with controlling male interpersonal violence in the Ionian Islands, a region from which many early Greek settlers in Australia came.[33] As Thomas Gallant notes, male violence in the Ionian Islands was highly prevalent and was rooted in an ethic of honor that was ritualized in knife combat. Viewing such ritualism as a form of lower-class dueling, the British attempted to remedy the prevalence to knife fighting through their colonial criminal justice system.[34] In this sense, despite the obvious similarities in each cartoon, we can view the cartoon of a dishonored Greek restaurant owner as an important visual example of how cultural specificity was imaginatively applied to the slur.

Returning to textual descriptions, the slur also straddled the color line, particularly when it was discussed within the binary racial logic of whiteness. In 1915, the anarchist Luigi Galleani, for example, wrote an article titled "Dagoes!" in the Italian-language journal *Cronaca Sovversiva* in which he observed that Italian migrants who were employed in building infrastructure projects in the United States were assessed as "something between the white and the black." Galleani, however, further added that "Dagoes" were not viewed as completely human: "The dago is not only the foreigner or the barbarian[,] he is ... in the anthropological classification, the bottom rung; something of a hybrid between man and gorilla."[35] The dehumanizing connotation that the slur validated was also extended to Australian shores.

For example, in 1917 *The Northern Herald* noted in an investigative article that reported on the introduction of Mediterranean labor in state of Queensland that "'The Dago' ... might be a bit white, and again might be a bit black. It's [sic] knowledge of the King's English," it was printed,

> as a rule don't amount to much, and its mode and manner of living is as mysterious as the witchcraft of our vanished abos. For, let me tell you, you will scarcely ever see the creature cooking, and as for eating, I have a fixed idea that he consumes sufficient during the silent hours of the night to carry him over the day's journey. He is generally as silent as the stagnant pool where the skeeters play. . . . But there is one point about the Dago . . . if you have a bit of work to do, you can always depend on the creature doing it, and as for rules and regulation and strictures and wasting the day's work by gazing on some cheap affair that is misnamed a timepiece, well it does not fall in line with the style of the Dago.[36]

Figure 1. "Cheap Fish and Fruit." *Truth*, 7 May 1911, 3, National Library of Australia, http://nla.gov.au/nla.news-article201555011 (accessed January 29, 2021).

Figure 2. "The Dago's Dilemma," *Truth*, January 14, 1917, 9, National Library of Australia, http://nla.gov.au/nla.news-article168755237 (accessed January 29, 2021).

Here the racial slur is fully debasing. As a secretive "creature" or "skeeter" who does not adhere to the rule of law and the workplace expectations of punctuality, "the dago" was racially positioned as fundamentally degraded. The comparison with "the witchcraft of vanished abos," in particular, revealed that the term could carry disdainful and tragic meaning within the dynamics of colonial intrusion that attempted to erase First Nations peoples. Indeed, comparing "the dago" with Aboriginals was to situate them alongside a group of people who race scientists routinely placed at the bottom of the evolutionary ladder.[37]

To Italian and Greek migrants who sought to mitigate their ambiguous racial standing when the term "dago" was applied to them, it may not have always been apparent whether such a process was a personal or group one, whether it required overpowering biology or changing cultural habits, and whether it was practicable or realistic. The alarmist, exclusionary, and degrading rhetoric that surrounded the use of "dago" seemed to be transnationally varied, yet persistent descriptions of a "dago deluge" that needed to be curbed, or representations of Greek and Italian workers as "dirty" and unwanted within the modern operations of labor, cut across national borders and ethnic differences or specificity. The ubiquity of the slur also ensured that the contestation over the slur's meaning also extended to migrants themselves.

Dirty Dagoes Respond

In 1905, *The West Australian* printed a letter that revealed that a migrant who was anxious to claim his Australianness while still acknowledging his Greek origins, believed that the persistent use of dago cut deeply. "Sir," the author penned,

> May I crave space in your valuable paper to ventilate a grievance at the way some honourable law-abiding citizens are being dubbed continually as "Dagoes." . . . Being an Australian native myself, of Grecian descent, it has often grieved me to hear Australians describe descendants of the noble Hellenic race as being other than white men. . . . Now sir, is it not time that

men in the street, as it were, should be informed (if he is so ignorant) that the Greeks, aye, and the Italians, in fact all Europeans, are as much entitled to the name white people as we ourselves are?[38]

The embraced white racial identity seemed to represent a commonly accepted, yet rapidly shifting, racial vernacular that tied "all Europeans"—like Italians and Greeks—into a single racially white category. Continual use of "dago" thus implied that heightened articulations of racial in-betweenness was seriously challenging the ability of "all" Europeans to claim whiteness.

Yet, the popular adoption of the term and how it challenged color race taxonomies was also considered a matter worthy of interrogation by migrant voices. "There is one little question I would like to ask, through your columns," Nicholas Leenos, a Greek migrant, wrote from Babinda, a sugarcane hub in northern Queensland:

> and that is the colour of a "Dago." It is a common thing to hear out here that so many white men and so many "Dagoes" are working on a job. Now, what get me is the colour of a "Dago." I was always under the impression that all Europeans were white, so it comes as a surprise to find that Spaniards, Italians and Greeks are not white. What I want to know is, are they black, brown, or brindle?[39]

Such a response reveals that the mobility of the word "dago" was complicating the process of white racial categorization, while also providing opportunities for "dagoes" themselves to challenge—or even mock—these processes. Indeed, the open questioning suggests how the confusing characteristics of "dago" contributed to how migrants learned of and interacted with the messiness of race. The suggestion of the more uncommon color/racial category of "brindle," in particular, acts as form of ridicule that calls into the question fantastical yet persistent rigidity of whiteness.

Furthermore, the movement of the term from the United States to Australia seemed to also inform the self-identifications of some migrant articulations. In 1921, for example, the *Brisbane Courier* printed an article by a migrant who went by the intriguing hyphenated name of "Greco-Italian." Titled "The Dago," the article noted that the use of the word was "common among the ignorant and uncouth" but was not "ever found on the lips of the educated and refined." As a self-identifying transcultural descendent, the author added,

> as a descendent of two nations, who in the brave days of the old were responsible for "the glory that was Greece and the grandeur that was Rome," I can afford to hold myself as high socially as the best Englishman, Scot, or Irishman. . . . Just look at what the Italians are doing with sugar in North Queensland. Why, sir, they will be the industrial salvation of tropical Australia! . . . The industry of Italians is proverbial. In New York city . . . my fellow countrymen are regarded as the most industrious of the labouring classes. The great New York weekly paper, "The Independent," has the following in its issue of July 23 last: "Recently an investigator found that out of every 28,000 Italians there was only one in the alms-house, while out of every 28,000 Irish there were 140. What a showing, when you recall that 85 per cent of New York's Italians are labourers!" . . . I think the Italians and the Greeks will make quite as good a showing as do the Italians in New York.[40]

In refuting the use of the slur as unrefined speech, the Greek-Italian spokesperson chose to promote the laboring efforts of Italians in New York and the civilizational attributes of both Greece and Rome. In doing so, engagement with the derogatory meaning of the term seemed to enforce a definite connection between two migrant groups who were strikingly *made into* "dagoes" through popular racial language. The merits of Italian labor efficiency and the civilizational heritage shared between Greece and Rome implied that both Italians and Greeks had something to offer Australia, like their counterparts there did for the United States. By virtue of the duality of his cultural ancestry, the articulations of "Greco-Italian" thus seemed to affirm the arrival of a new historical migrant subject that could draw upon a self-ascribed transcultural category for maximum effect. The desire to establish common purpose and experience was thus a powerful one in challenging the slippery and contingent racial debasement of people from the Mediterranean.

As the twentieth century started to reach its midway point, "dago" continued to be used in Australia with reference to the United States. Sydney's *Catholic Freeman's Journal* in 1940, for example, noted that "the very lowest level of American intelligence or unintelligence" was now commonly "using the word 'dago.'" "The historical implication of this phrase," it was added, was

> very amusing. The dago, generally speaking, is a member of those darker races which have colonised South America and whose original breeding ground is to be sought in the Peninsulas of the Mediterranean. The chief characteristics of the dago are knives, rages, romantic passions, reckless behaviour, garlic and guitars. With these things the beings in question create a perpetual disturbance quite out of proportion to their importance, or in other words, to their wealth; and have been a terrible nuisance to the more solid communities who are acquainted with the reign of law.[41]

The debasing rhetoric associated with the term had a lingering effect. Peter Veneris, for example, experienced the physical sting of the slur as a child of Greek background who lived in Lockhart in southwestern New South Wales. In an interview for an oral history project on Australia's Greek-run cafés, Veneris noted, "I was called a dago when I went to school. I didn't know what it meant, so I would fight and fight. We were proud of being Greek, but not of being called dagoes. When we got the café it changed from dagoes to greasy dagoes—greasy spoon dagoes."[42]

Frequent references to greasiness easily turned the slur into one associated with an unhygienic lifestyle and dirty labor practices. Moreover, the phonetic exactness between the words "grease" and "Greece" in the English language meant that the infliction of "greasy dago" could act as a rather piercing insult for Greeks and not Italians. Beyond the obvious connotation that being greasy meant being slippery, it could also imply that Greeks were susceptible to acting corruptly, since the popular saying "to grease someone's palm" was a popular euphemism for bribery. As Veneris's recollections attest, the use of the slur could thus leave Greek migrant families and individuals feeling totally isolated and unwanted.

Conclusion

In recent years scholars of race have started paying more serious attention to issues concerning the meaning or use of racial epithets and slurs. In addition, transnational historical scholarship has maintained that the social construction of whiteness should always be understood as relational and processual. In the case of Italian and Greek migrant experiences in Australia and the United States, however, scholarship has examined, with few exceptions, the operations of white racialization within a national frame of analysis. The ensuing analysis has resulted in singular narratives that, while accounting for changes in racial classification over time, have paid only cursory attention to transnational circulations of racial slurs and the overlaps and differences that were experienced by Greek and Italian migrant groups within the operations of whiteness. The transnational focus adopted here, with a preliminary examination of the contested meaning and use of the term "dago," provides a cautious comparative picture of how Greeks and Italian interacted in similar, yet distinct, ways within the settler colonial operations of race. Such a history demonstrates that the formation of Italian-Australianness and Greek-Australianness sometimes worked in tandem with the messy transnational historical dynamics of race in the United States.

Furthermore, the examples discussed here reveal how Greek and Italian migrants, as subjects whose full inclusion into whiteness was questioned, placed themselves within dominant racialist narratives. As a route to self-legitimation within the contested contours of whiteness, vocal Greek and Italian spokespeople challenged and resisted the demeaning slur. Often, they did so within the marginal pages of popular presses and periodicals as a means to seek visibility within the operations of popular race thinking while also presenting migrant-specific transcultural categories and solidarities. One of the effects of this anti-dago resistance, however, was that the transcultural linkages and identity formations shared between Greeks and Italians were mobilized within the powerful exclusivist racial paradigms from which the term "dago" emerged. Thus, it could be said that the circulations and contestation of the slur dago during the late nineteenth and early twentieth centuries marshaled Greek and Italian migrants to articulate solidarities with each other publicly while simultaneously reinforcing a dominant white racial ordering that excluded Asian populations and dispossessed First Nation peoples.

Different yet comparable migrant subjects from the Mediterranean region, like Greeks and Italians, were amalgamated within the exclusionary dynamics of the dominant racial language, but racialized forms of amalgamation could create firm migrant-specific articulations of difference, belonging, and solidarity. Although, as some studies suggest, "dago" became less insulting over time and evolved into a term of "endearment and intimacy," further research could focus more specifically on the contemporary everyday circulations and connotations of the racial slur.[43] Recently, in upstate New York, for example, a food truck called the "Wandering Dago" was banned from doing business because of its racially charged name. While "dago," as has been addressed here, was a racial slur that had demeaning connotations and an extensive circulation that cut across national boundaries, the truck's owner, Andrea Loguidice, argued that the branding of her business was a tribute to her Italian ancestors, who worked as laborers and were paid "as the day goes."[44] The positive appropriation of "dago" by a self-identifying Italian American, alongside the capacity of the term to be charged as a racial offense to this day, signals that the meaning and use of the word remain highly contested.

NOTES

This research has been supported by the Australian National University's Herbert and Valmae Freilich Project for the Study of Bigotry, The Griffith Centre for Social and Cultural Research at Griffith University, and the National Library of Australia. Zora Simic, who commented on earlier versions of the chapter, made this work a rewarding professional and intellectual experience. Insights by anonymous reviewers promoted me to broaden the scope of the chapter. Last but not least, I wish to thank Yiorgos Anagnostou, Theodora Patrona, and Yiorgos Kalogeras for their valuable comments and methodical editorial guidance.

1. "Re 'Dago,'" *The Sunday Sun*, March 12, 1905, 5.
2. Ibid.
3. "The Term Dago," *Goulbourn Evening Penny Post*, July 2, 1912, 2.
4. Jacobson, *Whiteness*, 2.
5. It should be noted that Greek migrants in the United States and Australia capitalized on the discourse of Hellenic civilizational exceptionalism to present themselves as legitimate members of the "white race." See, for example, Laliotou, *Transatlantic Subjects*, 123–25; Anagnostou, *Contours of White Ethnicity*, 43–46; Piperoglou, "The Memorialization of Hector Vasyli," 253–276; Piperoglou, "Border Barbarisms," 529–43; Piperoglou, "Migrant-cum-Settler," 447–71.

6. Roediger, *Working Towards Whiteness*, 1–34.

7. Lake and Reynolds, *Drawing the Global Colour Line*, 4. On "whiteness," see also Frankenberg, *White Women, Race Matters*; Roediger, *Wages of Whiteness*; Moreton-Robinson, *Talkin' up to the White Woman*; Moreton-Robinson, Casey, and Nicoll, *Transnational Whiteness Matters*.

8. "Re 'Dago,'" 5; Lake and Reynolds, *Drawing the Global Colour Line*, 4; See also Piperoglou, "Favoured 'Nordics' and 'Mediterranean Scum,'" 510–24; Piperoglou, "Migrant Acculturation via Naturalisation."

9. "The Dago," *The Northern Herald*, August 24, 1917, 35.

10. Roediger, *Working Towards Whiteness*, 37.

11. Stam and Shohat, "Transnationalizing Comparisons," 473–99; Loomba, "Race and the Possibilities of Comparative Critique," 518.

12. Lake and Reynolds, *Drawing the Global Colour Line*, 4.

13. See for example, Tamis, *Greeks in Australia*; Cresciani, *Italians in Australia*; Douglas, *From Italy to Ingham*; Cresciani and Mascitelli, *Italy and Australia*; Ricatti, *Italians in Australia*. On transnational historical whiteness, see Moreton-Robinson et al., *Transnational Whiteness Matters*; Boucher, Carey, and Ellinghaus, *Re-Orienting Whiteness*.

14. See Price, *The Great White Walls Are Built*; Huttenback, *Racism and Empire*; Markus, *Fear and Hatred*.

15. Price, *Southern Europeans in Australia*, 2.

16. Douglas, *From Italy to Ingham*, 47.

17. Burkholder, "From "Wops and Dagoes and Hunkie" to "Caucasian," and Baldassaro, "Dashing Dagoes and Walloping Wops," reveal that "dago" circulated in the media and classroom but provide little analysis on how the slur influenced migrant identities:

18. Luconi, "Black Dagoes?" 196.

19. It is also suggested that dago is tied to the word "dagger," hinting at the racial thinking that tied people from the Mediterranean region to having an angry nature, hot temperament, and tendency to settle disputes by stabbing their opponents. See Luconi, "Black Dagoes?"; Gallo, *Old Bread, New Wine*, 45. For anti-Italian insults in general, see also Donald Tricarico, "Labels and Stereotypes," in LaGumina et al., *The Italian American Experience*, 319–21.

20. Serra, *The Imagined Immigrant*, 27.

21. On the parallel dynamics between the United States and Australia, see Piperoglou, "Rethinking Greek Migration as Settler Colonialism."

22. For an analysis of how other racial slurs like "guinea," "greaser," and "hunky" traveled within the operations of labor and whiteness in the United States, see Roediger, *Working Towards Whiteness*, 37–54.

23. Jacobson, *Whiteness of a Different Color*; Gugliemo, *White on Arrival*.

24. Roediger, *Working Towards Whiteness*.

25. Pascoe, *What Comes Naturally*; Hattam, *In the Shadow of Race*; Baum, *The Rise and Fall of the Caucasian Race*; Goldstein, *The Price of Whiteness*; Williams, *The Social Sciences and Theories of Race*; Gerstle, *American Crucible*; Guterl, *The Color of Race in America*; Jacobson, *Barbarian Virtues*; Smedley, *Race in North America*; Gossett, *Race*; Bederman, *Manliness and Civilization*; Ignatiev, *How the Irish Became White*.

26. For a comprehensive analysis on the "provisional" or "probationary" dynamics of whiteness, see Jacobson, *Whiteness of a Different Color*.

27. Morgan, "What Shall We Do with the Dago?" *Hidalgo* was a word to describe a member of the Spanish or Portuguese nobility.

28. "The Dago Deluge," *Truth*, February 20, 1904, 2.

29. Lee, *At America's Gates*, 31.

30. "Cheap Fish and Fruit," *Truth*, May 7, 1911, 3.

31. Ibid.

32. "The Dago's Dilemma," *Truth*, January 14, 1917, 9.

33. On migration from the Ionian Islands to Australia, see: Piperoglou, "Border Barbarisms," and "The Memorialization of Hector Vasyli."

34. Gallant, *Experiencing Dominion*, 117–47; Gallant, "Honor, Masculinity, and Ritual Knife Fighting in Nineteenth-Century Greece."

35. Luigi Galleani, "Dagoes," *Cronaca Sovversiva*, August 28, 1915, cited in Tomchuk, *Transnational Radicals*.

36. "The Dago," *The Northern Herald*, August 24, 1917, 35.

37. For an analysis of the idea that Aboriginal Australians were doomed to extinction, see McGregor, *Imagined Destinies*.

38. "Dagoes and Greeks," *The West Australian*, April 15, 1905, 11.

39. "What Is White?" *Cairn Post*, April 27, 1917, 4. "Brindle," it should be noted, is a word used to describe a brown streak, pattern, or patchy coloring in the fur of cats, dogs, and other animals.

40. "The Dago," *Brisbane Courier*, September 29, 1921, 7.

41. "These Dagoes," *Catholic Freeman's Journal*, July 25, 1940, 9.

42. Janiszewski and Alexakis, "Telling Tales of Australia's Country Greek Cafes," 9.

43. Douglas, *From Italy to Ingham*, 304.

44. Ngoc Huynh, "Controversial Wandering Dago Food Truck Returns to Empire State Plaza," *Upstate NewYork.com* (June 13, 2018), https://bit.ly/3D5xkMW.

Bibliography

PRIMARY SOURCES

Brisbane Courier
Cairn Post
Catholic Freeman's Journal
Cronaca Sovversiva
Goulbourn Evening Penny Post
The Northern Herald
The Sunday Sun
Truth
Upstate NewYork.com
The Western Australian

SECONDARY SOURCES

Anagnostou, Yiorgos. *Contours of White Ethnicity: Popular Ethnography and the Making of Unstable Pasts in Greek America*. Athens: Ohio University Press, 2009.

Baldassaro, Lawrence. "Dashing Dagoes and Walloping Wops: Media Portrayal of Italian American Major Leaguers before World War II." *Nine: A Journal of Baseball History and Culture* 11, no. 1 (Fall 2005): 98–106.

Baum, Bruce. *The Rise and Fall of the Caucasian Race: A Political History of Racial Identity*. New York: New York University Press, 2006.

Bederman, Gail. *Manliness and Civilization: A Cultural History of Gender and Race in the United States, 1880–1917*. Chicago: University of Chicago Press, 1995.

Boucher, Leigh, Jane Carey, and Katherine Ellinghaus. *Re-Orienting Whiteness*. New York: Palgrave Macmillan, 2009.

Burkholder, Zoë. "From 'Wops and Dagoes and Hunkie' to 'Caucasian': Changing Racial Discourse in American Classrooms during World War II." *History of Education Quarterly* 50, no. 3 (August 2010): 324–58.

Coupland, Nikolas, ed. *Sociolinguistic and Social Theory*. New York: Routledge, 2001.

Cresciani, Gianfranco. *Italians in Australia*. Melbourne: Cambridge University Press, 2003.

Cresciani, Gianfranco, and Bruno Mascitelli. *Italy and Australia: An Asymmetrical Relationship*. Ballarat: Connor Court Publishing, 2014.

Douglas, William A. *From Italy to Ingham: Italians in North Queensland*. St. Lucia: University of Queensland Press, 1995.

Frankenberg, Ruth. *White Women, Race Matters: The Social Construction of Whiteness*. Minneapolis: University of Minnesota Press, 1993.
Gallant, Thomas. *Experiencing Dominion: Culture, Identity, and Power in the British Mediterranean*. Notre Dame, IN: Notre Dame University Press, 2002.
———. "Honor, Masculinity, and Ritual Knife Fighting in Nineteenth-Century Greece." *American Historical Review* 105, no. 2 (2000): 359–82.
Gallo, Patrick J. *Old Bread, New Wine: A Portrait of the Italian Americans*. Chicago: Nelson-Hall, 1981.
Gerstle, Gary. *American Crucible: Race and Nation in the Twentieth Century*. Princeton, NJ: Princeton University Press, 2001.
Goldstein, Eric L. *The Price of Whiteness: Jews, Race, and American Identity*. Princeton, NJ: Princeton University Press, 2006.
Gossett, Thomas F. *Race: The History of an Idea in America*. Rev. ed. New York: Oxford University Press, 1997.
Gugliemo, Thomas. *White on Arrival: Italians, Race, Color and Power in Chicago, 1890–1945*. Oxford: Oxford University Press, 2004.
Guterl, Matthew Pratt. *The Color of Race in America*. Cambridge, MA: Harvard University Press, 2001.
Hattam, Victoria. *In the Shadow of Race: Jews, Latinos, and Immigrant Politics in the United States*. Chicago: University of Chicago Press, 2007.
Huttenback, Robert A. *Racism and Empire: White Settlers and Coloured Immigrants in the British Self-Governing Colonies 1830–1910*. Ithaca, NY: Cornell University Press, 1976.
Ignatiev, Noel. *How the Irish Became White*. New York: Routledge, 1995.
Jacobson, Matthew Frye. *Barbarian Virtues: The United States Encounters Foreign Peoples at Home and Abroad, 1876–1917*. New York: Hill and Wang, 2000.
———. *Whiteness of a Different Color: European Immigrants and the Alchemy of Race*. Cambridge, MA: Harvard University Press, 1999.
Janiszewski, Leonard, and Effy Alexakis. "Telling Tales of Australia's Country Greek Cafes: A Project Insight." *Oral History Association of Australia Journal* 34 (2012): 3–13.
LaGumina, Salvatore J., ed. *The Italian American Experience: An Encyclopedia*. New York: Garland, 2000.
Lake, Marilyn, and Henry Reynolds. *Drawing the Global Colour Line: White Men's Countries and the Question of Racial Equality*. Melbourne: Cambridge University Press, 2012.
Laliotou, Ioanna. *Transatlantic Subjects: Acts of Migration and Cultures of Transnationalism Between Greece and America*. Chicago: University of Chicago Press, 2004.

Lee, Erika. *At America's Gates: Chinese Immigration during the Exclusion Era, 1882–1943*. Chapel Hill: University of North Carolina Press, 2003.
Loomba, Ania. "Race and the Possibilities of Comparative Critique." *New Literary Histories*, 40, no. 3 (2009): 501–22.
Luconi, Stephano. "Black Dagoes? Italian Immigrants' Racial Status in the United States—An Ecological View." *Journal of Transatlantic Studies* 12, no. 3 (2016): 188–99.
Markus, Andrew. *Fear and Hatred: Purifying Australia and California 1850–1901*. Sydney: Hale and Iremonger, 1979.
McGregor, Russell. *Imagined Destinies: Aboriginal Australians and the Doomed Race Theory, 1880–1939*. Melbourne: Melbourne University Press, 1997.
Moreton-Robinson, Aileen. *Talkin' up to the White Woman: Aboriginal Women and Feminism*. St. Lucia: University of Queensland Press, 2000.
Moreton-Robinson, Aileen, Maryrose Casey, and Fiona Nicoll. *Transnational Whiteness Matters*. Plymouth, MA: Lexington Books, 2008.
Morgan, Appleton. "What Shall We Do with the Dago?" *Popular Science Monthly* 38 (December 1890): 172–79.
Ngai, Mae M. *Impossible Subjects: Illegal Aliens and the Making of Modern America*. Princeton, NJ: Princeton University Press, 2004.
Pascoe, Peggy. *What Comes Naturally: Miscegenation Law and the Making of Race in America*. New York: Oxford University Press, 2009.
Piperoglou, Andonis. "'Border Barbarisms,' Albury 1902: Greeks and the Ambiguity of Whiteness." *Australian Journal of Politics and History* 64, no. 4 (2018): 529–43.
———. "Favoured 'Nordics' and 'Mediterranean Scum': Transpacific Hierarchies of Desirability and Immigration Restriction." *History Australia* 17, no. 3 (2020): 510–24.
———. "The Memorialization of Hector Vasyli: Civilisation Prestige, Imperial Association and Greek Migrant Performance." In *Australia, Migration and Empire*, edited by Philip Payton and Andrekos Varnava, 253–76. Cham, Switzerland: Palgrave Macmillan, 2019.
———. "Migrant Acculturation via Naturalisation: Comparing Syrian and Greek Applications for Naturalisation in White Australia." *Immigrants and Minorities* (2021). https://doi.org/10.1080/02619288.2021.1974405
———. "Migrant-cum-Settler: Greek Settler Colonialism in Australia." *Journal of Modern Greek Studies* 38, no. 2 (October 2020): 447–71.
———. "Rethinking Greek Migration as Settler Colonialism." *Ergon: Greek/American Arts and Letters* (2018). https://bit.ly/2YnAME1.
Price, Charles. *The Great White Walls Are Built: Restrictive Immigration to North America and Australasia, 1836–1888*. Canberra: ANU Press, 1974.

———. *Southern Europeans in Australia.* Melbourne: Oxford University Press, 1963.
Ricatti, Francesco. *Italians in Australia: History, Memory, Identity.* Cham, Switzerland: Palgrave Macmillan, 2018.
Roediger, David. *Wages of Whiteness: Race and the Making of the American Working Class.* London: Verso, 1991.
———. *Working Towards Whiteness: How American's Immigrants Became White—The Strange Journey from Ellis Island to the Suburbs.* New York: Basic Books, 2006.
Serra, Ilaria. *The Imagined Immigrant: Images of Italian Emigration to the United States between 1890 and 1924.* Madison, NJ: Fairleigh Dickinson University Press.
Smedley, Audrey. *Race in North America: Origin and Evolution of a Worldview.* 2nd ed. Boulder, CO: Westview Press, 1999.
Stam, Robert, and Ella Shohat. "Transnationalizing Comparisons: The Use and Abuses of Cross-Cultural Analogy." *New Literary History* 40, no. 3 (2009): 473–99.
Tamis, Anastasios. *Greeks in Australia.* Melbourne: Cambridge University Press, 2005.
Tomchuk, Travis. *Transnational Radicals: Italian Anarchists in Canada and the U.S., 1915–1940.* Winnipeg: University of Manitoba Press, 2015.
Tynan, Kathrine, and T. A. Daly. "The Poet of the Dago." *Irish Quarterly Review* 2, no. 7 (September 1913): 234–46.
Williams, Vernon J., Jr. *The Social Sciences and Theories of Race.* Urbana: University of Illinois Press, 2006.

A Greek American Vice President?

The View from the Italian American Community

Stefano Luconi

Participation in the ethnic revival and the elaboration of a white identity in response to African Americans' alleged encroachments were among the main features that shaped the experience of US national minorities, including Italian Americans, in the late 1960s and early 1970s.[1] In those years it seemed that Blacks had achieved a special status, as affirmative action programs best epitomized. This feeling caused the emergence of a mutual Caucasian sense of belonging after the members of the diverse groups from European backgrounds realized that they shared a common interest in curbing African Americans' claims and defending their own racial privileges. The battle cry of "Black Power" against white dominance also provided a model for white ethnic communities to rediscover and to promote their ancestral heritage. As prominent historian Rudolph J. Vecoli testified before the US House Subcommittee on Education in 1970, "'Black Power' ... brought forth echoes of 'Irish Power,' 'Italian Power,' and 'Polish Power.'

Heightened group antagonisms raised fears of polarization, not simply a black-white polarization, but one which would pit various ethnic groups against others."[2] In other words, two divergent forces resulting from the radicalization of the Black freedom struggle influenced ethnic communities of European extraction. The one encouraged them to merge into a larger interest group, namely white Americans, to safeguard their economic and social privileges, especially in response to affirmative action and busing to the benefit of African Americans. The other urged them to revitalize their national roots and to cherish their diversity, causing rivalries among European Americans.[3]

Subjected to such centrifugal stimuli, Italian Americans were pushed at the same time toward both the whitening of their self-perception and the rediscovery of Italianness.[4] These tendencies could coexist, producing a hybrid affiliation by which the assimilation and acculturation into the Caucasian mainstream of US society occasionally let people of Italian descent also retain symbolic ethnic feelings.[5]

Yet, the concurrence of a racial and an ethnic sense of belonging was not always possible. Politics was a case in point for the shortcomings in the generalization of such a pattern of double identity between the late 1960s and the early 1970s. On the one hand, following the rise in the number of Italian American candidates for elective positions as more and more members of their ethnic group entered the middle class and consolidated their standing in US society, thereby qualifying for a place on the ballots, voters from Italian background enhanced their inclination to cast ballots for politicians of the same national ancestry. Raymond E. Wolfinger has argued that bourgeois status maximized ethnic voting, and, as Salvatore J. LaGumina has suggested, Italian Americans had reached this condition by the mid-1960s, when almost half of their workforce held white-collar jobs.[6] On the other hand, out of a sort of racial defensiveness at the polls, Italian Americans often joined forces with voters of eastern and southern European extraction and supported Caucasian candidates who belonged to other European minorities, providing that the latter advocated whites' demands, in the effort to prevent the enactment of Black-oriented platforms and the election of either spokespersons for African American claims or Black politicians themselves. For example, in Boston's prevailing Italian American North End, the vote for Irish American Louise Day Hicks rose from 26.0 percent in 1961 to 56.1 percent in 1963 in her successful bids for the city's School Committee after she had come out against the enforcement of busing to ensure racial balance between Black and white students in local public education.[7] Likewise, in 1966, anti-Black feelings in the wake of African Americans' initial urban unrest enabled Democratic segregationist George P. Mahoney, of Irish ancestry, to obtain 75 percent of the vote in Baltimore's Little Italy in his albeit fruitless campaign for governor of Maryland.[8]

The sense of being white and an Italian self-perception as determinants of the vote overlapped when the standard bearer of the Caucasian electorate was of Italian ancestry. For example, in 1969, in Newark, New Jersey, Hugh J. Addonizio—the city's first mayor of Italian descent—carried the local Little Italy by 87.5 percent of the vote in his vain attempt at reelection against African American Kenneth A. Gibson in the wake of unrest in the local Black ghetto.[9] The disturbance broke out after two patrol officers of Italian ancestry had beaten an African American taxi driver, and it expressed Blacks' frustration at whites' virtual monopoly over positions with the municipal administration and the local police force.[10] Likewise, in 1971, in Philadelphia, bridging what had been theretofore considerable cleavages with Irish Americans, Polish Americans, and Jewish Americans, Italian Americans participated in a coalition with voters of these groups and elected to City Hall fellow ethnic Frank Rizzo, a former police commissioner who had made a name for himself nationwide for his strongarm methods to quell Black Power activists' demonstrations.[11]

The voters' racial consciousness and their ethnic awareness as factors for the choice of candidates were compatible especially in local and state races due to the multiplicity of offices at stake in these political contests. Conversely, such identity criteria could conflict with each other in federal elections, where fewer seats were available. Against this backdrop, many Italian American voters had to make a choice between their ethnic affiliation and their racial sense of belonging upon entering the polling station.

This was the political context of Spiro T. Agnew's bids for vice president on the Republican ticket in 1968 and 1972. His campaigns offer valuable case studies to test whether ethnic or racial determinants prevailed in shaping Italian Americans' electoral behavior. The following analysis shows that the latter started to become dominant in 1968. As such, it serves as an instance of how politics reflected Italian Americans' construction of a racialized identity in opposition to Blacks' claims. For comparative purposes, this chapter will also take into account Greek Americans' stand on Agnew's candidacy and their electoral behavior, helping elucidate two components in an emerging coalition of resentful and allegedly disprivileged members of white ethnic minorities that, with ups and downs, has subsequently contributed to shaping US politics in part at least until Donald J. Trump's presidency.[12]

Agnew vs. Volpe

Agnew was the son of a Greek immigrant, whose family last name was originally Anagnostopoulos. A Caucasian candidate who had antagonized Black radical groups in his capacity as the governor of Maryland, he would also become the spokesperson for Italian Americans' racial backlash at African Americans. Therefore, he was likely to benefit from the membership of both Greek Americans and Italian Americans in what Michael Novak, the leading theorist of the white ethnic movement, called PIGS. The acronym referred to the Catholic and Orthodox working-class and lower-middle-class underdogs of eastern and southern European descent—among whom Poles, Italians, Greeks, and Slavs were the largest nationality groups—as opposed to the WASPs, the socially established white Anglo-Saxon Protestants of northern European ancestry. In Novak's opinion, the unstable standing of the PIGS was threatened by Blacks' alleged ascent with WASPs' supposed complicity, and therefore the former had to join forces across previous ethnic rivalries and divisions to protect their rights and assert themselves.[13] Actually, Republican presidential candidate Richard M. Nixon slated Agnew as his running mate for the White House in 1968, partly in the effort to reach out to white ethnic voters in northern states, where this cohort of the electorate was more relevant than in the southern region.[14]

Greek American voters' identification with Agnew could not be taken for granted because the governor of Maryland was Episcopalian rather than Orthodox, spoke no Greek, had Americanized his last name, and was actually of Greek descent on his father's side only.[15] Nonetheless, in the eyes of many members of his ethnic community, he soon turned into the quintessence of both Greek Americans and their longing for accommodation within US society in the context of the paucity of elective officeholders from Greek background.[16] He won, for instance, the endorsement of the magazine of the American Hellenic Educational Progressive Association, Greek Americans' largest fraternal association in the United States, which praised him as the self-made "son of a poor immigrant from Messinia, Greece" who had "reached the political summit."[17] The *New York Times* similarly reported that Greek Americans became immensely "proud of Mr. Agnew's rapid rise to national political prominence."[18] Though in hindsight and as an interested party, Agnew himself has contended that "the Greek Americans all over the United States were so excited about the selection of the first vice-presidential candidate of Greek blood that they enthusiastically began pouring money into the Nixon-Agnew coffers."[19]

As for Italian Americans, Agnew's candidacy was not an unreasonable political gamble, either. Four years earlier, for instance, numerous members of this community in Baltimore had given in to presidential hopeful George C. Wallace's white supremacist appeal to race-sensitive working-class ethnics in his unsuccessful bid for the Democratic nomination against sitting President Lyndon B. Johnson.[20] Nonetheless, Nixon notably selected Agnew over John A. Volpe, the incumbent governor of Massachusetts and an apparently rising star in the Italian American political universe. As such, the Greek American vice presidential candidate might have dissatisfied several voters of Italian background with a strong ethnic consciousness and a less forceful sense of racial belonging.

Elected in 1966, Agnew was a former chief executive of Baltimore County and a one-term governor from a small state to whom few political commentators had paid attention at the national level until violent racial unrest, often demonized as "riots" and lasting for five days, broke out in Baltimore in the aftermath of Martin Luther King Jr.'s assassination on April 4, 1968. In response to such turmoil, notwithstanding his previous reputation of sympathy with Blacks' claims on the grounds of his earlier support for and enforcement of civil rights legislation, Agnew summoned the representatives of the local African American community and publicly reprimanded them for the disturbances. Specifically, he made a point of stating in front of the press and television crews that the upheaval and looting had been encouraged by the "circuit-riding, Hanoi-visiting, caterwauling, riot-inciting, burn-America-down type" of the local African American middle class and moderate leadership that had failed to distance itself from such key figures of the radical Black Power movement as Stokely Carmichael and H. Rap Brown. In Lee Sartain's words, Agnew was the politician who stood out "to speak to a growing suburban white constituency who were appalled by the 1968 riots."[21]

Agnew's reaction not only impressed Nixon and his campaign advisers. It also fit both Nixon's strong stand for "law and order" and his campaign strategy of reaching out to voters of European ancestry in traditionally Democratic constituencies in the South and working-class districts in the metropolitan areas of the North by pandering to the Caucasian electorate's call for the retention of its racial privileges, as opposed to whites' supposedly reverse discrimination, and backlash at African American accomplishments and claims for a more equalitarian society.[22] Furthermore, Agnew, with his anglicized last name and Episcopalian faith, was a thoroughly assimilated individual who had previously distanced himself from the Greek community and therefore easily personified white ethnics' quest for Americanization after enduring decades of humiliation and bigotry on the grounds of their ancestries. His disdain for intellectuals similarly echoed white ethnics' contempt for university-educated liberals of Anglo-Saxon heritage who had allegedly disavowed their whiteness and the ensuing prerogatives in the effort to speed up racial integration.[23] As Nell Irvin Painter has suggested, Agnew apparently fit into Nixon's representation of "ethnic whites as temperamentally honest and hardworking . . . against an alien race of black degenerate families judged lacking those self-same virtues."[24]

Contrary to Agnew, Volpe was a three-term governor of a large state and had achieved a national stature long before the spring of 1968. A self-made construction contractor, he served as President Dwight D. Eisenhower's first federal highway administrator, a subcabinet position to which he was appointed in 1956. He was subsequently elected governor of Massachusetts in 1960 against Democrat Joseph D. Ward. Defeated by a narrow margin by Endicott Peabody in 1962, he was reelected to the statehouse both in 1964 against Francis X. Bellotti and in 1966 against Edward McCormick.

Unlike the previous close victories, the latter was a landslide triumph. Volpe's three successful bids for governor in a traditionally Democratic state built up his reputation as an effective vote-getter. Most notably, two of his three elections occurred as John F. Kennedy and Lyndon B. Johnson won the presidency by carrying Massachusetts.[25]

"The projection of Gov. Volpe into the national spotlight," the *Springfield Republican* observed in December 1966, "is a logical result of the recent elections, in which Volpe scored the greatest percentage margin of victory of any GOP governor."[26] Counting on such an achievement, Volpe had placed his eyes on the vice presidency since early 1967, a few months after winning a third term in the State House, and acknowledged that he had some "nudges" in the late fall of that year.[27] For this reason, he threw his hat into the ring of Massachusetts' Republican primaries for the White House. He never dreamed of securing the nomination, but he hoped that a strong showing as his home state's favorite son would pave his way to secure the second place on the GOP ticket at the national convention in Miami Beach.[28] His plans, however, went adrift. Volpe was the only official candidate with his name printed on the ballot. Nevertheless, New York State's Governor Nelson A. Rockefeller managed to come out on top with 30 percent of the vote, as opposed to Volpe's 29.5 percent, by means of a write-in campaign that he launched a few hours after the polls opened in Massachusetts.[29]

In the wake of Volpe's stunning defeat, an editorial in the authoritative *New York Times* mercilessly remarked that he was "an estimable man, but like certain other governors in both parties," Volpe was "not of the White House stature."[30] Likewise, but less outspokenly and more diplomatically, the *Boston Globe*, Massachusetts' leading daily, pointed out that the outcome of the state's primary election revealed that voters were "more interested in picking a president rather than a favorite son" and that "the people want[ed] a choice among serious presidential candidates," implying that Volpe did not belong to such a level of statesmanship.[31] Both assessments, however, disregarded the candidate's ethnicity.

Unable to carry his home state in April, Volpe was pushed aside in the selection of the Republican vice presidential nominee in August. The fact that he had previously shunned the GOP primary in New Hampshire after announcing his bid for the second spot on the Republican ticket also questioned the size of the governor's political following outside Massachusetts.[32] As a result, Nixon eventually chose Agnew. Coeval rumors in the press, which found an echo in subsequent scholarship, had it that large donations from the Greek American community, primarily from Boston's import-export mogul and industrialist Thomas A. Pappas, to Nixon's war chest made the difference to the benefit of Maryland's governor.[33] Yet, Volpe's weakness at the polls did contribute to his eventual failure to become the Republican 1968 candidate for vice president, since one of the main functions of the running mate in any campaign is to bring out votes for the White House hopeful in the Electoral College, starting with their respective home states.[34] Nixon himself would later comment in his memoirs that the governor's rout in Massachusetts had been "embarrassing to Volpe" and "irritating to me."[35]

Italian Americans and Nixon's Dropping of Volpe

Regardless of the reasons for Volpe's exclusion from the Republican ticket, Agnew's nomination had the potential to displease many voters of Italian extraction, causing them to stay home on Election Day or to cast their ballots for the Democratic Party out of retaliation for Nixon's decision. Actually, in his analysis of the Republican National Convention, Giacomo Grillo, the editor of the Italian-language section for Boston's Italian American weekly *Post-Gazette* mentioned his fellow ethnics' "disappointment." He went on to stress the political marginalization of his own nationality group because none of its members was currently serving on the cabinet or the Supreme Court and expressed his regret that Nixon had missed an opportunity to heal such a wound by picking Agnew instead of Volpe as his running mate.[36] In the same issue, a front-page article lashed out at Nixon, significantly resorting to English: "How could you have ignored the selection of Governor John A. Volpe as your running mate?"[37] This periodical subsequently complained that "when the showdown came, he dunked Volpe in the Nixon watering trough just as he dunked several other nationally prominent Republicans in favor of the relatively unknown Gov. Agnew."[38] Another

Italian-language newspaper, *Il Popolo Italiano*, a monthly printed in Atlantic City, New Jersey, but also serving a large readership in Philadelphia and eastern Pennsylvania, denounced a climate of "hatred" that had allegedly shaped the convention in Miami Beach, although this ambience had been fueled by the ethnic press itself.[39]

New York City's *Il Progresso Italo-Americano*, perhaps the most influential Italian American periodical nationwide, stated that Agnew's nomination "surprised everybody."[40] It echoed the astonishment of other media as well. Most notably, the *Washington Post* called Nixon's choice "perhaps the most eccentric political appointment since the Roman emperor Caligula named his horse as consul."[41] Agnew himself admitted that he was "not a household name."[42] Yet, *Il Progresso Italo-Americano* went beyond this issue and attacked the Republican presidential candidate and his running mate directly. According to this daily, Agnew's nomination was Nixon's "first political big mistake" because he had chosen a candidate who "had no experience at all about international problems and no relevant knowledge of the complexity of domestic issues." *Il Progresso Italo-Americano* concluded that Agnew's place on the Republican ticket would eventually turn out to be an asset for the Democratic Party and its standard bearer for the White House, Hubert H. Humphrey, the incumbent vice president in the Johnson administration.[43] Political observers have subsequently shared this interpretation. For instance, Roger Stone and Mike Colapietro have remarked that Agnew's selection "was to be a blunder," while "Volpe would have been a naked grab with the Catholic vote."[44] *Il Progresso Italo-Americano* also reprinted an article by Drew Pearson, one of the best-known syndicated columnists in the United States, who praised Humphrey's inclusion of Joseph Alioto, San Francisco's mayor of Italian extraction, in his short list of tentative Democratic vice presidential nominees. In Pearson's opinion, slating Alioto would prove to be an effective choice to carry not only the Italian American community but also the vote of other white ethnic minorities.[45]

The Democratic nomination eventually went to Senator Edmund Muskie from Maine, a Catholic whose religious faith was expected to appeal to voters of Irish, Polish, and Italian descent.[46] Yet, the attention of *Il Progresso Italo-Americano* for Alioto's possible but short-lived candidacy revealed Italian Americans' growing interest in the top echelons of elective offices.

Indeed, Italian American leaders of Republican attachment such as Anthony A. Maisano, the president of the Columbian Republican League, and Philip A. Guarino, the chairperson of the Italian-American Section of the Nationalities Division of the Republican National Committee, mobilized to support Volpe's candidacy in the effort to empower their ethnic community both within the GOP and in national politics.[47] In particular, Guarino established a committee of fifty prominent Italian Americans to pressure Nixon into choosing Volpe as his running mate.[48]

A few rank-and-file voters of Italian descent, not only from Massachusetts but also from New Jersey, Pennsylvania, and New York State, also congratulated Volpe on his decision to seek the Republican nomination for vice president and took pride in such a move by a fellow ethnic, committing themselves to the governor of Massachusetts. For example, a woman by the name of Porfida Stella from Staten Island wrote to Volpe that "my husband and I will vote for you because I like to see an Italian to be in a high position." Likewise, to Judge Joseph Vinciguerra from Andover, Massachusetts, Volpe was "still our hero," even after he yielded the nomination to Agnew at Miami Beach.[49]

Other Italian Americans, as Grillo suggested, gave vent to their frustration for the selection of Agnew at the Republican National Convention. Upon hearing of the selection of Maryland's governor, Frank J. Pandolfo—the owner of a pharmacy in Somerville, Massachusetts—expressed his "regret and disappointment," out of ethnic pride, on the grounds that Volpe deserved a place on the ballot because his performance in office had "done much to uplift the attitude of others towards us, of Italian anncestory [sic]." Vinzo Comito of Newton, Massachusetts, maintained that he felt "disgusted and angry" for how the governor had been mistreated in Miami Beach. Anthony Magnacca even wrote to Volpe that Nixon "is not a man. He is a savage. If I were in your place, I would never look him in the face again." Rather than casting his ballot for Nixon and Agnew, Magnacca was ready to vote for Wallace, who was running again for the White House as the candidate of the American Independent Party on a segregationist platform.[50]

Italian Americans' resentment for Volpe's dropping and their indirect hostility toward Agnew were not confined to Massachusetts. For instance, according to Californian Basil Zolli Jr., "Nixon foolishly passed up" Volpe's "great appeal . . . to the Italian vote," and the Republican ticket had no chance to win with Agnew on it. Gino M. Pirrone, a resident of West Chester, Pennsylvania, and the national chairperson of the Italian American Citizens Council for Political Action, contended in mid-August that he was "still trying to overcome the shock I received in Florida."[51]

The Italian American Vote in 1968

According to *Il Popolo Italiano*, in 1968 "many Catholics, including millions of Italo-Americans, threw their weight behind the Nixon-Agnew Ticket."[52] Ultimately, although Pirrone might not have recovered from his upset by Election Day, a significant component—though not a majority—of the electorate from Italian background did. In spite of his initial frustration, Volpe himself made a point of campaigning for the Nixon-Agnew ticket.[53] The chairmanship of a special committee in charge of mobilizing ethnic voters (the Nationality Division of the United Citizens for Nixon-Agnew) and the promise of the appointment to the position of US ambassador to Italy, in case a Republican administration assumed charge, were enough to persuade Volpe to endorse Nixon and Agnew and to secure the favor of many Italian American voters for the GOP standard bearer and the latter's running mate.[54]

During the 1968 campaign Agnew engaged in a few ethnic slurs. He took on Japanese Americans and Polish Americans, but he notably spared Italian Americans, since the latter were a key constituency for the Republican Party.[55] Major Italian-language newspapers, such as *Il Progresso Italo-Americano*, made no endorsement in the presidential race and limited themselves to urging readers to go to the polls and to exert their political rights.[56] However, when the votes were counted in November, Nixon received overall roughly 40 percent of the ballots in the Little Italies nationwide. He was definitely more popular with voters of Greek origins or ancestry, who generally tended to support the Republican Party out of ethnic solidarity with Agnew. Surveys revealed that 53 percent to 81 percent of Greek Americans voted for the GOP in the 1968 race for the White House, while "the association between identification with Agnew as 'a fellow Greek-American' and candidate choice for the Republican presidential ticket [was] positive and statistically significant."[57] In particular, even if roughly 80 percent of Greek American eligible electors turned out to be registered as Democrats in 1968, an estimated four-fifths of them cast their ballots for the Nixon-Agnew ticket.[58] Although Nixon did not carry the Italian American community, his following underwent a significant growth among voters of this ethnic community as compared to his previous performance in the 1960 race for the White House against John F. Kennedy. Specifically, as evidence of Nixon's mounting popularity, between 1960 and 1968, the Italian American vote for him rose by 10 percent in Cleveland; by 13 percent in Brooklyn, where the Republican candidate carried the local Little Italy with 56 percent of the ballots; by 15 percent in Newark; and by 22 percent in Philadelphia. It increased, albeit by only 3 percent, in Boston, too, notwithstanding the exclusion of Massachusetts' favorite son from the GOP ticket. According to future Governor Christine Todd Whitman, Nixon carried New Jersey for the GOP for the first time in twelve years thanks to the electorate of Italian extraction.[59] Moreover, the forecast of a possible Italian Americans' bolt to Humphrey by *Il Progresso Italo-Americano* proved to be wrong. Indeed, the Democratic presidential hopeful won 50 percent of the Italian American vote, while Johnson had obtained 77 percent of the ballots in 1964 and Kennedy 75 percent in 1960.[60]

In order to offset Volpe's dropping from the ticket, GOP appeals to Italian American voters stressed that "under Republican President Richard Nixon . . . the American of Italian heritage will get his share."[61] In the end, however, ethnic pride played second fiddle to race-related fears. To the electorate of Italian background, Agnew was eventually a less displeasing candidate than he had seemed after snatching the Republican vice presidential nomination from Volpe's hands. Actually, Italian Americans were more worried about racial unrest than concerned about their own political representation and recognition at the federal level. For instance, *Il Progresso Italo-Americano* devoted a larger coverage to African Americans' rioting at Miami Beach in the days of the Republican National Convention than to the political maneuvering within the GOP.[62] Against this backdrop, appealing to whites' racial resentment in his campaign rhetoric,[63] Agnew became a satisfactory and reliable candidate on the grounds of his previous inflexibility toward Blacks in the aftermath of King's assassination the previous April. At that time, *Il Progresso Italo-Americano* made a daily assessment of the mayhem that the alleged "black hoodlum"—as the newspaper called it—had provoked city by city.[64] Specifically, after denouncing lootings, shootings, and arsons that had taken place in Baltimore, the periodical welcomed Governor Agnew's request to President Johnson for the dispatch of federal troops to Maryland's main city and credited it with the subsequent pacification of the racial turmoil.[65] Baltimore's mayor, Italian American Thomas D'Alessandro III, criticized Agnew's reprimand of the city's moderate African American leadership for its alleged collusion with Black extremism. Yet, his fellow ethnics, who had felt particularly vulnerable to the rioting because the city's Little Italy was near a Black public housing project, appreciated it.[66] Residents of Baltimore County who congratulated Agnew "upon the stand you took at the recent meeting with Negro leaders in regard to the civil disorders" included individuals with such Italian-sounding last names as Thomas J. Lorenzo Jr., Joseph Pedone Jr., Michale Quinto, Leonard Butta, Lawrence Borgetti, and Leo F. De Luca.[67]

In his analysis of the editorials in *Il Progresso-Italo Americano* about the Black freedom struggle in the first half of the 1960s, Eddy Menichelli has concluded that the daily supported African Americans' campaigns for civil and political rights, but it opposed such special programs as affirmative action and busing to make amends for past bigotry and to speed up Blacks' integration, which the newspaper considered tantamount to reverse discrimination against whites. Italian newcomers endured intolerance and prejudices upon arrival in the United States between the early 1880s and the mid-1920s, but they eventually worked their way out of destitution and social marginality by means of their hard work and personal sacrifices without any kind of government aid. Therefore, apparently unaware of the differences between slavery and voluntary migration, their offspring did not understand why African Americans should receive institutional support to overcome inequalities mainly in employment and education.[68]

Although *Il Progresso Italo-Americano* reiterated its criticism of special policies for Blacks during the 1968 presidential campaign, the newspaper also continued to distance itself from segregation and maintained that Wallace did not "deserve a role in the nation's political life" because he was an advocate of hatred, racism, violence and intolerance."[69] It can be easily suggested that the voice of this newspaper reflected the orientation of most members of the Italian American community. One of them remarked that he could not back Wallace because "he would have caused too much resentment among the blacks and split the nation in half. I don't like having second-class citizens."[70] Consequently, numerous voters of Italian extraction found a political spokesperson in Agnew. As historian Peter B. Levy has suggested, the governor of Maryland was no Wallace. Unlike the latter, Agnew did not win "fame by defending the Southern way, espousing 'segregation forever,' threatening to block the schoolhouse door, or preaching the doctrine of nullification." He distanced himself from "an open defense of Jim Crow" and "emphasized orderliness, personal responsibility, and the sanctity of hard work, the nuclear family, and the law."[71] Moreover, as he would reiterate in his vice presidential years, Agnew voiced whites' fears of social and economic dispossession to the benefit of Blacks, but he did not resort to an overtly racist discourse.[72] Election returns showed that few Italian Americans identified with a return to segregation. Indeed, contrary to Magnacca's commitment and as compared to the 40 percent of the ballots for the Nixon-Agnew ticket, Wallace received only 10 percent of the Italian American vote nationwide in 1968.[73]

Agnew had been elected as a Republican moderate in 1966, but he adopted a law-and-order approach on race issues after taking office as Maryland's governor.[74] Instead, Volpe moved in the opposite direction. In particular, he signed legislation in 1965 to ban racial imbalances in the state's schools and hailed it as "another page in the history of Massachusetts' leadership in education" and a demonstration of "our commitment to strike at the causes of prejudice."[75] As Jason Sokol has pointed out, "Volpe positioned the Massachusetts state government as the initial shaper of desegregation policy."[76] Subsequently, in Boston's 1967 mayoral campaign, he came out against Louise Day Hicks because of her opposition to racial integration and contributed to progressive Democrat Kevin H. White's election to City Hall.[77] He also encouraged affirmative action in both the public and private sectors in Massachusetts. For example, he urged Polaroid Corporation to give preference to African Americans in hiring workers for its plants in Cambridge and Waltham. These decisions were at variance with the stand of the Italian

American community. The *Post-Gazette*, for instance, reported that "the Volpe statement in which he emphasized that more Negroes should be appointed to state jobs brought an immediate roar of protest." The newspaper also accused Volpe of "granting preference in employment to Negroes to the discrimination of white applicants." Overall, the Italian American weekly criticized the governor and his political ally, Boston's mayor, for their alleged neglect of Caucasian residents: "Both Volpe and White are talking incessantly about the 'poor Negroes in the ghetto.' Neither ever mentioned the 'poor whites' who have become forgotten people."[78] It is hardly by chance that the *Post-Gazette* did not regret Volpe's defeat in Massachusetts' Republican primary against Rockefeller, listing "his persistence in demanding preference for Negroes" among the reasons for his rout.[79] *Il Progresso-Italo Americano*, too, implied that Rockefeller was a better candidate than Volpe.[80] Moreover, the newspaper's long-term contempt for life in African American ghettos seemed to find a responsive chord in Agnew's notorious campaign statement that "when you've seen one slum, you've seen them all."[81]

Conclusion

The Italian American vote in the 1968 presidential elections was in a state of flux as for the prevalence of ethnic or racial factors influencing the choice of candidates. On the whole, however, it reflected at least the beginning of the whitening of the Little Italies. A few Italian American newspapers discussed Agnew's Greek American ethnicity. This was the case of the Chicago-based and Catholic-oriented *Fra Noi*, which also reminded its readers of "the joys that might have been in this election year if we could have voted for an Italian-American as vice-presidential candidate."[82] Yet, political retaliation against Nixon out of ethnic redress for his failure to place Volpe on the GOP ticket was kept to a minimum and the Republican candidate underwent a significant increase in his share of the Italian American vote in comparison with his 1960 unsuccessful bid for the White House.

The Republican Party further consolidated its following in the Little Italies four years later. In 1972, 63 percent of the electorate of Italian background still identified with the Democratic Party in registration records nationwide.[83] But Nixon and Agnew received 52 percent of the Italian American vote in Ohio, 53 percent in Pennsylvania, 61 percent in New Jersey, and 68 percent in New York State.[84]

In the view of *Il Progresso Italo-Americano*, it came as no surprise that Agnew was slated for a second term in 1972.[85] The following year, when Agnew was forced to step down amid charges of bribery, extortion, and tax fraud during his terms as chief executive of Baltimore County and governor of Maryland, the Chicago-based *La Parola del Popolo* even regretted his resignation and, despite his personal faults, presented him as the embodiment of "patriotism, self-confidence, and pugnacity, all features that Americans usually regard as positive characteristics."[86]

It was only in hindsight that the most ethnically conscious members of the Italian American community realized what an opportunity they had missed with the 1968 nomination of a Greek American for vice president on the Republican ticket.[87] Following in Agnew's footsteps, Nixon gave up the presidency in 1974 to prevent his removal from office in the wake of the Watergate scandal. "If Nixon had chosen Volpe to be his running mate in 1968 (and 1972)," historian Frank J. Cavaioli has suggested, "the first Italian American would have become president."[88] In such a sort of retrospective and collective self-deprecation, Geno Baroni, a Catholic priest and ethnic activist who served as assistant secretary for Housing and Urban Development in the Carter administration, even revived rumors that the Greek American community had secured Agnew the vice presidency with a significant donation to Nixon's campaign funds.[89] However, igniting a belated competition between Italian Americans and Greek Americans in the political arena seemed a futile gesture because both communities had generally come to share common interests as white ethnics across the partisan spectrum, instead of antagonizing each other by means of conflicting goals as separate nationality groups. In particular, resistance to busing contributed to encouraging both Italian Americans and Greek Americans to switch from the Democratic Party to the GOP, strengthened their belonging to what Nixon's aide Michael P. Balzano Jr. has called "the New Majority" along the color line, and thereby consolidated their whiteness.[90]

In 1975 Baroni and other Italian American leaders established the National Italian American Foundation, a lobbying organization that intended to support the ethnic claims of the Little Italies and to promote candidates of Italian extraction to elective and appointive offices.[91] Yet, this initiative, too, was tardy, as ethnic identity was a determinant of electoral behavior for fewer and fewer Italian Americans. Remarkably enough, in 1984, when Democratic Congresswoman Geraldine Ferraro, a member of the board of the National Italian American Foundation, became the first politician of Italian ancestry to be slated by either major party for vice president, 61 percent of the voters of Italian descent cast their ballots for Republican Ronald Reagan and his running mate George H. W. Bush in the race for the White House.[92] It was the final stage of a trajectory toward the construction of a racial sense of belonging that had begun to loom in 1968 when four out of ten Italian American voters had forgiven Nixon for dropping Volpe and replacing him with a Greek American on the GOP ticket. Conversely, ethnic allegiance influenced Greek Americans' electoral behavior longer. When Michael Dukakis, Massachusetts' governor of Greek descent, ran for president on the Democratic ticket in 1988, he managed to win 55 percent of the Greek American vote, thanks primarily to his ancestral roots, although racial issues characterized the election campaign and Republican propaganda denounced him for being soft on African American crime, appealing to whites' fears.[93]

NOTES

1. Colburn and Pozzetta, "Race."
2. US House of Representatives, 91st Congress, 2nd Session, *Hearings*, 70–71.
3. Jacobson, *Roots Too*.
4. Alba, *Italian Americans*; Richards, *Italian American*; Aversa, "Italian Neo-Ethnicity."
5. Gans, "Symbolic Ethnicity," 7–8, 13–14.
6. Wolfinger, "The Development," 905; LaGumina, "Politics," 483–84; Van Horne, *Ethnicity*, 205.
7. Buell and Brisbin, *School Desegregation*, 61–66. For the opposition of Boston's Italian Americans to busing, see Formisano, *Boston against Busing*.
8. Levy and Kramer, *The Ethnic Factor*, 174.

9. Ibid., 174.

10. Tuttle, *How Newark Became Newark*, 42–46. African American writer Amiri Baraka sarcastically remarked that "Blacks are some 60 percent of the half-million people who live in Newark, a city where Italian Power must be second only to that in the Vatican" [as quoted in David Llorens, "Ameer (Leroi Jones) Baraka," *Ebony* 24, no. 10 (August 1969): 78].

11. Hamilton, *Rizzo*.

12. Berezin, "On the Construction Sites of History," 324; Szefel, "From Tall Ideas Dancing," 153.

13. Novak, *The Rise of Unmeltable Ethnics*.

14. Scammon and Wattenberg, *The Real Majority*. See also Sugrue and Skrentny, "The White Ethnic Strategy."

15. Peter Millones, "20,000 Greek Americans Having Word Here," *New York Times*, August 21, 1968, 47; Moskos and Moskos, *Greek Americans*, 124.

16. Botsas, "The American Hellenes," 40.

17. As quoted in Brock, "Ethnic Voting," 75.

18. Ben A. Franklin, "Greek Americans Rally to Agnew," *New York Times*, October 3, 1968, 40.

19. Agnew, *Go Quietly*, 63.

20. Durr, "When Southern Politics Came North," 327.

21. Marsh, *Agnew*, 158–62; Carter, *The Politics of Rage*, 331; Sartain, *Borders*, 175.

22. Ambrose, *Nixon*, 162–63; O'Reilly, *Nixon's Piano*, 296–308; Briley, *Nixon Rebuilds*, 183–84. For Nixon's subsequent endeavors to consolidate his own following among European ethnic groups after taking office, see Merton, "An Ethnic Presence in the White House?" 419, 423, 425–27.

23. Novak, *The Rise of Unmeltable Ethnics*, 116–34. For Agnew's efforts to downplay his ethnic roots, see also Manchester, *The Glory*, 476.

24. Painter, *The History*, 379–80.

25. Kilgore, *John Volpe*.

26. "Volpe as Vice President?" *Springfield Republican*, December 2, 1966, 6C.

27. Paul Driscoll, "Observers Believe Volpe May Try for 1968 Team," *Telegram and Gazette*, January 26, 1967; Howard S. Knowles, "Volpe Reports Some 'Nudges' to Be Nixon's Running Mate," *Evening Gazette*, December 9, 1967, clippings, John A. Volpe Papers, box 68, folder "Clippings," Snell Library, Northeastern University, Boston, MA.

28. Paul Driscoll, "Volpe Makes It Official: To Run as Favorite Son," *Telegram and Gazette*, January 11, 1968, 1, 3.

29. Timothy Leland, "Massive Write-In for Rocky," *Boston Globe*, May 1, 1968, 1, 24; Wainstock, *Election Year 1968*, 94.

30. "Upset in Massachusetts," *New York Times*, May 2, 1968, 46.
31. "Again, the Voters Surprise," *Boston Globe*, May 2, 1968, 20.
32. Cornelius Dalton, "Shaky Start for Volpe's Campaign," *Boston Herald Traveler*, January 11, 1968, 15.
33. Louis Kaufman, "Tom Pappas Pushed Agnew," *Boston Globe*, August 9, 1968, 1, 9; "A 'Good Word' for Agnew," *New York Times*, August 10, 1968, 12; Summers and Swan, *The Arrogance of Power*, 284–87; Reeves, *President Nixon*, 231, 659; Thomas, "Racial and Ethnic Construction," 264–67, 269.
34. Baumgartner, *The American Vice Presidency*, 105.
35. Nixon, *RN*, 302.
36. Giacomo Grillo, "Panorama politico americano," *Post-Gazette*, August 16, 1968, 12.
37. "How Could You, Mr. Nixon," *Post-Gazette*, August 16, 1968, 1
38. "What Did Nixon Offer?" *Post-Gazette*, August 23, 1968, 3.
39. "Nixon nominato candidato presidenziale," *Il Popolo Italiano* 33, no. 8 (August 1968): 6.
40. "Nixon sceglie S.T. Agnew per la vice-presidenza," *Il Progresso Italo-Americano*, August 9, 1968, 1.
41. As quoted in Roberts, *In the Shadow*, 399.
42. As quoted in Witcover, *The Resurrection*, 355–56.
43. "Un 'atout' per Humphrey," *Il Progresso Italo-Americano*, August 10, 1968, 1.
44. Stone with Colapietro, *Nixon's Secrets*, 313.
45. Drew Pearson, "Corriere di Washington," *Il Progresso Italo-Americano*, August 11, 1968, 1, 12.
46. Cohen, *American Maelstrom*, 283–84.
47. Anthony Maisano to Philip A. Guarino, June 20, 1968, Anthony Maisano Papers, box 4, folder 13, Historical Society of Pennsylvania, Balch Institute Collection, Philadelphia, PA.
48. Giacomo Grillo, "Un comitato elettorale italo-americano patrocinerà la candidatura di Volpe alla vice-presidenza," *Post-Gazette*, July 26, 1968, 12.
49. A. J. Caruso to Volpe, February 27, 1968; Porfida Stella to Volpe, February 28, 1968; Gus Lombardi Jr. to Volpe, April 2, 1968; Dan Montemarano to Volpe, April 15, 1968; Joseph Vinciguerra to Volpe, August 9, 1968, Volpe Papers, box 68, folder "Volpe—V.P."
50. Frank J. Pandolfo to Volpe, August 9, 1968; Vinzo Comito to Volpe, August 11, 1968; Anthony Magnacca to Volpe, August 13, 1968, Volpe Papers, box 68, folder "Volpe—V.P."
51. Basil Zolli Jr. to Volpe, August 9, 1968; Gino M. Pirrone to Volpe, August 15, 1968, Volpe Papers, box 68, folder "Volpe—V.P."

52. "Nixon's It," *Il Popolo Italiano* 33, no. 11 (November 1968): 8.
53. Sobel, *The Fallen*, 291.
54. "Volpe nominato aiutante di Nixon," *Il Progresso Italo-Americano*, September 4, 1968, 1, 16; "Volpe Eyes Embassy in Rome," *Il Popolo Italiano* 33, no. 9 (September 1968): 1.
55. Black, *Richard Milhous Nixon*, 543.
56. "Oggi parla l'elettore," *Il Progresso Italo-Americano*, November 5, 1968, 1.
57. Humphrey and Brock Louis, "Assimilation and Voting Behavior," 41–42 (quote 42); Brock, "Ethnic Voting," 79.
58. Paul, "A Study in Ethnic Group," 168–69.
59. Whitman, *It's My Party Too*, 94.
60. Rothenberg, Licht, and Newport, *Ethnic Voters*, 19–20.
61. Pasquale Pignato, "A Proud American Speaks His Mind," *Post-Gazette*, September 19, 1968, 7.
62. "Tumulti razziali e saccheggi a Miami per il secondo giorno," *Il Progresso Italo-Americano*, August 9, 1968, 1, 10; "Continuano i disordini nei dintorni di Miami," *Il Progresso Italo-Americano*, August 10, 1968, 1, 10.
63. Cottrell and Browne, *1968*, 231.
64. "L'esercito protegge la Casa Bianca," *Il Progresso Italo-Americano*, April 6, 1968, 1, 10; "Tutta la nazione sconvolta da disordini," *Il Progresso Italo-Americano*, April 7, 1968, 1, 14; "La tensione si aggrava," *Il Progresso Italo-Americano*, April 8, 1968, 1, 10.
65. "Ritorna la calma nelle città sconvolte dai moti razziali," *Il Progresso Italo-Americano*, April 9, 1968, 1, 10.
66. Durr, *Behind*, 141–43.
67. Raymond Sadler et al. to Spiro T. Agnew, November 16, 1968, Addresses and State Papers of Spiro T. Agnew, General File, MSA S 1041–1713 Archives of Maryland Online, https://bit.ly/3AfasbT.
68. Menichelli, *La questione*; LaGumina, "Discrimination."
69. "Il candidato George Wallace," *Il Progresso Italo-Americano*, September 24, 1968, 1.
70. As quoted in Rieder, *Canarsie*, 243.
71. Levy, "Spiro Agnew," 714.
72. Olson, "Whiteness," 705, 710–14.
73. Levy and Kramer, *The Ethnic Factor*, 172.
74. Conversely, for the thesis that Agnew always held conservative views on race relations and civil disobedience, see Csicek, "Spiro T. Agnew," 70–85.
75. As quoted in Delmont, *Why Busing Failed*, 82.
76. Sokol, "Uneasy Executives," 129.

77. Fred Blumenthal, "Gov. John Volpe: He Wants To Be No. 2," *St. Petersburg Times*, February 25, 1968, clipping, Volpe Papers, box 68, folder "Volpe—V.P."; Weinberg, "Boston's Kevin White," 91–92.

78. "No Mass Hiring at Polaroid," *Post-Gazette*, May 10, 1968, 1–2; "The Distressing Fact," *Post-Gazette*, August 2, 1968, p. 3.

79. "Primary Sweepings," *Post-Gazette*, May 10, 1968, 3.

80. "Nell'agone politico," *Il Progresso Italo-Americano*, May 3, 1968, 1.

81. "Difficile per i bianchi la vita a Harlem," *Il Progresso Italo-Americano*, May 10, 1964, 5; Agnew as quoted in "Spiro Agnew, Dead at 77," *The Greek American*, September 21, 1996, 3.

82. G. M. Lanzillotti, "'Ethnic' Voting Extends to National Scene," *Fra Noi* 9, no. 11 (November 1968): 1

83. Martinelli, "Italian-American Experience," 227.

84. Rothenberg, Licht, and Newport, *Ethnic Voters*, 20.

85. "Nixon fa il punto sulla sua politica," *Il Progresso Italo-Americano*, August 24, 1972, 1.

86. Marino de Medici, "Esce Spiro Agnew, entra Gerald Ford," *La Parola del Popolo* 23, no. 65 (September–October 1973): 15.

87. Bosco, "A Fateful Decision," 12–14.

88. Cavaioli, "Italian American Governors," 146.

89. Baroni, "An Address," 23.

90. Van Patten, "Reflections," 78; Balzano, "The Silent," 261.

91. Morton, "National," 183–84.

92. Ladd, "On Mandates," 14.

93. Davies, *Elections USA*, 62; Kitroeff, "The Limits," 147; Mendelberg, *The Race Card*, 3–4; Mayer, *Running on Race*, 211–14, 218–28.

Bibliography

Agnew, Spiro T. *Go Quietly . . . Or Else*. New York: Morrow, 1980.

Alba, Richard. *Italian Americans: Into the Twilight of Ethnicity*. Englewood Cliffs, NJ: Prentice-Hall, 1985.

Ambrose, Stephen E. *Nixon: The Triumph of a Politician, 1962–1972*. New York: Simon & Schuster, 1989.

Aversa, Alfred, Jr. "Italian Neo-Ethnicity: The Search for Self-Identity." *Journal of Ethnic Studies* 6, no. 2 (1978): 49–56.

Balzano, Michael P., Jr. "The Silent versus the New Majority." In *Richard M. Nixon: Politician, President, Administrator*, edited by Leon Friedman and William F. Levantrosser, 259–74. Westport, CT: Greenwood Press, 1991.

Baroni, Geno. "An Address by the Rt. Rev. Mons. Geno Baroni." In *Italian and Irish in America*, edited by Francis X. Femminella, 19–25. New York: American Italian Historical Association, 1985.
Baumgartner, Jody C. *The American Vice Presidency Reconsidered*. Westport, CT: Praeger, 2006.
Berezin, Mabel. "On the Construction Sites of History: Where Did Donald Trump Come From?" *American Journal of Cultural Sociology* 5, no. 3 (October 2017): 322–37.
Black, Conrad. *Richard Milhous Nixon: The Invincible Quest*. London: Quercus, 2007.
Bosco, Joseph A. "A Fateful Decision." *Italian America* 19, no. 2 (Spring 2014): 12–14.
Botsas, Eleftherios N. "The American Hellenes." In *America's Ethnic Politics*, edited by Joseph S. Roucek and Bernard Eisenberg, 29–45. Westport, CT: Greenwood Press, 1982.
Briley, John David. *Nixon Rebuilds: From Defeat to the White House, 1962–1968*. Jefferson, NC: McFarland, 2021.
Brock, Helen Theresa. "Ethnic Voting Behavior in an Urban Area: The Effect of Ethnic Identification upon Candidate Choice and Political Party Affiliation among Greek Americans." MA thesis, College of William and Mary, 1971.
Buell, Emmett H., Jr., and Richard A. Brisbin Jr. *School Desegregation and Defended Neighborhoods: The Boston Controversy*. Lexington, MA: Lexington Books, 1982.
Carter, Dan T. *The Politics of Rage: George Wallace, the Origins of the New Conservatism, and the Transformation of American Politics*. Baton Rouge: Louisiana State University Press, 2000.
Cavaioli, Frank J. "Italian American Governors." *Italian Americana* 25, no. 2 (Summer 2007): 133–59.
Cohen, Michael A. *American Maelstrom: The 1968 Election and the Politics of Division*. New York: Oxford University Press, 2016.
Colburn, David R., and George E. Pozzetta. "Race, Ethnicity, and the Evolution of Political Legitimacy." In *The Sixties: From Memory to History*, edited by David Farber, 119–48. Chapel Hill: University of North Carolina Press, 1994.
Cottrell, Robert C., and Blaine T. Browne. *1968: The Rise and Fall of the New American Revolution*. Lanham, MD: Rowman & Littlefield, 2018.
Csicek, Alex. "Spiro T. Agnew and the Burning of Baltimore." In *Baltimore '68: Riots and Rebirth in an American City*, edited by Jessica Elfenbein et al., 70–85. Philadelphia: Temple University Press, 2011.

Davies, Philip. *Elections USA*. Manchester: Manchester University Press, 1992.
Delmont, Matthew F. *Why Busing Failed: Race, Media, and the National Resistance to School Desegregation*. Berkeley: University of California Press, 2016.
Durr, Kenneth. *Behind the Backlash: White Working-Class Politics in Baltimore, 1940–1980*. Chapel Hill: University of North Carolina Press, 2003.
———. "When Southern Politics Came North: The Roots of White Working-Class Conservatism in Baltimore, 1940–1964." *Labor History* 37, no. 3 (Summer 1996): 309–31.
Formisano, Ronald P. *Boston against Busing: Race, Class, and Ethnicity in the 1960s and 1970s*. Chapel Hill: University of North Carolina Press, 2004.
Gans, Herbert J. "Symbolic Ethnicity." *Ethnic and Racial Studies* 2, no. 1 (1979): 1–20.
Hamilton, Fred. *Rizzo: From Cop to Mayor of Philadelphia*. New York: Viking, 1973.
Humphrey, Craig R., and Helen Brock Louis. "Assimilation and Voting Behavior: A Study of Greek-Americans." *International Migration Review* 7, no. 1 (Spring 1973): 34–45.
Jacobson, Matthew Frye. *Roots Too: White Ethnic Revival in Post–Civil Rights America*. Cambridge, MA: Harvard University Press, 2006.
Kilgore, Kathleen. *John Volpe: The Life of an Immigrant's Son*. Dublin, NH: Yankee Books, 1987.
Kitroeff, Alexander. "The Limits of Political Transnationalism: The Greek-American Lobby, 1970s–1990s." In *Greek Diaspora and Migration since 1700: Society, Politics, and Culture*, edited by Dimitris Tziovas, 141–53. Farnham, UK: Ashgate, 2009.
Ladd, Everett Carll. "On Mandates, Realignments, and the 1984 Presidential Election." *Political Science Quarterly* 100, no. 1 (Winter 1985): 1–25.
LaGumina, Salvatore J. "Discrimination, Prejudice, and Italian American History." In *The Routledge History of Italian Americans*, edited by William J. Connell and Stanislao G. Pugliese, 223–38. New York: Routledge, 2018.
———. "Politics." In *The Italian American Experience: An Encyclopedia*, edited by Salvatore J. LaGumina et al., 480–86. New York: Garland, 2000.
Levy, Mark L., and Michael S. Kramer. *The Ethnic Factor: How America's Minorities Decide Elections*. New York: Simon & Schuster, 1972.
Levy, Peter B. "Spiro Agnew, the Forgotten Americans, and the Rise of the New Right." *Historian* 75, no. 4 (Winter 2013): 707–39.
Manchester, William. *The Glory and the Dream*. Boston: Little, Brown, 1974.
Marsh, Robert. *Agnew, the Unexamined Man: A Political Profile*. Philadelphia: J. B. Lippincott, 1971.

Martinelli, Phylis Cancilla. "Italian-American Experience." In *America's Ethnic Politics*, edited by Joseph S. Roucek and Bernard Eisenberg, 217–31. Westport, CT: Greenwood Press, 1982.

Mayer, Jeremy D. *Running on Race: Racial Politics in Presidential Campaigns, 1960–2000*. New York: Random House, 2002.

Mendelberg, Tali. *The Race Card: Campaign Strategy, Implicit Messages, and the Norm of Equity*. Princeton, NJ: Princeton University Press, 2001.

Menichelli, Eddy. *La questione razziale negli Stati Uniti: Il racconto della conquista dei diritti civili sulle pagine de Il Progresso Italo-Americano, 1961–1965*. Anagni: Alcheringa, 2015.

Merton, Joe. "'An Ethnic Presence in the White House?': Ethnicity, Identity Politics, and the Presidency in the 1970s." *Presidential Studies Quarterly* 50, no. 2 (June 2020): 418–35.

Morton, Sean. "National Italian American Foundation." In *Italian Americans: The History and Culture of a People*, edited by Eric Martone, 183–84. Santa Barbara, CA: ABC-CLIO, 2017.

Moskos, Peter C., and Charles C. Moskos. *Greek Americans: Struggle and Success*. New Brunswick, NJ: Transaction Books, 2014.

Nixon, Richard M. *RN: The Memoirs of Richard Nixon*. New York: Grosset & Dunlap, 1978.

Novak, Michael. *The Rise of Unmeltable Ethnics: Politics and Culture in the Seventies*. New York: Macmillan, 1972.

Olson, Joel. "Whiteness and the Polarization of American Politics." *Political Research Quarterly* 61, no. 4 (December 2008): 704–18.

O'Reilly, Kenneth. *Nixon's Piano: Presidents and Racial Politics from Washington to Clinton*. New York: Free Press, 1995.

Painter, Nell Irvin. *The History of White People*. New York: Norton, 2010.

Paul, John Peter. "A Study in Ethnic Group Political Behavior: The Greek Americans and Cyprus." PhD dissertation, University of Denver, 1979.

Reeves, Richard. *President Nixon: Alone in the White House*. New York: Simon & Schuster, 2001.

Richards, David A. J. *Italian American: The Racializing of an Ethnic Identity*. New York: New York University Press, 1999.

Rieder, Jonathan. *Canarsie: The Jews and Italians of Brooklyn against Liberalism*. Cambridge, MA: Harvard University Press, 1985.

Roberts, Chalmers M. *In the Shadow of Power: The Story of the Washington Post*. Cabin John, MD: Seven Locks Press, 1989.

Rothenberg, Stuart, Eric Licht, and Frank Newport. *Ethnic Voters and National Issues: Coalitions in the 1980s*. Washington, DC: Free Congress Research & Education Foundation, 1982.

Sartain, Lee. *Borders of Equality: The NAACP and the Baltimore Civil Rights Struggle, 1914–1970*. Jackson: University Press of Mississippi, 2013.

Scammon, Richard, and Benjamin Wattenberg. *The Real Majority: An Extraordinary Examination of the American Electorate*. New York: Coward, McCann & Georghegan, 1970.

Sobel, Robert. *The Fallen Colossus*. Washington, DC: Beard, 1977.

Sokol, Jason. "Uneasy Executives: Governors and Civil Rights from the Bay State to the Old Dominion." In *A Legacy of Innovation: Governors and Public Policy*, edited by Ethan G. Sribnick, 124–48. Philadelphia: University of Pennsylvania Press, 2008.

Stone, Roger, with Mike Colapietro. *Nixon's Secrets: The Rise, Fall, and Untold Truth about the President, Watergate, and the Pardon*. New York: Skyhorse, 2014.

Sugrue, Thomas J., and John D. Skrentny. "The White Ethnic Strategy." In *Rightward Bound: Making America Conservative in the 1970s*, edited by Bruce J. Schulman and Julian E. Zelizer, 171–92. Cambridge, MA: Harvard University Press, 2008.

Summers, Anthony, with Robbyn Swan. *The Arrogance of Power: The Secret World of Richard Nixon*. New York: Viking, 2000.

Szefel, Lisa. "'From Tall Ideas Dancing' to Trump's Twitter Ranting: Reckoning the Intellectual History of Conservatism." In *American Labyrinth: Intellectual History for Complicated Times*, edited by Raymond Haberski Jr. and Andrew Hartman, 146–62. Ithaca, NY: Cornell University Press, 2018.

Thomas, Vaso. "Racial and Ethnic Construction of Greek America." PhD dissertation, New School University, 2003.

Tuttle, Brad R. *How Newark Became Newark: The Rise, Fall, and Rebirth of an American City*. New Brunswick, NJ: Rutgers University Press, 2009.

US House of Representatives, 91st Congress, 2nd Session. *Hearings before the General Subcommittee on Education*. Washington, DC: US Government Printing Office, 1970.

Van Horne, Winston A. *Ethnicity and the Workforce*. Milwaukee: American Ethnic Studies Coordinating Committee, 1985.

Van Patten, James J. "Reflections on the Future of Higher Education." *Journal of Thought* 16, no. 4 (Winter 1981): 74–84.

Wainstock, Dennis D. *Election Year 1968: The Turning Point*. New York: Enigma, 2012.

Weinberg, Martha Wagner. "Boston's Kevin White: A Mayor Who Survives." *Political Science Quarterly* 96, no. 1 (Spring 1981): 87–106.

Whitman, Christine Todd. *It's My Party Too: The Battle for the Heart of the GOP and the Future of America*. New York: Penguin, 2005.
Witcover, Jules. *The Resurrection of Richard Nixon*. New York: Putnam's Sons, 1970.
Wolfinger, Raymond E. "The Development and Persistence of Ethnic Voting." *American Political Science Review* 59, no. 4 (1965): 896–908.

Mediterranean Americans to Themselves

Jim Cocola

In Italian American representations of Greece, as in Greek American representations of Italian Americans, a self-reflective Mediterranean American imaginary begins to emerge. Rather than insisting on national distinctions still relatively inchoate at the point of emigration, we should regard these representations as self-representations, or, put another way, as representations of similarly situated otherness. Like many other Mediterranean emigrants and their descendants, Greek Americans and Italian Americans have been doubly and mutually othered in the imperial and national logics of diaspora: eclipsed not only by Anglo-Saxon settler colonist power structures upon arrival in North America, but first of all by incursions of Ottoman, Spanish, and British power—or by further refractions within the nascent Greek, Italian, and Turkish nation-states—occasioning their very departure from the Mediterranean.[1] Sharing in the largely appropriated legacies of classical antiquity, and struggling with the present-day vagaries of skin privilege and symbolic ethnicity, Greek American and Italian American expressive cultures are ripe for exercises in comparison, which might also lead to exercises in collectivity. This dual errand also provides a comparative analogue to those exercises in comparison and collectivity bringing Chinese, Filipino, and Japanese Americans under the umbrella of the Asian American field imaginary nearly half a century ago.

Italian Americans and Greek Americans have invoked one another, or their respective homelands, in many literary and filmic depictions. Mentions of Greece occur in the work of John Ciardi, Diane di Prima, and Gay Talese. Greece plays a role in Gregory Corso's plays, poems, and letters. And Elia Kazan's controversial film *Baby Doll* (1956) features a Sicilian American antagonist, Silva Vacarro.[2] While such texts cut across national origins, they also emanate from local roots in a commonly held bioregion, registering as cases of self-reflection by Mediterranean Americans. Whether conceived of as looking in the next mirror over or as looking in the selfsame mirror, whenever Greek American and Italian American audiences and authors—which is to say, Mediterranean American audiences and authors—consider their respective works in common, they create the conditions to achieve greater clarity in reflecting on questions of identity and performativity in more particular and more generalizable keys.

If emigrants from Sicily and Smyrna were propelled from their respective homelands for distinct reasons, upon arrival in America they faced similar cultural and social challenges, whether in Boston, Detroit, or San Francisco. For every Charles Atlas, the famed Italian American professional bodybuilder born Angelo Siciliano in Calabria, there is also a Jim Londos, the popular Greek American professional wrestler born Christos Theofilou in the Peloponnese. Particularly among succeeding generations, even as acculturation, language acquisition, and socialization proceeded apace in the period spanning immigration restriction and civil rights reform, Greek Americans and Italian Americans continued to depart from Anglo norms in terms of complexion, family structure, and religious practice. On the national political stage, for example, the rises and falls of Spiro Agnew and Frank Rizzo have their parallels, just as Mario Cuomo's triumphs and struggles in the political arena found their echo in those of Michael Dukakis. For some, the Mediterranean American identity formation may present an anachronistic and misrepresentative label when applied to figures who infrequently identified as such, yet the same objection could be applied to Asian American identity formation at the moment of its emergence in the 1970s. In fact, as a distinct watershed, the Mediterranean presents a geographical catchment area more definite and distinct than the more familiar but no less tendentious continental formations of Asia and Europe.

While the Mediterranean American identity formation remains nascent, Mediterranean studies stands as a well-established field, dating from Fernand Braudel's two-volume study *The Mediterranean and the Mediterranean World in the Age of Philip II* (1949), which posited the region's "unity and coherence," in an argument more frequently applied to the ancient and medieval periods than to the modern period.[3] More recently, Peregrine Horden and Nicholas Purcell's *The Corrupting Sea: A Study of Mediterranean History* (2000) questioned whether "the Mediterranean region as a distinct whole" could serve as an "indispensable framework" for "the *very recent* history and likely futures of its people," cautioning that "we should not take its unity as an uncontroversial geographical datum."[4] And yet, due to cultural and linguistic convergences in diaspora, present-day Mediterranean American populations present a more cohesive unit than any demographic unity spanning the contemporary Mediterranean itself. In the United States, as Greek Americans and Italian Americans have tentatively assimilated, some have striven to affiliate and others to disaffiliate from whiteness, slowly accruing or incompletely incorporating elements of white privilege. At the same time, the specific contours of their alterity have remained evident even as they have gradually amalgamated among themselves, following the tendency identified by Ronald Horowitz whereby a set of distinct ethnic groups combine to "form a new group, larger and different from any of the component parts."[5] Indeed, the very volume in which this essay appears can be read as evidence of such a tendency.

Whereas Anglo, African, and Asian American depictions of Greek Americans and Italian Americans have turned on complex processes of hostility and sympathy often harboring concealed reflections on their own distinct and separate identities, Greek American invocations of Italian Americans can be understood as vehicles for ventriloquized modes of self-reflection. So too, Italian American invocations of Greece offer opportunities for reflection on their ethnicity and identity. Such dynamics pertain not only in the American context, but also in Australia, as manifested in the works of writers including Rosa Cappiello, Angelo Loukakis, and Vasso Kalamaras.[6] In American and Australian spheres alike, the expressive cultures of several Mediterranean diasporas have been marked by fraught identifications that consistently trouble—and are troubled by—the discriminatory norm of whiteness.

As a demographic and geographical phenomenon, Mediterranean American identity formation draws on bioregional and racialized origins alike. Standing as a cousin to Michael Novak's favored acronym, "PIGS—those Poles, Italians, Greeks, and Slavs,"[7] the broader designation of Mediterranean American also allows for more distant and more recent arrivals from the Maghreb and the Mashriq. And yet, while Matthew Frye Jacobson has classed earlier new immigrant populations under the heading of "Ellis Island whiteness"—as distinct from "Plymouth Rock whiteness"[8]—whiteness as an identity formation brooks no qualifiers. During the 1920s, as the whiteness of Mediterranean populations was called into question, their access to Ellis Island was all but foreclosed. Many in subsequent generations of Mediterranean Americans have balked, following a trajectory identified by Yiorgos Anagnostou wherein "ethnicity is disarticulated from whiteness and rearticulated into an emergent ethos of interracial solidarity."[9] Rejection by and resistance to the dominant culture has brought members of the Italian and Greek diasporas together in their mutual distrust of—or, less honorably, in their desperate attempts to cling to—the invidious logics of American racialization.

Ottoman Greek emigrants like Kazan can be understood in the terms Robert Viscusi used to describe Italian emigrants, as "orphans of massive political catastrophes" whose expressive culture "does not belong to a national project" so much as to multiregional and translocal imaginaries. Insofar as the emergence of the modern Greek, Italian, and Turkish states was informed by Anglo and American imperialism in the Mediterranean, propelling emigrants into diaspora, it moved them not so much toward as away from the national, to which they remained tenuously attached in memory even as they were driven by and into larger, newer empires that ambivalently incorporated them. From emigrant figures like Kazan and Pascal D'Angelo to American-born descendants such as Gregory Corso and Jeffrey Eugenides, Greek American and Italian American artists and writers have contested what Viscusi describes as "the bourgeois Anglo order of prestige," aiming "to overcome its effects on their lives and literary ambitions."[10] Even as American citizens, their identities continue to pivot on Mediterranean descent, for as Ghassan Hage has observed, writing in the Mediterranean Australian context, "the acquisition of formal citizenship does not give any indication of the level of practical national belonging granted by the dominant cultural community," which "remains determined by questions of cultural descent far more than by state acceptance,"[11] in a dialectic of exclusion and inclusion redounding for several generations.

Whether asserting dubious claims to, striving for attendant privileges of, or resisting partial interpellations into whiteness, Italian Americans and Greek Americans have never fully transcended their regional and ancestral origins, nor have they fully assimilated into national identities, whether as emigrants or immigrants, whether as citizens or descendants. Although not co-ethnics, they have become co-nationals along similar trajectories, thereby accruing a kind of paraethnicity, linked through comparable but distinct descent lines, national origins, and subject positions. Here, *para*—comes from the Greek παρά (*pará*: beside; next to, near, from; against, contrary to), and *ethnicity* from the Greek ἔθνος and εθνικός (*éthnos*: custom, nation, tribe). Even as Greek American representations of the Italian and Italian American representations of the Greek retain particular distinctions and local manifestations, they nonetheless deserve to be read in a broader key as Mediterranean American self-representations, fashioned by proximate figures who stand next to one another: alongside, but not fully of—and thus, potentially poised against and contrary to—the American paradigms of white nationalism and white supremacy.

The Italian's Greece

Near the peak of Mediterranean immigration to the United States, around the turn of the twentieth century, the US Immigration Bureau devised a framework accounting for different categories of "race or people," partitioning Italian immigrants into two different classes. Per 1898 codifications subsequently incorporated into the US census, a panoply of over twenty racial categories included "Italian (north)" and "Italian (south)," while a 1903 refinement of these guidelines clustered "races or peoples" into "four or five recognized divisions," including the Teutonic, Celtic, Iberic, Slavic, and Mongolic. Although ostensibly unified in 1871, "Italian (north)" and "Italian (south)" were repartitioned through the racialized logic of the US Immigration Bureau, with "Italian (north)" classed as Celtic alongside "Irish, Welsh, Scotch, [and] French," and "Italian (south)" classed as Iberic alongside "Greek, Portuguese, and Spanish; also Syrian from Turkey in Asia."[12] This partition exemplified a process of racialization whereby southern Italian emigrants converged with Greek emigrants rather than with northern Italian emigrants, not only in terms of complexion and descent lines in the Mediterranean but also in terms of privilege and social position within the United States.

Recalling her childhood in Helper, Utah, Helen Papanikolas noted that "North Italian and South Italian miners fought each other over whether to call a strike" as the Klan met Mediterranean coal and rail workers with the warning: "Take the Greeks and Italians and get out of town."[13] Racialized dynamics also pertained for Gay Talese as an undergraduate in the 1950s at the "then lily white University of Alabama," where he counted himself among those "olive-skinned out-of-staters whose ancestry might be Jewish, Arab, or Greek," those "whom the Tuscaloosa chapter of the Ku Klux Klan saw as borderline whites," or, in another Klan formulation, as "marginally white."[14] But whereas the Klan racialized Italian Americans together with Greek Americans, Italian Americans themselves, particularly in the second and third generations, emphasized connections to Greek Americans on a more decidedly cultural basis. Thus, in his poem "A Five Year Step," John Ciardi described his family, emigrants from Campania to Massachusetts, as "Greeks who spoke ourselves in bad Italian" with "our saints/disguised as Catholic" but in fact "mountain-rank."[15] Meanwhile, in her memoir *Recollections of My Life as a Woman* (2001), Diane di Prima recalled the division of her immigrant family—with grandfather Pietro deciding "to stay in America" and his brother Giuseppe electing "to 'go home,' to return to Sicily"— as "a Mediterranean, or North African ritual, the splitting of a tribe," with "the makings of Greek tragedy."[16] Later rendered "outcast, outrider" after she dropped out of Swarthmore and returned to New York, di Prima began to "study Homeric Greek out of an 1890's grammar I had discovered in my Aunt's attic in Queens."[17] The framings of these returns do not so much as mention Italy as such, being more decidedly aligned to Greece, and to the Mediterranean.

More recently, in her memoir *The Anarchist Bastard* (2011), Joanna Clapps Herman emphasized the "deposits of Greek colonization" structuring her family's removal from Basilicata to Connecticut, bespeaking "a subtle layer, remnant of that Greek 'new world,' one inscribed in cultural mores and oral traditions." Tracing her heritage back to the Italian peninsula, she nonetheless positioned her deeper roots as Greek, turning, like di Prima, to Homer as the "author who acts as a useful guide to the land and tribe whence I came."[18] Such Greek and Italian fusions abound among Mediterranean American writers, from Don DeLillo's novel *The Names* (1982), set largely in Greece, but extending across the Near East to Lahore, to the fiction of Jeffrey Eugenides, who emphasizes Greek protagonists but also relies on related Mediterranean characters and references as a way of testifying to Mediterranean alterity in novels including *The Virgin Suicides* (1993), *Middlesex* (2002), and *The Marriage Plot* (2011). In a more autobiographical key, the poet Eleni Sikelianos reflects in *You Animal Machine (The Golden Greek)* (2014) on the intermingling of Greek and Italian strains across her family tree. Writers in the Mediterranean itself have also been alive to such synergies. For example, Greek novelist Kallia Papadaki's *Dendrites* (2015) narrates a Greek American immigrant's rise in the 1920s among an Italian American community in Camden, New Jersey—one that welcomes him only to rebuff him in turn, revealing the contingent and provisional nature of paraethnic solidarity.

Mediterranean American identity often solidifies in print, in diaspora, though it can also coalesce in person, at sea. Whereas Ciardi, di Prima, and Herman considered connections between Italian descent and Greek culture from perches within the United States, Gregory Corso traveled directly to Greece to engage that intersection, albeit reluctantly. In one 1958 letter, from Paris, he confessed being "very afraid to go to Greece because I always dream of Greece and if I see it I'll lose the dream"; in another, from Rome, he explained that "the ancient Rome of my dreams was a far greater ancient Rome, an ancient Rome that never existed," suggesting he could "devise far nobler Caesars, far colossus Coliseums, damned if I had gone to Greece and I would have forfeited that too, happily so."[19] But across his third and fourth volumes, *The Happy Birthday of Death* (1960) and *Long Live Man* (1962), Greece, not Italy, drives his imagination. In "Spontaneous Poem After Having Seen the Metropolitan Museum," Corso writes from Central Park, noting "I'm out here/and old Greece is in there," asking "what good my sitting here and Greece in there," while in "Mortal Infliction" he references Polyphemus and Ulysses.[20] Even in poems where Italy is invoked, such allusions point toward Greece. In "Marriage," Corso imagines fatherhood, proposing a nursery for his baby where he would "tack Della Francesca all over its crib/Sew the Greek alphabet on its bib/And build for its playpen a roofless Parthenon"; in "On Palatine," he begins by announcing "Via Sacra I look down upon you,/my ownself tribunal," and ends by declaring "I've an eye impure for sight;/I dare not visit Greece."[21]

Yet Corso did visit Greece, resolved "to prove my belief that the golden statue of Poseidon, the biggest ever, the Trojan gog God is two miles out beneath the Aegean."[22] Upon arrival, he found himself drunk in Athens, "crying all night putting down the Greek peasantry for having chased Poseidon away."[23] In the capital, Corso's failed errand was not Athens but the Aegean, less concerned to reify an imagined national community than to recover the ancient Greek god of the sea. Crete, rather than continental Greece, most captivated Corso, prompting anxiety and enthusiasm alike. In "Paranoia in Crete," he cursed the "Damned Minoan crevices, that I clog them up!" resolving to "Plaster myself away from everything, all that out there!" and "forfeit the Echinadian Isles." In "First Night on the Acropolis," with "pressed face against a pillar I cried/Cried for my shadow that dear faithful sentry/Splashed across the world's loveliest floor." In "Greece" he presented himself as "the once Grecian/Grecian no more."[24] Summing up his journey, in "European Thoughts 1959," Corso allowed that "Greece was a marvelous country/but of course I was not marvelous in it." Nevertheless, he formed some connections, however unlikely. In a section of "Some Greek Writings" titled "Phaestos is a Village with 25 Families," Corso recalled a day at the tavern with some Cretans, where "we could not speak each other's language / but drink after drink we talked about everything."[25]

A more seasoned Corso returned from Greece with equal parts nostalgia and pessimism. By 1961, weary of Europe, Corso wrote to James Laughlin that being in London came as "a relief after two years of alien tongues," positing, in "After Reading 'In the Clearing,'" that "my homeland were Greece and England / Shelley is my ichor—Demeter is my mother."[26] In regarding Corso as "the most frequent and explicit of all the Beats in his references to classical lore," Stephen Dickey, Shelia Murnaghan, and Ralph M. Rosen speculate that this might be "despite or because of the fact that he was the least formally educated,"[27] but it might also be understood as a function of Mediterranean descent: here was an autodidact who took the time to follow his roots back to their sources. And while Corso's Shelleyan tendencies might seem to betray an Anglophilic and ultimately Western taste in the Mediterranean, his interest emanated from and gravitated toward decidedly eastern and southern vantage points.

Corso's engagement with the Mediterranean did not confine itself to Europe, but also extended to North Africa. In "Bomb," he expressed anxieties about American hostility toward the Mediterranean in imagining "Penguins plunged against the Sphinx" and "The top of the Empire State / arrowed in a broccoli field in Sicily."[28] Corso also developed a taste for Tangier, maintaining, in a section of "Some Moroccan Writings" titled "The European Section in Tangier," that "one culture must blend with another culture / (ancient Phrygia can tell) / to maintain the separation it demands."[29] But even before arrival in Morocco, Corso had the Maghreb in mind. Nonplussed by the Parisian atmosphere in "The Sacre-Coeur Café," Corso kept his eye on North Africa, writing that "the Algerians / they don't go to the Sacré-Coeur Café," while in "Reflection in a Green Arena" he conjured "France Algeria" as a case of "sad geo-woe."[30]

Asked by Michael Andre if he was a classicist, defined as "someone who found great value in past civilizations, particularly Greece and Rome," Corso replied in the affirmative, explaining that "if anyone were to ask me about Carthage or Phoenicia, or about the Bogomils or about Sumer and *Gilgamesh*, I know the shot."[31] Significantly, when the subject turned to Greeks and

Romans, Corso's attention turned beyond Western European antecedents, extending to the Balkans, the Levant, the Maghreb, and Mesopotamia. Elaborating on his tendency to "go backwards," he explained that he did not stop with "Ancient Greece and Rome," but went from there "to Egypt, and from there to Sumer and wedges."[32] This interest in the ancient Near East also emerged in his affinity for *The Epic of Gilgamesh*, which he described as "the first thing written down," devoting an hourlong lecture to the text in a 1977 seminar at the Naropa Institute's Jack Kerouac School of Disembodied Poetics.[33]

Corso's eastern and southern orientations were apparent even before he broke into print, as manifested in his early closet drama *Sarpedon* (1954). According to legend, he wrote the play on a dare from a teaching fellow at Harvard who told him "if I could write a Greek play I could stay at Eliot House." Corso "did it overnight," drawing on elements of Homer in the tradition of Aeschylus, Sophocles, and Euripides.[34] "Like the great Greek masters," Corso explained, "I took off where Homer left an opening."[35] Drawing on an episode from Book XVI of *The Iliad*, Corso focused his attention on the titular son of Zeus, who nonetheless fought and died on the side of the Trojans against the Greeks during the Trojan War. Dead and unaccounted for, it is Sarpedon's very absence that structures Corso's play.[36] When Charon accepts a roll call of seventy newly dead, Hades objects, noting a list of seventy-one, including Sarpedon, whom he describes as "something special" and "unlike the common mortal," since "his mother was Europa / and his father, a bull."[37] Sarpedon here stands as a cipher for Corso, a son of Europe who could not be contained by Europe, identifying more strongly with the Near East than with the West.

Presenting himself as Greek and Anglo, rather than Italian or American, Corso displayed a preference for deeper civilizational origins stretching all the way back to Sumer, even while despairing of the prevailing cultural direction in America. His critique of the United States proved especially pitched in *Elegiac Feelings American* (1970), as, for example, in "Eleven Times a Poem," where he presented Athens as "the birthplace of liberty" and "wondered if my country were its grave."[38] Notes of Mediterranean American self-abnegation occur elsewhere in late Corso, as in "The Mirror Within," where he thinks "to see myself / like a battered Greek statue / slowly ruining away."[39] Taken together, it is striking to observe that some of the most prominent Italian American poets of the twentieth century—Ciardi, Corso, di Prima—prove less likely to identify themselves with the nation-state as such than with their specific regions of origin—Ciardi via Campania, Corso via Calabria, di Prima via Lazio and Sicily—and their deeper civilizational roots, drawn more decidedly to ancient Greece than to modern Italy.

The Anatolian's Sicilian

As one of the most conspicuous and provocative stage and screen directors of the twentieth century, Elia Kazan nevertheless proved reluctant to engage with his own origins, which he ventriloquized for decades before shifting to a career as a novelist, only then moving to address the contours of his Greek Ottoman and Anatolian American heritage, in *America America* (1962) and *The Arrangement* (1967), both adapted as films he directed, as well as in *The Anatolian* (1982) and *Beyond the Aegean* (1994).[40] In early work as film director, Kazan prevailed upon Irish ethnicity as a vehicle for exploring otherness: first, more explicitly, in *A Tree Grows in Brooklyn* (1945), and later, more implicitly, in *On the Waterfront* (1954), one of the few Hollywood films to treat organized crime without placing Italian Americans at the center of the power dynamic.[41] Kazan's most prominent Mediterranean character of the 1950s came in *Baby Doll* (1956), developed from a Tennessee Williams screenplay that Kazan brought to fruition. Yet, in keeping with the casting redlines of the day, the role of Sicilian American Silva Vacarro was not played by a Mediterranean actor. Originally hoping to draw Brando for the role, Kazan eventually settled on Eli Wallach, in his screen debut. Born to Jewish emigrants from Poland, Wallach had also portrayed Alvaro Mangiacavallo opposite Irish American actress Maureen Stapleton's Serafina Delle Rose in the 1951 stage premiere of Williams's *The Rose Tattoo*, a play about Sicilian Americans with an oliveface cast, populated almost exclusively by non-Mediterranean actors. Despite their once and future collaborations, Kazan demurred from directing Williams's *The Rose Tattoo* on stage or screen, preferring to concentrate on the development of *On the Waterfront*.

Thus, several years before treating Greekness on film, Kazan focused on a Sicilian. Moreover, several years before treating a Sicilian, Kazan focused not only on the Irish, but also on a pair of protagonists embroiled in racialized passing, with Gregory Peck as Philip Schuyler Green in *Gentlemen's Agreement* (1947) and Jeanne Crain as Pinky Johnson in *Pinky* (1949). Peck, an Anglo-Irish Catholic from California, was cast to type, portraying a journalist posing as a Jewish writer on undercover assignment to expose the social malaise of anti-Semitism in Manhattan. Crain, also Irish Catholic, portrayed a light-complexioned woman of partial African descent returned home to Alabama after crossing the color line in Massachusetts, through a dizzying filmic logic in which an actress regarded as white passed in portraying a character regarded as Black who had herself passed for a woman regarded as white. *Pinky* was met with considerable controversy, prompting a cross-burning at a drive-in screening in Macon, Georgia, where "newspapers reported that the Klan could not be definitively linked to the incident."[42]

For its critics, *Pinky* "embodies the mulatto through a white actress, producing an ambiguous interplay of audience identifications,"[43] with the casting of Jeanne Crain making "a far more successful movie but a far less honest one, too."[44] A related dynamic pertains in *Baby Doll*, with the casting of Wallach as Vacarro. Just as in *Pinky* "the mulatto woman becomes a physical absence in the very narrative that attempts to account for her presence and represent her story,"[45] so too in *Baby Doll* the Sicilian man is subjected to a similar dialectic of absence and presence. Nevertheless, Kazan's extended treatment of Vacarro emboldened him to include other Italian American characters with key supporting roles in later films, including Anthony Franciosa as Joey DePalma in *A Face in the Crowd* (1957) and Zohra Lampert—like Wallach, translating Eastern European Jewish identity into southern Italian identity—as Angelina Stamper in *Splendor in the Grass* (1961). Such roles offered further mouthpieces for the ventriloquism of Kazan's Mediterranean roots, laying the groundwork for his direct treatments of Greek American protagonists: Stathis Giallelis as Stavros Topouzoglou in *America America* (1963) and Kirk Douglas—this time translating Eastern European Jewish identity into Anatolian Greek identity—as Evangelos Arness in *The Arrangement* (1969).

Set in the fictionalized Tiger Tail County, Mississippi, and shot on location in Benoit, Mississippi, *Baby Doll* was based on a Tennessee Williams screenplay developed from two of his one-act plays: *The Long Stay Cut Short; or, The Unsatisfactory Supper* (1946) and *27 Wagons Full of Cotton* (1946). Principal filming began in November 1955 at the J. C. Burrus House, an 1858 Greek Revival mansion subsequently used as a Confederate hospital and headquarters for General Jubal Early. More immediately, Kazan was on location only a few months after—and only fifty miles from the site of—the lynching of Emmett Till. The irony of filming on location beneath a Greek architectural facade representing the redoubt of a waning white supremacy breached by an unwelcome Mediterranean newcomer was not lost on Kazan.

Baby Doll revolves around the unconsummated marriage of would-be-gentleman farmer Archie Lee Meighan, portrayed by Karl Malden, and his nineteen-year-old bride, Baby Doll Meighan, portrayed by Carroll Baker in her screen debut. Occupying a dilapidated, largely unfurnished plantation house, the Meighans find themselves disrupted by Sicilian interloper Silva Vacarro, whose shrewd management of the Syndicate Gin unsettles the pecking order in Tiger Tail County. While Ron Briley has read Archie Lee and Vacarro as "symbols of the Old and New South,"[46] Vacarro's place in the American South was far from assured. The film suggests an uneasy path to parity between Meighan and Vacarro, and Kazan's original intentions for the film's ending suggest that he meant Vacarro less as Southern symbol than as a Mediterranean American martyr, representing the foremost ethnic insertion in a county whose white majority grew increasingly defensive amid its shifting demographics. Even as Archie Lee finds himself piqued by Vacarro personally and professionally, Baby Doll fields attention from the Jewish dentist in town, and a pair of Chinese men watch bemusedly as the Meighans fight in public.

Vacarro's introduction in the film comes courtesy of an elder statesman described as "the old boy," who sings the Sicilian's praises only to be heckled and pelted by the audience for his pains. In Williams's script, Vacarro admonishes the assailants by declaring, "If anybody's got anything more to throw, well, here's your target, here's your standing target! The wop! The foreign wop!!"[47] These lines are dropped from the finished film, where fire consumes Vacarro's gin following a series of catcalls. While the hostility toward Vacarro proves largely implicit in the film, it reads much more plainly in the script, which describes a fire engine "lax in its efforts and inefficient," manned by firemen taking "an odd pleasure in the flames, which they seem more interested in watching than fighting." One can only imagine the unfilmed scenario in which Vacarro fights the firemen in order to seize the hose, attempting to extinguish the fire by himself, screaming "in a foreign tongue" before collapsing, surrounded by firemen, where, "lit by the victorious flames are a circle of faces which are either indifferent or downright unfriendly," some of whom "cannot control a faint smile."[48] Suppressed on screen, such pleasure in Vacarro's misfortune suffuses the script, where, after the fire, at the Brite Spot Café, "a holiday mood prevails," with the fire having "satisfied some profound and basic hunger and left the people of that community exhilarated."[49] In the film, this treatment is sharply minimized, reduced to Vacarro's line in the café that he has "never seen so many happy faces."

In one of the film's source texts, *27 Wagons Full of Cotton* (1946), Williams introduces Silva Vicarro as "a rather small and wiry man of dark Latin looks and nature," wearing "a Roman Catholic medallion on a chain about his neck"; Flora subsequently observes that Silva is "natcherally dark," a line that her equivalent, Baby Doll, also utters in the script and the film.[50] In the play, Jake, the basis for Archie Lee, notes that Silva's name is "like a silver lining," and Flora asks if it's "like a silver dollar"; in Williams's screenplay, Vacarro, his name slightly altered, appears as "a handsome, cocky young Italian" marked by "a certain watchfulness, a certain reserve," yet the animus toward him proves more pronounced and more collectively felt.[51] Vacarro does not hesitate to acknowledge the racialized slurs against him. Upon their meeting, Baby Doll observes that his "name sounds foreign," to which Vacarro replies, "I'm known as the wop that runs the Syndicate Plantation." Archie Lee objects by interjecting "Don't call yourself names. Let other folks call you names!" When Baby Doll follows up by asking "So you're a wop?" Vacarro responds "with ironic politeness," saying, "I'm a Sicilian."[52] In the film, under his breath, to himself, he can only incredulously repeat: "So you're a wop!" Later in the film, Archie Lee calls Vacarro a wop on several occasions: first in passing, then in anger, finally in murderous rage. When

Archie Lee resolves to "wipe that grin off your greasy wop face for good," Vacarro asks Baby Doll "Is my wop face greasy?" She kisses him but doesn't answer directly. Later, when Archie Lee slurs Vacarro as a "yellow-bellied wop," the intimation is cowardice, but the implication is racial.

If the Meighans offer an awkward portrait of white privilege in decline, then Vacarro, who may aim to accede to their station, cannot partake fully in their privilege. On the verge of brandishing his rifle, Archie Lee explains to Vacarro that he "ain't got the advantage" of those who "got position in this county" thanks to being "born and brought up" alongside "longstanding business associates and social." In the script, Archie Lee also proceeds to ask "ain't you a dago, or something, excuse me, I mean Eyetalian or something, here in Tiger Tail County?"[53] On the one hand, Vacarro can be read as Baby Doll's predator; on the other hand, he can be read as Archie Lee's prey. Vacarro links the violence against him to a longer history of racialized violence in the American South, telling Baby Doll that he believes in "ghosts" and "evil spirits," namely in "spirits of violence, cunning, malevolence, cruelty, [and] treachery," recalling that upon the burning of his gin, "the faces I saw were grinning," in a "manifestation of the need to destroy" by people "overrun by demons of hate and destruction," leading him to conclude that "this place—this house—is haunted." Baby Doll subsequently cautions Vacarro that "justice here is deaf and blind," warning him that her signed testimony will have little traction in a county—and a country—intent on preserving white supremacy at his expense and at the expense of his Black analogues and associates.[54]

Michele Meek has pointed to "the film's implicit challenge of the domesticated woman's role" and its "explicit portrayal of female sexual desire" as "an antiestablishmentarian perspective."[55] Crucially, the antiestablishment ethos in *Baby Doll* centers not only on female sexuality, but more precisely on female sexuality vis-à-vis interethnic, racialized desire. In Williams's script, Vacarro's Syndicate Plantation registers more obviously as a site of integration. When Archie Lee spots some of Vacarro's men walking past, he objects to the "*White an' black* mixed!" and resolves to "blast them out of the Bayou with a shotgun!"[56] In the finished film, this dynamic remains implicit, with the workmen briefly shown, but overtly linked neither to integration nor to Vacarro. Yet the racialized logics of the film remain apparent at its conclusion, with Archie Lee's final appeal to the authorities coming in the name of preserving his supremacy. "I ain't a white man?" he asks, urging them to "turn me on in but don't you leave my Baby Doll with him," making his plea "as one white man to another." Vacarro poses a threat not only to the sanctity of the Meighan marriage but also to the sanctity of whiteness itself, with Archie Lee appealing to law enforcement as the ultimate defender of white supremacy. Just as the film necessarily conformed to the logics of the Motion Picture Production Code by suppressing the implication of adultery, so too it necessarily suppressed the implication of miscegenation, though Kazan managed to suppress both of these dynamics in plain sight.[57] In *Baby Doll*, Vacarro telegraphs the specter of miscegenation: racialized as not quite white, he is hardly embraced and ultimately repulsed by the establishment figures of Tiger Tail County. While Williams's dramatic attraction to an amorous Sicilian male was made with implicit reference to the love of his own life, Frank Merlo, to whom he dedicated his play *The Rose Tattoo* (1951), Kazan had his own reasons for being drawn to Vacarro. As Kazan navigated a fraught marriage to Molly Day Thacher, Vacarro's titillations and tribulations offered him an opportunity to reflect on and refract his own sense of alterity vis-à-vis whiteness.

Kazan intimated an identification with Vacarro by explaining that he made *Baby Doll* "to get on film what I felt in the South."[58] Indeed, the film stands as a record of what any Mediterranean American man might have felt in the South of that era. Yet this identification also bespeaks an identification with Southern Blackness more generally—a connection not lost on Arthur Knight, who noted in *The Saturday Review* that "Kazan seems not unlike the Negroes in this film, watching everything with a quiet smile but personally disengaged," adding that "if he has any strong personal convictions about these people, any private resentment or objection to their way of life, it is kept well hidden behind the smile."[59] It is this coolness, finally, that unsettled the film's critics. For all its suggestiveness, the film never explicitly smolders beyond the burning of Vacarro's gin. As Meek points out, given the animus against *Baby Doll*'s immorality, "one would expect it to contain more than a few scenes of light petting," yet as Kazan himself observed, within a few decades such scenes would fail to "raise the most timid eyebrow."[60] What was condemned and suppressed in *Baby Doll*, then, was not so much seduction or sexuality in general, but seduction and sexuality between a controversial pairing.

If *Baby Doll* scandalized in part due to the youth of the titular lead, it also scandalized in part due to the representation of sexual conquest by a Mediterranean lothario who threatened to undo the color line and transcend the racialized ghetto, not only in the segregated South but also in the ethnically divided North.

What was perhaps most offensive of all in the North as in the South was the notion that an Italian male might be taken seriously as an object of desire, in a longstanding grudge dating back to the precipitous rise and sudden death of Rudolph Valentino. The threat of this specter was most clearly visualized by Kazan in a scene in which Baby Doll drinks a bottle of Coke as Vacarro begins to intensify his gradual advances toward her (Figure 1).[61] Here Kazan positions Baby Doll and Vacarro in a space simultaneously intimate and permeable: over Vacarro's shoulder, through a shattered window, a Black man looms in the distant background. Kazan thus locates the Sicilian between blackness and whiteness, suggesting a seduction that, triangulated, further signals the forbidden topic of miscegenation, still banned at the time in the Motion Picture Production Code, and still illegal at the time in twenty-six out of forty-eight states, including Mississippi.[62]

Released during the Christmas season in 1956, according to *Time*, Kazan's *Baby Doll* registered plausibly as "the dirtiest American-made motion picture that has ever been legally exhibited."[63] Condemned by the Catholic Legion of Decency as "morally repellant" in its "carnal suggestiveness," and its "unmitigated emphasis on lust" that proved "grievously offensive," the film was denounced as evil and immoral from the pulpit by Cardinal Spellman, who enjoined his charges to avoid the film "under pain of sin." In subsequent weeks, *Baby Doll* found itself banned in locales from Maine and New Hampshire to Memphis and Atlanta, partially censored in Providence, and disrupted by a bomb threat at a screening in Hartford before being pulled from general distribution by Warner Brothers.[64] Yet none of these controversies stopped *Baby Doll* from garnering four Academy Award nominations, including Carroll Baker for best actress in her titular role as Baby Doll Meighan.

Figure 1. Frame at 0.41.03 from *Baby Doll*, directed by Elia Kazan, with performances by Carroll Baker and Eli Wallach (Warner Brothers, 1956).

For all controversy surrounding the finished *Baby Doll*, the Code silently shaped many aspects of the film during production, particularly in terms of its denouement. As Albert J. Devlin has observed, "agreement on the elusive ending of *Baby Doll* was not forthcoming until the end of principal filming."[65] The contestation around this ending reveals a significant gap in the authorial visions of Kazan and Williams. As Ron Briley noted, "Kazan suggested that the final confrontation between Archie Lee and Vacarro conclude with the Sicilian being pierced by a frog-sticking pole wielded by Archie Lee during a swamp battle," after which Archie Lee "accidentally shoots and kills a black man." Williams objected less to the lynching of Vacarro than to the shooting that followed, arguing that such an ending was "false to the key and mood of the story."[66] Williams later praised Kazan for his plans to revise the ending of the "frog-gigging episode—its violence notwithstanding," redrawn to culminate "with Archie Lee shouting to the men on the bank of the bayou that he burned the Syndicate gin" before "one of the silent witnesses, goaded by Vacarro to acknowledge the forced confession, kills the outsider with a rifle shot."[67] Among other interpretations, the layers of this violent conclusion can be read as an elaborate and heavily sublimated allegory for the lynching of Emmett Till.

Williams's script had no such designs, culminating as "Vacarro drops out of tree and stands with arms lifted for Baby Doll," revealing a yawning gap between Williams's comedic notions and Kazan's tragic vision.[68] In the finished film, Archie Lee pursues Vacarro with a rifle, but nothing comes of it, and Vacarro slinks off as Archie Lee is perfunctorily hauled to jail for the night, with Baby Doll retreating to the house, concluding, "We've got nothing to do but wait for tomorrow, and see if we're remembered or forgotten." Though the Code ending of the film overrode Kazan's initial and modulated intentions for a conclusion, it could not disappear the evidence of what it suppressed. Kazan's design throughout the principal filming was for Vacarro's lynching, initially as impaled at the hands of Archie Lee, and in revision, as gunned down by an uncredited extra. But Vacarro's heroism and martyrdom could not play, even when murdered by a peripheral rather than central assailant: by the Code's logic, Vacarro could only be sinner and villain, not hero and martyr, even though Kazan himself continued to associate Vacarro with Christ. In Williams's play *27 Wagons Full of Cotton*, Vicarro explains that his is "an Italian name" and identifies himself as a "native of New Orleans,"[69] whereas in Kazan's film Vacarro explains that he is Sicilian and says he is from Corpus Christi, to which Baby Doll responds "Oh, how unusual!"

Received as salacious in its own time, in retrospect *Baby Doll* has been understood as "a far more subtle and subversive film than critics emphasizing its sexual content ever recorded."[70] In this regard, the film offers a pivotal link between Kazan's earlier and more broadly distributed explorations of ethnic and racialized difference in general and his subsequent turn to more focused explorations of his own ethnic and racialized difference in particular. As it happened, in the spring before Kazan went to Mississippi to film *Baby Doll* on location, he traveled to Greece and Turkey to do some preliminary research toward the project that would evolve into the novel and film titled *America America*. It was here that the Mediterranean came into clearer relief for Kazan, and here that Silva Vacarro likely emerged as a clear test run toward the protagonist that Stavros Topouzoglou would become.

On Mediterranean American Mutuality and Solidarity

In Corso's poetry and in Kazan's films alike, we see the ambiguous positions of Mediterranean Americans within the legacies of the European grand tour, the shifting discourses of civil rights, and the indefinite arrays of racialized identity. These commonalities transcend the particular distinctions that separate Mediterranean Americans in their respective descent lines. After all, the Calabrian American Corso spent more time thinking Greece than thinking Italy, and the Anatolian American Kazan relied upon a Sicilian American avatar in order to enable more extended reflections on his own ethnic identity. This mutual willingness to consider roots in relational and transnational terms is characteristic not only of their national origins, such as they are, but also of their Mediterranean heritage, a Mediterranean that has registered in antiquity and modernity alike as "a space of dynamic and multiple interconnections," and "a fragmented world which is nonetheless united by its very interconnectivity."[71] In the American context, such connections constellate not only to Greek and Italian points of contact, but also via the Iberian, to the Hispanic and Latin American imaginaries, via Egypt, to the Afrocentric imaginary, and, via the Mashriq, to the Asian American imaginary.

Many will nonetheless regard the Mediterranean American frame as unduly broad, constituted as it is of multiple national and religious affiliations, not to mention myriad local and regional identifications that overwrite any tendency toward interethnic coalition. Yet similar features also characterized the Asian American field imaginary as it coalesced around the work of editors Frank Chin, Jeffrey Chan, Lawson Inada, and Shawn Wong, who in their pathbreaking *Aiiieeeee! An Anthology of Asian American Writers* (1974) conjured "the first generation of Asian Americans to be aware of writing within an Asian American tradition." While this first effort included Chinese, Filipino, and Japanese American exemplars to the exclusion of Korean,

Vietnamese, and other Asian American ethnicities, it offered a starting point to be addressed in subsequent work, which was catalyzed in the context of US imperialism across the Asian and Pacific regions. As Chin, Chan, Inada, and Wong explained of this initial constellation of Asian American writers, "we know each other now. It should never have been otherwise."[72] Their bid for interethnic solidarity amid divisive—and correspondingly unifying—forms of racialization in the United States has a fainter, and perhaps diminished, but nevertheless parallel, and possibly reemergent analogue in the Mediterranean American imaginary, which, starting from Greek and Italian American connections, can further extend to Albanian, Moroccan, Syrian, and Turkish American cognates, among others. Such a formation does not stand distinct from but rather relates decisively to the Asian American case, not least because the Asian and the Mediterranean American formations hold the Near East in common. As the Italian legislator and sociologist Franco Cassano has argued, "to think the Mediterranean today means, first of all, to deconstruct the perspective of a clash of civilizations," insofar as "the Mediterranean, as a sea *between* lands that does not belong to any of them, is a *communal* sea."[73]

Just as philosopher Antonio Gramsci was taken up by literary critic Edward Said, and he in turn by Leila Ahmed, so too pop star Madonna presents a model not only for Lady Gaga but also for Bebe Rexha. Similar convergences of affect and alienation mark a trio of loosely autobiographical protagonists in recent examples of bildungsroman by Turkish American novelist Elif Batuman in *The Idiot* (2017), Italian American novelist B. G. Firmani in *Time's a Thief* (2017), and Moroccan American novelist Laila Lalami in *The Other Americans* (2019). As for similarities of affect and alienation linking Corso and Kazan, despite a prevailing late twentieth-century anthropological paradigm emphasizing the salience of honor and shame across various social formations in the Mediterranean, Corso's speakers, like Kazan's characters, shamelessly flout standards of honor, like the daring works from which they spring, made by Mediterranean Americans unafraid to upset the status quo even in the highly conformist 1950s.[74]

Ultimately, the expressive cultures of American artists and writers of Greek and Italian origin and descent cannot be fully discerned by recourse to Anglophone or European frameworks, much less to the exclusionary paradigm of whiteness. Such figures are finally best read in a Mediterranean key, and best understood not only separately but also together. The conditions for their convergence, their comparison, and their collectivity spring from what Mary N. Layoun has described as "the massive movements and dislocations of peoples in the modern period" which have led to "radical juxtaposition" among "different peoples and ideas and things that were hitherto not colliding with one another in quite the same close fashion."[75] In America, Greek and Italian immigrants and their descendants can confidently juxtapose themselves, for all their differences, as relatively similar peoples. We might think of them, after Marcel Detienne, as "neighboring configurations," who in their "particular differential features" reveal a "deviation from the norm that distinguishes, among a whole set of possibilities, the particular formula of a microconfiguration of politics."[76] If the tandem study of these neighboring configurations offers a version of "weak comparatism,"[77] it also offers a place to begin theorizing a Mediterranean American imaginary, and, potentially, to enact a Mediterranean American collectivity whose several constituencies, taken together, might illuminate one another after the examples of an Asian American imaginary and an Asian American collectivity.

One larger project would be to link earlier waves of Italian and Greek immigrant arrivals and their descendants to more distant and more recent waves of Maghrebi and Mashriqi immigrant arrivals in the United States. Though beyond the scope of this essay, this comparison suggests a further range of analysis, poised to explore the striking sets of parallels—migratory intensification, mandated restriction, persistent intersections of ethnic difference and religious alterity, and enduring stereotypes of imputed criminality emboldening racialized profiling—that have marked Mediterranean Americans from one century to the next. Today, even as Greek Americans and Italian Americans vacate longstanding ethnic ghettoes, finding themselves increasingly dispersed, their distribution across the American landscape remains relatively delimited. Moreover, the shift from concentrated ghettoization to gradual atomization only further underscores their dual distinction, described, nearly half a century ago, in terms of an "unmeltable" ethnic difference that has attenuated in some spheres but remains palpable in others.[78]

In any event, their forebears came cheek by jowl. Near the end of *America America*, as the *Kaiser Wilhelm* approaches Long Island, Kazan presents the "steerage passengers" first and foremost in bioregional terms, as "very poor and from every country served by the Mediterranean," near American shores but "still in their native clothes, their possessions bundled and always at their sides." Itemizing their several nationalities, from Italians, Romanians, and Albanians to Serbs, Croats, and Syrians, he links them once again by describing them as "fanatics" and "men alone."[79] United neither by their countries of origin nor by their various destinations, such migrants had the Mediterranean in common. It is time that their descendants listened more carefully to one another, and it is time for others to listen to them in the aggregate. To listen in this way serves not only the mutual interests of Mediterranean Americans but also the wider project of transcultural solidarity in an increasingly fragmented and increasingly interconnected multiethnic and multiracial America.

NOTES

1. While Robert Stam and Ella Shohat acknowledge the "mutual opposition and antipathy" in the two terms "Latin" and "Anglo-Saxon," they present them as "regional variants" of "Eurocentrism," particularly given "a Native American or an Afrodiasporic 'view from below'" that renders them "mere nuances within European whiteness." Yet, contrary to Stam and Shohat, such consolidations obscure internal differentiations *within* Latin and Anglo-Saxon formations, whereby southern Italian and Ottoman Greek populations in the Latin domain—like various Celtic populations in the Anglo-Saxon domain—have been ambivalently racialized into their own versions of a "view from below" that place them astride the trajectories of the colonizer and the grievances of the colonized. See Stam and Shohat, "Transnationalizing Comparison," 126.

2. Kazan's work paved the way for Greek American director John Cassavetes, who, after portraying the eponymous lead in the NBC drama *Johnny Staccato* (1959–60), also flagged solidarities between Greek and Italian American figures in his films *Husbands* (1970) and *The Killing of a Chinese Bookie* (1976), particularly through the casting of Ben Gazzara, his costar in *Husbands*.

3. Braudel, *The Mediterranean and the Mediterranean World in the Age of Philip II*, 2:14.

4. Horden and Purcell, *The Corrupting Sea*, 3, 7.

5. Horowitz, "Ethnic Identity," 115.

6. In Cappiello's *Paese fortunato* (1981), translated into English in 1984 as *Oh, Lucky Country*, a protagonist recently arrived from Naples traverses the migrant ghettos of Sydney among various Mediterranean Australian compatriots. Meanwhile, in Greek Australian short story collections including Kalamaras's *Other Earth* (1977) and Loukakis's *For the Patriarch* (1981) and *Vernacular Dreams* (1986), Greek and Italian Australian characters move in parallel and often travel together.

7. Novak, *The Rise of the Unmeltable Ethnics*, 63.
8. Jacobson, *Roots Too*, 7.
9. Anagnostou, *Contours of White Ethnicity*, 128.
10. Viscusi, *Buried Caesars*, xii, xiv, 22.
11. Hage, *White Nation*, 50.
12. For an analysis of these classifications, see Weil, "Races at the Gate."
13. Papanikolas, *A Greek Odyssey in the American West*, 264, 291.
14. Talese, *A Writer's Life*, 118, 123; Talese, *The Gay Talese Reader*, 245.
15. Ciardi, *Lives of X*, 72.
16. Di Prima, *Recollections of My Life as a Woman*, 20–21.
17. Ibid., 102.
18. Herman, *The Anarchist Bastard*, 8.
19. Corso, *An Accidental Autobiography*, 100, 179–80.
20. Corso, *The Happy Birthday of Death*, 25–26; Corso, *Mindfield*, 86.
21. Corso, *Mindfield*, 63; Corso, *Happy Birthday*, 63.
22. Corso, *An Accidental Autobiography*, 196. With high hopes, at the racetrack in New York in May 1959 before his journey to Greece, Corso admitted to Ginsberg that he had "lost at Belmont about $400 on such names as Aegean Cruise, Macedonian Way, Agamemnon all came in last or next to last. Can you imagine that and I who put so much faith in Greece. Damn Greece I say" (194).
23. Ibid., 196, 211.
24. Corso, *Mindfield*, 75; Corso, *Long Live Man*, 19, 27.
25. Corso, *Mindfield*, 106, 112.
26. Corso, *An Accidental Autobiography*, 292; Corso, *Long Live Man*, 89. Corso's Anglophilia can also be read as a brief against northern Italy. Drawn to the English over the Tuscan, Corso revealed his distrust of Dante in a 1961 letter to Laughlin, writing against "that kind of Italian who is cocksure, smart, granite morality and beautiful," who, nevertheless, "always irritated me," and noting that "I have no doubts about Shakespeare, Homer, Milton; I doubt Dante" (300).
27. Dickey, Murnaghan, and Rosen. "Introduction," 4.
28. Corso, *Mindfield*, 65–66.

29. Corso, *Long Live Man*, 65.
30. Corso, *Happy Birthday*, 85; Corso, *Long Live Man*, 28.
31. Corso, *The Whole Shot*, 54–55.
32. Ibid., 65.
33. Ibid., 67. The lecture in question, delivered on July 1, 1977, is available via archive.org.
34. Sayre, *Previous Convictions*, 203.
35. Corso, *An Accidental Autobiography*, 405–6.
36. Absence also marks C. P. Cavafy's early poem "The Funeral of Sarpedon," in which Zeus "mourns deeply" and prevents Sarpedon's "dishonor," and Apollo attends to his corpse as he "bleaches his skin" and "combs out the jet black hair." As George Savidis notes, this poem—likely written before 1892, first published in 1898 as "Ancient Days," and published in subsequent versions under its final title in 1904, 1908, and 1924—was, "though never actually rejected by Cavafy . . . not included in his mature collections," so that Cavafy simultaneously contended with and shielded an engagement with Sarpedon's legacy in an effort spanning a quarter of a century. Thanks to Yiorgos Kalogeras for suggesting Cavafy's Sarpedon in view of Corso's Sarpedon. For the text of Cavafy's poem and the relevant editorial note, see *Collected Poems*, 7, 218.
37. Corso, *Sarpedon*, 15.
38. Corso, *Elegiac Feelings American*, 32–33.
39. Corso, *Herald of the Autochthonic Spirit*, 39.
40. In the initial voiceover narration of *America America*, Kazan explains his heritage by saying he is "a Greek by blood, a Turk by birth and an American because my uncle made a journey."
41. Kazan and screenwriter Budd Schulberg took this approach deliberately, basing the film's protagonist, Terry Malloy, portrayed by Marlon Brando, on Italian American longshoreman Anthony DeVincenzo. By contrast, Arthur Miller grounded his treatment of longshoremen, *A View from the Bridge* (1955), squarely within the Italian American community of Red Hook.
42. McGehee, "Disturbing the Peace," 31.
43. Kydd, "The Ineffaceable Curse of Cain," 96.
44. Bogle, *Toms, Coons, Mulattos, Mammies, and Bucks*, 152.
45. Kydd, "The Ineffaceable Curse of Cain," 118.
46. Briley, *The Ambivalent Legacy of Elia Kazan*, 85.
47. Williams, *Baby Doll*, 32.
48. Ibid., 33–34.
49. Ibid., 40.
50. Williams, *Plays 1937–1955*, 313, 316; Williams, *Baby Doll*, 56.

51. Williams, *Plays 1937–1955*, 313; Williams, *Baby Doll*, 30.
52. Williams, *Baby Doll*, 50–52.
53. Ibid., 132.
54. As delivered in the film; equivalent passages in ibid., 78–80, 121.
55. Meek, "Marriage, Adultery, and Desire."
56. Williams, *Baby Doll*, 115.
57. The indeterminacy of Sicilians with respect to racialization, and, thus, to miscegenation law, had been established in neighboring Alabama by the legal precedent of *Rollins v. State*, 92 So. 35, 36 [1922]. For more on this case, see Novkov, *Racial Union*, 125–28.
58. Crowther, "The Proper Drama of Mankind."
59. Quoted in Briley, *The Ambivalent Legacy of Elia Kazan*, 80.
60. Meek, "Marriage, Adultery, and Desire"; Williams and Mead, *Tennessee Williams*, 209.
61. Other exemplifications of the consumption–miscegenation matrix come in an early scene from the film involving ice cream cones, and a transition cut from the script that dissolved from Baby Doll singing a lullaby to Vacarro in her crib to "Aunt Rose eating chocolate cherries" in the town hospital. For the latter, see Williams, *Baby Doll*, 107.
62. Susan Courtney notes that "from 1930 to 1956 the Production Code's sixth regulation on matters of 'sex' boldly declared: 'Miscegenation (sex relationship between the white and black races) is forbidden,'" though she mentions Kazan only in passing in a footnote in connection with his 1949 film *Pinky*. See Courtney, *Hollywood Fantasies of Miscegenation*, 105, 343.
63. Quoted in Briley, *The Ambivalent Legacy of Elia Kazan*, 81.
64. On resistance to *Baby Doll* from the pulpit and in the theatre, see "New Kazan Movie Put on Blacklist" and "Cardinal Scores 'Baby Doll' Film." For further commentary, see Briley, *The Ambivalent Legacy of Elia Kazan*, 81.
65. Kazan, *The Selected Letters of Elia Kazan*, 305.
66. Quoted in Briley, *The Ambivalent Legacy of Elia Kazan*, 74.
67. Devlin, in Kazan, *The Selected Letters of Elia Kazan*, 312.
68. Williams, *Baby Doll*, 139–40. As Meek notes, there is also the fact of "Williams's later adaptation into the play *Tiger Tail*, which concludes with the lovers unambiguously united," reverting to a comedic ending that attempts to overwrite Kazan's tragic sense and the film's ambiguous conclusion.
69. Williams, *Plays 1937–1955*, 317.
70. Philip C. Kolin, "Civil-Rights and the Black Presence in *Baby Doll*," 3.
71. Isabella and Zanou, *Mediterranean Diasporas*, 1.
72. Chin et al., *Aiiieeeee!* 38.
73. Cassano, *Southern Thought and Other Essays on the Mediterranean*, 142.

74. On early anthropological discourse on Mediterranean unity, see Peristiany, *Honour and Shame*; Davis, *People of the Mediterranean*; and Gilmore, *Honor and Shame and the Unity of the Mediterranean*.

75. Layoun, "Endings and Beginnings," 212.

76. Detienne, *Comparing the Incomparable*, 99.

77. Lincoln, *Apples and Oranges*, 27.

78. Robert Novak's *The Rise of the Unmeltable Ethnics*, first published in 1972, was revised in a second edition as *Unmeltable Ethnics* in 1995. It was reprinted as recently as 2018, suggesting the continuing solidity of the unmeltable paradigm.

79. Kazan, *America America*, 165.

Bibliography

FILMOGRAPHY

Cassavetes, John, director. *Husbands*. Columbia Pictures, 1970.
———. *The Killing of a Chinese Bookie*. Faces Distribution, 1976.
Kazan, Elia, director. *America America*. Warner Bros., 1963.
———. *The Arrangement*. Warner Bros., 1969.
———. *Baby Doll*. Warner Bros., 1956.
———. *A Face in the Crowd*. Warner Bros., 1957.
———. *Gentleman's Agreement*. 20th Century Fox, 1947.
———. *On the Waterfront*. Columbia Pictures, 1954.
———. *Pinky*. 20th Century Fox, 1949.
———. *Splendor in the Grass*. Warner Bros., 1961.
———. *A Tree Grows in Brooklyn*. 1945.
———. *Wild River*. 20th Century Fox, 1960.
Mann, Daniel, director. *The Rose Tattoo*. Paramount, 1955.

PRINTED SOURCES

Anagnostou, Yiorgos. *Contours of White Ethnicity: Popular Ethnography and the Making of Usable Pasts in Greek America*. Athens: Ohio University Press, 2009.
Batuman, Elif. *The Idiot*. New York: Penguin, 2017.
Bogle, Donald. *Toms, Coons, Mulattos, Mammies, and Bucks: An Interpretive History of Blacks in American Films*. 2nd ed. New York: Continuum, 1991.

Braudel, Fernand. *The Mediterranean and the Mediterranean World in the Age of Philip II.* 2 vols. Translated by Siân Reynolds. Glasgow: William Collins, 1972.

Briley, Ron. *The Ambivalent Legacy of Elia Kazan: The Politics of the Post-HUAC Films.* Lanham, MD: Rowman and Littlefield, 2017.

Cappiello, Rosa. *Oh Lucky Country.* Translated by Gaetano Rando. St. Lucia: University of Queensland Press, 1984.

"Cardinal Scores 'Baby Doll' Film: Spellman, in Pulpit, Warns Catholics to Shun It as 'Evil' Incurring 'Sin' Sponsors Termed 'Venal' Producer and Author Reply." *New York Times*, December 17, 1956, 28.

Cassano, Franco. *Southern Thought and Other Essays on the Mediterranean.* Edited and translated by Norma Bouchard and Valerio Ferme. New York: Fordham University Press, 2012.

Cavafy, C. P. *Collected Poems.* Edited by George Savidis. Translated by Edmund Keeley and Philip Sherrard. Rev. ed. Princeton, NJ: Princeton University Press, 1992.

Chin, Frank, Jeffrey Chan, Lawson Inada, and Shawn Wong, eds. *Aiiieeeee! An Anthology of Asian American Writers.* Washington, DC: Howard University Press, 1974.

Ciardi, John. *Elegiac Feelings American.* New York: New Directions, 1970.

———. *Lives of X.* New Brunswick, NJ: Rutgers University Press, 1971.

Corso, Gregory. *An Accidental Autobiography: The Selected Letters of Gregory Corso.* Edited by Bill Morgan. New York: New Directions, 2003.

———. *The Happy Birthday of Death.* New York: New Directions, 1960.

———. *Herald of the Autochthonic Spirit.* New York: New Directions, 1981.

———. *Long Live Man.* New York: New Directions, 1962.

———. *Sarpedon.* Arlington, MA: Tough Poets Press, 2016.

———. *The Whole Shot: Collected Interviews with Gregory Corso.* Edited by Rick Schober. Arlington, MA: Tough Poets Press, 2015.

Courtney, Susan. *Hollywood Fantasies of Miscegenation: Spectacular Narratives of Gender and Race, 1903–1967.* Princeton, NJ: Princeton University Press, 2005.

Crowther, Bosley. "The Proper Drama of Mankind: Some Thoughts on 'Baby Doll' and the Italian Film 'La Strada' Theatrical Skill Shallow People Melodrama Humanity." *New York Times*, January 6, 1957, D1.

Davis, John. *People of the Mediterranean: An Essay in Comparative Social Anthropology.* London: Routledge & Kegan Paul, 1977.

Detienne, Marcel. *Comparing the Incomparable.* Translated by Janet Lloyd. Stanford: Stanford University Press, 2008.

Dickey, Stephen, Shelia Murnaghan, and Ralph M. Rosen. "Introduction." In *Hip Sublime: Beat Writers and the Classical Tradition*, edited by Shelia

Murnaghan and Ralph M. Rosen, 1–14. Columbus: Ohio State University Press, 2018.

di Prima, Diane. *Recollections of My Life as a Woman: The New York Years.* New York: Penguin, 2001.

Firmani, B. G. *Time's a Thief: A Novel.* New York: Doubleday, 2017.

Gilmore, David D., ed., *Honor and Shame and the Unity of the Mediterranean.* Washington, DC: American Anthropological Association, 1987.

Hage, Ghassan. *White Nation: Fantasies of White Supremacy in a Multicultural Society.* New York: Routledge, 2000.

Herman, Joanna Clapps. *The Anarchist Bastard: Growing Up Italian in America.* Albany: SUNY Press, 2011.

Horden, Peregrine, and Nicholas Purcell. *The Corrupting Sea: A Study of Mediterranean History.* New York: Blackwell, 2000.

Horowitz, Ronald. "Ethnic Identity." In *Ethnicity: Theory and Experience*, edited by Nathan Glazer and Daniel Patrick Moynihan, 110–40. Cambridge, MA: Harvard University Press, 1975.

Isabella, Maurizio, and Konstantina Zanou, eds. *Mediterranean Diasporas: Politics and Ideas in the Long 19th Century.* New York: Bloomsbury, 2016.

Jacobson, Matthew Frye. *Roots Too: White Ethnic Revival in Post–Civil Rights America.* Cambridge, MA: Harvard University Press, 2006.

Kazan, Elia. *America America.* New York: Stein and Day, 1962.

——. *The Anatolian.* New York: Knopf, 1982.

——. *The Arrangement.* New York: Stein and Day, 1967.

——. *Beyond the Aegean.* New York: Knopf, 1994.

——. *The Selected Letters of Elia Kazan.* Edited by Albert J. Devlin with Marlene J. Devlin. New York: Random House, 2014.

Kolin, Philip C. "Civil-Rights and the Black Presence in *Baby Doll*." *Literature-Film Quarterly* 24, no. 1 (1996): 2–11.

Kydd, Elspeth. "'The Ineffaceable Curse of Cain': Racial Marking and Embodiment in *Pinky*." *Camera Obscura* 43 (2000): 94–121.

Lalami, Laila. *The Other Americans.* New York: Pantheon, 2019.

Layoun, Mary N. "Endings and Beginnings: Reimagining the Tasks and Spaces of Comparison." In *Comparison: Theory and Approaches*, edited by Rita Felski and Susan Stanford Friedman, 210–34. Baltimore, MD: Johns Hopkins University Press, 2013.

Lincoln, Bruce. *Apples and Oranges: Explorations In, On, and With Comparison.* Chicago: University of Chicago Press, 2018.

Loukakis, Angelo. *For the Patriarch.* St. Lucia: University of Queensland Press, 1981.

McGehee, Margaret T. "Disturbing the Peace: Lost Boundaries, Pinky, and Censorship in Atlanta 1949–1952." *Cinema Journal* 46, no. 1 (Fall 2006): 23–51.
Meek, Michele. "Marriage, Adultery, and Desire: A Subversive Subtext in *Baby Doll*." *The Tennessee Williams Annual Review* 12 (2011): n.p.
"New Kazan Movie Put on Blacklist: Catholic Legion of Decency Condemns 'Baby Doll'—Film Gets Code Seal." *New York Times*, November 28, 1956, 32.
Novak, Michael. *The Rise of the Unmeltable Ethnics: Politics and Culture in the Seventies*. New York: Macmillan, 1972.
———. *Unmeltable Ethnics: Politics and Culture in American Life*. 2nd ed. New York: Routledge, 2018.
Novkov, Julie. *Racial Union: Law, Intimacy, and the White State in Alabama, 1865–1954*. Ann Arbor: University of Michigan Press, 2008.
Papanikolas, Helen. *A Greek Odyssey in the American West*. Lincoln: University of Nebraska Press, 1997.
Peristiany, John G., ed. *Honour and Shame: The Values of Mediterranean Society*. London: Weidenfeld & Nicolson, 1965.
Sayre, Nora. *Previous Convictions: A Journey through the 1950s*. New Brunswick, NJ: Rutgers University Press, 1995.
Stam, Robert, and Ella Shohat. "Transnationalizing Comparison: The Uses and Abuses of Cross-Cultural Analogy." In *Comparison: Theory and Approaches*, edited by Rita Felski and Susan Stanford Friedman, 120–46. Baltimore, MD: Johns Hopkins University Press, 2013.
Sumner, Cid Ricketts. *Quality*. New York: Bobbs-Merrill, 1946.
Talese, Gay. *The Gay Talese Reader: Portraits and Encounters*. New York: Walker & Company, 2003.
———. *A Writer's Life*. New York: Knopf, 2005.
Viscusi, Robert. *Buried Caesars, and Other Secrets of Italian American Writing*. Albany: SUNY Press, 2006.
Weil, Patrick. "Races at the Gate: A Century of Racial Distinction in American Immigration Policy (1865–1965)." *Georgetown Immigration Law Journal* 15 (2000): 625–48.
Williams, Dakin, and Shepherd Mead. *Tennessee Williams: An Intimate Biography*. New York: Arbor House, 1983.
Williams, Tennessee. *Baby Doll: The Script for the Film*. New York: New Directions, 1956.
———. *Plays 1937–1955*. Edited by Mel Gussow. New York: Library of America, 2000.

PART II

Identity Construction in Two Ethnic Communities

Style and Real Estate

The Architecture of Faith among Greek and Italian Immigrants, 1870–1925

Kostis Kourelis

The American metropolis during the era of great migration (1870–1925) contained a number of diverse minorities that collectively made up an immigrant majority. More than 40 percent of the adult population in cities like Buffalo, Chicago, Cleveland, Detroit, Milwaukee, Minneapolis, or New York was foreign-born; adding their children (technically native-born citizens), the ethnic population made up 75–80 percent of those cities' total population.[1] This urban majority was fragmented into sectarian, national, and linguistic units that worshipped independently. As Martin Luther King Jr. pointed out in 1968, eleven o'clock on Sunday morning is the most segregated hour in America.[2] Places of worship became the de facto collective spaces for ethnic solidarity. Financially supported by parish members, Greek and Italian churches became expressions of prestige and economic power.[3] The Catholic Archdiocese (established in 1808) and the Greek Orthodox Archdiocese (established in 1921) oversaw the operations of each respective parish but counted on their financial autonomy reflected by each parish's collection plates. Protestant churches operated under a decentralized or "presbyterian" model where an assembly of elders (presbyters) controlled governance. This dominant ecclesiastical polity influenced the parish churches of the archdioceses.[4]

Earlier waves of immigration from Ireland and southern Germany had established a Catholic infrastructure that placed Italians into ethnic, linguistic, and cultural confrontation with earlier established hierarchies. The geopolitical fragmentation of Orthodoxy lacked the centralization of a global Catholic church. Greek, Russian, Ukrainian, Serbian, Macedonian, Romanian, Syrian, Coptic, and Unionist Orthodox Americans lacked an institutional oversight. In the early years, they worshipped together out of convenience. For the first thirty years of the oldest Greek Orthodox Church, in New Orleans (est. 1866), Greeks, Russians, and Serbians worshipped together in English and kept records in separate languages.[5] When the respective groups acquired enough numbers, they split off into their own congregations and eventually built archdioceses starting in the 1920s. Tensions between Irish and Italian Catholics led to the establishment of national parishes, but under the oversight of a single Catholic Archdiocese. A bottom-up Greek Orthodox process contrasted with a top-down Roman Catholic process.

Professional differences among Greeks and Italians supplemented linguistic, religious, and national divides. Italians dominated the construction sectors of the urban economy as contractors, stonemasons, quarrymen, and builders. More than any other immigrant group, Italians are responsible for the physical maintenance of the American metropolis. Although Greeks rose to prominence in construction after the 1960s, their contribution before World War II centered on the provision of organic rather than structural material. Flowers, sweets, shoeshines, and food preparation were the material media through which Greek immigrants prospered and financed the building of their churches. The construction industry required the centralization of labor (large team of workers) that was different from the decentralization of labor in the service food industry. Consequently, Italians congregated in neighborhoods that could access major building works, while Greeks dispersed into entrepreneurial opportunities throughout the city.

A comparative approach illustrates many themes on how Greek and Italian communities differed. In the building of churches, there are two productive points of comparison: style and real estate. Philadelphia will serve as our focal point. In 1910, Philadelphia was the third largest city in the United States (New York, 4.8 million; Chicago, 2.2 million; Philadelphia 1.5 million), with the second largest Italian and seventh largest Greek populations. Its Italian population (45,308) made 11.7 percent of the total, while its Greek population (589) made up only 0.15 percent. Comparable to national demographics, the proportion of Italians to Greeks in Philadelphia was tenfold (3 million Italians versus 350,000 Greeks immigrating to the United States in 1900–1920).[6]

Style

Christopher Morley, an astute observer of American life in 1920, captured a vivid moment in Philadelphia's Little Italy. "It was a day of entrancing sunlight, when all that lively district of Little Italy leaped and trembled in the fullness of light and appetizing fluent air. One saw a secret pathos in the effort to reproduce in the flat dull streets of a foreign city something of the color and mirth of Mediterranean soil."[7] One among many primary sources on the immigrant city, this passage makes it clear that the Italians of Philadelphia were engaged in the aesthetic construction of their urban environment and were the architects of their social experience. By repurposing spaces built by others before them, however, the scale and scope of their intervention were limited, and the precise nature of their agency is difficult for historians to reconstruct. Churches are one building type that affords relative clarity in how Greek and Italian immigrants exercised architectural agency. Both groups used their faith affiliation to construct social bonds and a sense of belonging. More important, both groups understood the prestige endowed by Western civilization on the architectural masterworks of their homelands. Whether rural or urban, rich or poor, young or old, male or female, the Greek and Italian immigrant had received an architectural education in the didactic buildings of their religious upbringing. The Mediterranean's Early Christian, Medieval, Byzantine, Renaissance, Baroque, and

Neoclassical churches were objects of admiration, touristic consumption, academic study, and imitation by the American mainstream. Church architecture did not simply provide a shelter in which immigrants congregated to form social identity; it also participated in the language of that identity formation through visual communication. The shared historical styles of the Mediterranean brought Greeks, Italians, and Americans into a dialogue with each other.

In the marketplace of self-presentation, Greeks and Italians possessed a currency from their pasts, a stylistic denomination that was disconnected temporally (the golden ages of the past) and spatially (left behind by immigration). Morley articulates the great aesthetic divide between "the loveliest land on earth" that they left behind and the "cheerless byways of American towns" in which they have landed. The immigrant attempts to bridges the cultural divide by reproducing the native color and mirth in the new streetscape. Doomed to failure by the sheer perfection of its original, this reproductive pathos highlights the inevitable failure in authenticity. At the end, the Italian immigrant cannot but "be pitied for losing the beauty and old tradition of that storied peninsula so far away." *Travels in Philadelphia*, in which "Little Italy" appeared, was directed to the city's natives, to whom Morley belonged; it offered an essayistic grand tour of a changing, diverse, and humorous city. Philadelphia's Little Italy was only a few blocks away from the commercial center, "and yet," Morley writes, "I daresay thousands of our citizens hardly suspect its existence." Morley was not unique in writing about immigrants, but his account differs from the prevalent genre by social reformers like Emily Dinwiddie, who targeted Little Italy as a housing problem that needed scientific description in order to be fixed.[8] According to the social reformer, immigrant architectural heritage was a liability (clutter of religious objects, comfort with cohabiting animals, etc.) that had to be eradicated in order for sanitary Americanization to take place. For reformer Jacob Riis, "the framework of Mediterranean exuberance" evident in the Italian slums of New York does not create a positive space of origin, but "reproduces conditions of destitute and disorder."[9] Riis goes as far as disparaging contemporary artists who took interest in the visual culture of the Italians.

Guided by his friend the Epicure, Morley's journey identifies an ethnoscape whose dimensions cannot be reduced to utilitarian pragmatism.[10] The essay highlights spaces for the consumption, production, and exchange of food. Morley begins a long tradition that privileges foodways as the premier cultural contribution of southern Europeans to the American scene. Both Greeks and Italians aggressively capitalized in the commodity niche of food services. The economic vitality of confectionaries, patisseries, bakeries, restaurants, pizza parlors, diners, cafes, and food markets circumscribed the spatial boundaries where Morley's natives rewarded Mediterranean superiority. In an arena of cultural reproduction, food could easily succeed.

In contrast, architecture could reproduce only thin slices of the monumental original. Architecture's rootedness to place, material, and climate could not be translated by the same ease as food. Morley's immigrant pathos for reproduction is experienced spatially, but the available spaces of observation are commercial. One locus where Greeks and Italians articulated their identities is religious. Greeks and Italians invested great reproductive resources in the expensive and communal church.

Starting in the early 1970s, the new disciplines of material culture identified cultural contributions made by nameless builders. The expansion of architectural studies to include makers outside the academic canon revealed that, along with foodways, immigrants successfully transported architectural ideas to the United States. Their contributions, moreover, were not minor footnotes in a larger story but central to what differentiates American architecture from its European predecessors. In 1986, Dell Upton edited the landmark collection *America's Architectural Roots: Ethnic Groups That Built America*, showcasing twenty-two distinct ethnic contributions. Greeks and Italians are both absent from this selection. Upton notes that "some well-known and conspicuous ethnic groups, such as the Italians, the Greeks, the Poles and the Jews are absent. Why is that? Large urban ethnic groups evidently built little that was distinctive but instead expressed their ethnicity through language, food customs, religion and social organization."[11]

A closer look at the immigrant churches of Greeks and Italians confirms that the identification of a single national style or a craft tradition is hard to find. There is no visual style that resonates as strongly as the culinary contributions of Greeks and Italians to popular American culture. Arguably, their foods have overshadowed their stones. Bringing together Greek and Italian churches during the early waves of migration helps us uncover the less visible architectural contributions of the two groups during the peak of their immigration (1870–1925). A comparative approach elucidates the shared complexities of self-representation and the structural differences that lead to different architectures.

Greeks and Italians encountered each other as foreigners in the public arena of the American city. They competed in a religious marketplace dominated by Protestantism and articulated their national, linguistic, and religious otherness through the single largest communal investment, their neighborhood church. Denominational differences aside, Greek Orthodox and Roman Catholic buildings adorned the same urban streetscapes and conversed with others in the civic theater. Radically different than Greece and Italy, America's "holy experiment" began with a principled rejection of styles as part of the religious reformation of culture from the authoritarianism of Catholicism. In the second half of the nineteenth century, however, American culture embraced the eclecticism of styles that defined architectural discourse. Whether ancient Greek, Roman, Byzantine, Romanesque, Gothic, Islamic, Renaissance, or Baroque, each stylistic revival solicited a psychological association with the civilization that created it. The very buildings that southern European immigrants left behind, thus, provided the linguistic vocabulary with which Americans conversed.[12]

Greeks and Italians brought to America a collective architectural history that was internally diverse and could not be reduced to a single iconic style. Italians could claim Roman, Early Christian, Romanesque, Gothic, Renaissance, and Baroque styles. Greeks could claim ancient Greek, Early Christian, Byzantine, Ottoman, and Neoclassical styles. The long and diverse past of both, however, had been superseded by the creation of recent nation-states in the Greek War of Independence and the Italian Risorgimento. In this respect, younger than the United States, both Greece and Italy promoted a singular national style of neoclassicism that self-consciously diminished periodic and regional differences. It stressed the glories of antiquity over the impure admixtures of the Middle Ages. The Royal Palace in Athens (1836) and the Victor Emmanuel II Monument in Rome (1885), two of the finest expressions of nation-building, were artificially new and did not reflect the older religious spaces that had matured over centuries. A typical southern Italian immigrant would have worshipped in a small but ornate Baroque building, while a typical Greek immigrant would have worshipped in a Byzantine or post-Byzantine-style building.

More important than the architectural choices that they might have brought from home, the new immigrants encountered a richer buffet of stylistic choices in the United States that incorporated the architectural legacies of other European countries, such as France, Germany, England, and Central Europe. Paradoxically, a Greek viewer would encounter many Byzantine buildings in the United States in the early 1900s that had nothing to do with Orthodoxy or Greece. Although the Byzantine style is now recognized as the indigenous ecclesiastical style of Greece and the natural vehicle for Orthodox spirituality, this was not seen as such before the 1930s. The popularization of Byzantium through the writings of John Ruskin in the Victorian period had so co-opted its meanings toward multicultural aestheticism that it no longer resonated with Greece. Instead, the Byzantine style (combined with Islamic and Romanesque elements) had become the iconic style of both Reform Judaism and Protestantism. Starting with the New Synagogue in Berlin (1866), Byzantium was disseminated through American congregations as a Levantine style of amalgamation and oriental splendor. The notion that synagogues defined themselves visually through Muslim architecture is a reality that seems irrational today, given the tensions in the Middle East following the foundation of Israel in 1948. Similarly, it seems unthinkable today that Hagia Sophia was not the paradigm of Greek Orthodoxy but the model for progressive Protestantism, such as in St. Bartholomew's Episcopal Church in Manhattan (1903). Like the Gothic Revival, the Byzantine Revival captured the popular imagination more widely than a denominational preference, as evident in the Byzantine architecture at Rice University's campus (1912) or the Nebraska State Capitol (1922).[13]

Whether populated by Irish, Polish, German, or Italian parishioners, Catholic churches before the Second Vatican Council were designed in historical styles ranging from Renaissance to Gothic, Romanesque, and on a few occasions Byzantine. Initially, Protestantism had rejected the Gothic as representing medieval Catholicism. In the 1840s, however, the Gothic Revival movement infiltrated British Protestantism and slowly reconfigured it as the official church style. The embrace of the Gothic by the Ecclesiological movement spread to the United States through the Episcopal Diocese of New Jersey. Although the Gothic flourished in medieval Italy (see the Orvieto, Siena, and Milan cathedrals), it carried stronger associations with the British Isles and consequently was embraced by Irish rather than the Italian Catholics. Irish Catholic churches shared the Gothic style with Protestant churches, denominationally different but culturally and linguistically united. In contrast, Italian churches stressed a Renaissance heritage. The first Italian ethnic church in America, St. Mary Magdalen de Pazzi (1852), was designed in a Renaissance style. The Cathedral Basilica of Sts. Peter and Paul, the head church of the Roman Catholic Archdiocese of Philadelphia (1846–1864), was also designed in a grand Renaissance style (Figure 1). In the American setting, the style had become the lingua franca of European humanism and stretched across all of northern Europe. Even as its first manifestations arose in the Catholic churches of 1420s Florence, the Renaissance style was global, safe, and secularized by the mid-nineteenth century.

The Cathedral Basilica of Sts. Peter and Paul in Philadelphia used the Renaissance style not to differentiate itself from mainstream America but rather to unite with it. The building was a direct response to the anti-Catholic riots of 1846, with windows placed high enough as not to be destroyed by nativists. The Cathedral had an architectural austerity and universalism that could be shared by the entire Catholic community. Its frescoes were executed by Constantine Brumidi, best known for his work in the Capitol in Washington. Although Brumidi's father was Greek, he grew up in Italy and received Italian academic training before migrating to the United States. Before the Civil War, the Italian community of Philadelphia originated from northern Italy. The High Renaissance of Florence was an appropriate style that could strike pan-Catholic sentiments. In contrast to the High Renaissance and the humanism of northern Italy, the Baroque's epicenter was Counterreformation Rome; as a style, it flourished in southern Italy and would have been the style of many Sicilian or Neapolitan

Style and Real Estate   113

FIGURE 1. Cathedral Basilica of Sts. Peter and Paul, Philadelphia.
Author photograph.

churches in which Italian immigrants worshipped. It would be recognizably different as more theatrical and exuberant. In France, Germany, and England, the Baroque was imported by the royal courts and thus became associated with the aesthetics of monarchy, whereas in Italy, the Baroque remained the primary language of the papacy.

The situation seems to change in the early twentieth century during the American Colonial Revival movement. The Colonial Revival movement appropriated the Renaissance as a weapon of white ethnic supremacy against new eastern and southern European immigrants. At this moment, the ethnic immigrants heightened their deployment of the Renaissance heritage in order to appropriate the Renaissance for an ethnic rather than Anglo-colonial heritage. St. Rita of Cescia, an Italian church in Philadelphia was designed in 1907 by Catholic (but not Italian) architect George I. Lovatt (Figure 2).

FIGURE 2. St. Rita of Cescia, Philadelphia. Author photograph.

Fronting the main thoroughfare of Broad Street, St. Rita is a proudly Baroque edifice that advertises ethnic Italian pride and is modeled after two famous Roman churches, Giacomo della Porta's Gesù (1573) and Carlo Maderno's Santa Susanna (1603).[14] St. Rita was commissioned by Patrick Ryan, the Irish-born Catholic Archbishop of Philadelphia, who employed prominent architects in each of the 172 churches and 82 schools built under his tenure, including the Italian parishes of St. Lucy (1906), Our Lady of Angels (1907), St. Donato (1910), and St. Mary the Eternal (1911). The Roman precedent was an explicit strategy by Archbishop Ryan to battle the proselytization of immigrants by Episcopal, Presbyterian, and Methodist missionaries who established Italian ethnic churches in their neighborhood. Architecture, thus, played a strategic role in grounding the Italians back to their Catholic roots. Although stylistically Italian and directed to a southern Italian audience, Archbishop Ryan gestured toward interethnic collaboration by giving an Irish narrative to the church's stained glass windows.[15] Although given architectural expression in the facades of their church, the Italian parish was kept under close check by Irish clergy who controlled dissent.

After St. Rita, the use of Baroque for Italian churches became more explicit. The church of St. Lucy in Scranton exemplifies the trend. It falls under the auspices of the Philadelphia Archdiocese and was designed by an Italian architect in 1915. After emigrating from Italy in 1902, Luigi Russoniello worked as a stone mason at the Italian-owned quarries of the Carlucci Cut Stone Company. Without much architectural training beyond correspondence school, Russoniello apprenticed in an architectural firm and eventually opened his own practice. St. Lucy illustrates how a blue-collar construction job led into a white-collar occupation of architectural design. St. Lucy translates the architect's direct experiences of the Italian Baroque as well as his craft-based understanding of how Baroque stones were carved. Most spectacularly, the church embodied Italy in a physical way thanks to the global export of Carrara marble, which Russoniello was able to acquire.[16] Over the course of his tenure, Archbishop Ryan consolidated the Baroque as an ethnically Italian style and orchestrated the elevation of immigrant craftsman into mechanisms of an urban growth and speculation.

Baroque architecture was a double-edged sword. It paid cultural homage to the Italian origins of Catholicism, but also claimed the style as universally Catholic. The multivalences of the Baroque are illustrated by its use among ethnically Polish congregations. The Polish Cathedral style that flourished in the Midwest is indistinguishable from the style of ethnically Italian churches. The Immaculate Heart of Mary Church in Polish Hill, Pittsburgh (1905), St. Mary of the Angels in Bucktown, Chicago (1914), and the Basilica of St. Josaphat in Milwaukee (1901) celebrate the apogee of Polish history that occurred in the sixteenth and seventeenth centuries under the Polish Commonwealth. Poland's embrace of the Baroque in this period (in churches like Sts. Peter and Paul, Krakow, 1597–1619) naturalized it as a Polish style. The grandiose oversized churches of the Polish communities made a double nod to St. Peter's Cathedral in Rome (whose ground plans they imitated) and to the great Baroque cathedrals of Poland.

The Italianification process in church architecture was not limited to urban metropolises like Philadelphia, but also operated in the labor frontier of mining towns. In the case of the Immaculate Conception in Iron Mountain Michigan, the agent of design was a lone priest. Iron Mountain, which takes its name from its mines, employed a multiethnic work force of Germans, French, Irish, and Italian miners. Without a Catholic church of their own, the Italian community built Immaculate Conception in 1902. The parish priest was characterized as "engineer, architect, manual bricklayer, parish (pastor) and priest proportionately (who was) always on the site to direct, assist and design."[17] Father Sinopoli's church was modest in size and material (compared to St. Rita or St. Lucy in Philadelphia and Scranton), but it was also modeled after the Baroque Roman church of Gesù. Another example comes from rural Vermont in 1906–1908, where an Italian Baptist minister used the Baroque to communicate the Italian origin of his recently converted Protestant flock. The Italian Baptist Church of Barre, Vermont, is a simple wooden balloon frame building with a brick veneer and granite columns that alludes to Baroque grandeur.[18]

It is difficult to speak of an Orthodox architectural style that resembles the centralized and disseminative work of the Catholic Church in the United States. Having access to many different ethnic communities, the Catholic Church was able to nourish an entire cadre of architectural offices continuously from the mid-nineteenth to the mid-twentieth centuries. Architects like Edwin Forrest Durang, Henry Dagit, and George I. Lovatt in Philadelphia sustained their entire careers with Catholic Church commissions. No such church-building practice emerged among the Greek Orthodox communities, making it difficult to engage in a cultural conversation about style, as could be done among the many Catholic publications devoted to the arts. Picking through some scant evidence, we have only one example of a Greek architect that managed to sustain a network of commissions. In 1909, Nikolaos Dokos advertised himself as "the only Greek architect and engineer in Chicago"[19] (Figure 3). Dokos had graduated from the Lewis Institute of Technology, whose curriculum was more technical than artistic. We know of at least one case where Dokos was subcontracted in the design of a church in the West. In 1924, the Greek community of Salt Lake City had outgrown its first church and hired local architects Hyrum Conrad Pope and Harold

FIGURE 3. Advertisement of Nikolaos Dokos's design for a church in Atlanta (never built), in Canoutos, *Greek-American Guide*, 431. Public domain.

FIGURE 4. Holy Trinity Church, Lowell. Author photograph.

William Burton (who specialized in Mormon temples) for its new building. Although the nature of collaboration is unclear, Pope & Burton consulted with Dokos in the design of Salt Lake City's Holy Trinity Church.[20]

Among the first Greek Orthodox churches designed in the United States was Holy Trinity in Lowell, Massachusetts (Figure 4). The community used local architect Henry L. Rourke, who also designed the church of Lowell's French Canadian immigrants, St. Jean Baptiste.[21] Both churches were a blend of Romanesque and Byzantine precedents. Rourke's qualifications included a trip to Constantinople and eyewitness understanding of Hagia Sophia.[22] Holy Trinity combines a sampling of features from Hagia Sophia, including transverse arches (but in the opposite direction) and a lead dome. Starting with Holy Trinity, the dome emerged as an iconographic signature of Greek Orthodox churches. In a similar way, domes with a bulbous shape became a Russian Orthodox signature starting with St. Theodosius in Cleveland (1913), funded by Czar Nicholas II of Russia. The Greek communities in the United States did not have any financial support from the homeland. Like Holy Trinity in Lowell, St. Nicholas in Cleveland was designed by Frederick Baird, a non-Russian local architect but based on models of the Cathedral of Christ the Savior in Moscow (which was indirectly modeled after Hagia Sophia in Constantinople).[23]

Since Lowell, the dome has been singled out as the premier iconic register of any newly constructed Greek American church. Although ubiquitous, the reference to Hagia Sophia as a model is not always substantiated by the buildings. Justinian's sixth-century cathedral is "the white elephant" that was never used as a model for any future church in Byzantium's long history. Paradoxically, it was Ottoman mosque architecture that first imitated the church nine centuries after its construction. Following the conquest of Constantinople, Ottoman sultans differentiated their dynasties by rejecting the standard mosque of earlier Islamic civilizations through the prototype of Hagia Sophia. The Fatih (1463), Bayezid II (1500–1505), Şehzade (1545), and Süleymaniye (1550) mosques consolidated an architectural image that was dispersed uninterruptedly from 1453 to 1922 across a wide geographical area spanning three continents. One distinctive feature of Hagia Sophia is that it is not symmetrical on four sides but sits on two transverse arches and two piers. More important, the Hagia Sophia dome is low and, in contrast to St. Peter's in Rome, it does not sit on a prominent high drum. This raises an important question of visual familiarity over the architectural particulars of a church that most parishioners would have never experienced. The ideological and poetic centrality that Hagia Sophia may have played in the Orthodox identity does not require a visual understanding of the monument. Modern Greece's ambitions of capturing what was once Byzantine territory in Turkey (the *megali idea*) flourished in 1897–1922 and utilized Hagia Sophia as a sacred destiny. Few Greeks outside Constantinople had experienced the building directly and knew it only through distant exterior views. The majority of churches in which rural Greeks actually worshiped date to the Ottoman period, when Orthodox churches were prohibited from having domes. Greece's post-Byzantine churches were basilicas without a dome. To use Hagia Sophia as a model in the American metropolis would have been foreign to many Greeks and risked being misunderstood as a mosque by non-Greeks.

St. Peter's Cathedral in Rome had been imitated by northern and central Europeans, both Catholic and Protestant (e.g., St. Paul's Cathedral in London). The Renaissance and Baroque style of architecture could play on visceral memories among the whole Catholic realm shared by Italians, Poles, and Spaniards (but not the Irish). The comparable icon for Orthodoxy, Hagia Sophia, had no such afterlife. In the architectural significations of the late nineteenth and early twentieth centuries, the iconography of Hagia Sophia had already been taken by mosques and muddled by other Western imitations. Hagia Sophia had a strong influence in American architecture during the nineteenth century, long before Greeks could claim it as an ethnic marker.[24] Most striking about the early Greek American churches purportedly inspired by Hagia Sophia is how little they actually resemble the prototype in contrast to other contemporary buildings in the American scene. As Protestant worship became increasingly theatrical in the late nineteenth century, configurations of round amphitheatrical spaces grew in popularity and the circle was often roofed by domes.[25]

If not Hagia Sophia, what was the cultural model for Greeks? If the Renaissance and Baroque style became an important paradigm for the configuration of Italian worship, what would be the equivalent configuration for the Greeks? The answer lies in the architectural church style that the national church of Greece promoted, namely the Romanesque Revival or *Rundbogenstil* (round arch style). The Metropolis Church of Athens, which like many of the first American churches was dedicated to the Annunciation, had a distinctive double-tower facade with no historical precedents in Byzantium. Designed in 1842 by the Danish architect Theophilos Hansen, the Athens Metropolis exhibits a pan-European cultural heritage. The *Rundbogenstil* combined Byzantine, Romanesque, and Renaissance elements into a conciliatory new style as fitting for Athens as for Vienna or Berlin.[26] The oldest newly built church of Chicago, the Annunciation of 1910, was explicitly based on the Annunciation Metropolis Church of Athens.[27]

In the minds of the Greek diaspora, this double-tower style reverberated with national ideas of Greece that were promoted in the new churches of provincial capitals after independence. This new Greek ecclesiastical architecture harked back to the church's Early Christian past in order to erase a perceived darker medieval Byzantine past. The Early Christian basilica, moreover, became the universal Christian church in both East and West before the split of the churches. The architects who designed the national ecclesiastical standard in the first churches of modern Greece (1842–1871) considered the Byzantine style "degenerate." Many of the Byzantine monuments were in fact demolished to make room for the modern and improved new churches.[28] As Kathleen Curran has shown, the same German style that inspired Greece's enlightened national church style had already taken root in the United States through its German immigrants.[29] Thus, the direct associations to Greece were legible only to those familiar with the new generation of churches sponsored by the nation-state during the few decades before emigration. The national Greek church had a high dome (resembling St. Peter's in Rome rather than Hagia Sophia in Constantinople), double towers in its facade, and only a few allusions to Byzantium (such as in the use of thin double windows).

Like the Italian parishioners who landed in an architectural milieu dominated by the Irish Catholics of a generation earlier, the Greek parishioners encountered an eclectic urban environment, where all of their potentially unique stylistic markers had been claimed by others (Germans, Jews, Baptists, Presbyterians, etc.). At a stylistic level, Italian Americans sought to rebrand the Renaissance away from its Protestant English associations with St. Paul's in London back to the earlier Catholic associations with St. Peter's in Rome. Similarly, the dome could reclaim for the Greeks a vague Byzantine prototype, which they never directly experienced in their worship space of Greek villages. The large domed churches constructed in Greece's provincial capitals (Patras, Aigion, Volos, etc.) after the revolution disseminated a modern Athenian style that sought to supersede the Byzantine and post-Byzantine churches of the countryside. With the money earned in the United States, Greek immigrants sent remittances to their villages to build new churches and clock towers that resembled the churches of Athens and the provincial capitals and were much larger than the village needs.[30] The churches that the Greeks built in America and the churches that they built in their villages shared a common Athenian aspiration in spite of the great geographical and cultural distance that divided those two arenas of architectural patronage.

It is easy to exaggerate the stylistic markers of ethnicity through few newly constructed monuments. Worshipping in a newly constructed space designed explicitly for your ethnicity was a rare privilege. For most Greeks and Italians alike, the spaces in which they worshipped were not new but hand-me-down remnants of an earlier generation. For Italians, it was older Irish churches, while for Greeks, it was rented or bought properties that had served a different liturgical, cultural, linguistic, and ethnic denomination. Consequently, the one experience that best characterizes Greek churches is recycling and reuse. For instance, all the church spaces that they reused came fitted with pews, an architectural feature that they would have never encountered in Greece. Greek parishes did not remove those pews but adjusted worship accordingly. Russian Orthodox immigrants, on the other hand, removed the pews in transforming Protestant into Russian Orthodox spaces. Some Protestant churches included a pipe organ, which had no function in Orthodox music. The multiplicity of sacred spaces that the Greeks appropriated in their various new cities had not internal coherence. Some were once churches, others were once synagogues, while others were theaters, commercial spaces, or masonic lodges. The one thing that all buildings had in common, however, is a departing group that sold or rented the building to the incoming Greeks. Depending on the long-term histories of the various American cities (some older, some newer), the church that each Greek community acquired had a different vintage. Depending on the patrons that commissioned it and the stylistic choices available at that moment of design, each reused church embodied different aesthetics and internal arrangements. The Italian experience, in contrast, was not subject to such vast variation. Since worship occurred in a Catholic (albeit Irish or German) space, the visual, spatial, and liturgical coherence was more uniform.

The art that decorated the interior of Catholic and Orthodox churches was of equal importance. The Catholic Church in the United States was able to sustain an active debate over artistic merits and execution of the religious art that decorated its church interiors through journals and guidebooks.[31] The popularity of the Gothic Revival movement among American Protestants provided a rich ecclesiastical market for Catholic artists. The career of Italian American artist Nicola D'Ascenzo is most instructive. His family emigrated when he was eleven years old. He studied mural painting at the Pennsylvania Academy of the Fine Arts and the craft of stained glass windows at the New York School of Design in 1900. He then toured Europe to document medieval prototypes. He established D'Ascenzo Studios in Philadelphia and became one of the most sought after stained glass artists, competing with Louis Comfort Tiffany and John La Farge in New York. Out of the seven hundred stained glass windows that D'Ascenzo completed, few are in Catholic churches.[32] A similar opportunity for Italian artists came in the marble quarries of Vermont and Indiana, where entire colonies of Italian stone carvers were established.[33] The craft traditions brought from Italy were so strong that they yielded craft-based social clubs such as the Venetian Club in Philadelphia, established by the stone cutters from Friuli in 1924.[34] In some instances, in fact, Italians were the masons who worked on Greek Orthodox churches. Unable to find Greek icon painters in the building of the Church of St. Andrew in Chicago, for example, Italians were hired instead.[35]

The Greek American community produced a significant cadre of modernist artists outside of the church in the 1940s (William Baziotes, Theodore Stamos, Aristodimos Kaldis, Michael Lekakis, Thomas Chimes, etc.) but did not support an active circle of artists in the 1900s. The portability of canvas icons made it simpler to import directly from Greece. Before the Greek Neo-Byzantine movement of the 1930s, America's churches were adorned by works made in the fashionable Nazarene School of Mount Athos, specifically the workshop of Kausokalyves Monastery (Figure 5). Immigrants bought canvases by Kausokalyves painters, rolled them up, brought them to America, and stretched them onto new wooden frames. A few Greek icon painters eventually crossed the Atlantic, such as Sofronios Afentakis (born in Alaçatı, Turkey) who established an icon workshop in Boston and worked around New England in the 1920s.[36] Due to its Western origins in German Romanticism, the Nazarene school of Kausokalyves was demonized by the Neo-Byzantine style of Photis Kontoglou. Many canvases were systematically destroyed and replaced by correct Byzantine frescoes. This purge did not reach the United States until after World War II (when

FIGURE 5. Ioannikios Kausokalyvitis, Saint George, 1927. St. George Greek Orthodox Cathedral, Philadelphia. Author photograph.

Kontoglou's students arrived). Consequently, a large sample of Athnonite art from 1900 to 1930 survives in churches in the United States and waits to be properly inventoried.

A few additional case studies need mention. Emmanuel Caravacos of Baltimore received a scholarship to study at the École des Beaux Arts in Paris in 1911 and carved funerary monuments in Baltimore's cemetery.[37] Theodore Tsavalas studied in the Art Academy in Athens before arriving in New York in 1912, where he continued taking classes at the Art Student League. His greatest commission came from Holy Trinity in Manhattan (a reused Gothic Revival Episcopal Church), which burned in 1927.[38] Another noteworthy artist was Constantine Triantaphillou, who painted in a Renaissance grand master style from the 1920s to the 1950s. He is responsible for a complete iconographic program at St. George Greek Orthodox Cathedral in Philadelphia (1939–1942), a mural on *The Adventures of Ulysses* painted in a restaurant in Brooklyn (1921), St. Nicholas in St. Louis (late 1940s), and the narthex of St. Nicholas in Chicago (1952). Finally, we have records for one established woodcarver, John W. Perates, who set up a workshop in Portland, Maine, and carved altar screens, icons, and furniture.[39] Even as these few named artists begin to enter art historical scholarship, their contribution cannot be compared to the work of their Italian peers, such as D'Ascenzo.

Sacred Real Estate

Differences in the management and organization of community life mark the divergent experiences between Greeks and Italians in the United States. For the Catholic administration, the building of an Italian church was bound with the demographic parish that sustained it. In planning parish churches, the Catholic Church was engaging in urban planning and a controlled network of neighborhoods. For the Greek administration, on the other hand, a Greek *paroikia* (community) involved no demographic management. In the Catholic Church, one's place of residence determined church affiliation, while in the Orthodox Church, the church was a single space that received parishioners from across the city. Greeks and Italians were separated by an additional organizational difference. Italian churches were subsumed under a preexisting central organization established to serve earlier waves of migration. Italians worshiped as a minority within a minority in spaces that had been constructed to reflect the Irish and southern German diaspora half a century earlier. And when ethnically Italian churches were constructed, it was the Catholic archdiocese that defined the borders between Irish, German, and Italian parishes. No such administration exercised control over the topographic planning of the Greek American religious experience. Greeks, Russians, Ukrainians, Romanians, Serbians, Albanians, Lebanese, Syrians, and Armenians inherited a fragmented Orthodoxy. Before emigrating, they lived in the collapsing Ottoman, Austro-Hungarian, or Russian Empires. Caught up in the disintegration of these empires and the formations of Balkan or Eastern European states, the respective churches became adversarial national churches. The fragmentation in southeastern Europe was mirrored in America.

Both Roman Catholic and Greek Orthodox churches are transnational organizations predating modern nation-states. They participated in earlier arrivals of colonization that preceded the mass immigration of Greeks and Italians in 1870–1925. Catholicism arrived in America from the south through Spanish and French colonization, while Eastern Orthodoxy arrived in America from the north through the missionary activities of Russian monks in Alaska. With the exception of the states of Maryland, California, New Mexico, and Louisiana (which had Catholics dating to the colonial period), Protestantism was the dominant religion of the United States. Having fled persecution from state religions, the Protestant mentality of American churches was embedded with strong anti-Catholic and anti-Orthodox sentiments. Catholicism entered into architectural visibility in the 1840s through the mass migration of Irish and southern Germans a whole generation before the mass arrival of Italians and Greeks.

The Roman Catholic Church was a hierarcical global organization with its headquarters in the Vatican. The Orthodox Churches, on the other hand, had splintered into multiple autonomous churches with the Patriarchate of Constantinople exercising partial control. The chaotic system of ecclesiastical control that Greeks encountered in the United States affirmed their lack of trust in centralized systems as authority wavered between Constantinople and Athens, causing multiple splits and cycles of upheaval. When

Italians arrived in the United States, they found a perfectly organized ecclesiastical system, albeit demographically dominated by the Irish. When Greeks arrived in the United States, there was no equivalent hierarchy. Although Orthodoxy arrived in North America in 1794, while Alaska was a Russian territory, the number of ethnic Russians in America before the nineteenth century was small. In 1905, the Russian Orthodox Church dioceses was transferred from San Francisco to New York and convened an all-American Council in 1907. Orthodoxy took roots with the mass migration of Eastern Europeans and Greeks, who arrived with diverse church affiliations. The dissolution of the Russian Orthodox Church by the Bolshevik Revolution in 1917, moreover, made the status of the older church foundations unstable. Greek, Bulgarian, Romanian, Georgian, Albanian, Ukrainian, Russian, Syrian, Palestinian, and Jordanian Orthodox Christians practiced haphazardly. Incorporated in the state of New York in 1921, the Greek Orthodox Church of North America was formalized at a time when many Greek communities had already established their own separate charters.[40] A push to found new churches would create loyalties to the new archdiocese that could, potentially, assert a coherent architectural identity; a top-down architectural standard was not pursued until Archbishop Iakovos in 1959. Even as a latecomer, the Greek Orthodox Church of America preceded the establishment of other national churches—Serbian (1926), Carpatho-Russian (1938), Ukrainian (1948), Albanian (1950), and a nonethnic Orthodox Church of America but with a strong Russian heritage (1924). Susceptible to "individualistic relativism" and to "crusading sectarianism," Orthodoxy in the United States could not consolidate its religious authority like the Catholic Church.[41] Political schisms in Greece, moreover, were mirrored in American communities, most notably in the national schism of 1910–1922 between royalist and republican factions.

The lack of a centralized church administration to plan for the devotional and social experiences of Orthodox immigrants led to what contemporaries observed as a notable lack of religiosity. Studying the life of a Pennsylvania mill town in 1910, Margaret Byington noted that church attendance among the faithful was mandatory only at Easter.[42] In the absence of a centralized church, the laboring communities established fraternal associations that served semireligious functions, such as guaranteeing a burial place to its members. Greeks established early fraternal societies based on the province of origin that formed the seeds for the establishment of a congregation. One of the earliest churches in Chicago, the Assumption, was formed by Laconians from the Peloponnese. When Greeks from the neighboring province of Arcadia joined the church, they were charged twenty-five cents. The Arcadians protested this tax by forming a new congregation, Holy Trinity, in 1897.[43] Thus, in addition to political infighting, the lack of central organization encouraged provincial divisions even among Greeks of the same province.

When Italian immigrants arrived in the United States, they were received by a well-oiled ecclesiastical machine that had already won major battles of acceptance. The anti-Catholic sentiment that flourished in the 1830s had targeted the Irish population and led to traumatic events like the 1844 anti-Irish riots in Philadelphia (which led to the foundation of the grand Renaissance cathedral).[44] The people of the American Catholic Church consolidated their cohesion after the destruction of churches and property and loss of life. Threatened by an encrypted missionary Protestantism in public education, they also funded a separate system of parochial education that by 1920 numbered 6,551 elementary schools. Catholic monastic orders were also active in the establishment of universities (Georgetown University in 1789, Villanova University in 1842, Notre Dame University in 1842). Although founded with the Irish populations in mind, the parochial schools eventually took national characteristics, focusing on the ethnic makeup of the parishes they served (Irish, Polish, Italian). The Greek Orthodox Church organized schools but failed to institutionalize them in the same way.[45]

The small first wave of Italian immigrants to the U.S. originated from northern Italy. The first ethnically Italian parish was St. Mary Magdalen de' Pazzi, founded in Philadelphia in 1852 (Figure 6). Bishop John Neumann, who was later canonized as a saint, recognized the ethnic solidarity of immigrant groups and initiated the first system of ethnic parishes.[46] St. Mary Magdalen de' Pazzi was intended to serve the Italian community of 1852, whose origins were centered on northern Italy, Liguria, and the Piedmont. Following the unification of Italy in 1861, the Italian government encouraged emigration from the poorer south and lead into a mass exodus. After 1861, the mass of Italian immigrants originated from south-

Style and Real Estate 129

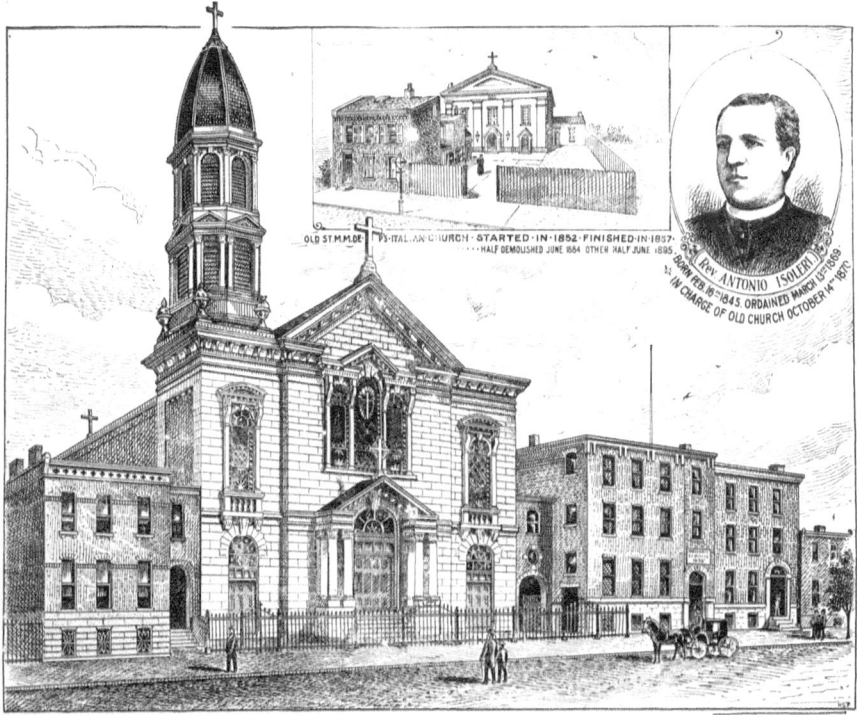

FIGURE 6. St. Mary Magdalen de' Pazzi Italian Church, Rectory, and Orphan Asylum, Philadelphia, 1900. Public domain.

ern Italy and Sicily and were antagonized by the older northern immigrants. The clergy of St. Mary Magdalen actively discouraged the new wave of southern Italians from joining the congregation, although Italian descent was the only requirement for admission. A second Italian parish, Our Lady of Good Counsel, was founded in 1898 as the first parish for southern Italians. Moreover, there was subdivisions of further regionalism within the southern region; immigrants from Calabria, for example, founded Our Lady of Pompeii.

During the second half of the nineteenth century, the Catholic Church in the United States initiated an aggressive system of architectural patronage known as the "Era of Brick-and-Mortar" in the 1910s and 1920s.[47] Recognizing its identity as a fundamentally urban religion, the Catholic Church developed a geographic system of parishes that covered the city and reflected ethnic segregation. Church officials closely followed the network of urban expansion, monitoring the laying out of new gas lines or rail tracks. By centralizing all church building campaigns, the Catholic Archdiocese could monitor trends of new housing and assure lower costs of buying property. New buildings defined the domains of new parishes and placed relative autonomy on the local level of neighborhood. This "parochial" strategy of managing the problems of the industrial city was successful. Protestant churches tried the same strategy but were less successful due to the decentralized nature of their organization. Whereas Protestant churches have congregations, the Catholic Church has parishes. Thomas Rzeznik describes how the Catholic parish carried a different theological understanding of the local church: "A parish, unlike a congregation, served a defined geographic area. With few exceptions, a person belonged to the parish within whose territorial boundaries he or she resided. Even ethnic parishes had defined boundaries in relation to one another. Since a parish was responsible for the spiritual care of all the souls within geographical boundaries, membership could not be selective or restrictive."[48]

In 1883, Philadelphia ranked as the second largest Catholic city, with a total of fifty-six parish churches, of which only one was Italian. By 1923, the Philadelphia archdiocese contained twenty-three Italian parishes.[49] As many of the working-class Irish left the neighborhoods that became dominated by new Italian immigrants, some of the Irish congregations flipped national focus. In addition to the two early churches in Little Italy (St. Mary Magdalen for northern Italians and Our Lady of Good Counsel for southern Italians), parishes became flagships in new neighborhoods of Italian expansion outside the Italian core of South Philadelphia.[50] Some of the churches included bilingual parochial schools that taught classes in both Italian and English. The framework of American Catholicism may have provided a structure of belonging among Italian immigrants, but it also created resentment. In Boston, New York, Newark, and Saint Paul, Minnesota, Italians worshiped in the basements of Irish churches. These "duplex parishes" eventually split but not after cultivating a strong sense of anticlericalism among the Italians.[51]

Fragmentation and centralization vis-à-vis the central ecclesiastical authority can also be seen in the history of Philadelphia's Greek Orthodox community. In contrast to the Italian immigrants who found a church hierarchy upon arrival, the first Greek communities had to invent one from scratch. The first Greek community in Philadelphia was established in 1901 and worshipped in rented houses or commercial spaces, until an Episcopal church was available for purchase in 1908. Like many other Greek communities, this first church was dedicated to the Annunciation. Its building was an unpretentious stone basilica that had served as an Episcopal outreach church. Two years before finding a permanent place of worship, the Greek community had chartered itself under the state of Pennsylvania and had created a logo that included the image of a church modeled on the facade of the Annunciation Metropolis church of Athens. The adapted Episcopal church did not resemble the idealized Athenian church graphic.

As was the case in most other urban congregations, the Greek community split into two during the great political schism between royalists and Venizelists. In 1921, a new church was purchased to house the second Greek Orthodox congregation of St. George, which, unlike the Annunciation, continues to worship in its original location. Fragmentation of churches and the proliferation of congregations can also be explained by the late date of the formal incorporation of the Greek Orthodox Archdiocese of America. When the archdiocese was formed in 1921, the 128 Greek churches already established were allowed to preserve their charters as guaranteed by the states in which they were incorporated. Communities established after 1921, however, were strictly tied to the charter of the archdiocese. Many of the pre-1921 churches were reluctant to give up their autonomy. Consequently, the archdiocese carried out a concerted effort to multiply the new churches in order to numerically overcome the older congregations.[52] In contrast, the Catholic Church had a top-down macro-management structure that predated Italian immigration and had been well tested by German and Irish predecessors. The foundation of new ethnically Italian parishes by the Catholic Archdiocese sought to extend ecclesiastical control while allowing for differentiation. The foundation of new Greek parishes by the Greek Orthodox Archdiocese, on the other hand, sought to create ecclesiastical control by encouraging dissent. Whether along ecclesiastical or national lines, dissent among the Greek churches in America was so extreme that in 1930, the Patriarch of Constantinople had to send a special emissary, Bishop Damaskinos, to broker a resolution between the factions. In 1938, Damaskinos was promoted as archbishop of the Orthodox Church of Greece; under the Axis occupation of Greece in 1940, Damaskinos distinguished himself in resisting the mass deportation of Greek Jews during the Holocaust.

A regional rift between north and south is evident in both Italian and Greek congregations. The provincialism of the homeland was also reflected in political differences that split communities. Within both Greek and Italian migration, there is an internal periodization of regional migration. The rift between northern Italians, who came earlier, and southern Italians, who came later, was as intense as between Italians and their coreligionist Irish. Although not defined as a north-south divide, immigration from Greece began in the Peloponnese and moved northward and eastward as the nation's physical boundaries were expanded through war. With most of northern Greece under Ottoman rule (Thessaly was annexed to Greece in 1881, Epirus and Macedonia in 1912, and Asia Minor temporarily in 1919), the Greeks who came from these newer provinces had different experiences and political affiliations than those from central Greece and the Peloponnese, the old Greece of 1829.

National groups also experienced religious conversion, as Protestant missionary activities succeeded in attracting small national congregations. Any discussion of Italian religious history would be incomplete without discussing conversion from Catholicism into distinctly Italian congregations created by the Presbyterian or Episcopalian churches. The variety of languages and national allegiances of Orthodox groups made them harder to proselytize than the Italians who lived in nucleated neighborhoods. This interethnic fissure complicates the architectural narrative of Italian churches. Thousands of Greeks drifted into other religions, particularly through marriage, but not in large enough numbers to establish ethnic Protestant churches.[53] Although a Greek Evangelical Church existed in Greece as early as 1858, the history of Greek Protestants in the United States remains to be studied. The architecture of ethnic mission churches is a topic not considered in this essay. Similarly, there is no discussion of the synagogue architecture of Greek and Italian Jews or Romani. Kehila Kedosha Janina Synagogue in New York warrants attention as a proudly Greek community with ancient roots that predate the Sephardic and Ashkenazi divisions.[54]

Conclusion

The golden age of Greek and Italian American architecture came in the 1960s after both groups achieved prominent status in the American mainstream. Their bold and iconic church architecture of the 1960s was a sharp break from the spaces they had worshipped in previous generations. Italians opted for the soaring simple forms encouraged by Vatican Council II (1962–1965).[55] This reform broke with architectural models and placed the clergy at the center of worship, imitating the communal experiences of Protestantism. Greeks also experimented with modernism in the 1960s: Frank Lloyd Wright's Annunciation at Wauwatosa, outside of Milwaukee (1961), Sts. Constantine and Helen at Merrillville, near Gary, Indiana (1971), and the Annunciation Cathedral in Atlanta (1968) are most noteworthy. Archbishop Iakovos instituted a return to traditionalism developed by his favorite architect, W. Stuart Thompson, and exhibited in the Church of the Archangels in Stamford, Connecticut (1958), and the chapel of the Greek Orthodox Seminary in Brookline, Massachusetts (1969). Thompson had worked in the American School of Classical Studies at Athens and was familiar with the restoration of the Holy Apostles in the Athenian Agora. The twelfth-century prototype became the model of traditionalism that flourished from the 1980s to today.

As Italians and Greeks moved to the segregated suburbs, they built churches on a tabula rasa of open land and drove to church every Sunday. Surrounded by a sea of parking, the suburban buildings stood as isolated objects to be looked at from afar and lacked the dense and multivalent relationships of the urban buildings that formed their earlier communities. Prosperity and dislocation by automobile allowed for a theatrical staging of a suburban Orthodoxy and Catholicism spatially separated from each other.

At the same time, the old ethnic neighborhoods became commercial simulacra of Greekness or Italianness through the touristic promotion of ethnicity as food markets and restaurants. These ethnoscapes of late capitalism are categorically different from the original ethnic neighborhoods. The overtly representational semiotics of postwar architecture and ethnic urbanism have produced an imagery so strong and simplified as to overshadow the architectural expressions of the first immigrant generations. The melting pot, as it were, had erased all the evidence of melting.

Christopher Morley observed a secret pathos among the Italians of Philadelphia to reproduce the color and mirth of their Mediterranean origins. The process of reproduction, however, was not a simple mirroring of singular prototypes. Greeks and Italians had inherited unique architectural traditions with their own historical afterlives. They also inherited institutional structures of real estate development that shaped the limits of reproduction. Greek Orthodox and Roman Catholic churches were the arena in which Greeks and Italians actively translated their communal identities in brick and mortar. Called national churches (before 1960) and ethnic churches (after 1960) these two minority religions played with dynamic elements of the marketplace and architectural heritage. Their buildings could not be reduced to a single style or a single episode of urban development. The processes through which each nationality negotiated and reproduced its difference implicates architecture at the center stage of the community's physical and cultural actualization. In the 1950s, assimilation, suburbanization, white flight, and urban renewal created a sharp break from the tools of engagement that southern Europeans used in their first period of migration. The second dislocation—this time, from city to suburb rather than from Europe to America—was a trajectory motivated by prosperity rather than poverty. The newly acquired financial assets of the middle class (and the demographics of a baby boom) propelled Greeks and Italians to rebuild their environment and, perhaps for the first time, command the design process of their churches from beginning to end. The building boom of postwar America and the decimation of its inner cities was so successful that it erased earlier episodes of amalgamation and bricolage. The style and real estate of Greek and Italian religious experience in 1870–1925 needs archaeological and museological attention. Excavations of Irish slums, Chinatowns, African burial grounds, and mining towns have generated a material turn in the scholarship on American immigration showing the way to future possibilities in the study of churches.[56]

NOTES

1. Golab, "The Immigrant and the City," 203–205.
2. Martin Luther King Jr., "Remaining Awake Through a Great Revolution" sermon, delivered at the National Cathedral in Washington, DC, on March 31, 1968. King was assassinated four days later. Even though ethnic diversity has increased since 1968, the majority of Americans still worship in segregated enclaves, according to Duke University's 2015 National Congregation Study: "The percentage of people attending congregations in which no ethnic group constitutes at least 80 percent of the regular attendees increased from 15 percent in 1998 to 20 percent in 2012." Chaves and Eagle, *Religious Congregations in 21st Century America*, 20.
3. The Revenue Act of 1913 that established federal income tax categorized religious institutions as 501(c)(3) nonprofit organizations exempted from taxation.
4. Conflict between local parishes and the synods of mainline Protestantism (Episcopal, Methodist, Presbyterian, Lutheran churches) are a central feature of American religious life, evident most recently over same-sex marriage and LGBTQ clergy.
5. Frangos, "Hellenic Spirit."
6. Golab, "The Immigrant and the City," 205. For an overview of Italians and Greeks in Philadelphia, see Luconi, "Italians," and Kitroeff, "Greeks."
7. Morley, *Travels*, 16.
8. Dinwiddie, *Housing Conditions*.
9. Riis, *How the Other Half Lives*, 31.
10. Appadurai, "Disjuncture and Difference."
11. Upton, *America's Architectural Roots*, 14.
12. Lewis, *American Art*, 7–25. The term "holy experiment" was used by Quakers in Pennsylvania, a colony of persecuted minorities.
13. Bullen, *Byzantium Rediscovered*.
14. Upton, *Architecture*, 82.
15. Morello, "Roman Catholic Church."
16. Sutton, "Vincent Russoniello"; Tatman, "Vincent Russoniello."
17. Rotherford, "Immaculate Conception."
18. Clark, "Italian Baptist Church."
19. Canoutas, *Greek-American Guide*, 431.

20. Papanikolas, "Holy Trinity."
21. Chiat, *America's Religious Architecture*, 52.
22. According to local stories, it was the Greek community that sent Rourke to Constantinople.
23. Williams, *Houses of God*, 178–79.
24. Nelson, *Hagia Sophia*, 187–213.
25. Kilde, *When Church Became Theatre*.
26. Bergdoll, *European Architecture*, 184–89.
27. Fiorentinos, *Ecclesia*, 50.
28. Metropolis, Zoodochos Pege, Agios Georgios Karytsis, Agia Eirine, Chrysospiliotissa, and Agios Konstantinos; see Philippides, *Νεοελληνική αρχιτεκονική*, 93–98, 140–43.
29. Curran, *The Romanesque Revival*.
30. There is no systematic survey of the architectural patronage and philanthropy of Greek immigrants, but a preliminary overview of the Peloponnese and central Greece reveals many surviving foundation inscriptions that name diaspora communities in the renovation of churches. See, for example, the churches of Schinohori and Lyrkeia, studied by the author as part of the Western Argolid Regional Project.
31. *The Liturgical Arts Journal*; Bliley, *Altars*.
32. Soria, *American Artists*, 70–74.
33. Audenino, "The Paths of the Trade."
34. Saverino, "Mapping Memories."
35. Fiorentinos, *Ecclesia*, 62.
36. Boston City Directories list his name from 1927 to 1946. His work can be found in the Dormition Church of Poughkeepsie (dated to 1939) and Lowell, Massachusetts.
37. Prevas, *House of God*, 33.
38. Katsaras, "Theodore Tsavalas."
39. Frangos, "The Greek Outsiders."
40. Kitroeff, *The Greek Orthodox Church*, 36–38.
41. Noll, *A History of Christianity*, 346.
42. Byington, *Homestead*, 161.
43. Fiorentinos, *Ecclesia*, 58.
44. Beyer-Purvis, "The Philadelphia Bible Riots."
45. Soumakis, "Greek Orthodox Education."
46. For a history of Philadelphia's Italian community, see Luconi, *From Paesani to White Ethnics*; Juliani, *Building Little Italy*.
47. Rzeznik, "The Church in the Changing City," "The Parochial Enterprise," *Church and State*.

48. Rzeznik, "The Parochial Enterprise," 12.
49. Consuela, "The Church of Philadelphia," 271, 280–281; Luconi, "Italians and Italy."
50. St. Lucy (1906) in Manyunk; St. Rita (1907) on South Broad Street; Our Lady of the Angels (1907) in west Philadelphia; St. Columba (1895) and St. Mary of the Eternal (1911) in north Philadelphia; St. Donato (1910) in Overbrook; Our Lady of the Rosary (1914) in Germantown; and Our Lady of Consolation (1917) in Frankford.
51. Linkh, *American Catholicism*, 104.
52. Gizelis, "Narrative Rhetorical Devices," 44.
53. Form, "Italian Protestants."
54. Ikonomopoulos, *In Memory*.
55. Osborne, *American Catholics*.
56. For a summary on the archaeology of race and ethnicity in the immigrant city, see Rothschild and Wall, *Archaeology*, 102–33. Historical archaeology, so far, has focused on sites of the African American, Asian American, Irish American, and German American experiences. Greek and Italian coal miners are the subject of two noteworthy excavations in Colorado and Pennsylvania; see Larkin and McGuire, *Archaeology*, and Roller, *Archaeology*.

Bibliography

Appadurai, Arjun. "Disjuncture and Difference in the Global Cultural Economy." *Theory, Culture, & Society* 7 (1990): 295–320.
Audenino, Patrizia. "The Paths of the Trade: Italian Stonemasons in the United States." *The International Migration Review* 20, no. 4 (1986): 779–95.
Bergdoll, Barry. *European Architecture, 1750–1890*. Oxford: Oxford University Press, 2000.
Beyer-Purvis, Amanda. "The Philadelphia Bible Riots of 1844: Contest Over the Rights of Citizens." *Pennsylvania History* 83 (Summer 2016): 366–93.
Bliley, Nicholas Martin. *Altars According to the Code of Canon Law*. Washington, DC: Catholic University of America, 1927.
Bullen, J. B. *Byzantium Rediscovered*. London: Phaidon 2003.
Byington, Margaret F. *Homestead: The Households of a Mill Town*. New York: Russell Sage Foundation, 1910.
Canoutas, Seraphim G. *Greek-American Guide and Business Directory*. New York: Helmis Press, 1909.

Chaves, Mark, and Alison Eagle. *Religious Congregations in 21st Century America*. Durham, NC: Duke University, 2015.

Chiat, Marilyn J. *America's Religious Architecture: Sacred Places for Every Community*. New York: Wiley, 1997.

Clark, Carol Ann. "Italian Baptist Church, Barre, Vermont." National Register of Historic Places. Washington, DC: US Department of Interior, National Park Service, 1975.

Consuela, Mary. "The Church of Philadelphia (1884–1918)." In *The History of the Archdiocese of Philadelphia*, edited by James Francis Connelly, 271–338. Philadelphia: Archdiocese of Philadelphia, 1976.

Curran, Kathleen. *The Romanesque Revival: Religion, Politics, and Transnational Exchange*. University Park: Pennsylvania State University Press, 2003.

Dinwiddie, Emily W. *Housing Conditions in Philadelphia*. Philadelphia: Octavia Hill Association, 1904.

Fiorentinos, Panos. *Ecclesia: Greek Orthodox Churches of the Chicago Metropolis*. Chicago: Kantyli, 2004.

Form, William. "Italian Protestants: Religion, Ethnicity and Assimilation." *Journal for the Scientific Study of Religion* 39, no. 3 (2000): 307–20.

Frangos, Steve. "The Greek Outsiders: Artists Lost to Hellenism Part Two." *The National Herald*. https://www.mgsa.org/Resources/Frangos.html.

———. "Hellenic Spirit Firmly Rooted in New Orleans." *The National Herald*, September 10, 2005, 1, 4.

Gizelis, Gregory. "Narrative Rhetorical Devices of Persuasion in the Greek Community of Philadelphia." PhD dissertation, University of Pennsylvania, 1972.

Golab, Caroline. "The Immigrant and the City: Poles, Italians, and Jews in Philadelphia, 1870–1920." In *The Peoples of Philadelphia: A History of Ethnic Groups and Lower-Class Life, 1790–1940*, edited by Allen F. Davis and Mark H. Haller, 203–30. Philadelphia: University of Pennsylvania Press, 1973.

Ikonomopoulos, Marcia Haddad. *In Memory of the Jewish Community of Ioannina*. New York: Bloch, 2004.

Juliani, Richard N. *Building Little Italy: Philadelphia's Italians before Mass Migration*. University Park: Pennsylvania State University Press, 1998.

Katsaras, Penelope Eleni (Gaitanis). "Theodore Tsavalas: America's First Greek Orthodox Iconographer." *The National Herald*, February 17, 2017.

Kilde, Jeanne Halgren. *When Church Became Theatre: The Transformation of Evangelical Architecture and Worship in 19th-Century America*. Oxford: Oxford University Press, 2000.

Kitroeff, Alexander. "Greeks and Greece (Modern)." *The Encyclopedia of Greater Philadelphia*. New Brunswick, NJ: Rutgers University Press, 2017.
———. *The Greek Orthodox Church in America: A Modern History*. Ithaca, NY: Cornell University Press, 2020.
Larkin, Karin, and Randall H. McGuire, eds. *The Archaeology of Class War: The Colorado Coalfield Strike of 1913–1914*. Boulder: University Press of Colorado, 2009.
Lewis, Michael J. *American Art and Architecture*. London: Thames and Hudson, 2006.
Linkh, Richard. *American Catholicism and European Immigrants, 1900–1924*. New York: Center for Migration Studies, 1975.
Luconi, Stefano. *From Paesani to White Ethnics: The Italian Experience in Philadelphia*. Albany: State University of New York Press, 2001.
———. "Italians and Italy." *The Encyclopedia of Greater Philadelphia*. New Brunswick, NJ: Rutgers University Press, 2017.
Morello, Celeste A. "Roman Catholic Church of St. Rita of Cascia." Nomination of Historic Building, Philadelphia Register of Historic Places. Philadelphia: Philadelphia Historical Commission, 2019.
Morley, Christopher. *Travels in Philadelphia*. Philadelphia: David McKay, 1920.
Nelson, Robert S. *Hagia Sophia, 1850–1950: Holy Wisdom Modern Monument*. Chicago: University of Chicago Press, 2004.
Noll, Mark A. *A History of Christianity in the United States and Canada*. Grand Rapids, MI: W. B. Eerdman, 1992.
Osborne, Catherine R. *American Catholics and the Church of Tomorrow: Building Churches for the Future, 1925–1975*. Chicago: University of Chicago Press, 2018.
Papanikolas, Helen Zeese. "Holy Trinity Greek Orthodox Church." National Register of Historic Places Inventory. Washington, DC: National Park Service, 1975.
Philippides, Dimitris. *Νεοελληνική αρχιτεκονική. Αρχιτεκτονική θεωρία και πράξη (1830–1980) σαν αντανάκλαση των ιδεολογικών επιλογών της νεοελληνικής κουλτούρας*. Athens: Melissa.
Prevas, Nicholas. *House of God . . . Gateway to Heaven: A Centennial History of the Greek Orthodox Cathedral of the Annunciation*. Baltimore, MD: Greek Orthodox Cathedral of the Annunciation, 2005.
Riis, Jacob. *How the Other Half Lives: Authoritative Text, Context, Criticism*. Edited by Hasia R. Diner. New York: Norton, 2010.
Roller, Michael P. *An Archaeology of Structural Violence: Life in a Twentieth-Century Coal Town*. Gainesville: University of Florida Press, 2018.

Rotherford, John Bryant, Jr. "Immaculate Conception Church, Iron Mountain, Michigan." National Register of Historic Places. Washington, DC: United States Department of Interior, National Park Service, 1989.

Rothschild, Nan A., and Diana diZerega Wall. *The Archaeology of American Cities*. Gainesville: University Press of Florida, 2014.

Rzeznik, Thomas. *Church and State: Religion and Wealth in Industrial Era Philadelphia*. University Park: Pennsylvania State University Press, 2013.

———. "The Church in the Changing City: Parochial Restructuring in the Archdiocese of Philadelphia in Historical Perspective." *Catholic Historian* 27, no. 4 (2009): 73–90.

———. "The Parochial Enterprise: Financing Institutional Growth in the Brick-and-Mortar Era." *American Catholic Studies* 121, no. 3 (2010): 1–24.

Saverino, Joan. "Mapping Memories in Stone: Italians and the Transformation of a Philadelphia Landscape." In *Global Philadelphia: Immigrant Communities Old and New*, edited by Ayumi Takenaka and Mary Johnson Osirim, 52–76. Philadelphia: Temple University Press, 2010.

Soria, Regina. *American Artists of Italian Heritage, 1776–1945: A Biographical Dictionary*. Madison, NJ: Fairleigh Dickinson University Press, 1993.

Soumakis, Fevronia K. "Greek Orthodox Education: Challenges and Adaptations in New York City Schools." In *Educating Greek Americans: Historical Perspectives and Contemporary Pathways*, edited by Fevronia K. Soumakis and Theodore G. Zervas, 9–40. London: Palgrave Macmillan.

Sutton, David H. "Vincent Russoniello." Manuscript Guide, Balch Institute for Ethnic Studies, Historical Society of Pennsylvania, December 1985.

Tatman, Sandra L. "Vincent Russoniello (1890–1980)." *Biographical Dictionary of Philadelphia Architects (1700–1930)*. Boston: G. K. Hall, 1985.

Upton, Dell. *America's Architectural Roots: Ethnic Groups That Built America*. New York: Wiley, 1986.

———. *Architecture in the United States*. Oxford: Oxford University Press, 1998.

Williams, Peter W. *Houses of God: Region, Religion, and Architecture in the United States*. Urbana: University of Illinois Press.

Ethnic Language Education

A Comparative Study of Greek Americans and Italian Americans in New York City

Angelyn Balodimas-Bartolomei and Fevronia K. Soumakis

For the last century, Greek Americans and Italian Americans have used institutions such as schools and community organizations to affirm and transmit their ethnic identity and heritage languages in the public forum. Both have advanced language education in a particular way and for different purposes. Greek Americans have concentrated on achieving their goals through church schools and to a lesser extent through private and public schools. Although Italian Americans did so through private organizations, they have mainly implemented Italian language programs through the American public school system. While sharing similar socioeconomic backgrounds, particularly during the early migration period, both immigrant groups also diverged in distinct ways throughout the course of the twentieth century. Among these is how they perceived authoritative figures in education, religion, and government. Such distinctions manifest themselves acutely in patterns of schooling, community organization, and the promotion of ethnic language education into the present.

Since the 1960s, scholars such as Joshua A. Fishman have elaborated upon the significance and persistence of ethnic languages and ethnic schools among generations of immigrant populations in the United States. This study draws from Fishman's work as well as from the research of bilingual education experts Ofelia García, Zeena Zakharia, and Bahar Otcu to compare the similarities and differences among Greek Americans and Italian Americans in New York City. García, Zakharia, and Otcu use the phrase "bilingual community education," which we have adopted for the purposes of this chapter, to expand our understanding of "ethnic mother-tongue schools, supplementary/complementary schools, heritage language programs or bilingual education programs."[1] By moving beyond simpler or restrictive notions of ethnic schooling and heritage language practices, the purpose of bilingual community education programs is "the *bilingual* development of American children living in a global multilingual context" that evolves out of the organization of parents and communities, the development of institutional partnerships, and the support of "diasporic plural networks."[2] While Greek American and Italian American community education programs reflect this model, the current comparative study probes further by specifically examining the strategies, objectives, and viewpoints utilized by each group within the context of educational developments in New York City. New York City is significant in that Greeks and Italians arrived in large numbers in the late nineteenth and early twentieth centuries, settled in similar New York City neighborhoods, and engaged in relatively comparable occupations. Set in a highly diverse multilingual city, New York City's public schools responded to the language needs of immigrant populations in various ways. Most groups were expected to "sink or swim" with instruction modeled around English immersion. Although the Bilingual Education Act of 1968 led to bilingual education for some minority groups such as Latinos, most immigrant populations continued to pursue their own agendas or develop their own schools as they began to do in the early 1900s. The urban institutional context has shaped the opportunities and limitations for each group. To that end, we examine and problematize two interrelated questions centered on ideology, religion, and policy:

Ethnic Language Education   143

1. Why have Greek Americans chosen to sustain Greek language education through their afternoon church, Saturday, or parochial day schools, whereas Italian Americans have more or less promoted Italian language education through the American public school system?
2. What strategies has each group utilized for designing and creating heritage language programs in New York, both within and outside of the American educational system?[3]

American sociologist Nancy Foner reminds scholars of the significance of "historical developments and the role of historically rooted social, political, and economic structures and institutions."[4] The migration, settlement, and socioeconomic patterns of early Greek American and Italian American communities will lay the groundwork for understanding the intersection of religion and education here. We will then examine the development and elaboration of collaborative networks that have manifested themselves within the past few decades along with the resurgent interest in bilingual education and innovative school models in New York City. These "diasporic plural networks" may help forge a more democratic society through bilingual community education.[5]

Religion and Schooling in the Era of Mass Migration

Although Italians began immigrating to the United States in the early 1800s and a small group of Greek entrepreneurs arrived in the 1850s, it was not until the late nineteenth and early twentieth centuries that the first large wave of Greek and Italian immigrants arrived and settled in the country. The number of Greeks who arrived on American shores was far less in number than their eastern and southern European counterparts. Between 1890 and 1920, nearly 1.5 million immigrants, predominantly eastern European Jews and southern Italians, arrived in New York City alone.[6] By 1910, the number of Italians living in New York City had reached 341,000.[7] The US census of 1920 shows the population of the Greeks in New York City to be 21,455.[8]

Greek and southern Italian immigration was propelled by diminished opportunities, political instability, and a depressed agricultural economy. The timing of migration and premigration conditions shaped and developed Greeks' and Italians' ecclesial organizations, secular community organizations, their relationship with the political establishment of their respective native countries, and their configuration into the political economy of the United States. Each group arrived bringing with them their unique cultures, traditions, and languages as well as their distinct political, religious, and educational experiences and worldviews—all of which greatly influenced the route that they would take in establishing their edifices. In order to better understand such initiatives, we must first examine the stance of education back in each group's country of origin.

GREEK IMMIGRATION, COMMUNITY FORMATION, AND THE GREEK ORTHODOX CHURCH

In the Kingdom of Greece, a national system of education had been in place since the 1830s, reflecting Western European secular models of education in terms of its centralized structure (elementary, middle, secondary, and higher education levels) and a curricular emphasis on ancient Greek and Latin.[9] Unlike the European educational models, the modern Greek state co-opted the Greek Orthodox Church into its broader educational objective of nation building "by reinventing the classical Hellenic and the Byzantine Christian traditions."[10] The Greek Orthodox faith became part of the formal curriculum, thus, the state and the church participated in shaping the ideological prerogatives of the educational system as elementary education expanded during the nineteenth century.[11] Two forms of Greek were in use at this time: the demotic, or the spoken vernacular, and a more formal Greek known as *katharevousa*, a hybrid of demotic and ancient Greek that was taught in schools and was the official state language until 1976. The investment in education, even if it provided for rudimentary skills and may not have been uniformly enforced, especially in the agricultural communities of southern Greece, was seen as a means to better employment opportunities by the time of mass migration (1890–1920).

In their comparative study of Greeks and Italians in the United States, Hans Vermeulen and Tijno Venema analyze Greek immigrants' social mobility during the period of mass migration within the framework of a trading diaspora model.[12] Exposure to markets which helped cultivate knowledge of trading practices, migration to cosmopolitan urban centers in the Eastern Mediterranean, and the Greek state's investment in education all correlated with a positive attitude toward education. In this respect, the Greek peasant background differed markedly from the Italian.[13] From 1860 to 1900, public education in Greece expanded at all levels.[14] Sociologist Caesar Mavratsas offers a similar explanation for Greeks' social mobility but also draws attention to several crucial factors that offer a contrast with the Italian case. Greeks who arrived in the United States displayed an overwhelming preference for small business ownership because of their prior experience and involvement in commercial activities in Greece. The work ethic that Greek immigrant entrepreneurs adopted or, as Mavratsas puts it, the "intensification of economic life,"[15] molded their social and political outlook.[16] In other words, "the social and political conservatism of Greek Americans" prompted a gradual, yet, acute emphasis on the family and the church, such that the Greek Orthodox Church came to play a central and profound role in the lives of the immigrants as a place to educate and socialize their children, as the public face of the broader Greek American community, and as a symbol of Greek identity.[17]

Nonetheless, this early wave of immigrants was made up of mostly poor, single, unskilled Greek males. By 1909, Greek men who settled in New York City operated shoeshine parlors, florists, lunchrooms, confectionaries, and fruit stores. A system of exploitation known as the padrone system came to characterize many of the trades, particularly the shoeshine business. Such a system was already in place in Greece, but in America it was dominated by the Italians. Padrones took advantage of young boys by making them work long hours and withholding their wages until the initial debt for passage to America had been paid. The padrone system was indicative of the poor working and living conditions of the early immigrants. Nearly half of the immigrant Greek population repatriated to Greece in the early years, but many returned to make the United States their permanent home. The arrival of

Greek women and the formation of families ensured the permanence of the Greek community.[18]

As soon as enough Greeks settled in an area, they were "quick to organize themselves" by forming a *kinotis*, a close-knit self-governing community, to administer the needs of the Greek Orthodox population.[19] The purpose of the *kinotis* was to build a church and school and to oversee the administration and functioning of these institutions. This communal model of organization was supported by the church but also served as a springboard for other activities and organizations. Early Greek community organization allowed for the interaction among middle-class entrepreneur Greeks and the laboring classes so that a wide array of formal and informal educational institutions was established, including the Greek-language press and an extensive network of fraternal, cultural, and business associations.

It is notable that churches and parish schools were pioneered by the immigrants themselves and not by the efforts of a centralized church authority before the 1920s. Independent of jurisdictional authority, the leaders of congregations requested priests from the Church of Greece or from the Patriarchate of Constantinople. According to one scholar, "these immigrant pioneers made several crucial decisions: that Greek would be the language of liturgy and worship, that each church would be incorporated locally and be self-governing, and that each church should sponsor educational programs designed to preserve Greek language and culture among its parishioners."[20] Between 1892 and 1931, approximately eighteen Greek Orthodox church communities were established in New York City. By the late 1930s, four parochial schools were established (two in Chicago, one in Massachusetts, and one in New York City) in addition to 450 afternoon schools educating nearly 25,000 students in the United States.[21]

The Greek Orthodox Archdiocese of North and South America (GOARCH), which was established in the early 1920s in an effort to unite Greek Orthodox churches in the United States under one governing body, attempted to organize the existing schools. In 1912, the Greek American Institute (GAI) was founded in the Bronx as a parochial school and "dormitory for the care of poor and destitute Greek children,"[22] but it was not affiliated with a church. By the early 1930s, however, and with the establishment of the GOARCH's Educational Council, the charter of the school was given over to the GOARCH. The latter's statistics for the 1941–42 academic year reveal the existence of seven secular Greek schools and ten church-affiliated Greek schools in Manhattan alone.[23] In 1949, the second parochial school was established in New York City and from the 1950s to 1980 ten additional church communities commenced with the building of parochial schools.[24] While a number of secular schools existed, the Greek Orthodox Church would become the dominant vehicle through which Greek language and cultural education would take place. It offered the ideological space through which immigrants could conceptualize their identity in ethnoreligious terms and the physical space where immigrants of all social backgrounds could cooperate to organize communal activities and raise funds. The added layer of organizational structure provided by the GOARCH allowed for significant lay participation in the government and management of the churches and schools. Once the task of church building had been completed, communities would be able to make the decision to invest in education according to their financial means.

Not all Greek Americans supported church affiliated education, however. It is well documented that Greeks participated in working-class movements to combat their poor working conditions during the early twentieth century. They became members of the Industrial Workers of the World (IWW), the Socialist Labor Party (SLP), and the Communist Party (CPUSA). A number of Greeks also emerged as organizers. In the Chelsea district of New York City, Haris Claron founded the Spartakos Workers Club which was active in organizing Greek food workers and furriers. An independent school affiliated with the Spartakos Workers Club was founded with seventy-five students in attendance and a curriculum that emphasized the creative and fine arts. Similar schools could be found in Brooklyn and other cities across the United States.[25] The Greek left was critical of the poor facilities of the archdiocesan schools and their instructional methods using *katharevousa*. Thus, its members sought to create schools independent of the more conservative-minded ethnic leaders and Greek Orthodox Church and more attuned to progressive American educational ideas that centered upon the child's development and interests. Greek working-class concerns were communicated in demotic Greek through a leftist press that ranged from the socialist paper *Organization* (*Organosis*) to the communist *Voice of the Worker*

(*Foni tou Ergatou*). An organized working-class movement among the Greeks, however, was not sustained due to the rise of McCarthyism and Greeks' movement into the middle class.[26]

SOUTHERN ITALIAN IMMIGRANTS, SCHOOLING, AND CATHOLICISM IN THE UNITED STATES

In contrast to the Greeks, most Italian immigrants arrived in the United States with an attitude of indifference toward education. By 1861, the process of Italian unification known as *Risorgimento* (Resurgence) brought together the independent and linguistically diverse states under the Kingdom of Italy. Standard Italian, used only by the literate few, was selected as the language of both government and instruction. It was hoped and expected that it would foster a new national identity; however, debates soon arose over the *questione della lingua* (language question). One of the biggest challenges was that the great majority of the Italians spoke dialects. Although formal schooling, especially at the elementary level, became mandatory in southern Italy after unification, parents felt that children should work and contribute to the household economy; thus, education was not necessarily valued or emphasized, and very few learned the newly prescribed standard Italian. This pattern persisted in the United States for several decades.[27] Before the mass wave of Italian immigration (1890–1920), two schools were founded in New York City. The first school was established in 1842 by the political youth movement La Giovine Italia. It was formed and led by Italian activist and politician Giuseppe Mazzini and modeled after Mazzini's first Italian school in London.[28] Besides teaching reading and writing Italian, along with some geography and religion, instruction focused on the *Risorgimento* and in creating a national consciousness of Italian youth. The second school was established in 1855 for children of itinerant laborers and located in the Five Points district.[29] Whereas most Italian immigrants to America traveled alone during this period, several Ligurians brought children whose parents were unable to support them. The children found jobs mostly as itinerant organ grinders or statue vendors. Other children were part of the padrone system in which they were shipped directly from Italy to function as street musicians.

The vast majority of Italians who arrived during the period of mass immigration were poor, illiterate, male peasants—often referred to as "birds of passage," for they came to America to work, make money, and then return home. Those who stayed settled in tenement neighborhoods with others from their region or village who spoke the same dialect. They eventually brought other family members over from Italy. During this time there was no single Italian language in Italy or America.[30] When there was a need to communicate with outsiders, the immigrants would use a hybrid language combining elements of English, dialect, and Italian.[31]

First-generation southern Italian children in the United States grew up learning and speaking their ancestral dialects exclusively in the family. Most never formally learned the dialects or standard Italian, since Italian language schools were rare and attending school was uncommon. From 1899 to 1910, about 54 percent of Italians entering America were considered illiterate,[32] whereas the illiteracy rate of Greek immigrants was about 25 percent.[33]

The Catholic Church, with its long history in the Western Hemisphere, established an extensive parochial school system concentrated mainly in the Northeast. Founded to counteract the anti–Irish Catholic, Protestant-dominated public schools in New York City, the parochial schools grew to educate Catholic immigrant students of different national backgrounds. Although Italians were the largest group of non-English-speaking Catholics in New York's archdiocese, Italian enrollment in the parochial schools posed a challenge.[34] In 1912, the enrollment for southern Italian children in parochial schools within twenty-four cities totaled 10,640. While appearing to be a large figure, the percentage was small (0.8 percent) compared to other Catholic ethnic groups such as the Irish (26.2 percent). Authors such as Phillip Marshman Rose blame the low school enrollment on unsupportive parents who preferred free secular education like that in Italy.[35] However, the low school enrollment was only a minor obstacle in comparison to the challenges that the Catholic Church was encountering with its Italian parishioners.

Throughout the United States, the Catholic churches were dealing with "the Italian Problem." Although southern Italians shared the same Catholic faith, their worship practices differed from those of other Catholics. As such, the southern Italians were considered superstitious and pagan-like for believing in and wearing religious charms and venerating statues, which they carried around in elaborate outdoor processions.[36] While religion played a significant role in their lives, the Italians were considered inadequate Catholics by the official church. Church attendance was infrequent, especially among anticlerical Italian men who viewed the church as an instrument of political, social, and economic oppression. Such differences often led to fights within the congregations among the Irish Catholics and Italian Catholics.

Few pastors were equipped to deal with the Italian immigrants. To accommodate their needs, some Irish-dominated churches allowed Italian priests to conduct services in church basements or annexes. After several complaints from both Italian clergy and parishioners, New York's Archbishop Corrigan sought help from the Vatican. The favored solution was the creation of Italian national parishes with schools where priests and teachers could minister in the Italian language, which differed, however, from local dialects. Bishops recruited priests from Italy, many of whom were affiliated with religious orders. By the 1920s, more than forty Italian national churches were established in New York City.[37] The institutions were invaluable for keeping Italian immigrants connected to their faith and protected from Protestant missionaries.[38]

Thus, in attempting to solve the Italian problem, the Catholic Church established national parochial schools. Their main objective was to preserve *"L'Italianità"* (Italian identity) and inculcate Catholicism through instruction partially conducted in Italian.[39] It is here that we see a parallel with the ethnoreligious orientation of the Greeks. However, because most children spoke different dialects, they were often unable to understand standard Italian spoken by educated priests and teachers. Thus, the implementation of standard Italian within the parochial schools created additional challenges, resulting in a low number of Italian language schools. Unlike the Greeks, language was not the unifying element or key marker of ethnic identity among southern Italians who spoke regional dialects, thus supporting Hofman's principle that language is only one variable of ethnic identity.[40] Furthermore, outside of the national churches, the Italian language was not used to instill Catholicism within most parishes, nor was religion used for language maintenance.

SCHOOLING, POLITICS, AND ETHNIC IDENTITY

While the Roman Catholic and Greek Orthodox churches approached Italian and Greek immigrant education in distinct ways, it was the public schools that educated the vast majority of immigrant students.

The Greek Orthodox Archdiocese in tandem with the Greek immigrant community advocated for Greek language instruction as well as recognition of Orthodox religious holidays. In October 1938, nearly one hundred Greek students enrolled in Straubenmuller Textile High School in New York signed a petition requesting "the inclusion of Greek in the day and evening curricula of the school on the same basis as the other modern languages [that] are now being taught."[41] On April 26, 1940, Archbishop Athenagoras wrote to the principal of the same school, thanking him for his "kind interest toward the Greek students of the famous Textile School," and he would write to the appropriate authorities in Albany "regarding the religious holidays of our Church."[42] This was in line with the voluntary Weekday Religious Education Program that was popularized in nearly all states since it was first conceived in 1914 in Indiana. Students in public schools could be released for religious instruction during the school day on public school premises.[43] Although rendered unconstitutional in 1948, what should not be overlooked in these seemingly benign requests is the level of engagement between church and state actors. It can be inferred that the Greek students with the support of the archdiocese and Greek community took the initiative to write up the petition, gather student names and addresses, and submit it to the American principal. An undated flyer with the title "Learn to Speak Greek: The Language of the Olympians" indicates they were successful, since modern Greek language classes were offered at the school on Mondays and Wednesday evenings and at the local YMCA, which also offered New Testament Greek. The engagement between the GOARCH, the Greek students, and city and state governmental authorities can be understood as something more than Greek immigrants' desire to incorporate Greek into the public school classroom. For many ethnic groups, utilizing the public schools for ethnic or linguistic preservation was not entirely a successful undertaking.[44] What was important was engaging with the political process that "mobilized" ethnic groups. This participation "represented recognition on the part of public authorities that a group had become a respected part of the American body politic."[45]

On the other hand, Italian language instruction became an important vehicle for creating a new Italian American identity as a function of two concurrent efforts.[46] The first was prompted by prominent Italian Americans in New York City, who advocated for all junior high and high schools to offer Italian as a foreign language option. Among the most instrumental advocates was Leonard Covello, the founder and first principal of Benjamin Franklin High School in East Harlem and then the head of Dewitt Clinton High School's Italian program, the first to be offered in any city high school. Covello was one of the first to promote intercultural education and affirm immigrants' cultures. Whereas Covello believed in cultural democracy and that public schools should prepare students for leadership and civic participation, he also felt that the community-centered school was the best means for promoting Americanization among second-generation Italian Americans and other ethnic groups. Through Italian language instruction, Italian American youth would develop an appreciation for their heritage. They would also develop language skills needed for better communicating with their immigrant parents and teaching them American ways.[47] Through his successful initiatives, several Italian American students studied the Italian language. Parents were proud to see the resurgence of Italian pride among their children. In 1922, prominent Italian Americans such as Alberto Bonaschi, a member of the Italian Teachers Association, succeeded in helping Italian become a high school foreign language along with French, German, and Spanish.[48] Two years later, colleges accepted Italian as a full credit language requirement.[49]

The second endeavor was initiated by Benito Mussolini and his fascist government, with language used as a tool for ideological and political indoctrination. Mussolini's main interest was to connect second-generation Italian Americans to their ancestral country and fascism through linguistic bonds.[50] With the aid of teachers and textbooks from Italy, children would learn Italian, develop a national consciousness, and acquire and embrace fresh and friendly images of Mussolini. They could then indirectly sway their parents to vote and influence the US government and Congress in ways that would benefit Mussolini.[51] As in the Unification period, Italian Americans were reminded that their language was "the expression of the Italian 'genius' and civilization" as well as "a vivid and active expression of a people" that connected their past glories and future "potentialities,"[52] and "a sacred attribute of a people, the unmistakable privilege of a race, [language] is what we learnt to babble on our mothers' knees. . . . Forgetting or disavowing it is an ignominy."[53] After living through decades of anti-Italian sentiments, a new national pride arose, with many Italian Americans hailing the charismatic leader of Italy as a modernizing, anti-Bolshevik hero.[54]

Through La Farnesina (the Italian Ministry of Foreign Affairs), the Dante Alighieri Society, and the consulates, language instruction at the time was incorporated particularly in parochial primary schools and some high schools and universities. Lessons were provided by mutual-aid societies, Italian communities, cultural organizations, and associations such as Columbia University's Casa Italiana—the oldest institution representing Italian culture in New York—and OSIA (Order Sons of Italy in America). Whereas the Italian government provided instructional material and some funding, language instruction was mainly supported by Catholic parishes and ethnic associations. Additionally, the regime established summer camps, educational exchanges for high achieving students, and free or discounted journeys to the homeland while also awarding teachers, priests, and cultural promoters for their efforts.[55] In 1921–22, enrollment for Italian courses in seven New York City public schools was at 898. By 1937–38, it rose dramatically, to 16,000 in fifty-five schools.[56] Despite the increasing enrollment, though, it never compared to that for French or Spanish. Even more, Mussolini's efforts were short-lived. For political reasons, the Italian language would once again lose its popularity among Italian Americans, as it had in the early days of the twentieth century.

On December 11, 1941, when Italy declared war on the United States, the image of Italians and their language completely shattered. Since Italian was now considered the language of the enemy, Italian language instruction was soon banned in schools, as was the production of Italian newspapers and radio programs. Whereas some Italian Americans ceased to speak their mother tongue in public, the knowledge and use of the Italian language gave rise to new opportunities in very controlled situations.[57] The Office of Strategic Services recruited Italian American men who had the ability to speak Italian like natives to serve behind the enemy lines, and in that context the Italian language became a vehicle for expressing American patriotism.[58] Many young Italian American men served in the US Army, while others assisted as American government translators. For unnaturalized Italian American immigrants, however, life was full of restrictions, which included curfew, the need for permission to travel outside of hometowns, and being prohibited from owning firearms, cameras, and shortwave radios.[59] Many were incarcerated or interned in concentration camps. Once more, Italian Americans experienced discrimination, resulting in many youths refusing to speak Italian even within the family. As the twentieth century moved forward, the Little Italies experienced a language shift to English among second-generation Italian Americans who were now becoming Americanized. As Pretelli mentions, it would take a long time for the Italian language "to regain the status of a glorious feature of the *italianità* in the American perception of both Italy and the Italian people."[60]

World War II had a different cultural and linguistic impact for Greek Americans than it did for Italian Americans. The Italian invasion of Greece on October 28, 1940, mobilized Greek Americans to the Allied cause. Ethnic pride and patriotism elevated the public image of Greek Americans as they labored through their church and secular organizations to support the war effort. Through the church, Greek American immigrants negotiated their overlapping identities without necessarily privileging one over the other. The church offered the physical and intellectual space to entertain multiple and overlapping configurations of ethnic, linguistic, and socioeconomic identities. The Brooklyn-based Greek Orthodox Church of St. Constantine's Annual Ball provides ample context for such expressions. Held in March of 1940, just seven months prior to Italy's invasion of Greece, the Annual Ball was the parish's major fundraiser, with the journal serving as a memento of the event. It highlights the event's organizers, the entertainment for the evening, special letters from dignitaries, photos of organizations, and journal advertisements. The 1940 event was the community's twenty-seventh, held in the now historic Hotel St. George in downtown Brooklyn. The Annual Ball featured the Andrews Sisters, the famous Greek American trio, who would entertain troops during World War II. Guests danced the foxtrot, rumba, tango, and waltz in between traditional Greek folk dances. Supporters of the journal included hoteliers, restaurateurs, importers and exporters, and other small business owners.[61]

By 1942, the same parish's journal included tragic stories of famine in Greece. Images of Greek and American flags adorned the front cover, along with the phrase "God Bless America." The Greek War Relief Association (GWRA) was formed within days after the Italian invasion. It was through this association that churches, philanthropic groups, and fraternal organizations, contributed money, food, and medicine to Greece. The country's heroic resistance to the Italian invasion and subsequent German invasion and occupation devastated the country. "The heroism of the Greeks was given laudatory coverage in the American media,"[62] as evidenced by the December 16, 1940, *Life* magazine cover featuring an image of a victorious Greek soldier. Archbishop Athenagoras, honorary chairman of the GWRA, appealed directly to Greek schoolchildren in one of his encyclicals:

> Today Hellas is fighting a difficult battle for her freedom and independence. I am deeply moved at having learned that you admire Homeland Greece, and that you are proud of her heroic accomplishments and boast of your Greek names.... You will demonstrate your pride even more, if you also offer some assistance to Greece. Even if you are young. Your small assistance will be great. Your teacher will instruct you as to what you need to do. I will rejoice to be informed that with your deeds, you are good Greek Americans.[63]

In another encyclical, the Archbishop informed Greek Americans that the Greek Teachers Society of New York, Athena, raised $200 in support of "embattled Greece" and announced that they were hosting a celebration of Greek schools in the metropolitan New York area to support the GRWA. In effect, schools were also mobilized to assist in the immediate war effort.[64] After the war, the anniversary of the invasion became a national holiday in Greece, known as OXI (pronounced *o-hee*) Day, or the "Day of No," to commemorate Greece's heroic resistance to the invasion. Since then, Greek school students in the United States have celebrated this anniversary with songs, poems, plays, and skits.

In summary, preimmigration attitudes toward education shaped the early educational experiences of Greek and Italian Americans as they settled in New York City. Despite challenges from the Greek left, the communal model of organization centering around the Greek Orthodox Church allowed for the growth of church afternoon and Saturday language schools, a model that would dominate throughout the course of the twentieth century. In contrast, the Roman Catholic Church made concerted efforts to bring Italian immigrants into the religious fold through the creation of national parishes and parochial schools with the purpose of preserving Italian identity, although language maintenance would not be emphasized and teaching standard Italian proved to be unpopular within the parochial schools. Both groups engaged with political processes available to them through the public schools to negotiate their ethnic identities. Greek Americans and the GOARCH advocated for both language and religious teaching while leading Italian American educators advocated for the teaching of Italian in high schools and colleges. The onset of World War II found Greeks and Italians on opposing sides of the war and challenged the image of Italians while bolstering that of the Greeks. Over the next few decades, changes in federal immigration and education laws helped strengthen and expand community and diasporic networks.

The Growth of Collaborative Networks from the 1960s to the Present

Having abandoned the national-origins system of the 1920s, the landmark 1965 Immigration Act opened the door for another wave of Greek and Italian immigrants to the United States. The strides made during the civil rights movement era not only underpinned the liberal immigration legislation but also bolstered ethnic pluralism, ethnic studies programs, and bilingual education through the Bilingual Education Act of 1968. Although Greeks and Italians arrived in this period in significant numbers, the post-1965 immigration was predominantly made up of Asian, Caribbean, and Latino groups.[65] The new Greek and Italian arrivals to the United States included an educated and professional urban class as well as immigrants from rural communities. Unlike the early immigration period (1880–1920), which was characterized by an overwhelmingly male population, the new immigrants arrived with their families. There were as many women as men who emigrated from Greece and Italy and who entered the labor force. Distinct settlement patterns and established institutions offered Greek and Italian immigrants familiar sights and surroundings.

GREEK AMERICAN COMMUNITY NETWORKS

Ten Greek Orthodox parochial schools were established in New York City between the 1950s and 1970s through patterns of community organization, institutional partnerships, and diasporic networks that were nurtured during the preceding decades. The growth of parochial schools reflects to a large extent the dispersal of Greeks throughout the boroughs. Early nineteenth-century Greek immigrants were scattered throughout New York City and the boroughs, while the post-1965 immigrants tended to settle in Astoria, Queens; Washington Heights, Manhattan; and Bay Ridge, Brooklyn. The most influential Greek American institution, GOARCH, was led by Archbishop Iakovos beginning in 1959. Throughout his tenure as archbishop (1959–96), he was a formidable advocate of Greek American educational interests. In addition, the Bilingual Education Act of 1968 and its subsequent reformulation mobilized educators to develop Greek bilingual education programs beginning in 1974 in New York City public schools; however, this programming was limited to a small number of schools concentrated in Queens and Brooklyn.[66]

A significant strand of the growing collaborative networks that supported Greek education in New York City was that of the partnership between the archdiocese and the Greek Ministry of Education. Together, they cosponsored teacher-training seminars to keep Greek teachers abreast of new educational developments. Beginning in 1973, the Greek Ministry of Education funded teachers serving in Greek schools to attend three-week seminars in Athens, which included lectures on modern Greek instruction, visits to museums and archaeological sites, and participation in a variety of cultural activities. The seminar in Greece was geared to enhancing the teachers' experience and bringing their knowledge of Greece into the classroom. The Greek Ministry of Education offered an additional boost to Greek teachers. They recognized the teachers in the archdiocesan elementary and high school system as being equal to those teaching in Greece for the purposes of retirement benefits, as long as they met a minimum teaching requirement.[67]

In the same year, the Archdiocesan Office of Education began holding yearly training seminars for its teachers in every district, including New York. These seminars included lectures and workshops on a wide range of topics, including teaching Greek as a foreign language, Greeks in the Diaspora, teaching foreign languages in New York, the use of audiovisual materials, the archdiocese's curriculum, teaching history, bilingual/bicultural studies, the problems of Greek American education, and cultural studies.[68]

These efforts arose out of an acute recognition for the need for better-trained Greek language instructors. However, the relationship between the archdiocese and the Greek government during Greece's military dictatorship (1967–1974) cast a shadow on Archbishop Iakovos, who was viewed by many as pro-dictatorship in his outlook. The archbishop, as far as education was concerned, had to consider the immediate interests of the archdiocese, which had spent nearly $500,000 constructing the Ionian Village summer camp in Greece for two hundred Greek American children. The "Ionian Sea beach property was pledged by the former Greek government and turned over to the American Archdiocese by the present military regime."[69] Attending the dedication service in 1970 were clergy from the Church of Greece, Greek government officials, the US ambassador, and a US congressman. In addition, three other important education-related projects were supported by the Greek dictatorship: books free of charge, a high school for Greek American boys in Greece, and the yearly three-week-long professional development seminar for archdiocesan teachers.[70] Speaking out publicly against the military regime would have compromised the future of these costly educational endeavors. This brief example, however, illustrates the complicated and problematic nature of such relationships.

By the late 1990s, however, declining enrollments, and issues related to curriculum, teacher training, materials, and finances became too large and too public to ignore. Archbishop Spyridon, recognizing "that the issues of Greek language and culture were in dire need of immediate attention" undertook a formal assessment of the archdiocesan school system in the United States.[71] The commission appointed with this monumental year-long task was made up of a diverse group of high-profile scholars and politicians. It was led by John Rassias, a Dartmouth College professor renowned for developing a method for intensive language instruction that engaged college students enthusiastically. The comprehensive 110-page report, known more widely as the Rassias Report, offered seventy-three recommendations around nine areas: morale, parental investment, organization, curriculum, educational materials, pedagogy, teacher preparation, compensation, and finances. The findings of the report were not implemented in any systematic manner, though, since they coincided with the end of Archbishop Spyridon's brief three-year tenure in 1999. The attention and high priority ascribed to Greek language education under Spyridon was evidenced by the scope of the report, the in-depth research, countless interviews, and surveys conducted across numerous schools in towns and cities. The commission, which included recognizable political heavyweights Michael S. Dukakis, Paul Sarbanes, and Olympia Snowe, gave the archdiocese's educational project gravitas. By harnessing the capacities and support of scholars and politicians into its framework, the archdiocese cemented its leadership role in matters concerning Greek language education.

Today, schools that offer Greek language instruction are mostly the Greek parochial and afternoon or Saturday schools that continue to operate under the Greek Orthodox Archdiocese of America in New York City.[72] The Direct Archdiocesan District Office of Education (DAD) falls under the archdiocese's Department of Greek Education and offers support to schools located in the New York metropolitan area, Washington, DC, and Maryland. The DAD provides assistance in the form of books and materials, curriculum guides, teacher workshops, and the administration of the regents' proficiency examination in modern Greek to eighth grade students. According to the DAD, the "day and afternoon schools offer a Greek program of studies that incorporates the teaching of the Greek Orthodox faith, the Modern Greek language and history as well as the universal Hellenic ideals, customs, and traditions."[73] The DAD represents and advocates for Greek Orthodox parochial schools at the federal, state, and local levels including the New York Standing Committee of Religious and Independent Schools Officials and the New York State Commissioner's Advisory Council for Nonpublic Schools. It has been instrumental in procuring federal funds for the parochial schools; during the period 2014–2016, the DAD received $144,655 in funding, which was utilized for teacher training and instructional resources.[74]

While the overarching mission of the DAD promotes faith, language, and "universal Hellenic ideals," a perusal of the mission statement of the Annunciation School of Greek Language and Hellenic Culture, one of Manhattan's historic church communities, reveals an increasing shift toward a pluralistic outlook that moves beyond the ethnic Greek community:

> Since its inception in 1892, the Annunciation Greek Orthodox Church community has believed that the ecumenical principles of Hellenism can institute positive transformation in the lives of all people. Our School of Greek Language and Hellenic Culture offers our parishioners, friends and neighbors the opportunity to expand their horizons through the learning of one of the world's most time-honored languages and culture. We currently offer language courses and folk-dance lessons for both children and adults. Our personalized approach to teaching helps meet the needs of individuals with little or no exposure to the Greek language and culture and those for whom the Greek language and culture is more familiar.[75]

The Greek government continued to offer modest support for Greek language initiatives for several decades.[76] In 1996, the passage of Greek Law 2413/1996 provided for intercultural education and education for Greeks globally. Essentially, this legislation offered systematic support for Greek schools abroad by providing trained educators, Greek textbooks, teacher training workshops, and consular officials dedicated to overseeing educational initiatives. Greek textbooks have been developed through partnerships with the Pedagogical Institute of Greece, the University of Crete, and the Aristotelian University of Thessaloniki. During the academic year 2003–2004, nine teachers entirely funded by the Greek government were placed in teaching positions in ten parochial schools and one afternoon school, where they taught Greek language in addition to history and culture.[77] The Center for the Greek Language in Thessaloniki was established in 1994 and operates under the auspices of the Greek Ministry of Education, Research, and Religious Affairs. Through this research institute, the Certificate of Proficiency in the Greek Language is administered by the Greek Consulate in New York City. The center outlines in detail the value of obtaining the certificate for professional advancement, to obtain government positions in Greece, to pursue higher education in Greece, and for high school students to receive the Seal of Biliteracy from their home state, which officially recognizes their proficiency in a foreign language. Of the 275 candidates who sat for the exam in 2003 in New York City, nearly 82 percent obtained the certificate.[78] Consular officials immerse themselves in the Greek community in New York City and attend community events. They are often invited as guest speakers at school events and student celebrations, thus cementing the Greek government's investment in Greek language programming in the diaspora.

ITALIAN AMERICAN COMMUNITY NETWORKS

Since the 1950s, Italian Americans—many of whom were now of the second and third generations and fully integrated into American society—began leaving the original Little Italies, where their ancestors had settled during the early immigration period. Most relocated to Astoria and Staten Island. During this time, several historical and political events helped in elevating the Italian image not only in America but throughout the globe. Thanks to the Italian "economic miracle" of the 1950s and 1960s, Italy transformed from a poor, agrarian country into a global industrial power and quickly became famous for its beauty, style, and design. As more American tourists began visiting Italy, a sudden growing interest in *Italianità* arose. Suddenly the Italian language became popular leading to the call for Italian language instruction. A few other factors increased this demand and popularity. In response to the significant immigration populations that had arisen in big cities such as Chicago and New York, the 1968 Bilingual Act was enacted, bringing a need for both Italian bilingual programs in public schools and Italian bilingual teachers who were trained in teaching Standard Italian—the language that was spoken by the majority of those who had arrived from Italy. By the 1970s, Italian bilingual programs were flourishing in New York City.[79]

Additionally, the revival of white ethnics in the 1960s and 1970s also helped the resurgence of the Italian language. As Italian language and cultural programs increased within American colleges and universities, so did student enrollments. By 1965 nearly 20,000 students were studying the language in American colleges and universities.[80]

For the past few decades, the Italian government has played an important role in shifting the focus of instruction from afterschool programs to elementary and high school curricula. The programs are overseen by the Italian Ministry of Foreign Affairs and the Education Office at the Consulate General of Italy in New York.[81] Through generous contributions from the Italian government, annual funds are distributed to various selected schools around the country by means of *enti gestori*, or nonprofit local and regional organizations. In New York City, the IACE (Italian American Committee on Education) serves this function and establishes partnerships with the state departments of education in the tristate area of New York, Connecticut, and part of New Jersey. It also oversees language instruction in K-12 public and private schools and afternoon programs. For more than thirty years, the IACE program has reached out to 37,000 students and 350 teachers of Italian, with more than 1,300 courses being taught in public schools.[82]

La Farnesina also collaborates with another government organization, the Istituto Italiano di Cultura (Italian Cultural Institute) of New York. The institute promotes Italian language and culture through numerous adult language courses and cultural events. Additionally, the education office oversees Italian instruction at the United Nations International School (UNIS), as well as La Scuola d'Italia Guglielmo Marconi in Manhattan. Founded in 1977 as a high school for children of Italian expatriates, it is the only bilingual English-Italian day school in North America, serving students from prekindergarten through grade twelve.

This nexus of community and international government relations has the potential to push bilingual education operating within a multilingual urban "eduscape" into a more prominent intellectual space among American educators. As we see in the Italian case, the more recent efforts of La Farnesina have been channeled into the American public school systems. While Greek language education has been limited to the Greek Orthodox schools, the individual efforts of even a small group of dedicated parents and instructors, in both the Italian and Greek cases, can have a long-term effect.

GRASS ROOTS ADVOCACY IN NEW YORK CITY PUBLIC SCHOOLS

Efforts to initiate and sustain bilingual education are not confined to more prominent organizations and institutions. In fact, effective leadership at the local level can have a far-reaching impact to the extent that different institutions are intentionally drawn into collaborative and transnational partnerships. Such has been the case with community advocates and the public schools. As of 2019, there are three New York City public high schools that offer Greek language instruction: Fort Hamilton High School, Brooklyn; Long Island City High School, Long Island City, Queens and William Cullen Bryant High School, Astoria, Queens.[83] One such program, which was first organized in the late 1970s, flourished under the leadership of bilingual educator Argyro Apostolou in Fort Hamilton High School (FHHS), Brooklyn, during her tenure from 1994 to 2015. Apostolou arrived at FHHS after having gained experience as a Greek language teacher in St. Demetrios Parochial School in Astoria. After earning her licenses to teach in public high schools as well as to teach English as a second language, she went to work building the Greek program at FHHS. In her long career there, Apostolou developed the curriculum for both Greek American students and nonnative speakers living in the Bay Ridge section of Brooklyn. She taught classes at the introductory, intermediate, and advanced levels. She also taught ancient Greek for several years at FHHS and modern Greek at St. John's University. Apostolou was supported by the Greek American community of Bay Ridge and by both the archdiocese and the Greek consulate, whose representatives attended programs and offered awards to students. Apostolou rounded out the language program with a dance group, Culture Day celebration, and fundraising events. Her students celebrated Greek Independence Day at the school through a yearly performance for parents and teachers during parent-teacher conferences. In addition, she organized a Greek Club for the students that is still popular today.[84]

The Bronx High School of Science (BHSS), one of the selective specialized New York public high schools, is another example in which a Greek program was developed by Greek American faculty members. In 1984, foreign language educators Stella Economou and Georgia Thanasoulis established the Greek program with funding from the Rockefeller Foundation. This grant supported Thanasoulis's writing of the textbook *An Anthology of Greek Literature: Works from the Classical and Modern Greek Period*. While the student population enrolled in the Greek classes was predominantly from a Greek background, by the late 1990s, the instructors received funding to reorient the program to accommodate language classes for non-Greek speakers. A collaboration between BHSS and the Alexander S. Onassis Public Benefit Foundation of Athens enabled the support for project HELLAS (Hellenic Ethos, Language, Literature, and Artistic Studies) through the funding of the Greek language program. The Onassis Hellenic Studies Program Grant at BHSS was renewed yearly through the 2015–16 academic school year.[85]

On May 3, 2018, the New York City Department of Education announced on its blog "The Morning Bell" that forty-eight bilingual language programs would be added, expanding upon the two hundred programs then in place. Many of these initiatives were prompted by the grass-roots organization of parents. The organized effort by parents to incorporate a Greek-English dual language program in Astoria announced a meeting with Department of Education officials through social media, indicating the attendance of officials from the Greek and Cypriot consulates in New York City.[86]

Declining Greek American parochial school enrollments in New York City during the 1980s challenged communities to explore alternative educational options such as charter schools, which are experimental taxpayer-funded and community-led schools. The Kimisis tis Theotokou Greek Orthodox Church community in the Park Slope section of Brooklyn took the opportunity to promote a Hellenic-centered theme and curriculum by converting the Soterios Ellenas Parochial School into a charter school. The refashioned Hellenic Classical Charter School (HCCS), whose motto is Knowledge–Wisdom–Truth, opened its doors in 2005 and has been under the guidance of Principal Christina Tettonis and local Greek American community leaders ever since. The growth and prominence of the school is striking in terms of the awards and high rankings it has garnered as well as the significant partnerships it has forged, including an eight-year partnership with Teachers College Columbia University's Reading and Writing Program and a twelve-year partnership with the Greek government. In 2017,

100 percent of all eighth graders passed the regents' examination in modern Greek administered by the archdiocese. The school's diverse student population is drawn through a lottery application. The leadership of the school expanded the HCCS vision and opened a second location at the Holy Trinity–St. Nicholas facility in Staten Island in September 2019. As part of the overall programming, students learn modern Greek, Latin, and Greek folk dancing and participate in cultural events such as the Greek Independence Day parade in Manhattan and the Brooklyn Borough President's yearly "Embrace your Hyphen Greek-American Heritage Celebration." The school's mission emphasizes "a rigorous classical education in a challenging and engaging learning environment" where "students will leave the school prepared intellectually, socially, and emotionally to gain entry to and succeed in the best high schools in New York City and contribute to the global community as responsible citizens."[87] HCCS, which is open to students from all socioeconomic backgrounds, is illustrative of the extent to which bilingual community education efforts have the capacity to invigorate public education at the local level while imagining far-reaching implications globally.

It is the Italian language, however, which has become one of the most studied languages in American high schools. During the 2005/2006 school year, the language was recognized as one of the thirty-eight Advanced Placement courses in the United States and Canada. AP classes enable high school students to take introductory-level college courses and earn college credits upon passing an exam. Due to low enrollment, AP Italian was suspended in the 2008–9 school year; through donations from Italian American associations, it was reinstated in the fall of 2011.

The study of Italian has also gained popularity in American nursery, primary, and middle schools. The type and availability of children's Italian language programs vary in format and are offered after school, on weekends, and in all-day schools through language academies, private organizations, and public/private education systems.

New York City has recently become home to two Italian dual-language programs in which students are taught literacy and content in both Italian and English. Considered the most effective way for obtaining bilingualism, such programs are growing in popularity across the country. Whereas the

New York Department of Education has offered Spanish and French dual-language programs for the past decade, several other languages such as Italian have currently been added. The first Italian-English dual-language program was established in 2015 at Lefferts Park Public School 112 in Bensonhurst, Brooklyn. It now consists of four classes ranging from pre-K to second grade.[88] The second dual-language program was initiated in September 2018 at the Young Diplomats Magnet Academy in Harlem, PS 242. The school which already has an International Baccalaureate certification, chose to pilot the pre-K and kindergarten dual-language program.

The programs have been made possible by two dynamic Italian "tiger moms," Stefania Puxeddu and Benedetta Scardovi-Mounie, who founded a nonprofit organization called "In Italiano." They began a campaign to introduce Italian dual-language programs in New York elementary schools and were soon supported by the Italian consulate and the Federation of Italian-American Organizations. With the help of IACE, each Italian dual-language school receives partial financial assistance for the Italian teachers, teaching materials, resources, and professional development.[89] After seeing the success of the two programs, interest has grown for establishing additional Italian dual-language programs among other schools in New York City.

Advocacy at the grass-roots level by parents and educators, as illustrated by both the Greek and Italian cases, sets in motion the creation of collaborative local and transnational networks. These networks leverage the political processes afforded them through legislation and public schooling to expand bilingual education. For Greek Americans, this process has prompted a more inclusionary outlook that had been promoted by Italian Americans many decades earlier. At the same time, this advocacy challenges public schools to embrace bilingual education community efforts as an invaluable resource.

Conclusion

In New York City today, Greek and Italian language instruction occurs through an array of public, private, and religious institutions, which are supported by an interlocking and overlapping network of local and international educators, philanthropists, religious and secular institutions, and other stakeholders. The historical development of these educational efforts reveals the "complexity" that García, Zakharia, and Otcu argue "is not fully captured by seeing them simply as 'heritage language' programs." As we have demonstrated throughout this chapter, several unique factors account for the differences that exist amongst Italian and Greek language instruction in the United States. Whereas both groups arrived on American land during the first wave of mass migration (1890–1920) and shared similar socioeconomic premigration backgrounds, they differed greatly in their social mobility, their respective organizational capacities, and their stakeholders' attention to education. Such differences can be attributed to their unique historical and political pasts, which greatly influenced their attitudes toward the church and education. Whereas the Greek Orthodox Church was deeply committed to Greek language education and became central to Greek American immigrant community life, the Roman Catholic Church was widely viewed by the Italian immigrants as an instrument of political, social, and economic oppression. Thus, for many, church attendance was sporadic and frequented only on special occasions. Unlike the Greek Orthodox Church, which is the pillar and promoter of the Greek language and identity, Italian identity and the Italian language have been mostly disengaged from the Roman Catholic Church in the United States outside of a few discrete historical periods. Thus, both groups have depended on different sources for financially supporting heritage language instruction. Additionally, language instruction has differed in the audience that it would address.

Throughout the twentieth century, Greek education, which took place mainly in church-sponsored schools, continued to be supported through the Greek Orthodox Archdiocese of America and often through the Greek government. The main goal of both was to pass on the language to subsequent generations of Greek Americans. On the other hand, Italian language instruction, particularly in public education has been mainly supported through the Italian Ministry of Foreign Affairs, consulates, and Italian organizations with little or no help from religious organizations. Italian American educators such as Leonard Covello were trailblazers for introducing

Italian in the New York City public school system during the early twentieth century, not only for Italian immigrant students but also for others interested in learning the language. This would end, however, during World War II, when the Italian language became viewed as the language of the enemy. Greek Americans, whose image was cast in a positive light due to their war efforts, continued to support Greek language education.

The stance of both Greek and Italian instruction in the United States changed greatly after the war. The post-1965 period saw a new wave of Greek and Italian immigrants to the United States. This resulted in an expansion of bilingual programming in American public schools and community networks for the immigrant students. The Italian language suddenly became popular as more Americans began traveling to Italy, resulting in a surge in Italian language courses throughout the United States and especially within New York. Several Greek schools opened throughout New York City, catering to first- and second-generation Greek Americans. Today, individual educators and parents continue to have a large and long-lasting impact on heritage language learning both within and outside of their ethnic communities. The study of Italian continues to gain much popularity on all levels of education especially within the public domain. Many initiatives have also been taken by the Greek government in supporting Greek language instruction and fluency of the language within various types of schools not only in New York City but also throughout Greek-diaspora communities worldwide.

Although this study has focused on Greek and Italian education instruction at the elementary and secondary levels, it is important to make note of the increase in programs offered in colleges and universities throughout New York, such as the Calandra Italian Institute and the Center for Byzantine and Modern Greek Studies, both offered through Queens College. Programs such as these merit a separate study in the near future.

With the rise of globalization and the realization that language learning promotes both global understanding and respect, heritage language programs are beginning to change. There is a new emphasis "on living these language practices in the present and providing students with life experiences and performances that will enable them to practice their bilingualism in a future global world."[90] Michael Damanakis demonstrates that opportunities are available to diaspora groups, to "build on the existing *local* and *inter-local* (in the same country) *cultural networks*, but also to expand them into *hyper-local, transnational* (networks between countries) so that they can function as cultural bearers and culture promoters."[91] Several heritage language communities, such as the Italian community, are realizing that it is their responsibility to ensure that their language is more than an ethnic language and that it should be available for all who want to study it. Greek American educators and community groups are collaborating and promoting Greek language education for a broader, socioeconomically diverse student population within a more inclusive framework. These dynamic yet understudied educational spaces, as García, Zakharia, and Otcu contend, activate diasporic networks to enable a vision for a more democratic society.[92]

NOTES

1. The authors emphasize "community" to denote bilingual education programs developed "within the particular bilingual community." García, Zakharia, and Otcu, "Bilingual Community Education," 4.

2. Ibid., 11, 33–42. The notion of "diasporic plural networks," according to García, Zakharia, and Otcu, moves beyond the conventional understanding of Joshua A. Fishman's "speech community" where members share the same language and social norms for its use. It deconstructs the persistent idea that ethnolinguistic communities are "autonomous and segregated groups." Rather, they are "fluid and heterogeneous," "a product of their constant interactions in plural networks both in the US context and globally."

The diasporic plural networks we refer to in this chapter encompass the institutions and stakeholders, national and international, who have committed in some part to the support of the Greek and Italian languages in the United States, and specifically in New York City. Their interests may be aligned entirely, partially, or not at all; their agendas might differ; they may be public and powerful groups, or smaller, community grass-roots activists; they may be working independently or interdependently.

Another useful way of understanding the functioning of networks is through Artemis Leontis's eloquent metaphor of the "network" in her research on women's handwork. The Greek "social network" involves "nodes of activity" or "interconnected threads of communication, associations, and institutions that comprise Greek America" and which can be applied to Italian Americans as well. Leontis, "The Intellectual in Greek America," 92–93.

3. According to the Center for Applied Linguistics, "A heritage language program is any language development program that is designed or tailored to address the needs of heritage language learners.... Heritage language programs may be at any level or setting, including community-based, K-12, or higher education." According to Joshua Fishman's research, "Community-based schools or programs are organized privately rather than within the public education system." The main goal is to pass on the language and culture from one generation to the other. While they differ in scope and reach, "they are organized by community members- families, community leaders, churches, or civic organizations." Center for Applied Linguistics. Heritage Briefs, 2010.

4. Foner, "A Research Comment," 54.

5. García, Zakharia, and Otcu, "Bilingual Community Education," 33.

6. Foner, *From Ellis Island to JFK*, 1, 10. According to Foner, Russian Jewish and Italian immigrants made up nearly one-fifth of New York City's estimated five million residents.

7. Ibid., 10.

8. US Department of Commerce, *Fourteenth Census*, 702.

9. Kazamias, "Modernity, State-Formation, Nation Building, and Education in Greece," 247–50.

10. Ibid., 244, 246.

11. Kalyvas, *Modern Greece*, 41.

12. Vermeulen and Venema, "Peasantry and Trading Diaspora, 135–39. However, the Greek Orthodox Church's dominance in education in the United States was not the pattern found in other diaspora communities. For example, in Egypt, wealthy Greek merchants created, funded, and operated secular communal institutions, including schools over which they maintained firm control and oversight. These Greek community organizations were independent of the Greek Orthodox Church, whose influence was greatly diminished as the Ottoman millet system was phased out. See Kitroeff, *The Greeks and the Making of Modern Egypt*.

13. Vermeulen and Venema, "Peasantry and Trading Diaspora," 124–49.

14. Kalyvas, *Modern Greece*, 41–42; Gallant, *Modern Greece*, 50.

15. Mavratsas, "Greek-American Economic Culture: The Intensification of Economic Life and a Parallel Process of Puritanization," 105. See also Yiorgos Anagnostou's insightful analysis of Caesar Mavratsas's work, "Caesar V. Mavratsas."

16. Mavratsas, "Greek-American Economic Culture,"107–8. Mavratsas utilizes the term "puritanization" to describe the notion of Greek Americans' "intensification of economic life." According to Mavratsas's analysis, "purita-

nization involves a social and political conservatism, a more ascetic life-style with less emphasis on literary and artistic pursuits, an expanded role for the family and church, and a more conventional morality, with less tolerance for bohemian life-styles."

17. Ibid., 111–17.

18. Moskos and Moskos, *Greek Americans*, 31–33; Hatzidimitriou, "Greeks"; Saloutos, *The Greeks in the United States*, 47–58; Saloutos, "Greeks." It is also important to note that not all Greeks belonged to the Greek Orthodox faith. There were approximately fifty thousand Greek Jews who settled in New York City during the early twentieth century. For an extended discussion on the history of the Greek Jewish population and their settlement in New York City, see Ikonomopoulos, "The Romaniote Jewish Community of New York."

19. Vermeulen and Venema, "Peasantry and Trading Diaspora," 138.

20. Hatzidimitriou, "Church-Community Relations in the United States," 69–70.

21. Moskos and Moskos, *Greek Americans*, 66; See also Soumakis, "Greek Orthodox Education," 14, 20. For an analysis related to the educational material produced for Greek American children in the early period, see Kaliambou, "The First Schoolbooks for Greek American Children."

22. Burgess, *Greeks in America*, 76. See also Canoutas, *Greek American Guide and Business Directory*, 474. Canoutas identified seven schools in New York City under the heading "Schools": 3 language schools with the name of the head teacher or tutor, 3 schools of music, and the Greek American Institute.

23. Statistikos pinax scholion, mathiton, kai didaskalon tou scholikou etous 1941–1942 (Statistical table of schools, students, and teachers for the school year 1941–1942), June 10, 1942, Box VII, Folder DF, Archives of the Greek Orthodox Archdiocese of America (hereafter GOARCH). Enrollment information was not provided for every school.

24. These were The Cathedral School (1949), Chelsea School of St. Eleftherios Church (1955), St. Demeterios Astoria (1957), The Theodore P. Tsolainos-Constantine Goulandris Parochial School of St. Spyridon (1959), Argyrios Fantis Parochial School of Saints Constantine and Helen (1963), Soterios Ellenas Parochial School of Kimisis tis Theotokou (1966), St. Demetrios Jamaica (1967), Transfiguration School Corona (1967), Three Hierarchs Parochial School (1975), William Spyropoulos Parochial School of St. Nicholas Flushing (1977), and Dimitrios and Georgia Kaloidis Parochial School of Holy Cross (1980). See Soumakis, "Greek Orthodox Education," 20.

25. Karpozilos, "Greek American Laborers," 303.

26. Georgakas, "Greek-American Radicalism," 207–32; Moskos and Moskos, *Struggle and Success*, 110–12.

27. Cohen, *From Workshop to Office*, 21–22. Twenty percent of students in roughly grades one to three were enrolled in school in all of Italy during the 1907–8 school year.

28. Rossi, *The Image of America in Mazzini's Writing*, 24–25.

29. Brown, "The Archdiocese of New York before the Great Migration," 21–22.

30. Carnevale, *A New Language, A New World*, 21.

31. Ibid., 26.

32. Puleo, "From Italy to Boston's North End," 29.

33. Vermeulen and Venema, "Peasantry and Trading Diaspora," 131–33. Illiteracy in southern Italy was 68 percent in 1901 and 57 percent in 1907 in Greece. Drawing upon several data sets, Vermeulen and Venema write that Greek immigrants to the United States "were more literate than the Greek population as a whole." Carlo M. Cipolla bases his figures on Winthrop Talbot's data, which show a 24.6 percent illiteracy rate for Greek immigrants and 52.4 percent for southern Italian immigrants between 1900 and 1914. See also US Department of the Interior, *Adult Illiteracy*, 32–33; Cipolla, *Literacy and Development in the West*, 97; Waters and Lieberson, "Ethnic Differences in Education," 174, 177; US Immigration Commission, *Reports of the Immigration Commission*, 99.

34. Brown, "The First Generation and the National Parish System," 48.

35. Rose, *The Italians in America*, 86–87.

36. Iorizzo and Mondello, *The Italian-Americans*, 179.

37. Liptak, "Ethnic Catholicism," 16.

38. Vecoli, "Prelates and Peasants," 252.

39. Rose, *The Italians in America*, 86–87.

40. Hofman, "Mother Tongue Retentiveness in Ethnic Parishes," 136.

41. Greek American Students to Dr. William H. Dooley, October 1938, Box VII, Folder AS, GOARCH.

42. Archbishop Athenagoras to Dr. William H. Dooley, 26 April 1940, Box VII, Folder AS, GOARCH.

43. Fraser, *Between Church and State*, 138–40.

44. Zimmerman, "Ethnics against Ethnicity."

45. Olneck, "American Public Schooling and European Immigrants in the Early Twentieth Century," 112.

46. Carnevale, *A New Language, A New World*, 136.

47. Ibid., 137.

48. Ibid., 138.

49. Ibid., 139.

50. Ibid., 137.

51. Pretelli, "Culture or Propaganda?" 172.
52. "La diffusione della lingua e della cultura italiana nel mondo,: *Il Legionario* (October 7, 1933), cited in ibid., 180.
53. Piero Parini, the director of the Bureau for Italians Abroad, in The General Bureau of the Fasci Abroad cited in ibid., 175.
54. Luconi, "Forging an Ethnic Identity," 94.
55. Ibid., 183.
56. Fucilla, *The Teaching of Italian in the United States*, 263.
57. Carnevale, "No Italian Spoken," 4.
58. Ibid.
59. Cannistraro and Meyer, *The Lost World of Italian-American Radicalism*, 23.
60. Pretelli, "Culture or Propaganda?" 191.
61. St. Constantine's Annual Ball Journal, 1940, Archives of Saints Constantine and Helen Cathedral, Brooklyn, NY.
62. Moskos and Moskos, *Struggle and Success*, 66.
63. Archbishop Athenagoras, Encyclical, November 16, 1940, in Constantelos, *Encyclicals and Documents of the Greek Orthodox Archdiocese of America*, 355–57.
64. Archbishop Athenagoras, Encyclical, January 7, 1941, in ibid., 360–61.
65. By this time, significant changes occurred. While the first generation of Greek Americans had achieved success as business owners despite their limited education, nearly 50 percent of the second generation attended college, according to the 1970 federal census. See Moskos and Moskos, *Struggle and Success*, 142–44. On the other hand, Italian Americans were still ranked academically as one of the lowest-performing European groups in the country. See Gambino, *Blood of My Blood*, 230.
66. Anemoyanis, "Greek Bilingual Education in Historical Perspective," 177. In 1974, Greek bilingual education programs were created to serve the needs of Greek students with limited English proficiency. They served nearly 150 students in Community School District 30, which included Astoria, Long Island City, Jackson Heights, Woodside, Corona, and East Elmhurst; this number quadrupled by the 1980s. Supporters of Greek parochial schools opposed bilingual education programs because they saw them as a threat to their schools. They believed that parochial schools and afternoon schools alone could successfully impart Greek language instruction while educating students for participation in American society. They also feared a decrease in enrollments as well as a loss of teaching staff to the public schools. According to bilingual educators, however, Greek parochial schools were not equipped to meet the needs of first-generation Greek immigrant children, who

benefited from the transitional nature of the bilingual programs. See also Spiridakis, "Greek Bilingual Education," 73–90.

67. Emmanuel Hatziemmanuel, report to Clergy-Laity Congress, July 1972, Box V20, Folder AA, Education Collection, GOARCH.

68. Emmanuel Hatziemmanuel, report to Archdiocesan Board of Education, 30 January 1974, 13 March 1975 and 13 November 1975, Box V13, Folder AG, GOARCH; Hatziemmanuel to the Directors and Teachers of Greek-American Schools, 1 November 1977, 7 November 1978, 2 December 1978, Box V17, Folder HK, GOARCH; Hatziemmanuel, Progress Report, 14 April 1976, Box V13, Folder AH, GOARCH.

69. 1971 Yearbook of the Greek Orthodox Archdiocese of North and South America, pp. 145–147, Box E53, Folder 1971, GOARCH.

70. Curriculum and Instructions, 1971–1972, Box V12, Folder SD, GOARCH; Minutes Archdiocesan Board of Education Meeting, 15 December 1972, Box V13, Folder FF, GOARCH.

71. *Future of the Greek Language and Culture in the United States*, 1.

72. One reason this trend continues today is that the local Greek Orthodox churches or parishes offer a measure of stability that could ensure the operation of the schools: space for classrooms in addition to financial support and a potential teacher applicant pool that could be drawn from the wider Greek community. Another reason speaks to the early development of the church in the United States and the systematic efforts of the archdiocese to assert control over education and other nonreligious activities in an effort to combat the influence of Protestant congregational practices. From the 1930s onward, as the hierarchical structure of the archdiocese was solidified, both secular and religious activities came under the purview of the parish. For an extended analysis on the early church in the United States, see Kitroeff, *The Greek Orthodox Church in America*.

73. Direct Archdiocesan District Office of Education (DAD), School Directory.

74. Direct Archdiocesan District Office of Education (DAD), "Report on Parochial School Education."

75. Annunciation School of Greek Language and Culture.

76. For an insightful analysis on Greece's diaspora policies, see Vogli, "The Making of Greece Abroad," 14–33.

77. *A Hellenic Education Plan for America*, 2–3.

78. Ibid.; see also Center for Greek Language.

79. Haller, "Italian in New York," 140.

80. Ibid., 134.

81. Italian Consulate of New York, "Education Office."

82. Ibid.
83. *2019 NYC High School Directory.*
84. Argyro Apostolou, Interview, April 10, 2019.
85. As of this writing, BHSS no longer offers courses in Greek language. Email communication to BHSS regarding the Hellenic Studies program went unanswered. *A Hellenic Education Plan for America*, 28–32.
86. Greek-English Dual Language Program in NYC Public Schools.
87. Hellenic Classical Charter Schools. See also Gulosino, "A Case Study of Hellenic Classical Charter School," 81–102.
88. PS 112, "Italian Dual Language Program."
89. Puxeddu and Benedetta, "Mommies and Daddies of New York."
90. García, Zakharia, and Otcu, "Bilingual Community Education," 10.
91. Damanakis, "Identity, Language, and Language Policies in the Diaspora," 688–89.
92. García, Zakharia, and Otcu, "Bilingual Community Education," 41–42.

Bibliography

2019 NYC High School Directory. New York: New York City Department of Education, 2019.

Abbott, Grace. "A Study of the Greeks in Chicago." *American Journal of Sociology* 15, no. 3 (November 1909): 379–93.

Anagnostou, Yiorgos. "Caesar V. Mavratsas: Contributions to Greek American Sociology." *Ergon: Greek/American Arts and Letters* (2017).

Anemoyanis, Vivian. "Greek Bilingual Education in Historical Perspective." In Psomiades, Scourby, and Zenelis, *The Greek American Community in Transition*, 171–80.

Annunciation School of Greek Language and Culture.

Archives of the Greek Orthodox Archdiocese of America, New York.

Archives of Saints Constantine and Helen Greek Orthodox Cathedral, Brooklyn, New York.

Balodimas-Bartolomei, Angelyn. "On Being Ethnic in the Twenty-First Century: A Generational Study of Greek Americans and Italian Americans." *Italian American Review* 7, no. 1 (2017): 40–63.

Brown, Mary Elizabeth. *Churches, Communities, and Children: Italian Immigrants in the Archdiocese of New York, 1880–1945.* New York: Center for Migration Studies, 1995.

Burgess, Thomas. *Greeks in America: An Account of Their Coming, Progress, Customs, Living, and Aspirations, with an Historical Introduction and the Stories of Some Famous American-Greeks*. Boston: Sherman, French & Co., 1913.

Cannistraro, Philip, and Gerald Meyer, eds. *The Lost World of Italian-American Radicalism: Politics, Labor and Culture*. Westport, CT: Praeger/Greenwood, 2003.

Canoutas, Serapheim G. *Greek American Guide and Business Directory*. New York: Helmis Press, 1912.

Carnevale, Nancy. *A New Language, A New World*. Chicago: University of Illinois Press, 2009.

———. "'No Italian Spoken for the Duration of the War': Language, Italian-American Identity, and Cultural Pluralism in the World War II Years." *Journal of American Ethnic History* 22, no. 3 (Spring, 2003): 3–33.

Center for Applied Linguistics. Heritage Briefs. 2010. https://bit.ly/3Agldeo.

Center for Greek Language. Greek Language Certification. https://bit.ly/3moDpNR.

Cipolla, Carlo M. *Literacy and Development in the West*. Baltimore, MD: Penguin Books, 1969.

Cohen, Miriam. *From Workshop to Office: Two Generations of Italian Women in New York City, 1900–1950*. Ithaca, NY: Cornell University Press, 1992.

Constantakos, Chrysie M., and John N. Spiridakis. "Greek in New York." In Orfanos, *Reading Greek America*, 161–92.

Constantelos, Demetrios J., ed. *Encyclicals and Documents of the Greek Orthodox Archdiocese of North and South America: Relating to Its Thought and Activity of the First Fifty Years (1922–1972)*. Thessaloniki: Patriarchal Institute for Patristic Studies, 1976.

Contopoulos, Michael. *The Greek Community of New York City: Early Years to 1910*, vol. 11. New Rochelle, NY: A. D. Caratzas, 1992.

Covello, Leonard. *The Social Background of the Italo-American School Child*. Leiden: E. J. Brill, 1967.

Damanakis, Michael. "Identity, Language, and Language Policies in the Diaspora: Historical-Comparative Approach." In *Handbook of Research and Practice in Heritage Language Education*, edited by Peter Pericles Trifonas and Themistoklis Aravossitas, 671–90. New York: Springer International, 2017.

Deffenbaugh, Walter, and Ward Keesecker. *Compulsory School Attendance Laws and Their Administration*. Washington, DC: US Government Printing Office, 1939.

Direct Archdiocesan District Office of Education (DAD). "Report on Parochial School Education." 43rd Biennial Clergy Laity Conference July 3–8, 2016.

———. School Directory. https://bit.ly/3a5znEh.

Fass, Paula. *Outside In: Minorities and the Transformation of American Education.* New York: Oxford University Press, 1991.

Foner, Nancy. *From Ellis Island to JFK: New York's Two Great Waves of Immigration.* New Haven, CT: Yale University Press, 2000.

———. "A Research Comment: What's New about Super-Diversity?" *Journal of American Ethnic History* 36, no. 4 (Summer 2017): 49–57.

Fraser, James W. *Between Church and State: Religion and Public Education in a Multicultural America.* New York: St. Martin's Press, 1999.

Fucilla, Joseph G. *The Teaching of Italian in the United States.* New Brunswick, NJ: American Association of Teachers of Italian, 1967.

The Future of the Greek Language and Culture in the United States: Survival in the Diaspora: A Report from the Archbishop's Commission on Greek Language and Hellenic Culture. New York: Greek Orthodox Archdiocese of North and South America, 1999.

Gallant, Thomas. *Modern Greece.* New York: Oxford University Press, 2001.

Gambino, Richard. *Blood of My Blood.* New York: Doubleday, 1974.

García, Ofelia, and Joshua A. Fishman, eds. *The Multilingual Apple: Languages in New York City.* New York: Mouton de Gruyter, 2002.

García, Ofelia, Zeena Zakharia, and Bahar Otcu. "Bilingual Community Education: Beyond Heritage Language Education and Bilingual Education in New York." In García and Zakharia, *Bilingual Community Education and Multilingualism,* 3–42.

García, Ofelia, and Zeena Zakharia, eds. *Bilingual Community Education and Multilingualism: Beyond Heritage Languages in a Global City.* Buffalo, NY: Multilingual Matters, 2012.

Georgakas, Dan. "Greek-American Radicalism: The Twentieth Century." In *The Immigrant Left in the United* States, edited by Paul Buhle and Dan Georgakas, 207–32. Albany: State University of New York Press, 1996.

Glazer, Nathan. "The Process and Problems of Language-Maintenance: An Integrated View." In *Language Loyalty in the United States,* edited by Joshua A. Fishman, 358–68. The Hague: Mouton, 1966.

Gordon, Milton. "Assimilation in America: Theory and Reality." *Daedulus* 90, no. 2 (Spring 1961): 263–85.

Greek-English Dual Language Program in NYC Public Schools. Facebook Group. https://bit.ly/3Bp53kh.

Gulosino, Charisse. "A Case Study of Hellenic Classical Charter School." In *Proud to be Different: Ethnocentric Niche Charter Schools in America*, edited by Robert A. Fox and Nina K. Buchanan, 81–102. Lanham, MD: Rowman & Littlefield, 2014.

Haller, Hermann W. "Italian in New York." In García and Fishman, *The Multilingual Apple*, 119–42.

Hantzopoulos, Maria. "Going to Greek School: The Politics of Religion, Identity and Culture in Community-Based Greek Language Schools." In García and Zakharia, *Bilingual Community Education and Multilingualism*, 128–40.

Hatzidimitriou, Constantine G. "Church-Community Relations in the United States." In Ioannides, *Greeks in English-Speaking Countries*, 69–90.

———."Greeks." In *The Encyclopedia of New York City*, edited by Kenneth Jackson, 503–4. New Haven, CT: Yale University Press, 1995.

Hatziemmanuel, Emmanuel. "Hellenic Orthodox Education in America." In Psomiades, Scourby, and Zenelis, *The Greek American Community in Transition*, 181–90.

Hellenic Classical Charter Schools. https://bit.ly/3D8jPwo.

A Hellenic Education Plan for America. New York: Hellenic Link, Inc. 2005.

Hofman, John H. "Mother Tongue Retentiveness in Ethnic Parishes." In *Language Loyalty in the United States*, edited by Joshua A. Fishman, 127–55. The Hague: Mouton, 1966.

Ikonomopoulos, Marcia Haddad. "The Romaniote Jewish Community of New York." *Journal of Modern Hellenism* 23–24 (Winter 2006–2007): 141–68.

Ioannides, Christos P., ed. *Greeks in English-Speaking Countries: Culture, Identity, Politics*. New Rochelle, NY: Aristide D. Caratzas, 1997.

Iorizzo, Luciano J., and Salvatore Mondello. *The Italian-Americans*. New York: Twayne, 1971.

Italian Consulate of New York. "Education Office." https://bit.ly/3tdrENx.

Kaliambou, Maria. "The First Schoolbooks for Greek American Children." In Soumakis and Zervas, *Educating Greek Americans*, 41–70.

Kalyvas, Stathis N. *Modern Greece: What Everyone Needs to Know*. New York: Oxford University Press: 2015.

Karpozilos, Kostis. "Greek American Laborers, the Communist Movement and Trade Unions, 1900–1950." PhD dissertation, University of Crete, 2010.

Kazamias, Andreas M. "Modernity, State-Formation, Nation Building, and Education in Greece." In *International Handbook of Comparative Education*,

edited by R. Cowen and A. M. Kazamias, 239–56. New York: Springer, 2009.
Kitroeff, Alexander. *The Greek Orthodox Church in America: A Modern History.* Ithaca, NY: Northern Illinois University Press, an imprint of Cornell University Press, 2020.
———. *The Greeks and the Making of Modern Egypt.* Cairo: American University in Cairo Press, 2019.
Kopan, Andrew T. *Education and Greek Immigrants in Chicago, 1892–1973: A Study in Ethnic Survival.* New York: Garland, 1990.
Kourvetaris, George A. *Studies on Greek Americans.* New York: Columbia University Press, 1997.
La Scuola d'Italia. Mission Statement. https://bit.ly/3mlg9Ap.
Leontis, Artemis. "The Intellectual in Greek America." *Journal of the Hellenic Diaspora* 23 (1997): 85–109.
Liptak, Dolores Ann. *Ethnic Catholicism, European Immigrants and the Catholic Church in Connecticut, 1870–1920.* New York: Center for Migration Studies, 1987.
Luconi, Stefano. "Forging an Ethnic Identity: The Case of the Italian Americans." *Revue française d'études américaines* 96 (2003): 89–101.
Mavratsas, Caesar. "Greek-American Economic Culture: The Intensification of Economic Life and a Parallel Process of Puritanization." In *New Migrants in the Marketplace: Boston's Ethnic Entrepreneurs*, edited by Marilyn Halter, 97–119. Amherst: University of Massachusetts Press, 1995.
Modern Language Association. "Language Enrollment Database, 1958–2016, Italian 1983." https://bit.ly/2Yjl6Br.
Moskos, Peter C., and Charles C. Moskos. *Greek Americans: Struggle and Success.* 3rd ed. New Brunswick, NJ: Transaction Publishers, 2014.
Olneck, Michael. "American Public Schooling and European Immigrants in the Early Twentieth Century: A Post-Revisionist Synthesis." In *Rethinking the History of American Education*, edited by William J. Reese and John L. Rury, 103–41. New York: Palgrave Macmillan, 2008.
Orfanos, Spyros D., ed. *Reading Greek America: Studies in the Experience of Greeks in the United States.* New York: Pella Publishing, 2002.
Orfanos, Spyros D., Harry J. Psomiades, and John Spiridakis, eds. *Education and Greek Americans: Process and Prospects.* New York: Pella Publishing, 1987.
Perlmann, Joel. *Ethnic Differences: Schooling and Social Structure among the Irish, Italians, Jews, and Blacks in an American City, 1880–1935.* New York: Cambridge University Press, 1988.

Pretelli, Matteo M. "Culture or Propaganda? Fascism and Italian Culture in the United States." *Studi Emigrazione/Migration Studies* 43, no. 161 (2006): 171–92.

PS 112. "Italian Dual Language Program." https://bit.ly/3pi59Gf.

Psomiades, Harry J., Alice Scourby, and John G. Zenelis, eds. *The Greek American Community in Transition*. New York: Pella Publishing, 1982.

Puleo, Stephan. "From Italy to Boston's North End: Italian Immigration and Settlement, 1890–1910." PhD dissertation, University of Massachusetts, Boston, 1994.

Puxeddu, Stefania, and Benedetta Scardovi. "Mommies and Daddies of New York, Voice Your Preference: Go Italian! The Role of NYC Families in the Promotion of Bilingual Programs at Public Schools." *La Voce di New York*, April 24, 2018.

Rose, Phillip Marshman. *The Italians in America*. New York: Doran, 1922.

Rossi, Joseph. *The Image of America in Mazzini's Writing*. Madison: University of Wisconsin Press, 1954.

Saloutos, Theodore. "Greeks." In *Harvard Encyclopedia of American Ethnic Groups*, edited by Stephan Thernstrom, 430–40. Cambridge, MA: The Belknap Press of Harvard University Press, 1980.

———. *The Greeks in the United States*. Cambridge, MA: Harvard University Press, 1964.

Sandis, Eva E. "The Greek Population of New York City." In Psomiades, Scourby, and Zenelis, *The Greek American Community in Transition*, 65–92.

Soumakis, Fevronia K. "Greek Orthodox Education: Challenges and Adaptations in New York City Schools." In Soumakis and Zervas, *Educating Greek Americans*, 9–40.

———. "A Sacred Paideia: The Greek Orthodox Archdiocese, Immigration, and Education in New York City, 1959–1979." PhD dissertation, Teachers College, Columbia University, 2015.

Soumakis, Fevronia K., and Theodore G. Zervas, eds. *Educating Greek Americans: Historical Perspectives and Contemporary Pathways*. New York: Palgrave Macmillan, 2020.

Spiridakis, John. "Greek Bilingual Education: Policies and Possibilities." In Orfanos, Psomiades, and Spiridakis, *Education and Greek Americans*, 73–90.

Tsoucalas, Constantine. "Some Aspects of 'Over-Education' in Modern Greece." *Journal of the Hellenic Diaspora* 8, nos. 1–2 (Spring–Summer 1981): 109–22.

US Department of Commerce, Bureau of the Census. *Fourteenth Census of the United States Taken in the Year 1920: Volume III, Population, 1920, Composi-*

tion and Characteristics of the Population by States, by William C. Hunt. Washington, DC: US Government Printing Office, 1922.
US Department of the Interior, Bureau of Education. *Adult Illiteracy*, by Winthrop Talbot. Bulletin No. 35. Washington, DC: US Government Printing Office, 1916.
US Immigration Commission. *Reports of the Immigration Commission*, by William Paul Dillingham. Washington, DC: US Government Printing Office, 1911.
Vecoli, Rudolph R. "Italians." *The Electronic Encyclopedia of Chicago*. Chicago: Chicago Historical Society, 2005.
———. "Prelates and Peasants: Italian Immigrants and the Catholic Church." *Journal of Social History* 2, no. 3 (Spring 1969): 217–68.
Vermeulen, Hans, and Joel Perlmann, eds. *Immigrants, Schooling and Social Mobility: Does Culture Make a Difference?* London: Macmillan, 2000.
Vermeulen, Hans, and Tijno Venema. "Peasantry and Trading Diaspora." In Vermeulen and Perlmann, *Immigrants, Schooling and Social Mobility*, 124–49.
Vogli, Elpida. "The Making of Greece Abroad: Continuity and Change in the Modern Diaspora Politics of a 'Historical' Irredentist Homeland." *Nationalism and Ethnic Politics* 17, no. 1 (2011): 14–33.
Waters, Mary C., and Stanley Lieberson. "Ethnic Differences in Education: Current Patterns and Historical Roots." *International Perspectives on Education and Society* 2 (1982): 171–87.
Zimmerman, Jonathan. "Ethnics against Ethnicity: European Immigrants and Foreign-Language Instruction, 1890–1940." *Journal of American History* 88, no. 4 (March 2002): 1382–1404.

PART III

Ethnic and Gender Identities in Literature and Music

Identity, Family, and Cultural Heritage

Narrative Polymorphy in Let Me Explain You and Catina's Haircut

Eleftheria Arapoglou

When, in 2004, in her presidential address to the American Studies Association conference, Shelley Fisher Fishkin posed the question, "What would the field of American Studies look like if the transnational rather than the national were at its center?" (21), she used a conditional to ponder the possibilities that a transnational approach would afford American studies—a field in which the nation-centered model was, at the time, still prevalent. Fishkin was not the first to coin the term transnational in the context of discussing US society and culture. As early as 1916, Randolph Bourne, counteracting the patriotic Americanization campaign during World War I, openly rejected the concept of America as a melting pot shaped by Anglo-Saxon ideas and exposed it as a failed project. Conversely, Bourne pioneered the concept of a "trans-national America"[1] which, in his vision, was made up by a back-and-forth weaving of different threads of various sizes and colors (262)—the same threads that Fishkin would foreground as research foci by means of her hypothetical question in 2004.

Fishkin's call to leave behind the "national" origin of reference as a critical tool has resulted in various strategies of analysis and intellectual shifts in American culture studies in the last fifteen years. In turn, these shifts have produced interpretive projects that have made visible new forms of connection and difference in the field of American studies. For example, scholars in the fields of Italian American and Greek American studies—which are of particular interest in this chapter—have gone beyond the borders of the "nation state" as an object of analysis in the fields of ethnic or diaspora studies. More specifically, work by Yiorgos Kalogeras (1998, 2007), Yiorgos Anagnostou (2009), Martha Klironomos (2009), Vangelis Calotychos (2002), Fred Gardaphé (2004), Mary Jo Bona (2010, 2016), Edvige Giunta (2002), and Louise DeSalvo (2003), to name but a few, has specifically addressed the transnational routes of Greek American and Italian American literary texts. The work of these scholars represents a wide-ranging, highly charged debate that challenges the view of American culture as homogeneous, and highlights the multiple cultural differences within "American culture as a whole." More specifically, scholars in the fields of Greek American and Italian American studies have redefined "culture" in American culture studies beyond the monolithic pluralism of confined, territorialized cultures, and along the lines of "border" discourses such as hybridity, diaspora, or the study of intercultural contact zones. Ultimately, the transnational turn in American studies[2] has allowed the space for scholars such as those in Greek American and Italian American Studies to decenter the US perspective and take views from the "periphery" of Greek America or Italian America as cofoundational; address the intracultural diversity and hybridity of US culture(s) and transnational interactions; map the complex web of interactions within social and cultural processes in the United States in innovative and critical ways; and, emphasize international and transnational dialogue within the frame of US cultures.

In 2017, Yogita Goyal edited the timely *Cambridge Companion to Transnational American Literature*. In the introduction to the volume, Goyal does not shy away from the debate around the transnational turn in American literary and cultural studies, going as far as to include doubts about the very rubric "transnational" and the uses it can be put to. For instance, she wonders whether "transnational," in the context of literary studies, essentially functions as a euphemism for minority, ethnic, or multicultural US literature. Although I acknowledge the premise of such critiques, I wish to argue that satisfactory alternatives do exist, but only if we conceive American studies as "transcultural," rather than "transnational." A transcultural American studies frame of reference opens up critical possibilities for American literary studies. More specifically, in the case of such fields as Greek American and Italian American studies, a transcultural interpretative frame highlights the dynamic exchanges between the two groups, emphasizes the past and present interdependence and interconnectivity of their peoples, sustains cross-cultural dialogue, and provides invaluable analytical tools for cross-ethnic comparative work.

My argument for a transcultural approach echoes Günter Lenz's call for a wider-ranging, self-reflexive, and self-different methodology to explore "the multivoiced and multidirectional . . . transcultural dynamics" (29) in American studies. The advantage of this approach, as Lenz elucidates, is that it "works *through*—in the double sense—and works *with* cultural differences in terms of race, ethnicity, gender, class, and so forth without dissolving them or claiming a new synthesis" (7, emphasis added). In my view, a transcultural approach to American studies allows its practitioners something that is not possible within the frame of transnational American studies: that is, to explore the dialogics, contestations, and negotiations of intercultural relations from a multiplicity of sociocultural, political, and economic locations—both within and outside the United States. More specifically, the practice of transculturality in the field of American literary studies initiates a dialogue between groups that have, mostly, been seen as distinct communities within US culture(s).[3] A case in point is the literature by Greek American and Italian American women. As Edvige Giunta has pointed out in "Persephone's Daughters," even though the two groups of writers have not, thus far, "encountered" each other, they share a rich cultural heritage that has enhanced their cultural production and self-understanding (769, 781–82). In my view, any meaningful attempt to explore the parallels, intersections, but also disparities across the historical and cultural experiences of Greek Americans and Italian Americans necessitates a transcultural approach. In particular, a transcultural reading of the works of Greek American and Italian American women reveals that, if their voices are "heard" collectively, they form an artistic community that crafts its fictional responses to the experience of migration on a dialogic aesthetic.

Here I read across Annie Liontas's debut novel *Let Me Explain You* (2016) and Paola Corso's *Catina's Haircut: A Novel in Stories* (2010) in a transcultural, dialogic fashion. In my analysis, the transcultural frame heightens the discursive possibilities of the individual texts, while "dialogic" is conceptualized along the lines of Bakhtinian notions of dialogism.[4] More specifically, I am particularly interested in the ways in which the dialogic element functions within the narrative discourses of Liontas and Corso, placing relationships—rather than individual subjectivity—at the heart of the text. It is my contention that, despite the two authors' distinct ethnocultural perspectives, the polyvocal organization of their works privileges relational models of subjectivity established through dialogue. In my view, a dialogic perspective is necessary if one is to consider literature as a mediating vehicle within a dialectical transculturalism. Considering that the key question in transcultural American studies is not so much cultural identity or autonomy, but rather the question of cross-cultural dialogue, of new forms of connection and difference that are cross-racial and cross-ethnic and that arise from transcultural permeations, it seems only fitting to contextualize works such as those by Liontas and Corso within a dialogic transcultural frame. Such a frame elucidates two levels of dialogic transculturalism: on one level, the "dialogue" is established among the multiple narrative voices existing within the two novels themselves; on a second level, the two novels, both of which negotiate experiences (such as ethnicity and cultural affiliation) by means of discursive narrative practices, "talk" to each other.

My discussion of *Let Me Explain You* and *Catina's Haircut* is based on the premise that the two novels share a dialogic narrative model of identity constitution. On the one hand, *Let Me Explain You* employs narrative polymorphy in the form of numerous narrative voices that speak of themselves in both first and third person. In a strikingly similar gesture of narrative polymorphy, *Catina's Haircut* morphs into a novel out of eight stories that are both self-contained and interdependent. The narrative polymorphy that is common between *Let Me Explain You* and *Catina's Haircut* performs two functions: first, it evidences a dynamic and relational sense of selfhood that is performed in and through the multilayered narrative structure of the two novels; and second, it bears witness to complex family patterns and practices of relating to collective memory and cultural heritage in the Greek American and Italian American communities.

Narrative Polymorphy

One night, Stavros Stavros Mavrakis, Greek immigrant and proud owner of the Gala Diner in Annie Liontas's *Let Me Explain You*, has a nightmare about a goat. The next day, out of nowhere, an actual goat shows up at Stavros's diner. In a culturally significant gesture that connects the immigrant character to his preimmigration superstitious beliefs, Stavros interprets his nightmare and the mysterious appearance of the goat as "omens," leading him to the conviction that he is destined to die in ten days. Liontas's debut novel opens on the tenth day with the scathing email that Stavros sends his ex-wife and three daughters, in which he announces his imminent death and lists his wishes for how they each might better live their lives. As the novel counts down, we watch Stavros draw up his will, meet with his ex-wife, Dina, his girlfriend, Rhonda, his three daughters, Stavroula, Litza, and Ruby, and his estranged compatriot friend, Hero. We also witness Stavros's booking his funeral. Overall, in *Let Me Explain You*, the narrative meanders around a very broad spatiotemporal terrain with no sense of urgency, though with a general, albeit inconsistent, feeling of forward motion. Thus, readers move from the narrative present set in contemporary New Jersey—to which Stavros has immigrated, raised his family, and built his diner business—to Stavros's preimmigration past set on the island of Crete, and back to the narrative present. This move happens on the wheels of the different characters' reflections, since *Let Me Explain You* is told from multiple perspectives, with particular emphasis on Stavros's, Stavroula's, and Litza's.

Narrative polymorphy in Liontas's book effectively articulates the complexity and variety of the immigration experience. Indeed, the many voices that tell their stories in *Let Me Explain You* illuminate distinct yet interdependent immigrant communities, such as first-generation versus second-generation immigrants or patriarch immigrant fathers set against their oppressed immigrant daughters. For instance, Stavros and Hero both represent ethnic patriarchs in the United States: their hard work and entrepreneurial spirit have earned them financial success, but their old world beliefs and patriarchal values have cost them healthy, fulfilling relationships with their families. The two men speak to, but also of, the second generation in a derogatory manner. Subsequently, Stavroula, Litza, and Ruby emerge as a triptych representing the generation that is caught between two countries, two cultures, and two histories. Subjected to emotional abuse, social devaluation, and spatial confinement by their immigrant father, the characters of Stavroula, Litza, and Ruby expose an authoritative and parochial immigrant world, in which the social and emotional growth of immigrant daughters is stunted. Considering these observations, it becomes clear that on one level *Let Me Explain You* functions as a typical immigrant narrative that tries to understand how the experience of immigration impacts multiple generations. On a second level, the novel purposefully relies on multivocality to highlight alienation—from the intimate and public place the characters inhabit, from those surrounding the characters, and from the characters themselves—as an essential aspect of the immigrant characters' identity formation.

The "conversation" that is established as the many voices in *Let Me Explain You* speak to and of each other generates dialogic reflections on the themes of identity, family, and community. In particular, over the course of the ten days that the novel narrates, all characters return to the Gala Diner, where they meet on several occasions to discuss the emails they received from Stavros, look for his will, or discuss his memorial services. During these meetings, they also end up discussing their relation to their home and host countries and cultures. To do that, they reflect upon their past(s) and revisit the immigrant webs that thread them together. The characters' personal reflections, as representations of diverse cultural experiences, push against singular narrative discourses relying on monologic paradigms. Thus, they escape the limitations of the singular narrative voice that may, at times, essentialize the cultural experience of immigration by personalizing it. Alternatively, the individual narratives of Stavros, Hero, Marina, Stavroula, Litza, and Ruby exemplify variations on the theme of immigrant identity enactment as a process determined by multiple variables: gender and sexual orientation, age/generation, class, family dynamics, place of origin, education, etc. In effect, the interconnecting narrative voices driving the narrative in *Let Me Explain You* point to an important cultural function the book performs by means of its narrative structure: namely, the distinctive stories told in the diverse characters' voices bear witness to the complex and dynamic nature of the immigration experience that cannot be neatly summed up in a single, uniform category.

Utilizing a storytelling mode that also relies on multivocality, Paola Corso's second book, *Catina's Haircut: A Novel in Stories*, is another example of a work where narrative techniques function as representations of complex immigration experiences. As its subtitle indicates, *Catina's Haircut* morphs into a novel out of eight stories that are both self-contained and interdependent. The web of retrospective references that each story makes offers readers a comprehensive overview of an immigrant family history—the del Negros—that spans four generations and two continents. In a similar fashion to Liontas's work, the setting in Corso's novel stretches transnationally from the brutally poor and barren Calabrian village of San Procopio in post-unification Italy, to the congested neighborhoods of Pittsburgh's Bloomfield section set against the confluence of the three rivers commemorated in the novel's epigram—the Allegheny, the Monongahela, and the Ohio. Tightly interweaving eight stories, Corso creates a saga of immigration to the United States that brings together, in one book, the Fata Morgana, the Risorgimento, and the Pittsburgh Steelers. The sweeping spatiotemporal perspective in Corso's novel, in like manner to the constant narrative shifts in Liontas's text, allows readers to better grasp the historical trajectory of immigrants—the majority of them female characters—of southern European origin in the United States. Furthermore, the multifarious narrative aesthetic in *Catina's Haircut*—similarly to the narrative structure in *Let Me Explain You*—points to Italian American identity as a complex construct in which present and past, America and Italy, as well as history and folklore, intersect.

In both *Let Me Explain You* and *Catina's Haircut*, the use of different speaking voices disrupts the linear unfolding of events and, as a result, problematizes the two books' narrative unity. In my view, reading the two novels as a purposeful layering of different dialogic "texts," spoken by distinct voices that appear, disappear, and reappear in the course of the narrative, illuminates the process by which Liontas and Corso review both the history of immigration and female immigrant subjectivity in the United States in the twentieth century. In fact, Corso's and Liontas's stylistic techniques and coded language trigger a cross-cultural conversation on the topics of identity, family, and cultural heritage and operate within the same discursive space of feminist resistance to the limiting horizons of a patriarchal ethnic culture that prescribes female subservience. As a result, the two books' narrative structures perform two functions: first, they valorize the silenced, disenfranchised, and marginalized voices of female immigrants and their American-born daughters by placing female narrators center stage and foregrounding their perspective. Second, by favoring multivocality, the two works insist on the multivalenced nature of the immigrant experience, and they suggest that immigrant identities are multidimensional, continuously configured, negotiated, and reinvented. Complicating the notion of a fixed immigrant identity perceived to unite all participants in a projected ethnic community, the two novels by Liontas and Corso illuminate the multiple forces operating on the ever-evolving process of identity enactment: class, gender, region, and personal history.

    The dialogic narrative model that is common between *Let Me Explain You* and *Catina's Haircut* conceptualizes identity formation within a transcultural frame, which is dynamic and involves continuous transitions. Transcultural forms of identity construction are fluid and flexible; they are also mobile and involve ever-changing subjects who live both "here" and "there," in the present and in the past, for themselves and for others. In both works, the intertwined forces of family history and affective ethnic ties, as well as individualism and rational civic affiliation operate simultaneously on the ethnic characters' identity enactment across Greek American and Italian American families. Giorgio del Negro is an excellent case in point. Readers first meet Giorgio in the opening chapter of *Catina's Haircut* as an eleven-year-old boy who witnesses his parents' murder during a socialist uprising in 1919 San Procopio. In the chapter entitled "St. Odo's Curse," readers encounter Giorgio again, this time married, with a family of his own, and loathing to leave their struggling farm for America. In both chapters,

Giorgio does not know himself as "Italian," but as a member of the del Negro family, rooted in San Procopio, and speaking Calabria's dialect. Giorgio's primary allegiance is to the social institution of the family—an allegiance that bestows upon him emotional warmth and a strong sense of belonging. Nevertheless, Giorgio's identity is not merely relational: it reflects and re-inflects southern Italy's folkways: the sense of an arboreal identity that connects individuals to a family tree whose roots go deep in Calabrian soil, and the sense of belonging to a communal past made up of superstition, hard work in the fields, constant struggles, and the hope/promise of prosperity. These same folkways bear upon Giorgio's life in the United States, when readers meet him again in "Giorgio's Green Felt Hat." Giorgio is now a grandfather who takes his ten-year-old granddaughter, Celeste, on strolls in Riverview Park. English has taken over Italian; Giorgio is part of the Italian American community in Ohio, he has achieved middle-class status, and Calabria is a distant memory. Yet, Giorgio refuses to give up Calabrian folkloric traditions, evidenced by his attachment to his green felt hat, the hat he wore the day he set foot in America. It is, in fact, these traditions that, in Giorgio's case, as in the case of many characters in both Corso and Liontas, function as a means of resisting the oppressions of class and ethnicity in the host country.

To Giorgio, the green hat is both a symbol of the past and an emblem of family legacy (Gardaphé 419) and cultural identity, which is why he refuses to take it off when his wife insists that it makes him "look like a peasant" (Corso 63). Ironically, his resemblance to a Calabrian peasant is exactly the reason that Giorgio "[would] wear [the hat] in the shower if he could figure out a way it wouldn't get wet" (Corso 63). In Giorgio's eyes, the hat speaks of the family's past in Italy as a generative force in the family's present life in America. More specifically, for Giorgio, his green hat is a signifier of the family's success: having turned the struggles and poverty of agrarian life in Calabria into the financial stability of middle-class life in America. Hence, by wearing his green felt hat, Giorgio is making the statement that his middle-class identity as an immigrant in the United States neither dissolves nor erases his agrarian Calabrian identity. Rather, the green felt hat is a signifier of Giorgio's dynamic and relational sense of selfhood and a constant reminder of how intertwined his affective ethnic ties and adopted civic affiliation are. As Giorgio's example illustrates, *Catina's Haircut* stretches the boundaries of "belonging" to accommodate the multiple identifications, flexible subjectivities, and deterritorialized identities of its immigrant characters.

In *Let Me Explain You*, two characters that bear witness to complex patterns and practices of dynamically constructed identity models are Stavroula and Litza—Stavros's daughters from his first wife, Dina, who was Greek. Both of them were born in the United States, were sent to Greece to live with their grandparents when their mother and father divorced and their father got sole custody of them due to the mother's drug addiction, and then moved back to the United States at elementary school age, when Stavros married his second wife, an American. Stavroula and Litza's forced moves at a tender age complicated their identification processes and subsequent socialization as second-generation immigrants. Furthermore, the trauma they experienced as a result of their mother's substance abuse and father's cruel parenting undermined their self-image, their connection to their family, and their sense of belonging to a wider ethnic community. Consequently, as the novel unfolds, Stavroula and Litza appear in constant negotiation of their self-identities at the conflictual space(s) between group and individual identity. Stavroula, at thirty-one, is the oldest; she is the one who seems to have overcome her childhood traumas—their mother's substance abuse, their father's tyranny, their parents' divorce—and who acts as a surrogate mother to her younger sisters. Stavroula loves people, "the messy noise of them" (59), and feels compelled to earn their love by being "The Way They Want" (74). Professionally, she is a cook who experiments with dishes and designs menus as a way to express her love for the daughter of the owner at the restaurant where she works. Stavros's second daughter, Litza, is twenty-nine. She is resentful because their father kicked her out after she called the police to report child abuse at age twelve. Subsequently, she expresses her resentment toward her family by means of physical violence: she smashes the dessert case at Stavros's diner with a stool, and she breaks the window of Stavroula's car. In a desperate cry for attention, Litza marries and divorces her husband in one week. Then she has an affair with a nineteen-year-old rebound boyfriend. Ultimately, Litza's habit of contemplating people via the ailment codes she uses at the insurance company where she works becomes her emotional coping mechanism.[5]

The stories of Stavroula and Litza showcase the series of struggles, negotiations, and compromises involved in the lives and identification processes of second-generation immigrant daughters. Through the characters of Stavroula and Litza, Liontas effectively explores the ways immigrants "devour" one life to create another. In one of the most powerful sections in the novel,[6] Marina speaks about the two women as immigrants: "you belong to a race of people who must carry everything they own in their own mouths. All of their luggage, they squeeze into their mouth. You can only fit so much of the old place . . . or so many stories, or so many people, or so much soup before you must spit and take a breath; and then a very different world fills you up. It is not unwelcome, it is just reinvention. This is immigration" (Liontas 306). The powerful metaphor of immigrant identity as the places, stories, people, and food immigrant daughters "own" and "carry" with them, like "luggage," in their "mouths," until they "spit" them out to ingest something else points to different modalities underlying their identification processes. More specifically, Marina argues that Stavroula and Litza experience immigrant identity as a choking burden they have to carry, but also as something they "own" as a result of choice and reinvention. Furthermore, when Stavroula mentions the Greek phrase "'Εφαγα τον κόσμο να σε βρω. *I ate the whole world to find you*" (Liontas 319, emphasis in original), the idea of having to first stuff oneself, before finding someone or something, surfaces again. In *Let Me Explain You*, immigrant daughters ruminate and "spit" out, but also "breathe" in and process, aspects of their identity in a unique manner. Hence, in Liontas's fiction, the experience of immigrant daughters is represented as selective internalization and subsequent consumption of multiple identity aspects: spatial, temporal, verbal, communal, cultural—the places, language, people, and food. Furthermore, the significance of the synecdochic use of the "mouth" as a mediator of identity-relevant immigrant experiences cannot be overlooked. Since the mouth is not just the organ by which food is consumed but also the organ that is essential in the production of speech, the figure of carrying and generating one's identity "in the mouth" points to immigrant identity enactment as both an act of nourishment as well as an act of verbal expression and resistance. In this sense, Stavroula's and Litza's characters bear witness to immigrant women's stories not only as acts of individuation but also as discursive practices that resist oppressions of silence within the Greek American community.

The combined forces of Litza's and Stavroula's characters, more so than the mystery of what will happen to Stavros when the self-imposed countdown ends, determine the narrative arc in *Let Me Explain You*. Structurally, the book is divided into three parts: Part I counts down from Day Ten to Day Three in nineteen numbered chapters; Part II is made up of six chapters bearing the names of characters ("Stavros Stavros Mavrakis"; "Dina Lazaridis"; "Stavros and Dina Mavrakis"; "Stavroula Mavrakis"; "Litza Mavrakis"; "The Rebirth of Stavros Stavros Mavrakis"); Part III narrates Days Two and One in two numbered sections entitled "Acceptance" and "Denial" respectively. In Part I, Stavros, Stavroula, and Litza alternate as narrators in a plotline that counts down the days to Stavros's impending death, and associates these days with the three characters' oscillating emotional reactions to it. More specifically, Day Ten is subtitled "Acceptance," Days Nine and Eight "Denial," Day Seven "Anger, Rage," Day Six "Acceptance," Day Five "Bargain: Beg," Day Four "Acceptance," and Day Three "Depression."[7] Part II functions as a flashback to the lives of the three main characters—Stavros, Stavroula, and Litza. In terms of the purpose they serve with respect to the novel's plot, these flashbacks not only trace the family history back to important events that are obscured in Part I (Stavros's motive to emigrate, the reasons leading to his divorce from Dina, Litza's report of child abuse), but they also illustrate the intersections among the characters' life threads. More specifically, readers find out that Stavros's decision to move to New York was a desperate reaction to his mother's refusal to lend him money to open his own business, a *kafenio* (coffee shop) in Crete. To move to New York, Stavros entered an arranged marriage to Dina Lazaridis, daughter of a fellow villager who had moved to New York years ago. Part II also uncovers Dina's past of substance abuse as a teenager, her struggle with addiction after she and Stavros got married, her subsequent abandonment of her family, the resulting trauma the two daughters suffered, as well as Stavros's second marriage to Carol and his success as a restaurateur assisted by Marina. Part III returns the story to the narrative present, featuring Stavros's funeral, Marina's killing and cooking of the mystery goat, and Stavros's reappearance and speech about his encounter with death. If one considers the numerous stories and sections that make up the plot of *Let Me Explain You* as narrative fragments that are intertwined, then a weaving pattern emerges as a result of the constant narrative shifts. On the surface, most characters in the novel seem to lead solitary lives, characterized by estrangement, isolation, alienation, fear, and abuse. Nevertheless, a closer look at the ways in which these lives intersect, and the paths that they take as a result of these intersections, reveals a fascinating pattern. Granted, the pattern is not uniform, but rather haphazard and erratic; nevertheless, it bears testimony to interconnectedness and the structure of a network at the heart of the immigration experience.[8]

The pattern of constant narrative shifts that is central in *Let Me Explain You* is also evident in *Catina's Haircut*, in which the del Negro family's tribulations—one generation after another—are related by numerous speaking voices and from multiple perspectives, namely, first or third person. What is of extreme significance in Corso's complex entanglement of intersecting narrative threads is that the eight chapters in *Catina's Haircut*, although vastly different in terms of their distinct settings and plot lines, nevertheless come together in a coherent narrative frame reinforced by two things: first, the connections embodied in the family relationships among characters; second, the book's overarching multivocal narrative discourse that encourages readers to read the stories against each other. More specifically, seven out of the eight chapters in the book are narrated by women, all of whom are related to the only male narrator, Giorgio del Negro, whose voice we hear in the book's opening chapter. In this chapter, entitled "The Rise and Fall of Antonio del Negro," eleven-year-old Giorgio recalls the death of his father and mother, Antonio and Celina, during a socialist uprising in 1919 San Procopio. By a tragic twist of fate, Celina's hopeful vision of the family someday owning their own land gives Giorgio the strength to overcome his fear of heights and climb to the roof of their house, where he finds his mother mortally wounded from a stray bullet. Celina's view of territorialization as an integral aspect of identity enactment is a thematic thread that runs through all eight chapters in the book, unifying characters and reinforcing narrative structure. Indeed, as the book reveals, despite the dispersion due to emigration, the del Negro family maintains its unity because of their sustained connection to the land they inhabit—be it Italy or the United States. Considering the book's shifting narrative structure, it can be argued that *Catina's Haircut* ultimately represents the characters' history of growing up immigrant in the United States in a richly complex fashion: not as a linear unfolding of events, but rather as a messy entanglement of diverse yet interconnecting narrative voices, united by their common need to root themselves in their place of residence.

Relational models of subjectivity and community dynamics are at the heart of Liontas's narrative, too. However, neither are they driven by the need for rootedness, nor are they mediated through the characters' connection to the land. Rather, in *Let Me Explain You*, identification with a community—whether involving the narrow frame of family, or the wider frame of ethnic community—is interrelated with individuation efforts. A careful look at all female characters in Liontas's novel reveals a dynamic and relational sense of selfhood that is performed in and through the characters' efforts at establishing lasting relationships. An episode that illustrates the way in which shifting narrative perspectives highlight relational models of subjectivity is the powerful interaction between Marina and Stavroula which takes place in chapter 18, on the third day of the countdown. The two women are cutting carrots in Stavros's restaurant kitchen, and Marina tries to encourage Stavroula to open up: "You are worried about your father? . . . You are troubled by something? . . . You walk around wanting to believe that you are whole when actually you are pieces. . . . I think maybe I have spent a lot of time teaching you how to be strong and not enough how to be open" (165, 166). Marina's insistent questions about Stavroula's state of mind and her plea to Stavroula to embrace her fragility overwhelm Stavros's daughter:

> She held on to the tears, would not let them fall. She was trying to conceal herself from Marina, and she was trying to make herself known. She was fifteen all over again, shaking and hoping no one and everyone could tell. Marina, the person Stavroula had admired since she was a little girl, Marina, the person she loved the most. The reason she has hidden all this time. . . . All Stavroula needed to say: This is who I am, *thea*. If I am who I am on the outside, I am who I am on the inside. But she couldn't. (168, italics in original)

The flashback to Stavroula's teenage years allows readers insight into her relationship to Marina and the importance of that relationship with respect to Stavroula's performance of individual subjectivity—in particular, her frustrated attempts to conceal and suppress her sexual orientation. When Stavroula was a teenager, Marina had refused to serve a gay couple, confessing to Stavroula that gay couples made her uncomfortable (167). Being afraid of "losing the one person whose love had felt as everlasting as bread" (169), Stavroula prioritized emotional ties—Marina's love and sustenance—and a sense of belonging over the road to selfhood. Nevertheless, years of repression have resulted in the vexing oscillation between "trying to conceal herself" and "trying to make herself known." The way in which the narrative discourse in *Let Me Explain You* dramatizes Stavroula's struggle with her gender identity as well as her anguish over community acceptance is by means of shifting perspectives. More explicitly, the "dialogue" that Marina initiates with Stavroula at the narrative present evolves into a "dialogue" between Stavroula and herself stretching back to the narrative past. This shifting narrative structure foregrounds the interdependent aspect of individual lives woven together in a "threaded net" that visualizes the relational process of identity enactment. The resulting text is a dynamic chronicle that charts the female characters' constant negotiation of life stances and self-identities within the interlaced canvas of interpersonal relationships.

Dialogicity in the two novels effectively retraces the characters' akin struggles to assert their individuality within, but also against, their home and adopted communities. In the first chapter of Part II of *Let Me Explain You*, entitled "Stavros Stavros Mavrakis," Stavros examines his life retrospectively. His flashback mode makes readers feel as if he is both there and not there, watching and watched, evoking the mood and sensibility of his pre-immigration self, and relating it to the present:

> He was too young to stay buried under his mother and eleven Stavroses, nothing new in life but the name of the village whore. Whatever he needed to do to get out, he would do it. . . . In that moment, he began to belong to the masses who dream America, the land too good for peasant Greeks. . . . What better place to be a man? To work, to earn, to imagine a life richer than his parents', to prove his eleven brothers wrong, to make something his own, to make children who would honor him and gratefully inherit his fortune. What

better place to reinvent himself—to reinvent the world? To make it bigger? To make it big enough to fit Stavros Stavros Mavrakis? In America, he would open a *kafenio*, hire Americans to clean the floor, buy crates of blue jeans and ship them back for all his brothers, especially Stavros Nikos. He would send back dollars, not drachmas, so they understood who he was. (197)

In this excerpt, Stavros, Greek immigrant and proud owner of the Gala Diner in New Jersey at the narrative present, reflects back to his decision to immigrate to America, and speaks about himself in the third person. What this narrative gesture of detachment does is that it draws attention to Stavros's struggle to assert his individuality within, but also against, his community of "peasant Greeks." The fact that Stavros is able to identify the exact moment when he "began to belong to the masses who dream America" as well as the reasons that brought about this self-identification reveal identity formation as a dynamic process that involves a reworking of the characters' relationship with the past. Furthermore, Stavros's detached perspective showcases a degree of ambivalence in his identification. Namely, on the one hand, he admits that there is no better place to be a man than America, boldly asserting his hard-won individuality, and, thus, his Americanness. On the other hand, he is unable to completely disengage himself from the home country and its people, as is revealed when he admits that his goal of sending "back dollars, not drachmas" was so that "they [his parents and brothers] understood who he was." In this excerpt, as in many other episodes in the book,[9] Stavros is torn between connecting to and detaching himself completely from his homeland. Importantly, Stavros's realization in the book's final chapter that he is "a man of two lives—one in Greece, one in America," brings the story full circle and provides insight into the development of his immigrant consciousness as a Greek living in the United States in the twentieth century. Stavros's view of himself as "a man of two lives" positions his identity representation at the intersection of Greekness and Americanness. Stavros's identity discourse in the closing chapter betrays a dynamic notion of cultural identity that is dialogically constituted, not just in terms of its dualism but also by nature of the transcultural permeation it suggests. Articulated at the end of the narrative, Stavros's statement about his identity is the culmination of purposeful reflexivity. Ultimately, the

"Stavros" who emerges in the book's final pages is a product of the novel's shifting narrative discourse and exemplifies immigrant identity enactment as reflexive reinvention—as "Stavros the man thinks on life" (337)—and not as a prescribed, static discourse.

What I hope has become clear by now is that in both *Let Me Explain You* and *Catina's Haircut*, interwoven narrative voices perform the function of cultural criticism of a number of issues, such as, for example, immigrant patriarchy in the case of Liontas, or the need for rootedness in the case of Corso. These voices function dialogically, in the sense that they disentangle the complexities in the immigrant characters' identity enactment by interrogating both the individual forces operating on their identity formation and their community allegiances. A case in point is found in the second and third chapters of Corso's novel. In the second chapter, "St. Odo's Curse," set against the backdrop of fascist Italy, Giorgio, Antonio and Celina's orphaned son, is married with children. His son and daughter, Coco and Celestina, turn to the village sorceress in hopes of bringing rain to their father's drought-stricken farm. Despite the extreme poverty and deprivation that the family suffers, Giorgio resists the idea of abandoning the "hungry and thirsty" land (25) of San Procopio to "go to America" (50). However, Giorgio's wife, Aida, does not share her husband's reservations. When she sees that, in the summer months, crevices open up in the earth and "swallow" pedestrians, she resolves to save money and pays to take her family to the New World against her husband's wishes (44). Much to the family's disappointment, though, nature is just as unforgiving in America as it is in San Procopio. In the third chapter, entitled "Hell and High Water," the del Negros, who have by now moved to America, fall victims to the 1936 flood in Pittsburgh. The narrator in this chapter is Giorgio's granddaughter, Celeste, whose confession as the chapter opens suggests her disillusionment at her adopted country and longing for her home country: "I cannot sleep at night. I am afraid to wake up and find my head under water. In San Procopio there are groves with big olive trees to climb high, but in America, no" (63). It is impossible to pull any one thread out of the complex weave of the characters' lives. In fact, readers cannot make sense of Celeste's reaction to the Pittsburgh flood unless they read Celeste's story against the story of the family's struggle to survive in drought-stricken San Procopio. This is because, in Corso's work, the characters personally witness and collectively give witness to poverty, despair, discrimination, victimization, nostalgia—just to name a few—as major aspects of the immigrant experience in the United States in the twentieth century. Moreover, the characters' distinct individual voices not only echo but are also heard through the collective of voices that speak of immigrant subjectivity as a complex living experience that cannot bear a uniform label of ethnic identification. It is by means of this narrative gesture that Corso's characters, similarly to Liontas's, speak in a collective voice, making their communities heard and allowing them control over their experiences, subjectivities, identities, and social categories.

One of the most memorable narrators in *Catina's Haircut*, whose personally vested excavation of the family's history speaks of the collective experience of her people, is Celestina's daughter, Celeste. In the final story in Corso's book, "Mirage," Celeste returns to San Procopio, hoping to experience the Fata Morgana mirage along the Strait of Messina. Celeste's pilgrimage pays homage to her mother's faith in the powerful hope the land of Calabria holds. The pilgrimage brings the family history full circle: "A story told and retold through the generations: father to daughter, grandfather to granddaughter and on to her children. It rises like a dark mountain that bears witness to family history but whose rock is a castle lit with towers and windows to envision a future. Ours" (103). The sentence spoken by Celeste in the book's final chapter circles back to Celina's view of the land in the book's opening chapter. As a story passed down from one generation to the next, it captures one of the del Negro family's core values—attachment to land—and hence bears witness to what Celeste has been told safeguards the family's future. Celeste's story seems to suggest that although almost a century has passed since her family's immigration to the United States and that English has taken over Italian, the sense of identifying with a communal past can be kept alive by the power of storytelling. On the one hand, the dialogue that is established between the first and last chapters of the book, at the intersection of Celeste's and Celina's stories, validates a single perspective, that of the peasant communal past. At the same time, the fact that Celeste's story authorizes a dialogue rather than a traditional monologue, with the communal past indicates a multilayered project that transforms the interaction between the individual voices into contested sites of meaning for the community.

In *Catina's Hair*, through storytelling, the characters keep returning to the same founding moments recorded in the first chapters set in Calabria. By means of this narrative gesture, they not only recall the peasant communal past but also connect to it. An example of the way in which the multilayered context of storytelling activates transcultural dialogue in *Catina's Haircut* is the book's title story. In it, fifty-year-old Catina is desperately searching for a barber who will be able to cut her hair, which reaches her ankles. When all the barbers she visits fail to cut her hair, Catina decides to try cutting her hair with a scythe "like the one her father used day after day to cut wheat and brush in the slopes of Calabria" (83). Even though her act of desperation is not successful, she nevertheless confesses that "it was only when she used that tool on her hair that she came to realize the reason her father brought his family to this country" (83). Catina's realization establishes a narratively articulated dialogue with her father and illustrates a personal level of transcultural negotiation. For most of her life, Catina could not understand why her family moved to the United States: "If we would have stayed in San Procopio, we wouldn't be so poor" she would complain to her mother (80). Catina would even dismiss her mother's statement that "when farmers in Calabria reach out their hands for something in return for their labor, they're filled with calluses" (80). Nonetheless, when calluses start growing on her hands as she struggles to cut her hair, she thinks back to the calluses on her father's hands. Thus, a figurative dialogue is established between Catina's present and the family's past that highlights the shifting boundaries of transcultural positioning and narrative representation. A second example in which transcultural dialogue is animated in the practice of storytelling is chapter 7, entitled "Flash Light." In this chapter, Celestina's cousin, Maria Ungaro, struggles to recover a sense of herself lost in US suburbia, where people prefer to "keep to themselves" (89). In the process of Maria Ungaro's transcultural identity negotiation, images of the closely knit community of World War II Sinopoli, where neighbors "had daily conversations out of their third-floor windows as they watered the geraniums in the flowerboxes" (89), keep surfacing. Maria Ungaro, in a similar gesture to other narrators in *Catina's Haircut*, attempts a magical leap in the landscape and in time, in an effort to experience feelings of deep belonging. Away from her relatives and alienated from her neighbors, she resorts to storytelling as a means of sustaining a community of belonging. Appropriating an oral tradition that is embedded in communal memory, Maria Ungaro—alongside Celestina, Celina, and Celeste—is propelled into new generations and a new world. Ultimately, just like Catina's cutting her fifty-year-long hair can be read as a gesture of coming to terms with the past in agrarian Italy as a precondition for membership in the adopted industrial Pittsburgh community, the recurring epigraph of Celina's words performs an important function. The epigraph bespeaks the pressing need to pass on familial stories to the younger generations as a means of bridging the chasm between a past that is easy to forget and a future that is waiting to be experienced.

Greek American and Italian American Narrative Encounters

Framing the discussion of *Let Me Explain You* and *Catina's Haircut* within transcultural American studies effectively addresses two challenging questions that surface when researching Greek American and Italian American narrative encounters: How do the works by contemporary Greek American and Italian American women—such as Liontas and Corso—showcase the shared transcultural and transgenerational complexities of these women's identities, origins, and journeys? And how do the narrative identities that are negotiated in the two novels point to intersections across the cultural imaginaries of the respective Greek American and Italian American women authors? My reading of the works of Liontas and Corso has offered a venue to access the stories of two "ethnic" women authors who are transculturally affiliated through their respective narrative discourses. In this sense, I have argued for the ways in which the discursive strategies of Liontas and Corso are acts of self-authorizing that illuminate the overlapping experiences of Greek American and Italian American women as dominated peoples whose cultural practices resist oppressions of silence.

The two novels—as vehicles of cultural expression—interact, work together, and affiliate in various degrees. The two novels—as Greek American and Italian American cultural expressions—converge in terms of the cultural function they perform by means of their narrative structure. Mainly, multivocality as a narrative strategy represents the immigrant experience, both personal and communal, as textured and diverse, rather than uniform and homogeneous. This is because the dialogic narrative structure that is common in the two works both illustrates and dramatizes the rethinking of distinct perspectives and positions on cultural and ethnic affiliation and family obligations. At the same time, the two novels diverge in terms of the aspect of the specific immigrant experience that they foreground. In *Let Me Explain You*, alienation is at the heart of the Greek American immigrant experience, while in *Catina's Haircut* the search for rootedness is the essence of the Italian American immigrant experience. Ultimately, the advantage of reading works such as those by Liontas and Corso within a dialogic transcultural frame is that the complexities of immigrant women's identities, origins, and journeys are not obscured by a homogenizing frame of reference serving hegemonic interests. Rather, a transcultural exploration of the narrative discourses of ethnic authors like Liontas and Corso sheds light on the disparities, parallels, and intersections across their cultural/ethnic imaginaries, and allows us to probe not only the convenient consistencies but also the perplexing irregularities in the cultural representations of the many groups making up the United States.

NOTES

1. Bourne's essay "Trans-national America" was published in the *Atlantic Monthly* in 1916. In it, Bourne, a committed leftist intellectual, promoted a vision of the United States that replaced the "melting pot" metaphor with the metaphor of the "loom." Although Bourne's vision has, since, been criticized for its oversights—its exclusive reference to European immigration, its lack of engagement with aspects of US history such as the transatlantic slave trade, American settler colonialism, ethnic cleansings and genocides, and its oversimplification of "national communities" (see Stroebel, "The Hyphenated Hyphen")—it remains a visionary piece that challenged the status quo of mainstream American society and culture at the time.

2. For an excellent discussion of Transnational American Studies in a time of globalization, see Lenz, "Toward a Politics of American Transcultural Studies."

3. Greeks and Italians in the United States were discussed together for the first time in 1971, when Michael Novak published *The Rise of the Unmeltable Ethnics: Politics and Culture in the Seventies*. The publication of Novak's book was the result of a particular cultural politics. More specifically, Novak's work defied nation-centric approaches to the study of history, and categorized Poles, Italians, Greeks, and Slavs under the ostentatious acronym PIGS. Subsequently, *The Rise of the Unmeltable Ethnics* spearheaded a white ethnic revival, making ethnic history fashionable and academically marketable. The "white ethnic" social category that Novak popularized in the 1970s in an effort to "collectively empower" the descendants of new immigrants has since been deconstructed by works such as Yiorgos Anagnostou's *Contours of White Ethnicity*. Today, American and ethnic studies scholars as well as cultural anthropologists defy the uniform construct of a panethnic identity that Novak advocated and expose it as "victimizing populism" (Anagnostou 57), tied to a very specific social and political context—that of minority civil rights activism. Subsequently, works such as Aste, Postman, and Pierson, *Greece and Italy*, and Patrona, *Return Narratives* (2017), have examined the cultural lives of Greek Americans and Italian Americans contrapuntally, highlighting not only their similarities and continuities, but also their differences and discontinuities. Such works document a wide range of transcultural connections and cross-cultural interfaces between the two groups that cannot be overlooked and that point to promising new research directions.

4. My dialogic transcultural approach moves beyond a binary philosophy of the "double" or the "dyad." This is because, although the prefix "dia" has conventionally been associated with dualism because of its etymological root in Greek—"δύο" is Greek for the number two—in ancient Greek "dia" [διά] also denotes "across," "through," and "thorough." Hence, the function of "dia" as both preposition and numeral indicates relations across difference or separateness.

5. The novel's Greek chorus is complete with five other female characters, who nevertheless are not as fleshed out as Stavroula and Litza are: Ruby, Stavros's younger daughter, pretty and immature; Dina, Stavros's first wife through an arranged marriage back in Crete; Carol, Stavros's second wife, an American; Marina, Stavros's business partner, daughter of the village priest back in Crete, who has stood by him like family; and Rhonda, Stavros's African American girlfriend at the novel's narrative present.

6. In an interview she gave to Dana Spiotta on July 15, 2015, following a book reading at the Strand Bookstore in New York, Liontas herself admitted that this quote is "the beating heart of the book for [her]."

7. The subtitles in these chapters are direct references to the five stages of grief as described by Elisabeth Kübler-Ross and David Kessler in their book *On Grief and Grieving* (2014).

8. Consider Artemis Leontis's "The Intellectual in Greek America," a fascinating discussion framed by the metaphor of weaving/embroidery: "Net-work suggests that we not look for a continuous, well-circumscribed plane in America densely occupied by Greeks and their offspring. Instead we should think of the different locations where Greek interests coincide or collide. We should consider nodes of activity—some interconnected, some isolated, some few and far between" (93).

9. Consider, for example, the opening scene when Stavros interprets his nightmare as an omen, thus illustrating his deep embeddedness in Greek superstitious beliefs.

Bibliography

Anagnostou, Yiorgos. *Contours of White Ethnicity: Popular Ethnography and the Making of Usable Pasts in Greek America*. Athens: Ohio University Press, 2009.

Aste, Mario, Sheryl Lynn Postman, and Michael Pierson, eds. *Greece and Italy: Ancient Roots and New Beginnings*. Boca Raton, FL: Bordighera Press, 2005.

Bona, Mary Jo. *By the Breath of Their Mouths: Narratives of Resistance in Italian America*. Albany: State University of New York Press, 2010.

———. *Women Writing Cloth: Migratory Fictions in the American Imaginary*. Lanham, MD: Lexington Books, 2016.

Bourne, Randolph. "Trans-national America" (1916). In *The Radical Will: Selected Writings 1911–1918*, edited by Olaf Hansen, 248–64. Berkeley: University of California Press, 1992.

Calotychos, Vangelis. "Φαντασιακοί Χάρτες Ανάγνωσης" ["Imaginary Maps of Reading"]. In *Σύγχρονη Ελληνική Πεζογραφία: Διεθνείς Προσανατολισμοί και Διασταυρώσεις* [Contemporary Greek Prose: International Orientations and Crossings], edited by Dora Tsimpouki and Angeliki Spyropoulou, 205–19. Athens: Alexandreia, 2002.

Corso, Paola. *Catina's Haircut: A Novel in Stories*. Madison, WI: Terrace Books, 2010.

———. "From Without and From Within." *Glimmer Train*, Available at https://bit.ly/3D8IkJy.

DeSalvo, Louise, and Edvige Giunta, eds. *The Milk of Almonds: Italian American Women Writers on Food and Culture*. New York: Feminist Press, 2003.

Doyle, Laura. "Toward a Philosophy of Transnationalism." *Journal of Transnational American Studies* 1, no. 1 (2009): 1–30.

Fisher Fishkin, Shelley. "Crossroads of Cultures: The Transnational Turn in American Studies: Presidential Address to the American Studies Association, November 12, 2004." *American Quarterly* 57, no. 1 (2005): 17–57.

Fluck, Winfried. "A New Beginning? Transnationalisms." *New Literary History* 42, no. 3 (2011): 365–84.

Gardaphé, Fred. "Italian-American Literature and Working-Class Culture." *Annali di Italianistica* 32 (2014): 409–28.

———. *Leaving Little Italy: Essaying Italian American Culture*. Albany: SUNY Press, 2004.

Giunta, Edvige. "Persephone's Daughters." *Women's Studies* 33, no. 6 (2004): 767–86.

———. *Writing with an Accent: Contemporary Italian American Women Authors*. New York: Palgrave, 2002.

Goyal, Yogita, ed. *The Cambridge Companion to Transnational American Literature*. Cambridge: Cambridge University Press, 2017.

Herlihy-Mera, Jeffrey. *After American Studies: Rethinking the Legacies of Transnational Exceptionalism*. New York: Routledge, 2018.

Kalogeras, Yiorgos. *Εθνοτικές Γεωγραφίες: Κοινωνικο-πολιτισμικές Ταυτίσεις μιας Μετανάστευσης* [Ethnic Geographies: Sociocultural Identifications of a Migration]. Athens: Katarti, 2007.

———. "The 'Other Space' of Greek America." *American Literary History* 10, no. 4 (1998): 702–24.

Klironomos, Martha. "The Topos of Home in New Greek-American Writing." In *Greek Diaspora and Migration since 1700: Society, Politics and Culture*, edited by Dimitris Tziovas, 239–53. Burlington, VT: Ashgate Publishing, 2009.

Kübler-Ross, Elisabeth, and David A. Kessler. *On Grief and Grieving: Finding the Meaning of Grief Through the Five Stages of Loss*. New York: Scribner, 2014.

Lenz, Günter H. "Toward a Politics of American Transcultural Studies—Discourses of Diaspora and Cosmopolitanism." *Journal of Transnational American Studies* 4, no. 2 (2012). https://bit.ly/3uGNqtF.

Leontis, Artemis. "The Intellectual in Greek America." *Journal of the Hellenic Diaspora* 23, no. 2 (1997): 85–109.

Levander, Caroline. "The Changing Landscape of American Studies in a Global Era." In *Working Together or Apart: Promoting the Next Generation of Digital Scholarship: Report of a Workshop cosponsored by the Council on Library and Information Resources and the National Endowment for the Humanities*, 27–33. Washington, DC: Council on Library and Information Resources, 2009.

Liontas, Annie. "Annie Liontas and Dana Spiotta: *Let Me Explain You*." https://bit.ly/3l9skAY.

———. *Let Me Explain You*. New York: Scribner, 2015.

Morgan, Nina, Alfred Hornung, and Takayuki Tatsumi, eds. *The Routledge Companion to Transnational American Studies*. New York: Routledge, 2019.

Novak, Michael. *The Rise of the Unmeltable Ethnics: Politics and Culture in the Seventies*. New York: Macmillan, 1971.

Patrona, Theodora D. *Return Narratives: Ethnic Space in Late-Twentieth-Century Greek American and Italian American Literature*. Madison, NJ: Fairleigh Dickinson University Press, 2017.

Simal-González, Begoña. "Disrupting Globalization: Transnationalism and American Literature." Special Forum of *Journal of Transnational American Studies* 9, no. 1 (2018). https://bit.ly/3Bb6T86.

Stroebel, Will. "The Hyphenated Hyphen: Turkish-in-the-Greek-Script American Literature." *Ergon*, December 18, 2018. https://bit.ly/3ozbnSu.

Wald, Priscilla. "Minefields and Meeting Grounds: Transnational Analyses and American Studies." *American Literary History* 10, no. 1 (Spring 1998): 199–218.

Ethnic Investigations of the American Crime Scene

Comparing Domenic Stansberry and George Pelecanos

Francesca de Lucia

Stemming from precursors such as Dashiell Hammett and Raymond Chandler, the subgenre of hard-boiled detective fiction has developed in different directions throughout the decades. As observed by John T. Irwin, characters like Sam Spade and Philip Marlowe emerged in the years surrounding World War II and differ from the previous model of detective found, for instance, in Edgar Allan Poe's narratives or in the English mystery novel tradition. Indeed, while precursors to crime fiction can be found as early as the eighteenth century, the origin of the genre is traditionally identified with the publication, in the 1840s, of short stories by Edgar Allan Poe such as "The Murders of the Rue Morgue" and "The Purloined Letter." Subsequently, the genre flourished predominantly in England, its most famous representatives being Wilkie Collins's *The Moonstone* (1868) and, later, the stories of Arthur Conan Doyle, G. K. Chesterton, and Agatha Christie. In the United States, authors such as Hammett, Chandler, and

James M. Cain developed what would be called the "hard-boiled" detective novel, as a reaction to the perceived affectation of the English model.[1]

The specifically American tradition of the hard-boiled novel has been famously discussed by Chandler himself in his essay "The Simple Art of Murder" (1950), in which he underlines the importance of Hammett's work: "Hammett gave murder back to the kind of people that commit it for reasons, not just to provide a corpse; and with the means at hand, not with hand-wrought dueling pistols, curare and tropical fish. . . . He was spare, frugal hard-boiled."[2] Here Chandler is explicitly detaching himself from a tradition represented by the likes of Conan Doyle, Christie, and Dorothy Sayers. The emphasis is not on puzzle-solving abilities but on representations of manhood. Classic elements of this type of detective fiction include emphasis on cityscapes, disenchanted protagonists, and the trope of the femme fatale. As Dennis Porter has pointed out, while the English detective novel can be read as a comedy of manners, the hard-boiled American one is indebted to the American realist literary tradition.[3]

Domenic Stansberry (b. 1952), an Italian American, and George Pelecanos (b. 1957), a Greek American, use some of the recurring motifs of the genre, placing a particular emphasis, for instance, on drab urban environments and on disillusioned, potentially morally ambiguous detective figures. Hard-boiled detective fiction is closely interrelated to different forms of popular narratives, including, in particular, the nineteenth-century western and the "dime novel." Cynthia S. Hamilton observes that both "are built around the testing and confirmation of key American values, especially individualism, and are closely tied to the myth of the American dream."[4]

In their bleak and disenchanted depiction of urban America, both Hammett and Chandler express social themes. In his introduction to Hammett's Continental Op novels, Stephen Marcus indicates that Hammett offers a "proto-Marxist critical representation of how a certain kind of society works. Actually, the point of view is pre- rather than proto-Marxist, and the social world that is dramatized in many of these stories is Hobbesian rather than Marxist. It is a world of universal warfare, the war of each against all, and of all against all."[5] Most studies of hard-boiled detective fiction emphasize the importance of three classic authors: Chandler, Cain, and Hammett. Both Stansberry and Pelecanos, for their parts, point to the importance of another author, Jim Thompson. While Thompson is currently not so well known in the United States, his work is quite popular in France, and several of his novels have been adapted into films by directors such as Sam Peckinpah, Stephen Frears, and Michael Winterbottom.[6] According to J. Madison Davis, Thompson's narratives lack the redemptive elements that remain present in Chandler and Hammett, and his outlook can be considered "nihilist."[7] Not only does Stansberry include Thompson's name in his overview of detective fiction "Noir Manifesto" but, more important, he also has published a fictionalized account of Thompson's final days, *Manifesto for the Dead*.

Pelecanos also points directly to the importance that Thompson's work has for him, listing Thompson among authors that sparked his interest in hard-boiled fiction and including several articles on Thompson's works on his website.[8] Both Stansberry and Pelecanos often focus on alienated protagonists who struggle with personal failure and substance abuse, not necessarily conforming to Chandler's idea "the hero is everything" of what the detective figure should be.[9] From this point of view, the "nihilist" perspective endorsed by these two ethnic noir authors can be associated with Thompson rather than the better-known Chandler and Hammett.

Megan Abbott identifies three defining traits in the traditional protagonist of the hard-boiled detective novel: maleness, whiteness, and isolation.[10] The characters created by Stansberry and Pelecanos partly adhere to these conventions, yet, at the same time, the authors reinterpret them as a result of the legacy of their immigrant background. Carmen Garcia also notes that early examples of the hard-boiled novel relegate members of minorities to the margins: people of color or immigrant groups typically remain associated with the criminal element. Hence, for example, *The Maltese Falcon* notoriously interweaves racial and sexual ambiguity in the character of Joel Cairo, whereas Chandler's representation of Los Angeles resists racial diversity, producing alienating descriptions of predominantly Black environments.[11] However, this situation has shifted in more recent decades, starting in the 1950s, with Chester Himes's reinterpretation of the genre within an African American context.[12]

Drawing from their background as the descendants of Italian and Greek immigrants respectively, Stansberry and Pelecanos complicate the tropes of the hard-boiled detective novel by giving a specifically ethnic dimension to their work, encompassing issues related to definitions of whiteness. Individuals of Italian or Greek descent found themselves in a better position within the racial hierarchy of the United States than Blacks or Asian immigrants, yet they were still the object of sometimes vicious discrimination. Individual studies of Italian and Greek Americans underline this situation and a subsequent shift, in both cases, to a clearer white identity. Thus, according to Thomas Guglielmo,

> beginning in earnest with the onset of mass migration from Italy (particularly Southern Italy) . . . racial discrimination and prejudice aimed at Italians . . . were fierce, powerful and pervasive. And some of this anti-Italian sentiment and behavior questioned Italians' whiteness on occasion. In the end, however, Italians' many perceived racial inadequacies aside, they were still largely accepted as whites by the widest variety of people and institutions.[13]

The situation of Greek immigrants is similar. While their whiteness might have been put into question by giving them more limited opportunities and exposing them to nativist violence, like Italians they benefited from privileges such as the possibility for naturalization, and since the second half of the twentieth century they were increasingly perceived as white, something that entailed a series of benefits and opportunities for upward mobility and integration. Writes Yiorgos Anagnostou, "At stake in these negotiations [with whiteness] were privileges associated with the right to citizenship, union membership, access to middle-class white neighborhoods as well as social networks of power, including intermarriage. Not many Greek American cultural producers—academics, filmmakers, journalists—venture to explore this politically loaded terrain."[14]

Nevertheless, debates surrounding ethnic whites persisted in the postwar period, in juxtaposition with the developing role of minorities of color and with the perceived "elite" position of WASPs and Jews. This perspective was most famously elaborated by Michael Novak, who significantly placed Italians and Greeks within the infamous acronym of "PIGS" (Poles, Italians, Greeks, Slavs). In this context, ethnicity becomes closely connected to a working-class or middle-class status; an immigrant background is seen as being parallel with a situation of cultural and political disenfranchisement.[15] This notion of "the unmeltable ethnics" (again in Novak's words), however, did not persist in the final decades of the twentieth century. Rather, at a later stage where the descendants of Eastern and Southern immigrants, including Italian and Greek Americans, were more likely to have achieved in turn a middle-class, suburban status, distancing themselves from their origins, the dominant idea to emerge was that of "symbolic" or "optional" ethnicity.

Championed most famously by Herbert Gans and Mary Waters, this conception of ethnicity suggests that white ethnicity does not hold much depth and can be endorsed and discarded at leisure. However, the perspective implying that the descendants of Southern and Eastern European immigrants (including Italian and Greek Americans) have merged into a broader white mainstream and that ethnic culture has been reduced to mere tokens has been rejected more recently. Hence, Rudolph Vecoli directly attacks Gans's ideas of ethnicity, perceived as "a static quantity, a commodity which, once dissipated, is gone for ever. . . . [Rather, it is a] subjective sense of peoplehood based in common memories."[16] In the case of Greek Americans, Anagnostou points out that the widespread idea of ethnicity as the result of the individual's deliberate choice neglects the presence of psychological or sociological factors that cannot always be controlled directly: "identification is a matter of deep psychic and cultural processes often beyond an individual's rational control. It requires deciphering, both for the subject who experiences it and the cultural analyst who approaches the self as a culturally constructed category."[17] Deconstructing the notion of symbolic ethnicity in a broader fashion, he also observes that "white ethnics make and transform their immediate social worlds through dispositions and practices that are not always recognized as ethnic."[18]

Stansberry and Pelecanos insert their respective backgrounds within the formula of this specific subgenre of crime fiction. A comparative analysis of Italian American and Greek American hard-boiled detective narratives is particularly relevant in light of the position of racial ambiguity in which both of these groups historically found themselves. As will be addressed in more detail further on, the traditional hard-boiled novel centers heavily on whiteness and notions of mainstream American identity; therefore, it is interesting to consider examples of the genre by members of these two groups. This approach allows for the exploration of themes such as perceptions of ambiguous whiteness, different ethnic categories, and symbolic ethnicity.

Two Ethnic Crime Writers

Born in 1952 and raised in California, Domenic Stansberry is a descendant of Italian immigrants on his mother's side. He is best known for his North Beach series, which follows the character of Dante Mancuso. His San Francisco setting mirrors Dashiell Hammett. While his influence is obviously present in Stansberry's work, his fiction also presents some commonalities with that of other West Coast–based Italian American novelists, namely John Fante and Dorothy Calvetti Bryant. The experience of Italian immigrants and their descendants in California differs from that of their better-known counterparts of the northeastern United States in different ways. First, West Coast Italian communities tended to include more individuals originating from northern and central Italy, rather than simply from the Mezzogiorno, the impoverished regions east and south of Rome from which the majority of immigrants originated. Secondly, the ethnic and racial context was different, being marked by a stronger presence of nonwhite groups, in particular Latinos and Asians. Works such as John Fante's *The Bandini Quartet* or Dorothy Bryant's *Miss Giardino* illustrate well how this situation altered the position of Italians within the racial hierarchy of the United States. Indeed, both Fante and Bryant portray interactions between Italian American characters and individuals of Asian or Mexican descent. In Fante's seminal work *Ask the Dust*, Arturo Bandini reiterates his sense of Americanness (and by extension his whiteness) in contrast to his Mexican love interest, Camilla, whereas the titular Miss Anna Giardino of Bryant's novel points out that she was looked down upon as a "dago" at the beginning of her career and as a "racist" toward the end.[19]

Moreover, as noted by Kenneth Scambray, Californian Italian American authors generally do not evoke the immigrant enclave that is so typical of much of the group's literature. When it is represented, as is indeed the case in Stansberry's work that centers heavily on North Beach, much emphasis is placed on a sense of change and loss in the years following World War II.[20]

George Pelecanos (b. 1957) is a Washington, DC–born Greek American novelist and screenwriter of Spartan origin, best known for his role in the creation and production of the HBO crime show *The Wire*. Like Stansberry, he makes an innovative use of the traditional motifs of hard-boiled detective fiction; the setting of his novels, for example, is Washington, a rather unconventional location in terms of genre. As he has said, "My city had been underrepresented and misrepresented. I don't write novels about politicians or power-mad generals roaming the halls of the Pentagon. The Federal City is only a very small part of this town. We [Washingtonians] have our own culture, our own music, our own language. I was just trying to shine a light on it and the people."[21]

In both Pelecanos's and Stansberry's writings, ethnic elements deriving from Italian and Greek immigrant culture are placed within the traditional framework of the hard-boiled detective novel. Moreover, both share, in a similar vein, a deeper interest in the intricacies of race and ethnic identity in contemporary American society.

Pelecanos's desire in particular to represent his city in a more authentic fashion parallels his attention to the racial dynamics of Washington. Indeed, Pelecanos notes that this city reflects a strong African American legacy, pointing out that for him, Washington will always be a city profoundly influenced by African American culture. He has explicitly set out to portray this previously neglected aspect in his fiction.[22] Along with Greek American figures, Black characters feature prominently in Pelecanos's novels, sometimes serving as protagonists and/or narrative points of view. As Anagnostou observes:

> [Pelecanos] navigates an uncharted terrain in Greek American history, doing so from a unique vantage point. Instead of focusing on ethnicity alone, it concentrates on race relations. Pelacanos' work demonstrates that in addition to ethnicity, racial issues also shape Greek American lives. In this respect, it rings a bell for artists, researchers, and educators. It signals that cultural and historical renderings of Greek America will remain one-sided unless one situates Greek America in the wider landscape of U.S. racial relations. In other words, the novel cautions against speaking about ethnicity as if ethnicity is a self-contained entity insulated from wider national issues.[23]

Pelecanos's interest in African American culture extends to the importance of music in his work. Pelecanos has actually created playlists for several of his more recent novels, which include a significant number of African American artists and genres. Such elements suggest that Pelecanos, and

Stansberry too, combine the formula of the classic hard-boiled narrative with elements derived from their respective ethnic backgrounds.

Investigating the Past of North Beach in The Last Days of Il Duce

The Last Days of Il Duce is described in Stansberry's own website as a sort of "prequel" to the North Beach series. While it has a similar setting that centers on San Francisco's Italian community but encompasses other ethnic and racial groups, in particular Chinese Americans, this novel is set in an earlier historical time, shifting from the present of the 1980s to reminiscences of the war years. As hinted by its title, *The Last Days of Il Duce* focuses on the repercussions of fascism and World War II on West Coast Italian Americans.

The novel is narrated by Niccolò "Nick" Jones who, like Stansberry himself, has a mixed background, being Italian on his mother's side. In spite of his very common and Anglo-Saxon sounding surname, he largely identifies as Italian American, to the extent that he recalls he and his brother being known during their childhood as the "Abruzzi boys," after their mother Rose Abruzzi, within the Italian American neighborhood. This suggests that the implicit pressure of origins remains strong even for a protagonist who is not fully Italian American.

Nick presents the traits of maleness, whiteness, and isolation that Abbott attributes to the "tough guy" protagonist of the hard-boiled novel. His cynical, detached first person echoes that of classic characters of the genre such as Chandler's Philip Marlowe or Hammett's Continental Op. However, Nick is not actually an investigator, but rather finds himself embroiled in the book's mystery. Therefore, from this point of view *The Last Days of Il Duce* reads more like what is defined as a "noir," since the protagonist is not actually carrying out an investigation and moral boundaries become particularly hazy and unstable.[24] Indeed, in the conclusion of the narrative, Nick ends up committing a murder and being arrested; his actions push him toward further marginalization and do not restore order or establish justice.

When he is first introduced, Nick is in prison, suggesting early on that the narrative will not have a positive resolution. As the story starts to unfold in flashback, Nick is shown leading a marginal, semilegal existence, working for a Chinese gangster. The plot is set in motion by the murder of Nick's brother, Joe, with whose first wife, Marie, Nick had had an affair. Joe's death prompts him to discover a convoluted plot that stretches back to the 1940s. In this context, Marie, who is the most prominent female character, disrupts traditional perceptions of Italian American women; while the emotional center of the household, she is shown trysting with both brothers. In other words, her character complies with the trope of the femme fatale, a figure who typically challenges the detective's masculinity and works against his better interests. Veronika Pituková sees the interaction between these two characters as a "clash of desires":

> The American hard-boiled detective novels present femme fatale as a dame with a past, a spider woman, and the detective as a tough, solitary hero with no future, caught in her web of intrigues. The only way out for the detective, we are told, is to suppress the sexual desire for the woman and hold strong to his professional and moral code. The femme fatale's desire for a better life and greed for wealth is deadly and dangerous for those who succumb to her lure, but the detective's desire for truth and maintain[ing] morals can be fatal for the dark lady, too. When the detective frees himself from the sexual lure of the fatal woman he has a chance to live and even bring her to justice, but she can still escape or decide herself what to do with her destiny.[25]

Furthermore, Joanna M. Smith points out that in Hammett's *The Maltese Falcon* and Chandler's *The Long Goodbye*, the two detectives must eliminate the femme fatale as a way to avenge a male friend.[26] *The Last Days of Il Duce*, however, subverts this dynamic, since Nick's murder of Marie is not carried out to avenge a comrade, as in the case of Sam Spade and Philip Marlowe, or even as a form of self-preservation; Nick accepts fatalistically the consequences of his crime, suggesting that he retains an outlook closer to the archaic world of his Italian roots. Indeed, in the aftermath he feels "only a dumb awareness that fate had worked itself out and was in some ways satisfied."[27]

The historical elements in the novel are closely intertwined with the ethnic ones, which encompass not only the Italian American aspect of San Francisco but also other different immigrant communities and underline

Nick's generalized sense of alienation. Stansberry evokes World War II and Italian American history in particular, focusing on American perceptions of Mussolini and fascism, which had lasting effects on some Italian Americans, affecting their relationship to roots as well as causing intergenerational conflicts and conflicts with other groups.

In spite of his own part-Italian background, Nick views older, less assimilated Italian Americans with condescension, referring to them as "wops," something that may be attributed to his own not entirely Italian background and possible sense of ethnic and cultural detachment. At the same time, he is aware that he is the object of their criticism, as a result of his failed ambitions and his hybrid descent: "It wasn't hard for me to guess the kind of things they were saying. *A mama's boy, that one. UCLA. Law School. Little Rose Abruzzi nearly died giving birth to him. Big shot office downtown, Mr. Lawyer, but look at him now. A bum in the park. That's what you get, you mix an Abruzzi and a Jones*"[28] (italics in the original). Winifred Farrant Bevilacqua points out that a constant in the novel is Niccolò's ambivalent attachment to North Beach: "On the one hand, his strongest sense of self-identity is represented by his bittersweet memories of childhood as one of the 'Abruzzi boys' as he and [his brother] Joe were called by their neighbors (despite being only half Italian). On the other, his attitude towards old Italians still living in the neighborhood is one of ridicule."[29]

Prejudice extends to Nick's perception of different, significantly nonwhite groups. The face of an Asian prostitute, for instance, reminds Nick of a mask, while the syncretic Catholic rituals performed by his Mexican sister-in-law make him feel a mixture of familiarity and spite. Throughout the novel, he perceives with a combination of fascination and revulsion the ethnic diversity of San Francisco, implying that it serves as a reminder of his own fragmented identity. In the conclusion of the narrative, when he is about to be arrested, Nick detachedly observes, "I wondered for a minute about those other cops behind her, whether they would be men or women, and whether their skin would be brown or yellow or white as the driven snow. In this city it was impossible to say. They could be any color at all, I thought, but one thing I knew for certain, their uniform would be midnight, the deepest shade of blue."[30]

In this context, Nick's hypersensitivity to differences of skin color and race may be linked to his own ambiguous identity in terms of race as a descendant of Italian immigrants who, moreover, also has a part-WASP background. His attitude toward questions of race and immigrant identity reflects his own shattered self-perception and leads to alienation and failure rather than the development of interethnic solidarity.

The actual investigation is triggered by Nick's frustration with the police, who explained away his brother's murder as a botched drug deal. Thus, Stansberry uses the traditional Italian motif of the family as a starting point for his mystery narrative. Quickly, the plot shifts toward a group of older Italian Americans, chiefly represented by the powerful Micaeli Romano. This allows Stansberry to explore the little-known issue of the internment of West Coast Italian Americans,[31] as well as the social and political turmoil within the community as a result of divided loyalties. The murder is ultimately connected to the killing of "Mussolini's favorite general" in the United States shortly after the end of World War II. Hence the narrative draws a link between a problematic time in Italian and Italian American history and the novel's present. Stansberry uses a setup based on the legacy of ethnic history to explore various issues such as rifts between ethnics of different generations and issues of identity and national loyalty. Early on, older characters muse on the loss of ethnic culture caused by wartime anti-Italian policies. Reflecting on the arrest of a newspaper editor (possibly based on the editor of the San Francisco Italian American periodical *La Parola*), an old woman points out, "The reason the government put him in jail was not because he was a fascist. It was Italian culture he was writing about. And Roosevelt did not want us to be Italians anymore."[32] Later, in the course of his investigation, Nick encounters an old man who, unlike the majority of Italian Americans, had not given up on his fascist ideology and became an object of derision as a result:

> Johnny Bruno was . . . one of those San Francisco Italians who had been snatched up and penned inside the Western States internment camps during the war. When those men came back to San Francisco, most did not stay long. . . . Shame and shame again, because how else could it be, all North Beach celebrating and then these men, aliens now, walking about with their heads hanging in everybody's hoopla. Most gathered their families and scattered as soon as they could.[33]

Moreover, as obviously suggested by the title of the novel, the figure of Mussolini has a highly symbolic role. Stansberry's perspective seems to ignore the devastation wrought on Italy by the Fascist regime. Rather, he romanticizes Mussolini and his execution as part of the immigrant community's mythology: "All over North Beach, they were always telling it, the same story, the last days of *Il Duce*. It was the story in which everybody wanted a part. The old man, father of Italy. The young mistress. The jealous communists who murdered them both."[34] Through Nick's reflections with older Italian Americans, Stansberry alludes to the complexities of the United States' relationship to fascism, which started out, in the 1920s, as approval for the regime by mainstream American society. Robert Viscusi writes that: "no corpse has more relevance to post-war Italian American history than [Mussolini's]. Italian Americans found that Mussolini spoke powerfully to their predicament."[35] It must be noted however, that prominent Italian Americans such as authors Jerre Mangione and Constantine Panunzio expressed antifascist sentiment early on and that Italian American support of fascism waned as America moved toward war with Italy. Ultimately, immigrants and their descendants felt greater loyalty toward their adopted homeland than their ancestral one. They enthusiastically took part in the American war effort and overall rejected the ideology of the Fascist regime, as noted by Salvatore J. LaGumina in his study of wartime Italian American communities, *The Humble and the Heroic* (2006).

The emblematic use of Mussolini extends to the narrative's portrayal of different immigrant groups and becomes a representation both of the connection to roots and of intergenerational conflicts. Thus, for instance, at one point Nick recalls how a demonstration of Maoist second-generation Chinese sparked the ire of older immigrants who "hated Mao more than they hated the dirt itself."[36] In the case of Italian Americans, it is older individuals who are more likely to approve of Mussolini, whereas in the case of Chinese Americans the younger generation embraces Mao Zedong. In both cases a highly controversial figure becomes a symbol of torn loyalties toward the old country. Later, the narration expands on this idea, making an explicit comparison between Mussolini and historical figures occupying a similar role: "All these different groups, they had their politics and their figureheads.

They had their Maos and their Chiang Kais, their Ho Chins and their Madame Nhus. Yes, I thought, they all have their *Il Duces*, whom they argue over night and day, weeping and hollering, and whose pictures hang on their bedroom walls."[37] This suggests a commonality of immigrant experiences among different groups and races, since ethnics seek a connection to roots that emerges symbolically through potentially problematic historical figures. In this context, the figure of *"il Duce"* goes beyond representing Mussolini, but rather reflects a more universal ethnic dimension.

In *The Last Days of Il Duce* Stansberry uses the conventions of hard-boiled and noir literature to depict the multiethnic reality of postwar Northern California. This allows him to explore the "ethnic waves" that succeeded one another on the West Coast, especially in light of the Asian and Mexican presence and, even more significantly, the impact of fascism. Stansberry's later works share some elements with *The Last Days of Il Duce* but adhere more closely to the traditional hard-boiled formula by using the character of a private investigator, as in the first volume in the North Beach series, *Chasing the Dragon*.

An Italian American Detective Chases a Dragon

The North Beach mysteries are at least in part closer to the model of the California-based detective model established by Hammett and Chandler. Unlike *The Last Days of Il Duce*, they are narrated in the third person, which creates a more detached perspective, removing the element of the casual, disenchanted narration that is so closely associated with Chandler's Philip Marlowe. However, these novels also have a certain number of elements in common with Stansberry's previous work. First of all, the setting is similar to Hammett's, San Francisco, if more specifically its Italian American community. As suggested already by the title, as well as much of the plot of the novel, once again the scope of the narrative encompasses the diverse nature of Californian society, including in particular an interest in Asian Americans. Much of the intrigue is based on the detective Dante Mancuso's own familial background. Indeed, the action opens with Dante's living in distant New Orleans while his father is dying: "It was August in New Orleans, and Dante Mancuso was far from San Francisco, far from his dying father."[38] Dante's character resembles Nick in other ways too: they are both Italian American men who have become detached from their backgrounds but whose attempts at gaining positions of prestige in mainstream American society have been unsuccessful. While Nick's career as a lawyer has failed, reducing him to a semilegal existence, a disastrous investigation cut short Dante's work in the police force, leading him not only to a geographical detachment from his roots but also working in the service of a mysterious government organization. A further notable point in common is an interest in the echoes of the war period on West Coast Italian Americans; while this element is not as prominent as in *The Last Days of Il Duce*, it is mentioned that the power and wealth of the German/Italian Visconti family has dwindled as a consequence of wartime suspicions.

Opening in New Orleans, the narration of *Chasing the Dragon* quickly widens the scope of the character's experience by alluding to Dante's recent "assignment" in Bangkok. Dante is to a great extent a typical figure of Italian American literature: his personality is largely shaped by his background as a descendant of immigrants from southern Italy, but he also moves in a much broader and more complex context. Indeed, *Chasing the Dragon* represents Dante's symbolic return to San Francisco's ethnic neighborhood, the world of his origins. Yet, while much of the mystery is closely related to Dante's own family and personal legacy, it also involves a broader ethnic dimension.

The presence of San Francisco's Chinese population, which was already visible in *The Last Days of Il Duce*, becomes even more relevant. Stansberry's earlier work had already introduced the character of the Chinese American policewoman Leonora Chinn; in *Chasing the Dragon*, Detective Ying almost acts as a foil to Dante. The presence of Chinese American characters complicates the ethnic discourse in these novels and hints at the presence of racial hierarchies on the West Coast. The third-person point of view allows Stansberry to adopt Ying's perspective, revealing, for instance, some details about the character's home life, his connection to his own ethnic background as represented by an elderly first-generation grandmother, as well as his own occasionally alienated view of Italian Americans. For instance, in Ying's eyes

Dante appears exotic and racialized: "He had hard, angular features. His nose was prominent, his skin dark, his lips thin—with a downward turn, almost sensuous—and altogether had about him the look of the old world, Moorish and cruel, but handsome too."[39] The Chinese theme of the novel turns out to have an even more significant part since the intrigue is closely related to a sprawling transpacific organized crime network involving the powerful Wu clan. Overall, the elaborate murder mystery offers Stansberry an opportunity to reflect on the diverse and often dramatic history of various ethnic and racial groups in Northern California. Stansberry's representation of interactions between different immigrant communities suggests reciprocal misunderstandings but, at the same time, an ultimate sense of commonality. Hence, while he destroys a journal in Chinese at the end of the novel, Dante ponders "the secret life of Chinese laborers. Guns and drugs smuggled in container ships. . . . There was so little left of the old days, how could he betray them."[40] Dante and Ying bond over both having fishermen ancestors. As a result the narrative remarks that "it was likely. The red-hulled [Chinese] junks had been here first. When the Luccans came, they forced the Chinese out. North to San Rafael, to China Camp, and Point Richmond. South to Monterey. Then the Sicilians came and forced out the northern Italians too."[41] Thus, the novel highlights a situation of greater ethnic and racial complexity than the one represented by most East Coast–based Italian American authors.

Stansberry combines aspects of the traditional hard-boiled novel that is deeply rooted in the classic California setting closely associated with this genre, with ethnic motifs that come not only from his immigrant background but also, more specifically, from the experience of West Coast Italian Americans, thus encompassing a situation of major diversity and the legacy of wartime internment. The work of George Pelecanos has some points in common with that of Stansberry, since both instill their group's background into the formula of the detective novel. However, at the same time, Pelecanos makes a different use of both these elements. Stansberry makes Italian American elements central to the plot, whereas in Pelecanos's work elements derived from his own immigrant roots remain in the background; instead, it is the city of Washington that takes on a central place. His perspective is multiethnic and multiracial.

The Greek American Hard-Boiled Novel in Washington

Both Pelecanos's first novel, *A Firing Offense*, and his later *The Cut* feature Greek American protagonists and references to Greek immigrant culture. While Nick Stefanos has a fairly conventional background as a descendant of Greek immigrants, Spero Lucas is the adopted child of a Greek couple, whose birth name is Sean. This device allows Pelecanos to explore themes of identity and race. Thus, for instance, the narrative mentions that Spero and his brother Leonidas (generally called Leo) are of different races without alluding directly to the skin color of either. In this perspective, Greek identity is not necessarily linked to actual descent, but is rather a matter of belonging and culture.

Both Stansberry and Pelecanos eschew the conventions of the ethnic or immigrant novel, since as detective writers they are detached from traditional themes such as cross-cultural clashes, ethnic discrimination, or reminiscences of the old country. However, while Stansberry places elements related to immigrant communities, familial structures, and history at center stage (albeit combining them with other elements), making them a crucial part of the intrigue, Pelecanos tends to place ethnic aspects in the background as a way to flesh out his protagonists' characters and to elaborate on his representation of the city of Washington. From this point of view, Pelecanos is in strong contrast with that tradition of Greek American writing which emphasizes "the social conditions in the donor country (Greece), a definition of the American dream and its effect on the immigrant; the archetypal odyssey, the journey to the promised land, the attitudes of the receiving community; alienation, the 'suspended souls,' the pull from two cultures, the ethnic enclaves, Greek Town . . . from myth to Zorba to gyros."[42]

However, Pelecanos too makes use of the traits of the hard-boiled novel identified by Abbott and Hamilton, namely the isolation of the male and (sometimes ambiguously in this case) white protagonist and the deconstruction of American values. The cityscape is an integral part of the hard-boiled narrative: "the American city, where criminal dangers, aggressive modern women, crooked judicial systems and urban decadence lurk at every corner."[43] Abbott points to the importance, in this context, of the Californian setting, and specifically of Los Angeles. This is strongly associated with the myth of the frontier and the implicit legacy of the western narrative. Hence, Pelecanos breaks away from this tradition by using as backdrop for his detective fiction Washington, a city more popularly associated with political thrillers. As previously mentioned, Pelecanos acknowledges the influence not only of the lesser-known, bleaker noir author Jim Thompson on his work, but also, significantly, that of the Greek American novelist and screenwriter A. I. Bezzerides.[44] The Ottoman-born Greek Armenian Bezzerides wrote novels showcasing the Greek immigrant experience, including their gradual shift toward whiteness. However, he is possibly best remembered for having written the screenplay of Robert Aldrich's adaptation of Mickey Spillane's novel *Kiss Me Deadly*. Yiorgos Kalogeras points out that Bezzerides endows the film with an "ethnic context" that is absent from Spillane's work, introducing Greek, African, and Italian American characters.[45] Thus, it is not only Bezzerides's specifically Greek American legacy that influenced Pelecanos; rather, it is a perspective that encompasses a global multiethnic and multiracial perspective on American society.

A Firing Offense introduces the character of Nick Stefanos, who is a disenchanted first-person narrator in the vein of Chandler's Marlowe or Hammett's Continental Op. According to convention, Stefanos is a private investigator, even though his initial occupation in the opening of the novel is that of advertising copywriter. Pelecanos himself points out in interviews the semiautobiographical nature of this character, a young man with a working-class background who is involved in a variety of different jobs. To an even greater extent than Nick Jones in *The Last Days of Il Duce*, Stefanos is marked by substance abuse, his alcoholism causing him to spiral further down as the trilogy unfolds. From this point of view, neither Stansberry nor Pelecanos endorse a conventional representation of success and assimilation of the descendants of immigrants, since they create characters who do not truly find a place in the fabric of mainstream American society. According to Stuart Sim, Stefanos does not adhere to Chandler's depiction of the detective: "this is someone else who would fail Chandler's test of what a detective ought to be: 'the best man in the world and good enough a man for any world.' Nick does not like the world the way it is . . . and is losing the battle to cope with the demands it is making on him and its failure to live up to what he wants."[46]

Stefanos's Greek American background is signaled clearly by his name, but it does not really emerge until the middle of the narrative, when he pays a visit to an elderly immigrant friend. The interaction with Costa allows Pelecanos to represent the ethnic culture and to develop his protagonist's background. As a younger, more assimilated ethnic, Stefanos views members of the first generation with a sense of detachment and alienation, pointing out that "some of these guys didn't really assimilate themselves too well into the American culture."[47] Subsequently, the physical description of Costa is fairly stereotypical: "he was short and solid, with thick wavy black hair that was gray at the temples and slicked back, and a thin black mustache below his bumpy nose."[48] This episode of the novel takes on an ethnographic tone, since Stefanos has the opportunity to explain the custom of covering mirrors as a sign of mourning and to refer to traditional food and coffee. Language is also mentioned, Stefanos referring to his "marginal command" of Greek.[49] The dialogue also reveals that, like Pelecanos himself and significant numbers of Greek immigrants since the late nineteenth century, Stefanos originates from Sparta and has been raised by his immigrant grandfather. Costa's character also allows the narrative to shed light on the concerns of immigrants and the potentially illusory, yet powerfully persistent nature of the American dream in an impoverished and violent section of Washington: "'Do you think you'll go back to Greece?' I asked, wondering why anyone would remain a prisoner in a house like this, in a city where the only common community interest was to get safely through another day. 'No I plan on dying here. Believe me, Niko,' he said, without a trace of irony, there is no place in the world like America.'"[50] Stefanos's own personal history is further fleshed out in the next chapter, where he decides to call his estranged mother, currently living in Greece. He notes, "We spoke superficially about our lives. She ended most of her sentences with, 'my boy' or 'my son.' I tried not to confuse the ethnic inflection with concern or, especially love. As our conversation pared down to awkward silences between pleasantries, I began to wonder, as I always did, why I had called."[51]

The strained relationship between Stefanos and his mother or the reason for her return to Greece are not further investigated, thus pointing to an ambivalent relationship to roots. The rift between Greek Americans of different generations, and, more specifically, a broken mother-son relation can be associated with the legacy of Bezzerides. Indeed, Bezzerides's novel *Thieves' Market* (1949) stages a young Greek American man (significantly named Nick) who views his mother with open hostility, as an overbearing figure who has "no capacity for forgiving, just a capacity for loathing, her life consumed with loathing,"[52] and whose "voice [is] nasty with the sibilance of Greek."[53] While the ethnic mother figure plays a much smaller role in *A Firing Offense*, in both cases she embodies a broken link to the world of origins. Interestingly, in a later instance a doctor initially assumes that Stefanos is Italian, suggesting that (presumably) mainstream individuals enact a blurring of different southern European identities. Ultimately, however, it is the memory of his namesake grandfather, "Big Nick," that continues to signal Stefanos's immigrant-derived identity, even at times when he is succumbing to alcohol abuse. As a result, toward the end of the narrative, before the climatic resolution of the mystery, a drunken Stefanos visits the cemetery, pausing to look at the tombs of Spartan immigrants. The closing pages of *A Firing Offense* take on an almost hallucinatory quality, as the memory of his grandfather makes a ghostlike appearance:

> I bought what was the first of many rounds. . . . With time came darkness, and the rain continued to fall outside and into the barroom. My friends told jokes and sang, then joined me in a toast, a Greek immigrant everyone had called Big Nick. For a moment I wondered what he would think, seeing me now, so twisted and far away from home: that moment burned away with my next taste of whiskey, stronger than reason, stronger than love.[54]

In the subsequent Spero Lucas novels, Pelecanos creates a different type of Greek American detective figure, also enacting a shift from first- to third-person narration.

Fluid Greek American Identity in The Cut

Published in 2011, *The Cut* is the first installment of the Spero Lucas series. While the Stefanos series belongs to the early phase of Pelecanos's career, this novel came out once he had become well established not only as a novelist but also as a television screenwriter and producer. Nevertheless, Nick Stefanos and Spero Lucas have a certain number of points in common, both being first presented as young men with a Greek American working-class background who are deeply immersed in the reality of urban Washington. In other ways, Lucas is different, being a more self-assured and better-adjusted character. Early on, Lucas contemplates his life thus: "this is what I dreamed of when I was overseas: a nice big comfortable bed in a place of my own, money in my pocket, good-looking young women to laugh with, sometimes just to fuck, sometimes to make love to."[55]

He is marked by his experience as a marine in Iraq and by the close relationship with his adoptive mother and brother. This latter element leads to an exploration of Greek identity which is not directly connected to actual descent and can even encompass nonwhite ethnicities.[56] The narrative focuses for instance on Spero's relationship with his schoolteacher brother, Leo, who is implied to be Black. Consequently, when Spero visits his class, "Leo let the murmurs die down. He wasn't about to explain the color difference between him and his brother. It was more fun to let the boys wonder."[57] This representation highlights a sense of race as a racial construct, and of immigrant culture as something that potentially can be partaken beyond actual origins.

The hybrid nature of the Lucas family has been foreshadowed earlier on: "an odd-looking bunch to outsiders but perfectly normal to them—two Greek American adults, two black kids, two white kids, and various yellow mutts."[58] Both Spero and Leo are shown partaking of Greek culture, including the food, language, and religion. In this context, Pelecanos does not ignore the possibility of anti-Black racism within the Greek American community, though it had a positive resolution in Leo's case:

> Leo had been a standout point guard in high school, and in the church league he tore it up. He was thirty years old and it had been twelve years since he had last played GOYA [Greek Orthodox Youth of America league], but in the Baltimore-Washington corridor Greek guys of his generation, even those who had cursed him at one time, and a few who had muttered racial epithets under their breath at him, now spoke of *Mavro* [Black] *Leo* with reverence.[59]

This specific background affects Lucas's overall view of the city of Washington. He points out on one occasion, "this is a black city, far as I'm concerned. Always will be" (107).

Greek Orthodox Christianity also plays a small part in the novel. Like Stefanos in *A Firing Offense*, Spero visits the Glenwood cemetery as a way to reconnect, in this case to an adoptive ethnic legacy, represented here by his deceased father, Van. Interestingly, ethnic Christianity intermingles with folk religion in Spero's character, since he is shown wearing a *mati* talisman (protection against the evil eye) along with a crucifix.

In Nick Stefanos and Spero Lucas, Pelecanos establishes portrayals of different young Greek American working-class men, exploring the legacy of immigration from the point of view of family, language, and religion. In both cases, the connection to the ethnic background is closely linked to the memory of a deceased older male relative, as represented respectively by the elder Nick Stefanos's and Lucas's adoptive father. Both characters inhabit a larger American context yet shift effortlessly into the world of origins in certain circumstances, such as visiting older immigrant friends or family members. The sense of a fluid ethnic identity is further emphasized in the character of Spero Lucas, since he is not Greek by birth but rather was raised in a Greek American family, something indicating that, in Pelecanos's perspective, modern forms of ethnic culture go well beyond specific descent, as shown also by the fact that Spero's Black brother can partake of this particular form of "Greekness." In his representation of Washington, DC, Pelecanos aims at moving away from stereotypical representations that tend to emphasize almost exclusively the political aspects of the city. Consequently, he sheds light on its diversity and, in particular, on its significant African American component, placing Greek American identity within this broader context. As a result, he creates a new version of the hard-boiled narrative, moving away from some of the common tropes of the narrative.

Conclusion

The novels of Domenic Stansberry and George Pelecanos have a certain number of points in common. Both writers draw from the well-established tradition of the hard-boiled novel, a subgenre of detective fiction that focuses not so much on mystery-solving as such but rather on an exploration of society, an emphasis on the urban landscape and a focus on a typically white, male protagonist holding a detached and disenchanted outlook on life. The influence of the model created by Chandler, Cain, and Hammett is particularly visible in Stansberry's *The Last Day of Il Duce* and Pelecanos's Nick Stefanos trilogy, which are first-person narratives. Both Stansberry and Pelecanos further adhere to the conventional formula by creating unromantic cityscapes. Within this typical framework, they draw attention to elements deriving from their own ethnic backgrounds as the descendants of Italian and Greek immigrants respectively. Traditionally, figures belonging to minorities were relegated to a position of marginality in hard-boiled detective fiction, the two authors instead place them at center stage by creating detective characters of Italian or Greek origin. This allows Stansberry and Pelecanos to adopt innovative perspectives, detaching themselves from the almost ethnographic tone of many traditional immigrant narratives. When they incorporate references to ethnic customs they do so occasionally, and only as elements within a broader cultural fabric. Another commonality between the two authors can be seen in a deeper interest in ethnic and racial questions that go beyond their own groups. Stansberry's fictional San Francisco and Pelecanos's fictional Washington both display racial diversity, whether it relates to immigrants from Asia in California or the strong African American presence in Washington. Like most groups deriving from the 1880s to 1920s migration from eastern and southern Europe, both Italians and Greeks in the United States can be considered what Matthew Frye Jacobson calls whites "of a different color" who, when they first settled in the United States, had an ambiguous racial status but ultimately enjoyed the privileges associated with whiteness. This is reflected in the way in which both Stansberry's and Pelecanos's characters inhabit a US space; although they might not fit completely within the fabric of US society, they nevertheless experience it differently from individuals of African, Asian, or Latin American descent.

 This general background potentially influences the two authors' view of nonwhite minorities. While Stansberry puts more emphasis on the themes of alienation and atavistic relationship to roots, Pelecanos underlines fluid forms of identity and draws attention to systemic discrimination against African Americans. Indirectly, the attention given by the two novelists to the presence of people of color in San Francisco and Washington emphasizes the fluid ethnic identity of their protagonists.

A significant difference exists, however, in the use the two authors make of their respective ethnic legacies. The ethnic family of the detective figure occupies a central place both in *The Last Days of Il Duce* and *Chasing the Dragon*; as a result, the Italian motifs are closely interwoven with the actual resolution of the mystery. On the other hand, in Pelecanos's works the Greek origins of his protagonists tends to remain in the background: while immigrant-derived identity helps develop the characters and contributes to the representation of Washington, it does not inform the plot directly.

The hard-boiled novel started out as a fairly monolithic genre but has diversified in more recent years. As noted by García:

> As is the case with most genre fiction, the formulaic quality of detective fiction has been recently amended to include developments both intra-literary such as in post-modern revisions of the genre, and extra-literary, insisting on literature as the product of a cultural and social time which must respond to changes in society if it wants to stay representative of and meaningful to its readership, a quality ever desirable in the case of genre fiction, subjected as it is to the forces of the economic market. Developments in the last sixty years that foreground the role of ethnic minorities and women as protagonists could not be ignored by detective fiction.[60]

Indeed, the novels of Stansberry and Pelecanos can be considered a part of this "revision of the genre," endowing the tradition with a specifically ethnic twist. They also represent an innovation within the canon of immigrant literature, using the formula of a genre to incorporate Italian or Greek themes with a broader analysis of contemporary urban America. Critics of the hard-boiled novel such as Megan Abbott emphasize the importance of the city environment for this kind of narrative, in particular in relation to representations of California. This becomes particularly relevant for Stansberry, who stages his work in a Bay Area context potentially reminiscent of Hammett's, yet uses this specific environment to highlight a relatively unfamiliar facade of the Italian immigrant experience, that of West Coast communities that confronted experiences such as greater interaction with individuals of Latin American or Asian descent and the legacy of war. Pelecanos, on the other hand, shifts the focus to the more unusual background of Washington, DC, downplaying the political element traditionally connected with this city and highlighting instead its African American dimension. Consequently, both authors present Italian American and Greek American characters respectively interacting closely with nonwhites, thus shedding light on the historical racial ambiguity of individuals of southern European descent in the United States. Furthermore, the use of this specific subgenre of detective fiction, which is typically marked by a disenchanted and pessimistic worldview, allows Stansberry and Pelecanos to distance themselves from the stereotypical immigrant "success story" by creating protagonists at the margin of American society. Globally, the work of these two authors can be considered not only as a deconstruction of the hard-boiled detective novel, which they infuse with ethnic elements, but also of the conventional immigrant novel itself. At the same time, different ethnic legacies imply different attitudes toward the chosen narratives, while Italians and Greeks in the United States present a number of similarities, namely in terms of their status upon arrival in America from impoverished rural areas as well as their racial position.

Nevertheless, significant differences also exist between the two groups, namely in relation to the experience of World War II. Whereas Italy was the enemy of the United States and some Italian Americans adhered at least initially to fascism, Greece was in the position of ally to the United States. This discrepancy has a long-lasting impact: Stansberry's novel *The Last Days of Il Duce* is deeply rooted in the experience of World War II. The trauma of fascism and of the internment of some of California's Italian Americans can explain a sense of lingering detachment from the fabric of American society. Stansberry's protagonists interact with individuals of different immigrant backgrounds and races, yet retain a sense of detachment. On the other hand, by focusing on the more unconventional setting of Washington, emphasizing the Black presence in this city and staging racially hybrid Greek American families, Pelecanos goes beyond the representation of "unmeltable ethnics."

By exploiting a genre that is traditionally perceived as being quintessentially white and "American," namely because of its association with the western and the dime novel, Stansberry and Pelecanos put into discussion traditional ideas related to US identity.

NOTES

1. Priestman, "Introduction."
2. Chandler, *The Simple Art of Murder*, 15.
3. Porter, "The Private Eye," 97.
4. Hamilton, *Western*, 1.
5. Marcus, "Introduction," xiii.
6. Gifford, "The Godless," 55.
7. Davis, "No Man," 39–40.
8. Cutter, "An Interview."
9. Chandler, *The Simple Art of Murder*, 18.
10. Abbot, *The Street*, 6.
11. English, "Private," 17–33.
12. García, "Private (Brown) Eyes," 70–82.
13. Guglielmo, "No Color," 30.
14. Anagnostou, "Rethinking."
15. Anagnostou, "White Ethnicity," 101.
16. Vecoli, "Are Italian Americans," 154.
17. Anagnostou, "Re/Collecting," 162.
18. Anagnostou, "A Critique."
19. Bryant, *Miss Giardino*, 131.
20. Scambray, *Queen Califia's Paradise*, 19.
21. Athens, "Greek of the Week."
22. Meyer, "George Pelecanos."
23. Anagnostou, "Greek Americans and African Americans."
24. Abbott, "Megan Abbott."
25. Pitukovà, "Clash of Desire," 25.
26. Smith, "Hard-Boiled," 79.
27. Stansberry, *The Last Days*, 167.
28. Ibid, 13.
29. Farrant Bevilacqua, Review, 112–13.
30. Stansberry, *The Last Days*, 168.
31. The internment of nonnaturalized Italians was prompted by Franklin D. Roosevelt's signing of Executive Order 9066 on February 19, 1942. While this event is best known for having triggered the mass internment of Japanese Americans, it also led to the evacuation and reclusion of about ten thousand Italians living in "restricted areas" of coastal California, as well as individuals occupying prominent positions within immigrant communities. Anti-Italian measures were removed on Columbus Day 1942, as Roosevelt became increasingly aware that he would need the support of Italian Ameri-

cans in the war effort. While the internment of Italian American was not as devastating as the experience of Japanese Americans, it had lasting impact on individuals and communities, leading, for instance, to the repression of the ancestral language and culture ("Una Storia Segreta").

32. Stansberry, *The Last Days*, 64–65.
33. Ibid., 79.
34. Ibid., 108.
35. Viscusi, *Buried*, 193.
36. Stansberry, *The Last Days*, 111.
37. Ibid., 127.
38. Stansberry, *Chasing*, 2.
39. Ibid., 76.
40. Ibid., 302.
41. Ibid., 176.
42. Karanikas, "Greek American."
43. Abbott, *The Street Was Mine*, 9.
44. Cutter, "An Interview."
45. Kalogeras, "Working," 66–81.
46. Sim, *Justice*, 227.
47. Pelecanos, *A Firing Offense*, 17.
48. Ibid., 128.
49. Ibid., 130.
50. Ibid., 131.
51. Ibid., 132.
52. Bezzerides, *Thieves' Market*, 5.
53. Ibid., 6.
54. Pelecanos, *A Firing Offense*, 132.
55. Pelecanos, *The Cut*, 18.
56. The representation of nonwhite Greek identity seems to reflect Pelecanos's own experience as the adoptive father of two Brazilian-born Black sons, one of whom, he notes, "is black, all his friends are black, but he also believes he's Greek" (Raphael, "Murder He Wrote").
57. Pelecanos, *The Cut*, 116.
58. Ibid., 163.
59. Ibid., 46.
60. García, "Private (Brown) Eyes," 71.

Bibliography

Abbot, Megan. "Megan Abbott on the Difference between Hard-Boiled and Noir." Interview with Annie Adams. https://bit.ly/3Fhe7tH.
———. *The Street Was Mine: White Masculinity in Hard-Boiled Novels*. New York: Palgrave Macmillan, 2002.
Anagnostou, Yiorgos. "Greek Americans and African Americans in Conflict and Solidarity." https://bit.ly/3D5NZ2W.
———."Re/Collecting Greek America: Reflections on Ethnic Struggle, Success and Survival." *The Journal of Modern Hellenism* 15 (2015): 148–75.
———. "Rethinking Greece: Yiorgos Anagnostou on Greek America, Greek American Studies and the-Diasporic Perspective as Syncretism and Hybridity." *Greek News Agenda*. https://bit.ly/2ZQk1S9.
———."White Ethnicity: A Reappraisal." *Italian American Review* 3, no. 2 (Summer 2013): 99–128.
Athens, Maria. "Greek of the Week Features Best-Selling Author George Pelecanos." https://bit.ly/3mlk9AV.
Bezzerides, A. I. *Thieves' Market*. Berkeley: University of California Press, 1949.
Bryant, Dorothy. *Miss Giardino*. New York: Feminist Press, 1978.
Chandler, Raymond. *The Simple Art of Murder*. New York: Vintage, 1988.
Cutter, Weston. "An Interview with George Pelecanos." *Kenyon Review*, August 29, 2011.
Davis, J. Madison. "No Man Is Prophet in His Own Land." *World Literature Today* 81, no. 6 (November–December 2007): 39–40.
De Lucia, Francesca. *Italian American Cultural Fictions: From Diaspora to Globalization*. Bern: Peter Lang, 2017.
English, George Brooks. "Private Eyes and Little Helpers: Doormen, Gatekeepers, and Racial Trespass in Chandler's *Farewell, My Lovely* and Mosley's *Devil in a Blue Dress*." *Pacific Coast Philology* 47 (2012): 17–33.
Farrant Bevilacqua, Winifred. Review of *The Last Days of Il Duce*. *Italian Americana* 19, no. 1 (Winter 2001): 112–13.
García, Carmen Mendez. "Private (Brown) Eyes: Ethnicity, Genre and Gender in Crime Fiction in the Gloria Damasco Novels and the *Chicanos* Comic Series." *AltreModernità* 15, no. 5 (2016): 70–82.
Gifford, Barry. "The Godless World of Jim Thompson." *Western American Literature* 21, no. 1 (Spring 1986): 55–56.
Guglielmo, Thomas A. "'No Color Barrier': Italians, Race, and Power in the United States," in *Are Italians White? How Race Is Made in America*, edited by Jennifer Guglielmo and Salvatore Salerno, 29–43. New York: Routledge, 2003.

Hamilton, Cynthia. *Western and Hard-Boiled in America: From High Noon to Midnight.* London: Macmillan, 1987.
Irwin, John T. *Unless the Threat of Death is Behind Them: Hard-Boiled Fiction and Film Noir.* Baltimore, MD: John Hopkins University Press, 2012.
Jacobson, Matthew Frye. *Whiteness of a Different Color: European Immigrants and the Alchemy of Race.* Cambridge, MA: Harvard University Press, 1988.
Kalogeras, Yiorgos. "Working Through and Against Conventions: The Hollywood Career of A. I. Bezzerides." *The Journal of Modern Hellenism* 32 (2016): 66–81.
Karanikas, Alexander. "Greek American Literature." https://bit.ly/3BfRMKA.
Marcus, Stephen. "Introduction." In Dashiell Hammett, *The Continental Op.* New York: Vintage, 1992.
Meyer, Lily. "George Pelecanos: A Novel for the New Washington D.C." https://bit.ly/3a4fMnZ.
Pelecanos, George. *The Cut.* London: Orion, 2011.
———. *A Firing Offense.* London: Orion, 2013.
Pituková, Veronica. "Clash of Desire: Detective versus Femme Fatale." *Journal of Art and Humanities* 1, no. 1 (August 2012): 25–32.
Porter, Dennis. "The Private Eye." In *The Cambridge Companion to Crime Fiction,* edited by Martin Priestman, 95–114. Cambridge: Cambridge University Press, 2006.
Priestman, Martin. "Introduction: Crime Fiction and Detective Fiction." In ibid., 1–6.
Raphael, Amy. "Murder He Wrote." https://bit.ly/2ZcS339.
Scambray, Kenneth. *Queen Califia's Paradise: California and the Italian American Novel.* Madison, NJ: Fairleigh Dickinson University Press, 2006.
Sim, Stuart. *Justice and Revenge in Contemporary Crime Fiction.* London: Palgrave Macmillan, 2015.
Smith, Joanna M. "Hard-Boiled Detective Fiction: Gendering the Canon." *Pacific Coast Philology* 26, nos. 1–2 (July 1991): 78–84.
Stansberry, Domenic. *Chasing the Dragon.* New York: St. Martin's, 2004.
———. *The Last Days of Il Duce.* New York: St. Martin's, 2010.
"Una Storia Segreta: The Internment and Violations of Civil Liberties during World War II." Italian American Museum of Los Angeles. https://bit.ly/3Dg5BJH.
Vecoli, Rudolph. "Are Italian Americans Just White Folks?" *Italian Americana* 13, no. 2 (Summer 1995): 149–61.
Viscusi, Robert. *Buried Caesars and Other Secrets of Italian American Writing.* New York: SUNY Press, 2006.

Imaginative Living in Mediterranean New England

Panayotis League

Like so many diasporic children, I grew up shuttling back and forth between a number of immigrant contexts, feeling simultaneously (and often, it seemed, quite randomly) at home and out of place at their intersections with each other and with the baseline of what I always oversimplified in my head as "mainstream American culture." In my particular case, the two originary references, the two Old Countries, the two Back Homes That Had Never Been Home to Me, were Greece (specifically the Ionian island of Cephalonia and the coastal town of Galaxidi down the mountain from Delphi, whence departed my maternal great-grandparents in the early twentieth century, bound for the Greek sponge-diving community of Tarpon Springs, Florida) and the Irish counties of Clare and Fermanagh. I was always acutely aware of my in-betweenness, not only by dint of being a "half-breed," one of the "mixed children" that seemed so uncommon in Tarpon's superficially homogenous Greek enclave, but also because of the dominance there of migrants from the island of Kalymnos in the eastern Aegean—the other side of the Greek world, whose music, poetry, dancing, and culinary traditions were so different from those of my own family. The product of these traditions became my model of mainstream Greekness because of their ubiquity and dynamism in my insular home community, and they fascinated and drew me in from an early age.

I learned much later, as a young man spending time in other, larger Greek American centers like New York, Boston, and Chicago (not to mention Greece itself), how unusual my understanding of "mainstream Greekness" was. Kalymnos, I discovered, occupies an extraordinarily peripheral spot on the diasporic map. As a musician dedicated to interpreting and sustaining Kalymnian traditional arts—playing violin, *laouto* (steel-string lute), and *tsambouna* (goatskin bagpipe), and singing *mantinades* or rhyming couplets at weddings, baptisms, saint's day feasts, and folk dance troupe performances—I began to meet musicians and dancers from other parts of the American-based diaspora, each with their own references and connections to various corners of the Greek world and their own understandings of what bound us all together as people who think of themselves, to some degree or other, as Greeks. Yet most of these people came from families that were Greek on both sides, regardless of when their ancestors immigrated, and I usually got the impression that, at least on the surface, most of them thought of themselves as moving back and forth between two large-scale social and imaginative contexts: a Greek one and a non-Greek or American one. For many of my friends and acquaintances, the Greek context was frequently broken down into regional affiliations with their respective cultural and linguistic differences—a mother from Crete and a father from Epirus near the Albanian border, say, or Athenian grandparents on one side and Peloponnesian ones on the other—but, in their speech at least, they tended to draw a line down the middle of their lives between their Greek and American identifications.

It wasn't until I moved to the Boston area in the early 2000s that I started meeting significant numbers of people who, like myself, were of mixed Greek and other immigrant ancestry, had Greek folk music and dance at the center of their social lives, and understood their place in the Greek diaspora in large part through their experiences growing up between several different migrant communities, as I had. New England's mills, factories, and wharves attracted a diverse cross-section of European workers, including large numbers of Greeks, in the early twentieth century before the Johnson-Reed Act of 1924 severely limited immigration from southern and eastern Europe (not to mention banning it from Asia).[1] In particular, the Boston area received thousands of Ottoman Greek refugees in the wake of the Greco-Turkish War and the "population exchange" between Greece and the new Turkish state in 1923. Some of my new acquaintances were of mixed Irish and Greek ancestry, like myself; some, particularly those from New Hampshire, were descended from the conjugal meeting of Greeks and French Canadians (and to my great amusement jocularly self-styled themselves as "Freeks"). But, for a constellation of reasons having equally to do with serendipity, aesthetic preferences, and ideological resonance, I gradually realized that many of the people who became my dearest friends and most frequent collaborators on New England's Greek folk scene had grown up in or were currently inhabiting homes built around shared Greek and Italian traditions.

Over the years, I became particularly close with four of these musicians and dancers, all of whom occupied central places of my life, sometimes together and sometimes apart. *Santouri* (hammer dulcimer) player Dean Lampros and his husband, guitarist and oud (fretless lute) player Joe Teja, were among the first musicians I met and began playing with after moving to Boston, and though we specialize in different regional styles of Greek music—Dean and Joe primarily play repertoire from the coast of Asia Minor and its associated islands, particularly Lesvos—we immediately forged a musical partnership and friendship that was among the strongest of my fifteen years in Boston and continues to this day. Their home in the Hyde Park neighborhood was the site of weekly rehearsals and dinners that were a perfect encapsulation of this meeting of Mediterranean socialities, Ottoman-era modal dance music preceded by home-cooked Italian and Greek delicacies and accompanied by Lesvian ouzo. Dean, born in 1969, grew up in the industrial town of Lynn just north of Boston, the grandson of immigrants from the island of Lesvos and the Peloponnese, and learned music from his uncle Nicky Kereakoglow, a pianist, trumpeter, and bouzouki player who himself played music with the Italian and Greek employees at his barbershop in Lynn and absorbed Asia Minor and Lesvian repertoire from his father Konstantinos, a noted instrumentalist and bandleader from the Lesvian village of Kapi.[2] Joe, or JT, born in 1962, of Italian and Spanish descent, grew up in New Jersey playing jazz piano, spent formative years studying in Florence, and fell in love with Greek and Turkish music after meeting Dean when the two were in graduate school. Today they are both active in a number of Boston-based ensembles playing regional Greek music, including their own group Skordaliá, though neither plays music full time for a living; Dean, or DL, holds a PhD in American studies from Boston University and teaches at the Rhode Island School of Design, and JT practices patent law.

I met singer Sophia Bilides, henceforth SB, born in 1954, through Dean and Joe, with whom she had worked in the past, when she invited the three of us to accompany her for performances at a Boston-area Balkan music and dance festival and the Montana Folk Festival in Butte, where she was a featured artist.[3] Sophia was raised in New Haven, Connecticut, the granddaughter of Neapolitan migrants and Turkish-speaking Greek refugees from the village of Permata in central Turkey. Her musical identity is correspondingly pluralistic: she specializes equally in the melismatic modal vocal music of urban Asia Minor Greeks and the cabaret-style classics of the Great American Songbook that JT grew up with. Rounding out this quartet is dance researcher and instructor Joe Kaloyanides Graziosi, born in 1954, who was raised in the Boston-area neighborhood of Waltham with grandparents from Campania and Abruzzo on his father's side and from Ottoman Greece (Eastern Thrace and Istanbul) on his mother's. Today Joe, henceforth JKG, is one of the best-known and most in-demand Greek folk dance instructors outside of Greece, traveling all over the world to teach workshops in many different regional styles and conducting original research in Greek archives and across the Greek countryside. I've played for his classes and danced alongside him at festivals and parties for almost two decades.

In addition to all the time we've spent together on stages and dance floors, all four of these artists were among my primary informants for my doctoral dissertation research, and I interviewed each of them several times during my fieldwork. But, although the five of us were all in the same room many, many times during that period—I have particularly fond memories of JKG dancing the sinuous nine-beat *karsilamas* to our music at the 2015 Balkan Night festival in Concord, Massachusetts, and of all of us laughing in a line of dancers at an Apokries or Greek Carnival party—I never managed to record any of the many conversations that we had about interactions between the Greek and Italian aspects of their families and personal sense of self. When the call for contributions to this volume of essays appeared, I knew I had to make it happen, and on a snowy night in February 2019 the five of us came together over fragrant tea, lamb kofta, and oven-roasted eggplant at a Turkish restaurant a short drive down Massachusetts Avenue from the Orthodox church dedicated by Anatolian Greek refugees in 1923.

We quickly began to interview each other about our simultaneously parallel and divergent experiences of in-between white ethnicity—though, as we will see, race largely remains in the background, rather than the foreground, of the conversation. For the most part I was able to stay out of the way, participating less as a researcher hoping to elicit responses to particular questions and more as an equal partner in an organically unfolding conversation. Accordingly, rather than follow the more common ethnographic technique of parsing select quotes from oral histories and informal discussions in support of a larger theoretical argument, I have opted here to foreground my interlocutors' voices, allowing them to set and maintain the tone and the direction of the conversation—almost as it happened in real time.

Despite its limitations, I think that this dialogic microethnography is good practice, both in terms of staying true to the broad theme of this volume and in terms of staying true to the nature of my relationship with my subjects.[4] First and foremost, we are friends and colleagues who spend a great deal of time hanging out together. Our version of hanging out inevitably involves long conversations and debates about exactly the topics covered here, typically over meals full of flavors that inspire even more reminiscences about the exchange of sensorially and semantically rich substance over lifetimes of engagement with cultural forms both inherited and assimilated. My presence at this meeting was certainly that of a researcher, but one among many; everyone else who was at the table that evening also conducts research both ethnographic and archival in their professional and artistic lives. This commonality of inquisitive practice is a hallmark of our particular version of sociality as a *parea*, a group of friends, and I believe that this collaborative group interview is the best way to explore the issues raised here.

Bearing this in mind, I am guided in my approach to writing this chapter by Mieke Bal's suggestion that we focus on a concept-based, rather than an abstractly theoretical, model of cultural analysis. Clearly defined concepts, argues Bal, are "tools of intersubjectivity" that facilitate discussion based on common language and how it is understood and used, producing miniature, highly specific, context-based theories and methodologies.[5] The core concept at work here—in this chapter, certainly, but also more broadly in my relationships and histories with each of these musicians, dancers, and friends—is *conversation*. As in the improvisational *zeibekiko* dance at the heart of festive sociality in the Asia Minor Greek community, where dancers move around each other in time to the music, responding in the moment to their partner's extemporaneous changes in directions, shifts in body weight, and gestures with hands and snapping fingers, the thoughts and sentiments exchanged around those dinner tables and conveyed here in print build upon each other to tell a collaborative story of encounters between two specifically situated migrant communities and the people who make them real. Rather than broadly generalized comparison between two upwardly mobile white ethnic groups struggling among themselves, with each other, and with American society writ large against the backdrop of industrial New England at the end of the long twentieth century, here we have intimate reflections about particular lives that happen to be joined in significant ways by circumstance and affinity.

I hope that what follows will provide a useful perspective on localized Greek and Italian encounters in this corner of their respective diasporas, highlight the heterogeneity of experience even among people with remarkably similar backgrounds and personal stories, and provoke reflection about how these migrant groups' trajectories both converge and diverge in matters of music, sensory memory, and affect. While our conversations suggest that the Greek has tended to absorb the Italian in these specific encounters between people and practices to the point of near-hegemony (at least in the realm of expressive culture)—and while I am sure that we could easily find another group of half-Greek/half-Italian New Englanders for whom the opposite is true—I believe that what my interlocutors have to say here portrays both cultural references as essential ingredients in a more broadly inclusive creative frame of imaginative living that they have all curated in their domestic, social, and artistic lives.

One of the first things we talked about in our dinner conversation that evening in February 2019 was language. All of my friends at the table speak some Greek, at least at a simple conversational level, but no one grew up with the language as their primary means of interacting with family and the wider world. Beyond their upbringing in families that spoke some Greek at home, DL and JKG both lived in Greece for extended periods and read the language comfortably, while SB and JT have some baseline Greek language skills picked up as adults through musical study and traveling. What particularly fascinated me about this part of our conversation was the tension between ethnic and linguistic identity, as various labels slide on and off of people depending upon context and representational goals.

I began asking about usage of the Greek language in the more Italian American suburb of Waltham, relatively far from the Asia Minor enclave of Somerville, where I erroneously assumed JKG had been born.

> JKG: So, actually, I wasn't born in Waltham, I was born in Somerville, and we moved to Waltham when I was four. I was born in the house where my mother was born and grew up in. Triple-decker, one floor per brother—my grandfather and his two brothers. On my father's side Italian, half Campania, half Abruzzo. My grandmother was a one-year-old immigrant; my grandfather was born on Long Island but as a child moved back with his parents to the village and came back to the US as an adult. On my mother's side, Greek, all from the Ottoman Empire.
>
> SB: So I was also born in a triple-decker, but we didn't have porches—things were much smaller in New Haven. I grew up in a third-floor attic apartment, my Greek grandparents on the second, my Greek godmother on the ground floor.
>
> PL: What was the language situation?

SB: Both my *yiayia* (grandmother) and *pappou* (grandfather) spoke mostly Turkish—my father spoke Turkish to them, broken Greek to the community, and English to us. And in the house, there was Greek on the first floor from my Peloponnesian *nona* (godmother), Turkish on the second floor, and English in the attic apartment.

JKG: One linguistic thing to add: my mother mentioned several times that when their parents didn't want them to understand something, they'd switch from Greek to Turkish. Turkish was a second language for them, but my grandfather was fluent. My grandfather's brother would read the Agape service on Sunday, the gospel, in Turkish.[6]

SB: My grandparents were from Permata near Akşehir. My grandfather got out just before the Catastrophe because they heard they were coming for the men, so he left, but my yiayia was marched and lost a sister, I think in 1922.[7] So she settled in Thessaloniki in a refugee camp, and eventually my grandfather got enough money to bring her over—an arranged marriage, you know . . .

DL: I didn't know, Sophia, that your Greek side were Turkish speakers.

SB: Yeah, they grew up speaking Turkish.

DL: So they were Orthodox at the time of the exchange.

SB: Spoke Turkish, cooked Turkish, but went to Greek church.

JT: But broken Greek, picked up Greek here?

SB: That's my assumption.

DL: So there are such varying degrees of this. They were Turkish speakers, very little Greek. But they knew enough Turkish that they could switch back and forth. I had an uncle by marriage who was like that. Then there are others who were in close proximity with Turks but only had words or phrases that they didn't even know were Turkish.

JKG: I was going to point out that in New Haven most of the early Greeks were from that same village, Permata—all Turkish speakers.

PL: Sophia, you've told me that you that would go to affairs at the church when you were a kid, and the linguistic situation was mapped out generationally and spatially, like in your house.

SB: Yeah, all the elders sitting around the sides of the room would be speaking in Turkish, the middle-aged folks from the greater Greek diaspora in Greek at the central tables, the kids in English, running around the hall.

PL: And there was an old-timer playing oud?

SB: Always an oud and dumbek (goblet drum) player, then the generic Greek stuff.

JKG: Was the oud player Achilleas Poulos? Predominantly Turkish-speaking and singing oud player from Balıkesir, wound up living in West Hartford. His sister was there, his sister's husband was in the coffee business like my mother's family. But he died in Hartford.

PL: Did he record a lot?

JKG: He made ninety-something sides of just Turkish songs from 1924 to 1926, old 78 rpm records, all at a studio in Jersey.

DL: So what did the larger New Haven community think of them as? Turks, Greeks?

SB: Well, they came there first. The Turkish-speaking refugees, I mean—we arrived before the other Greeks.

DL: No, I mean the larger mainstream white Anglo New Haven people.

SB: Oh, as Greeks. Everything was under the standard of the Greek Orthodox church, St. Barbara's right in the middle of New Haven, so that's how they knew us. There was a restaurant, Basil's—there wasn't really a Turkish subculture to look at.

DL: I'm just thinking, if you were a white Anglo in 1915 in New Haven and you're looking at all these foreigners coming and you couldn't tell the difference between Greek, Italian, and Turkish anyway.... I don't know. They called themselves Greeks, so I guess that's what made the difference.

SB: And by the time I was growing up the neighborhood was predominantly Black, so I didn't see a lot of interplay between the Greeks and the whites.

JKG: Sophia, your brother told me that Basil—the restauranteur you mentioned—growing up, he thought he was speaking Greek but then he found out that Greek was Turkish![8] He knew *he* was Greek, and he thought the language he was speaking with his parents was Greek, but it turns out it was Turkish!

DL: Didn't they write with Greek letters?

JKG: Yes, Sophia, I remember your brother showing me some letter, and it was Turkish, but written with Greek letters. This happened to me too! I was in contact with one of Poulos's relatives, who doesn't know Greek at all; she showed me a notebook in which he had written down the lyrics to all his songs. And they were all in Turkish, written with Greek letters! She didn't want to believe that it was Turkish, of course. "I'm gonna get a Greek to translate this!" she said. But it's not Greek! He sang in Turkish!

DL: Of course, all the *amanedes* . . .[9]

JKG: So Turkish song texts with Greek letters, written phonetically. *Karamanlidika*.[10]

This conversation reminded me of an interview I had conducted with Sophia in late 2016, in which she reflected on the frustration of being a monolingual English speaker whose passion, and livelihood, is singing the Ottoman Greek repertoire that she heard as a child:

PL: So how would you characterize your own relationship with the Greek language?

SB: It's very frustrating, because I didn't start trying to learn Greek until my twenties, since that's when I decided I wanted to focus on Greek music. Our home was 100 percent English; neither of our parents tried to teach us any Greek or Italian, which was later a huge disappointment to my brother and me. It was like, oh God, we could have been trilingual! We were strictly English-speaking and didn't go to Greek school. My grandparents were very reserved, and my pappou died very young from smoking. Yiayia didn't talk much, she was very quiet. I didn't even learn bits of Turkish. I heard Greek in church, that's about it. The language itself was always on the periphery. So in my twenties I had this degree from New England Conservatory and I said, wait, I want to do Greek and American cabaret. So that's when I started to learn it, and I was miserable at it! I took daily classes for a year at UMass (University of Massachusetts–Boston), then after that I took night sessions. Academically I was a straight-A student, but if someone tried to talk to me, there was a disconnect for some reason, so it's always been frustrating because even after years and years of transcribing songs I still need help. I'll sit there with my dictionary. I've always felt at a real disadvantage. There's a very real comfort level when I do American cabaret; when I do Greek there's a split-second editing going on, a hesitation that I don't feel with the English stuff. And I wish I had that fluency so I didn't have that step in between. I know what I'm singing about but it doesn't make for a very good conversation topic! The words I've learned don't make for a very good conversation, like "Oh, your eyebrows!" I know five different words for heroin, I can tell you that your eyes have burnt my heart, but I can't really talk about the weather. But I'm stubborn and I love the songs, so I've gone past that.

Back at the table at the Turkish restaurant, I asked JKG and SB—the two half-Greek, half-Italian members of the group—if there was much interaction between their Greek and Italian communities. This led to an extended reflection on previous generations' attitudes about cultural mixture, and some of the confusing incongruities inherent to growing up between languages.

> JKG: No, not really. I grew up in Waltham, a suburban development from the 50s, and there were Italian families, but it wasn't really an ethnic neighborhood. The interaction between Greeks and Italians was on a family level. My father had Italian relatives, but their relationship wasn't very solid so after several years we stopped seeing them. I didn't grow up with my Italian relatives, and to this day I have first cousins I haven't met.
>
> PL: But it's not like that on the Greek side, right?
>
> JKG: No, the Greek cousins, we were always at each other's houses! It was very aggressively social.
>
> PL: So how did your parents meet?
>
> JKG: They both were working at a fashion distribution house in Cambridge. My mother was working for New England Coffee, the family business, after her dad passed, but she didn't last long because they expected a relative would work for free! So one day she took the

typewriter and threw it in the garbage and walked out. *(Laughter and applause)*

DL: What year was your mother born?

JKG: 1925, my father in 1930.

DL: So not quite a generation older than mine—my mother in 1940, my father in '34.

DL: So did your grandparents have a problem? My mother was fifteen years younger than your mother, and she could *never* have come home and said, "I'm marrying an Italian." Not an option. And she was the last of eight kids! Americanized siblings, and she could not have married a non-Greek.

JKG: My mother's father had already died. I asked this question bluntly, and my father said he had no problem with my mother's relatives, including her mother, very unusual. He willingly converted to Orthodoxy. He had a very good relationship with my grandmother. I can't tell you how many times during the week after dinner she got up with her little *briki* (metal coffee pot) and made my father Turkish coffee. If my grandfather had been alive, maybe it would've been different, I don't know. She was the only one out of all the cousins except for one who didn't marry a Greek; she had one first cousin born in Bulgaria who married a Maine-iac.

DL: You mean from the Mani in the Peloponnese? A Maniot?

JKG: No, from Maine!

SB: That could've gone any number of ways.

DL: That's fascinating. My grandfather died two weeks after my parents got married—my mother was twenty-one years old—maybe if she had been twenty-three she would've had other options if her father wasn't around.

JKG: I understand because I grew up with that older generation—not only did they want their kids to marry Greeks, they wanted them to marry Greeks from the right part of the country.

DL: Exactly! And that's something that you don't really see so much anymore. My father not being from Mytilene was probably an issue, but the families knew each other. But for my grandfather, his daughter marrying somebody from the mainland—he still remembered the days a generation before when they were fighting over Venizelos and the king, and went to different coffeehouses.[11] My other grandfather was dead by then, but if he were alive, they might have had issues. . . . My dad was dating Greek girls, but he could've dated other girls. My grandmother, what was she gonna say?

JT: Well, it was different for boys.

DL: But he still married a Greek girl.

JKG: My mother was very independent . . .

SB: Well, I'll say! She was throwing typewriters.

PL: Sophia, how did your parents meet?

SB: They met at a Greek wedding. My father was in the bridal party, and my mother was invited by one of her girlfriends, and she did not want to go. "I'm not going to know anyone there, they're all Greek." But her girlfriend begged, so she went.

PL: Did they meet on the dance floor?

SB: Of course. They were looking at each other, and my father gestured as if to say, do you want to dance? Which for him was very talkative. And she just said no. And then she thought, you fool! So toward the end of the evening, when he was going around offering the candied almonds, he came up to her and she looked up at him and said, "Would you dance with me?"

DL: What's fascinating about stories like this is that we're moving into an era where everybody's story is going to be "we met online." These are stories of . . . classic stories from the mid-twentieth century . . .

SB: With the band playing Glenn Miller.

DL: And so . . . those stories won't exist in another generation, less.

SB: In our case, my yiayia—not sure how pappou felt, he was easygoing, but it was *not* okay with her. It was a Greek tragedy that her son married an Italian. Or not that she was Italian, but that she wasn't Greek. It didn't matter what she was, you know? I'm assuming because it was a son, and not a daughter, she couldn't do much about it. After they got married she didn't talk to my mother for like a year—and they were living in the same triple-decker! I thought about it when I was grown: how did my mother put up with that? Must have been intense. But then she gave her her first grandson, and all was forgiven. Now, my Italian grandparents on the other hand, they were thrilled to death! My grandmother had twelve kids, and she had to get rid of them! My grandfather was a cobbler, he didn't have any money.

JKG: Wow. When my parents got married, they got a small apartment, and my grandmother was still living in that place in Somerville. My mom's older daughter got married after my mother, and my grandmother asked my parents to move back in with her—my grandmother had no problem with her Italian son-in-law. So when we moved to Waltham she went with us. I was eighteen when she passed away. I don't know how we communicated though—her English was horrendous.

SB: I never spoke with any of my grandparents, really.

PL: Neither of you grew up speaking Italian?

SB AND JKG: No.

JT: Speaking of this: my father's mother was three-quarters Italian, and I lived with them for a short time as a kid—we lived with my father's parents for about a year when I was seven or eight. And my Neapolitan great-grandmother lived with us all. She only spoke Napolitano. And my father's mother spoke English very well, but spoke Spanish, Portuguese, and Italian too. They had a grocery in Newark, so they learned languages—I mean, my grandfather was Spanish, came here in the '20s, and he brought his parents from Spain. My Neapolitan grandmother was very close to her mother-in-law, so they had to speak all these languages in the same sentence. But I remember my great-grandmother very readily in the morning, cooking—and I don't know how we communicated. She was always there, she adored my sister, fawned over her—but we didn't speak a word of Napolitano. I don't know how that worked.

JKG: I'll tell you a story from when I was a kid. We lived in Waltham off Trapelo Road, and I used to walk to Waverly Square to pick up the bus to Harvard. I remember once I went—I was pretty young—and got on the bus and there were two or three old ladies in the back of the bus with me. You know, the hair, a little bit of blue tint. And they were speaking perfect English to each other. And I was shocked! I was like, I realized that this was the first time in my life that I had seen someone with white hair speaking perfect English.

JT: I know exactly that feeling!

JKG: I thought it didn't happen! It was so incongruous to me! How can they speak English? They have white hair! I grew up in a suburban neighborhood where all my friends were the kids of immigrants, so how could it be?

SB: I remember that too, hearing elderly people speaking English with no accent and being surprised.

JKG: We're probably the last generation of European immigrants with this experience.

PL: Yeah, I guess you're right . . . I can't imagine large-scale European migration to the US anytime soon.

JT: My grandmother and her sisters all grew up speaking Italian except for my great-aunt Florence—she was sent away to a convent so she learned English there. She spoke British English, perfect. No accent whatsoever.

DL: My aunt Dotty is a bit like that . . . but also nice Greek. But there are so many women and men of their generation who have an accent in one or both languages. My dad used to joke with Nicky, his father-in-law, "How is it possible that you were born here and your sister was born in Greece?" Because she had a thick American accent in her Greek, and he spoke English like he was from the North Shore and Greek like he was from the village.

JT: Language is weird that way. I lived in Italy for two years in college, and during that time spent some time in my grandmother's village. For those few years I didn't speak English at all. Part of my time I spoke the dialect I heard as a kid, by osmosis. When I started school in Florence I got teased a lot because my Italian was so dialect, like I was from the Italian Louisiana. But when I came back to the States my dad was like, "What's with you?" So there was something about the way I spoke English for a while that perplexed people. Something was triggered in my brain, it went back to those early childhood sounds.

I was particularly curious to hear what my friends had to say about why they all gravitated toward genres of music and dance from Asia Minor, which in the larger Greek and Greek American contexts are fairly marginal (if high-profile because of their nostalgic associations with lost homelands). I wondered if being of mixed ethnic heritage and always being a little bit outside the Greek mainstream had anything to do with not only their attraction to these music and dance forms, but also their individual foci on deep historical research and historically and ethnographically informed performance.

> JKG: Well, in our context growing up, that stuff wasn't marginal. When we moved to the Watertown church, it was very heavily Mytilene, people from Lesvos. And Asia Minor. My mother grew up in Somerville, heavily Asia Minor, all those refugees from the Turkish coast. So the music we heard, the church dances—we danced with the Armenians too, remember, all the Ottoman minorities together—we grew up with the five typical Greek American dance tunes. But I also noticed that in Watertown they'd play one or two *tsamika*[12] at night—and one of the two would be one of (art music composer Manos) Hadzidakis's songs, not folk music at all. But they would play five, six, seven *zeibekika*,[13] and not modern zeibekika. Mostly old style zeibekika, for dancing face-to-face. And everybody would get up and dance together. It was normal. Later I found that it was not normal in other communities—it was that "hey, look at me," show-off solo dance that guys do at the end of the night. So for us, it wasn't marginal. I mean, there weren't heavy *amanedes* and such, but . . .
>
> JT: I think it explains, accidentally, his question, though, right? Accidentally for you, in your microcosm, it was normal.
>
> DL: Well, when you're centered on the margins . . .
>
> JKG: And in Boston in those days, when all the teenagers wanted to go out and hear music at restaurants and what not—this was the height

of those mixed ethnic orchestras. Armenian, Greek, Arab . . . at the old Averof nightclub, for example, it was very common. And that's what I liked.

SB: Yeah, I remember just zeibekika and *tsiftetellia*[14] from when I was a kid. When I moved to the greater Boston area and went to dances with mainland Greeks, I was like, what are all these circle dances?

PL: What did the Italian relations think of the Greek music stuff?

SB: In my experience, never crossed paths. I was going to Greek dances, and my mother was playing opera at home. I mean, she would come with us, she learned to dance, converted culturally just like she did religiously. . . . I don't know if that's a Greek thing, non-Greeks tend to convert, the Orthodox are more stubborn . . .

JKG: My Italian father became, you know, a member of the Orthodox church board, learned to do simple circle dances, and could flap around a little bit for a *zeibekiko*.

DL: It's funny, almost all of my cousins married non-Greeks. And the only one of the spouses that converted was an Italian who became Greek Orthodox. None of the others converted.

SB: So funny, my mother was a choir conductor in the Orthodox church, a little Italian lady.

JT: There's the pattern!

PL: Funny, on the Irish side of my family, there's plenty of intermarriage with Italians up in Philly and Jersey—makes sense, the Catholic thing. And my Irish Catholic dad married my Greek mom in the Orthodox church in Tarpon, though he didn't convert. But I'm still waiting to see the first case of Greeks and Italians getting married.

DL: You're practically Italian anyway, being Cephalonian.[15]

PL: Watch yourself! Them's fightin' words. *(laughter)*

JKG: My father isn't religious—I mean, a lukewarm Catholic who converted to Orthodoxy so he could marry my mother—but he always makes a point when we're talking to people, "Oh, (eventual Greek Orthodox Archbishop of North America) Iakovos converted me!" because he was the parish priest at the Watertown church then. He baptized me and converted my father.

In a previous conversation with JKG at his home on Cape Cod in early 2016, I had asked him whether he had grown up conscious of having a Greek identity that was outside of the mainstream Greek American experience because of his Asia Minor heritage, whether in terms of food, language, or the music and dance forms mentioned above. His initial answer was that no, he didn't, because most of the Greeks he and his family associated with were also of Asia Minor descent, and also because for most second- and third-generation migrants geographic origins weren't as important as a general Greek American identity. He felt more self-conscious about his non-Greek last name, especially when he moved out of the community in which he grew up, where everyone knew him. But this prompted him to relate a fascinating anecdote about his maternal grandmother, who had grown up in Istanbul.

JKG: Well, I remember asking her what kinds of dances she knew, and being from Istanbul I thought she was going to say other things—you know, more typically Eastern stuff—but she said, "Well, we learned polkas and mazurkas, quadrilles, waltzes," you know, I said "Hmmm, okay," but then I realized that it makes sense. She came from a solid middle-class background, her father was a butter and yogurt merchant, and she received a very good education, went to a prestigious girls' school in Istanbul. So it makes sense. But she never exhibited any great interest in music and dance that I knew. And then one day we were at a cousin's house, and we were listening to an LP that I had, *Nightlife of the Greeks* by Mike Hart (Michael Hartofillis), and it was all instrumental except for two tunes, one of the first LPs I ever owned. And one of the songs was an instrumental *zeibekiko*. And out of the blue my yiayia got up, and to everyone's huge surprise, she must have danced a minute's worth of music to this tune, in perfect rhythm. I mean, you know, a *zeibekiko*, that old style of *zeibekiko* rhythm, which really shocked me, because I had no idea she knew anything about this kind of music. So it goes deep!

These anecdotes about domestic performance prompted me to recall a conversation that I had recorded several years earlier, in March 2013, between

DL, JT, and myself, focusing on the active, conscious reimagining of home. I had always been struck by what I perceived as their deliberate curating of the aesthetic and intellectual experience of everyday life and how they drew upon particular aspects of their respective cultural backgrounds in order to set the tone at social gatherings. But because their musical activity as a couple seemed to me to be almost exclusively oriented toward Greek music, I was particularly curious about JT's experiences entering that world as an Italian American.

> PL: Joe, how do you feel about all this stuff, not being ethnically Greek, about being around all these people who are obsessed with Greek folk music and dance?
>
> JT: Well, certainly at first it was intimidating, but it was all softened by the shroud of love. Being introduced to it by someone like Dean, my perspective was unusual, having had the music as part of our earliest bonding.
>
> DL: Yeah, but you know what, Joe? We are so *not* immersed in any kind of Greek American . . . I mean, we don't go to church, we don't go to Greek festivals, our Greek ethnicity as a couple is rooted in our home. It's not about going to church, it's not about being part of a larger community . . .
>
> JT: I don't know if that's the question he was asking . . .
>
> DL: No, but what I'm saying is that it means that it's so domestic, it's such a domestic phenomenon for us, it's about what we do in our home, the holidays spent with my family, now your family, our friends. For you it was going to be a much more inviting thing than say if I were involved in a church or going to Greek festivals all the time, where you would be inclined, you would feel like an outsider. You know what I mean?
>
> JT: But remember how it happened with us. We played music together. It was a strange coincidence, you played Greek music, I had played jazz but had not been playing for years, I had my folk guitar up from college with me . . . as an excuse to be close to you, we played music together. This was long before . . . I mean, it was coincident with the recognition that we came up in similar families. One happened to be

Greek and one happened to be Italian, but for all other intents and purposes, identical . . .

PL: Right.

JT: Neither one of which was terribly musical, actively. So that's the subtle difference. I agree about all that bonding glue that's domestic, out of which our more recent endeavors in music have grown.

DL: Yeah, but dating somebody who's from a different ethnic community, you're learning about their culture, there's something strange and wonderful about it and maybe familiar if you're Italian and he's Greek, but my only point—and I don't think I'm wrong, I will say—is that if my ethnicity, and therefore the ethnicity that is either going to feel foreign or feel familiar to you, is rooted in a domestic setting, it's going to make a big difference.

JT: Okay. Let me again remind you: in the early days, before we had . . .

DL: Early on, we had barely dated for six months, and then I went to Greece.

JT: But these are the early impressions that leave an anchor.

DL: But think about what was going on at that time. Just by sheer coincidence, before I met you, I had fallen in with a group of Turks. Right? So there was, in that sense, there was this other thing that we shared that was kind of close to Greek but also . . .

JT: Right, exactly.

DL: But also foreign to me too, and so this was this whole kind of broader Middle Eastern thing that was going to be foreign and familiar at the same time to both of us, so we could share that both as outsiders but kind of insiders at the same time, so we could approach it in a completely different way. We approached it in a way that was just completely different than a Greek American boy meeting a non-Greek girl, you know, a boy whose Greek family is involved in church and all this stuff . . .

JT: That part I did not feel. But that's still not to say that before I knew that the fabric of the community itself was fabricated in a way, in a lovely way, and knew the respective people involved, that whole block of caricature in the first months of knowing you was a big deal. You know, they were all big personalities, and going to the church services with all the incense and the drama, going to some of the more animated festivals, which we never had in my Italian American culture. All of that made a huge impression on me. And I thought, all these Greeks do this every summer, five times a summer, they all know each festival, they go travel to each festival and they know the bands and the musicians, before I knew the machinery behind it . . .

PL: So, two things: one, the point about the domesticity of the music that you guys play, that we all play together: I think that would be the case regardless, because . . . even if, for example, Joe, if you were Greek American, or if you had gone native or whatever you want to call it, if you guys did go to church and did go to bourgeois Greek American functions, still everything you do in your music-making would still be rooted in your home. One of the things that I find so delicious about playing music with you guys is that your home—it's just so welcoming and wonderful and a great place to be, and you guys are so hospitable and you create this environment that's so conducive to relaxing and being able to concentrate on playing music and expressing oneself and being together . . .

JT: Just doing it.

PL: And just doing it. I mean, your home and everything you've created is just so warm and wonderful in that way. It's specifically because of your individual and collective interests, cultural, intellectually, and musically, and the way you decorate your home, the kind of food you cook, the fact that you always have the right bottle of ouzo and the right bottle of wine, the fact that you're both great cooks—you know, you have all these Ottoman maps of Istanbul and Lesvos or whatever on the walls, that's all really important.

DL: There's a material aspect to it. And when you get right down to it, it's personal. I mean, there's a larger cultural context, but there is a sort of personal, psychological factor involved. And for Joe and me, there are—you were talking about special moments, magical moments that are part of a larger story, part of a larger narrative of how we construct our identity, and Joe and I have been—I want to say fortunate, because there was sort of a random element to it, there was nothing inevitable . . . we hadn't even been together two years as a couple when, you know, Joe came to Greece three times, you know, we were there, and I was studying *santouri*, Joe saw the folk school and we had lunch with my teacher and his wife . . . you know, these were very romantic settings, sitting outside in the kitchen in the far-off suburbs of Athens with this shining star of Greek folk music in his kitchen, you know, with the plant twirling around the kitchen . . . there's something so storybook authentic about it, with the food and his wife, it was so quintessentially, if you wanted to write a book about what it would look like, that's what it would be like. And then we had our wedding, and we happened to have a friend who was living on the island of Büyükada near Istanbul, the only place on the planet still where you can hear Greek and Ladino and Turkish and English and French all still spoken on the same street corner. Here we're just now discovering this world and kind of recreating it in our own corner of Boston and here we go and we experience it firsthand, and we meet the old Constantinopolitans, you know, the old Greek families who are exiled to this little island where all the minorities live . . . and then going to Lesvos and having my teacher throw together these little impromptu music symposia for us . . . you couldn't have asked for a more romantic situation . . . I mean, here I am, sitting with the Gulf of Kaloni, the shining turquoise gulf twenty feet away, being bathed in this music that I love . . . how lucky have we been that our story, our identity is made up of these moments that have constructed this narrative, and they've been amazingly beautiful moments. It didn't have to happen. A lot of people are bereft of that experience. How could you not fall in love? How could you not fall in love with that?

JT: Eating sardines at that little tavern . . .

DL: Yeah, I mean, the dulcimer hammers I use, he gave me that day. He gave me his hammers. And those are the ones I still use now. It's like, we've been incredibly fortunate in that regard, and we've taken bits and pieces of that and we've brought them home, both materially and nonmaterially.

The conversation then turned to a mutual friend, a former jazz saxophonist who joined our circle through his interest in the modal improvisation in Balkan traditions, fell in love with Greek and Turkish clarinet music, and became both a regular at our weekly dinners and music sessions and one of our closest friends.

> DL: The bottom line is, we may be constructing this hybrid thing based on our imagined ideals about Ottoman sociality or whatever, but I'd like to think that we're very inclusive. Like our friend CV. Here he was, experimenting with Balkan brass music for a while, but wasn't really doing much Greek music per se, kind of Serbian, Bulgarian stuff.... He was getting worn out by that, and so we met him, you met him, so we wound up playing music together. He's half Greek, half French Canadian, doesn't speak a word of Greek, but you know, grew up with these Greek traditions, and in some ways there's a solid Greek element in his life, in his childhood. So he comes in and we've been, all of us together, we have really been part of his adult Greek identity and sort of taking what was in his childhood and now taking it to the next step, what that means to him as an adult, what does that look like. And having that piece missing as a grownup ... you know, moving away from home, you're not living with your parents and your grandparents or your aunts and uncles, he's hours away, married to a non-Greek. What does it mean to be Greek American? Maybe not playing brass music, but so he finds us and all of a sudden it's like this is what being Greek American means to him.
>
> PL: And so he's participating with us in that very lived, imaginary ... not imagined, not imaginary world, but *an imaginary*, you know what I'm saying?
>
> DL: Yeah, it's constructed.
>
> PL: Yes, constructed.... I'm curious, both of you eloquently answered the question I wanted to ask which was about all that stuff, all those experiences which become part of the ... I don't know what the right word is.
>
> DL: It's sort of a constellation of experiences that ...
>
> PL: That informs living, imaginative living.

DL: And that's not the same type of immersion that someone who grows up with that has.

JT: It's more evocative. Having the experiences that accidentally leave an impression on us, we say "That's something I want to carry elsewhere and share."

DL: You are creating it, though, you are re-creating it.

JT: Yes, you can't carry it elsewhere physically. Maybe we can carry something . . .

DL: Well, we can carry it physically. We carry our instruments with us, we carry songs.

JT: I was going to say, sometimes we carry representations of things physically which evoke other things or represent what we want to carry, sometimes just emotional carrying or storytelling carrying or the music or the food or a recipe or . . .

DL: Yes, you carried an oud back from Turkey with you. I carried my teacher's hammers.

JT: Right, so . . . It's just an ad hoc combination of a whole bunch of stuff that goes toward recreating an imagined something that we want to share.

Conclusion

As I reread all of these conversations and recall the shared meals and music that accompanied and inspired and followed them, it strikes me that the common thread running through them all is not only my four interlocutors' choices to structure their lives around the artistic legacy of the post-Ottoman Greek world, or their baseline of engagement with the encounter between Italian and Greek ways of being in urban New England. More than that, what binds their experiences together is exactly what JT was talking about at the end of the above excerpt. It's the recognition that it's not always possible to carry the physical artifacts of home with us as we move through life, and that even when we can, changing contexts change those artifacts' emotional resonance, as we move in time from childhood to adulthood and set up our own homes, our own families, our own expanding and contracting social circles. But we can, and constantly do, strive to create and re-create that imagined something, whatever it may be for each of us, that we need to live with, and that we feel compelled to share—and, by sharing it, give it new life, new power, new imaginative dimensions.

The conversations that I've included here also point toward the degree to which my friends and their forebears—specific members both of heritage communities (Asia Minor Greeks and Italians in New England) and of several overlapping affinity communities (including the Greek and pan-Balkan folk music and dance scenes)—have made conscious decisions related to the active construction of ethnic belonging, to curating cultural forms; and how, in nearly every case, the specifically Asia Minor Greek (be it music, dance, the Orthodox church, or to a lesser extent, Greek *and* Turkish language and food) seems to have absorbed or dominated the Italian. Only rarely have the two references remained somewhat distinct, if domestically copresent, and never in these anecdotes and reflections have we seen the Italian come to the fore.

Just as important, neither have we seen my interlocutors express any real interest in deconstructing the reasons *why* Greekness always seems to subsume or neutralize Italianness in their particular lives and extended family contexts. Several possibilities occur to me; perhaps it has to do with the regional specificity of their Asia Minor Greek traditions and cultural values and their doubly minoritarian status in the American and diasporic Greek context, as opposed to the regional diversity of their respective Italian origins and the relative embeddedness of Italian diasporic identity in American popular culture. Perhaps it has to do with the explicitly performative and, crucially, *participatory* music and dance traditions that are such a fundamental part of Asia Minor Greek sociality, and remain such a vibrant and compelling anchor for social life in these communities, in contrast to the relative lack of such folk music and dance practices among Italian Americans. Regardless, it's clear that these particular musicians and dancers both recognize the dominance of the Greek/post-Ottoman over the Italian in the imaginative construction, maintenance, and constant re-creation of their pan-Mediterranean models of sociality, and perhaps even take it for granted.

This exposes one of the limitations of this dialogic ethnographic method: while it foregrounds and prioritizes the voices of ethnographic subjects, it allows for relatively little of the "thick" description and interpretive analysis that has been the gold standard in ethnographic writing for half a century. During the conversations presented here, I consciously tried to avoid the role of interviewer, allowing my friends to discuss what was on their minds rather than push them toward my own priorities. Consequently, many of my more pointed research questions went unanswered on these particular occasions and remain unaddressed by this essay.

Foremost among these questions are those having to do with race in general, and whiteness in particular. Interrogating the political and ideological consequences of the Greek American transition to whiteness over the course of the twentieth century is, to my mind, one of the most pressing issues facing Greek American studies, and one that scholars are just beginning to explore.[16] Investigating how Greek Americans discuss race and whiteness informally among themselves would doubtless be an extraordinarily productive project, and since I know all of my interlocutors here as articulate and incisive critics of American constructions of racial identity, I had hoped for more explicit deconstruction of white ethnicity in these conversations. But as we have seen, aside from a few comments setting Greek migrants apart from their Anglo neighbors, these topics went relatively untouched upon, if not necessarily avoided. Perhaps this is indicative of the degree to which the Greek (and Italian, for that matter) transition to whiteness has blunted the collective memory of racial otherness that so marked the lives of first-generation migrants; even among this progressive crowd of academics and artists, the normativity of their ethnic whiteness gets no comment.

Despite its shortcomings—or perhaps because of them—I think that this approach to ethnography does raise questions about interethnic interactions in the urban American context that might not have emerged out of more standard ethnographic projects such as my other publications on the Asia Minor Greek community in New England (see the references). And these questions emerge precisely because of the focus on *conversation* as a concept guiding both ethnographic practice and analysis: conversation as a collaborative, emergent negotiation of the collective production of knowledge about self and other.

First and foremost among these questions is the one alluded to earlier: Why is race in this particular Greek American context—one defined by living beside and with other white ethnics—not a more pressing point of conversation? But also, how do other Americans of mixed Mediterranean heritage imagine, practice, and articulate their belonging to wider transnational and intercultural networks of aesthetic affinity? How do the contours of these practices map onto, or diverge from, each other, and why? And, perhaps most urgently in the context of America's spiraling political, moral, and environmental crises as we approach the quarter-mark of the twenty-first century, how does interrogation of racial identification (or lack thereof) on the part of white ethnics intersect with political consciousness and engagement?

Ultimately, I think that the conversations presented here suggest an understanding and practice of ethnicity and belonging that is quite different both from the generalized symbolic ethnicity frequently reported among white American ethnics—that is, identification with ethnicity through contextually evoked and easily dropped symbols and practices[17]—and from the mainstream sociopolitical context of a diaspora defined in relation to the modern Greek polity. Here, the rhetoric and practice of belonging have relatively little to do with a wider ethnonational ideology, since the dominant cultural reference was brought to New England a century ago by refugees from a state that no longer exists. Rather, my friends' ruminations speak to the conscious cultivation of danced, sung, spoken, and tasted ethnicity at the intersection of these Mediterranean migrant groups as a deeply personal act of imaginative living across generations, an act that both reproduces beloved aspects of inherited cultural practice and necessarily begets its own fields and contexts. Here is world-creating, and world-sharing, on a human and home-sized scale—a realm of practice not only typical, but fundamentally constitutive, of North American ethnicity, white and otherwise.

NOTES

1. See Moskos, *Greek Americans*.
2. See League, "Genealogies of Sense and Sound" and *Echoes of the Great Catastrophe*, for case studies focusing on the significance of the Kereakoglow family's musical activity in the late Ottoman and post-Ottoman Anatolian Greek diaspora.
3. See League, *Echoes of the Great Catastrophe*, for an ethnographic account of these performances.
4. Thanks to Yiorgos Anagnostou for suggesting this apt term.

5. Bal, *Traveling Concepts*, 22.

6. In the Orthodox liturgical tradition, the Gospel according to John (20:19–25) is read aloud in a variety of languages on the morning of Easter Sunday in order to proclaim the joyous news of Christ's resurrection throughout the world and the triumph of his love for humanity; accordingly, the service is known colloquially as the "Sunday of *Agape* (Love)."

7. Greeks refer to the end of the Greco-Turkish War and the subsequent refugee crisis as *I Megali Katastrofi*, the Great Catastrophe. See Hirschon, *Heirs of the Great Catastrophe*, for an ethnography of refugees in the Athenian port of Piraeus, and his *Crossing the Aegean* for an enlightening collection of essays on the legacy of the population exchange from both Greek and Turkish perspectives.

8. Sophia's brother, David Bilides, is an accomplished percussionist who lives in Seattle and is active on the West Coast Balkan music scene.

9. *Amanedes* (the plural of *amanes*) are a genre of melismatic song popular among Turks, Greeks, Armenians, Sephardic Jews, and other Ottoman peoples in which the singer explores the contours of a given melodic mode while repeating the interjection *aman, aman*, "mercy." Achilleas Poulos was particularly known for his recordings in this genre. See Graziosi, "Turkish Music in the Greek American Experience."

10. The phonetic rendering of Turkish with Greek characters is generally known in modern Greek as *karamanlidika*, "the language of the inhabitants of the province of Karaman," since that region of Turkey was home to a large population of Turkish-speaking Orthodox Christians before the population exchange of 1923. Today the term is often used to refer to any dialect of Turkish written with the Greek alphabet, regardless of whether or not it is associated with Karaman; see Balta, *Beyond the Language Frontier*.

11. Known as the National Schism (*Ethnikos Dichasmos*), the political conflict between Greek Prime Minister Eleftherios Venizelos, who supported the Allied cause and advocated for Greece's involvement in World War I, and King Constantine I, whose pro-German stance advocated for neutrality, deeply divided the Greek population at home and throughout the diaspora. In the United States, migrants from the politically conservative Greek mainland tended to support Constantine, while those from outlying islands and territories that had only recently become part of the Greek state favored Venizelos's policies. The disagreements were so fierce that they frequently resulted in physical violence, and many migrant communities split into factions that refused to even socialize with each other. See Kitromilides, *Eleftherios Venizelos*, for an exhaustive analysis of Venizelos's political career and its ramifications for the twentieth-century Greek state.

12. A moderate-tempo dance associated with the rural Greek mainland and said to symbolize patriotic bravery (and named after the Cham Albanian ethnic group).

13. The *zeibekiko* is a slow to moderate-tempo dance characterized by languid movements of the legs and arms and particularly favored by Asia Minor Greeks, who practice it as a dialogic, improvisational dance between two partners who circle around each other in loose time to the music. For an analysis of the Anatolian Greek *zeibekiko* as a space of agonistic masculine debate, see League, "Grooving Heavy, Dancing Drunk."

14. *Tsiftetellia* is a sensual, often solo, dance popular among Greeks, Turks, and the other Balkan peoples; often glossed as "belly dancing."

15. The Ionian island of Cephalonia, off Greece's western coast, belonged to the Venetian Republic for nearly three hundred years and retains a great degree of Italian influence in local language, cuisine, music, and culture in general.

16. See, in particular, Anagnostou, *Contours of White Ethnicity* and "Forget the Past, Remember the Ancestors!"

17. See Gans, "Symbolic Ethnicity."

Bibliography

Anagnostou, Yiorgos. *Contours of White Ethnicity: Popular Ethnography and the Making of Usable Pasts in Greek America*. Athens: Ohio University Press, 2009.

———. "Forget the Past, Remember the Ancestors! Modernity, 'Whiteness,' American Hellenism, and the Politics of Memory in Early Greek America." *Journal of Modern Greek Studies* 22, no. 1 (May 2004): 25–71.

Bal, Mieke. *Traveling Concepts in the Humanities: A Rough Guide*. Toronto: University of Toronto Press, 2002.

Balta, Evangelia. *Beyond the Language Frontier: Studies on the Karamanlis and the Karamanlidika Printing*. Istanbul: Isis Press, 2010.

Gans, Herbert. "Symbolic Ethnicity: The Future of Ethnic Groups and Cultures in America." *Ethnic and Racial Studies* 2, no. 1 (January 1979): 1–20.

Graziosi, Joe. "Turkish Music in the Greek American Experience." In *Greek Music in America*, edited by Tina Bucuvalas, 149–64. Oxford: University Press of Mississippi, 2019.

Hirschon, Renee. *Heirs of the Great Catastrophe: The Social Life of Asia Minor Refugees in Piraeus*. New York: Berghahn Books, 1998.

Hirschon, Renee, ed. *Crossing the Aegean: An Appraisal of the 1923 Compulsory Population Exchange between Greece and Turkey.* New York: Berghahn Books, 2003.

Kitromilides, Paschalis, ed. *Eleftherios Venizelos: The Trials of Statesmanship.* Edinburgh: Edinburgh University Press, 2006.

League, Panayotis. *Echoes of the Great Catastrophe: Re-Sounding Anatolian Greekness in Diaspora.* Ann Arbor: University of Michigan Press, forthcoming.

———. "Genealogies of Sense and Sound: Home Recordings and Greek American Identity." *Journal of Greek Media & Culture* 2, no. 1 (2016): 29–47.

———. "Grooving Heavy, Dancing Drunk: Mimetic Metaphors in Anatolian Greek Music." *Ethnomusicology* 63, no. 3 (2019): 393–417.

Moskos, Charles. *Greek Americans: Struggle and Success.* New Brunswick, NJ: Transaction Publishers, 1990.

PART IV

Ethnic Identities and Visual Culture

An Ethnic Can't Be Like Other People?

The Construction of Greek Americans and Italian Americans in Kojak

Sostene Massimo Zangari

"To what does one assimilate in modern America?" This question appears in the introduction to *Beyond the Melting Pot*, Nathan Glazer and Daniel Moynihan's influential 1964 work about the major ethnic communities in New York City. The answer given at the time, that "assimilation has taken on the color of an ethnic group,"[1] anticipated the increasing incorporation of ethnic identities into the American mainstream. In particular, the "new syntax of nationality and belonging"[2] that emerged, according to Matthew Frye Jakobson, in the latter part of the twentieth century created new visibility for the non-WASP offspring of immigrants from Europe at the center of American culture: in popular perception, the symbolic starting point of "authentic Americanness" gradually shifted from Plymouth Rock to Ellis Island. The narrative of penniless and illiterate "nobodies" who became assimilated middle-class US citizens gave shape to an updated version of the

American tale of success, the "Ellis Island epic," and consequently paved the way for the increasing public presence of European hyphenated populations in American society.

The late 1960s and early 1970s were crucial to this cultural restructuring. The language of identity employed by African Americans to articulate their grievances during the civil rights era was appropriated by descendants of European immigrants to forge a new perception of themselves as distinct from an America that, both at home and abroad, was increasingly looked down upon as an oppressive and aggressive superpower. As hyphenated Americans, they could claim a history of struggles and deprivation at the fringes of US society and separate from that of the ruling elite. In particular, it was Michael Novak, a scholar and public intellectual, who articulated this peculiar positioning of white ethnics inside 1970s US society: the offspring of European immigrants upheld an ethos of "loyalty, hard work, family, discipline and gradual self-development"[3] that projected an Americanism steeped in the traditional rhetoric of opportunity and freedom, disclaiming the inegalitarian politics at home as well as the imperialistic ventures abroad. At the same time, this ethos provided a language of regeneration for American society as a whole: by appropriating the set of values associated with this new language, by putting the "Ellis Island struggle" at the core of its identity, America could recover a new "virginity" in reaffirming its traditional identification as the land of opportunity for the "wretched refuse of foreign shores." The white ethnic, therefore, became the new American cultural hero—the legitimate standard bearer of the founding values of the country.

Television was a driving force behind this cultural shift. In a matter of few years, network schedules increasingly made room for series like *Julia*, *Arnie*, *Columbo*, *Sanford and Son*, and many others, which featured a variety of ethnic leading characters. This move was part of the turn toward "relevance," a label that signaled a new strategy contrived by network executives in the early 1970s to pursue "more open confrontation with contemporary issues"[4] in TV projects. New trends, from the "vague but pervasive post-Watergate mistrust . . . of the political and economic institutions"[5] to the growing awareness of the TV audience as stratified and heterogeneous, meant that between 1969 and 1972 "the tacit and explicit rules governing production routines and programming shifted ground"[6] and paved the way for the inclusion of a more diverse roster of heroes and heroines on TV screens. No longer confined to marginal parts based on a limited set of stereotypes associated to ethnic groups, non-WASP characters became the focus of an increasing number of programs and their characterizations gained depth beyond established norms.

The police drama *Kojak*, which aired on CBS from 1973 to 1978, was one of the signature productions of this ethnic turn. Starring Greek American actor Aristotle ("Telly") Savalas in the role of Lieutenant Theo Kojak, the show became one of the most popular programs of the decade.[7] Kojak, the son of Greek immigrants, is a tough, resolute cop working at the Manhattan South precinct: wary of protocols and hierarchies, he is nonetheless committed to work within the system and bring criminals to justice. From drug dealers to collusions between politics and business, the series deals with a whole array of crime that, in its variety, reveals the complex social and ethnic stratification of the contemporary metropolis as well as its "hidden" power structures. Focus on contemporary issues and on ethnicity provided the "relevant" content that the audience demanded from TV. This was coupled with another major stylistic point: the decision to promote audience identification featuring a "language of intimacy," whereby the hero as well as the supporting cast were granted emotional depth and a personal private life beyond their public role as police officers, suggesting that colleagues were part of one big family.

The transformation of the workplace through the language of family was a common pattern in TV serial entertainment of the early 1970s. Turning the office or police headquarters into a family was the response to an era pervaded by "anxiety, pessimism and foreboding about the collapse of community and the growing fragmentation of social life."[8] According to Ella Taylor, the familiarization of the workplace expressed a cultural clash between "the yearning for meaning and community in the workplace" and "the fear of the power of corporation and of professionals in corporate settings."[9] Whereas business organizations increasingly reduced individual agency to the serial performance of tasks, and consequently turned people into soulless entities, the family appeared as the sanctuary where meaningful relationships could be nurtured. Therefore, in order to elicit empathy from the audience, workplaces on TV emphasized friendship, love affairs, mentoring, and other family-like relationships between colleagues.

This tension between family and the corporate world offers a valuable key to understand the discourse on ethnicity pursued in *Kojak*. In fact, in the effort to imagine ethnic characters as individuals who are no different from the public on the other side of the TV screen, writers attempted to frame the former within the same dichotomy between family and corporate world—with characters haunted by fear of being destroyed by a cold, corporate reality and craving for the warmth and safety of a family nest or a community. Paraphrasing the words uttered by detective Nick Ferro in the second episode of the first season ("A cop can't be human? He can't be like other people?"),[10] it is possible to summarize the project pursued by *Kojak* with the question "an ethnic can't be human, can't be like other people?" The show's aim is to present members of the different ethnic groups as individuals who are moved by the same feelings and passions as those of the predominantly WASP majority watching the show.

In its five seasons, *Kojak* promoted a new "human" portrayal of ethnic groups, white as well as nonwhite. The series presented characters of Greek and Italian origin as fitting within the family versus corporate frame, thus producing a common new image for both, distinct from the stereotypical representation that had dominated the mainstream media up to that point. The ethnic characters struggle to retrieve a family dimension that they have lost: they have either forsaken their parents or have been betrayed by close relations. In both cases, their estrangement is connected to pursuits that deny the very ethnic ethos of loyalty, hard work, and family identified by Novak and therefore suggests a self-indulging, hyperindividualistic vision of the American dream, an "over-assimilation" that alienates characters from their kin.[11]

Further, the chapter highlights how this project of "humanization" of the ethnic wasn't part of the original idea surrounding the Kojak character. The prequel where Kojak made his first appearance, the TV movie *The Marcus-Nelson Murders*, aired in March 1973, had a different focus. The movie sets a conflict between Lieutenant Kojack (spelled with a *c*, later lost), a generic ethnic with no specific national connotation, and a group of bad officers that includes several Italian Americans. The conflict is seen through the lenses of the civil rights movement, with Kojack coming across as the concerned cop aware of the bias against African Americans and confronting a department where racist attitudes are the norm. In the transition from prequel to series, however, the lieutenant "becomes" Greek. By centering the program on Savalas, who seldom missed a chance in his public life to refer to his origins, the main actor's personal traits were given more prominence, and the lieutenant transitioned from generic ethnic to Greek American. This, in turn, promoted a fresh look on other ethnicities as well, in an attempt to avoid stereotyping any of them with specific labels and in particular to disconnect Italians and Irish from the role of offenders they were given in the TV movie. Thus, Savalas's Greekness proved crucial in steering a mainstream product toward a new representation of the ethnic.

However, in becoming more "human," and thus made to appear not much different from the audience, the ethnic groups lost their cultural specificity: there is no mention of the particular histories of either Greeks or Italians in the United States, and no reference to issues concerning the meaning of being Americans of southern European origin. Prime-time TV is built upon the values of the audience, predominantly white and middle-class, whose interest in engaging with the foreign and marginal was thought to be limited to depictions as exotic curiosity. Within these structural constraints, *Kojak* attempts to make room for the multicultural fabric of New York: the wide range of characters from the different communities, often given meaningful roles in the economy of a single episode, present a social reality that expands the spectrum of American citizenship.

Relevant and Intimate: Reviewing the Formula of Police Dramas

According to Paul Cobley, among the distinctive style signifiers of *Kojak*, and one of the reasons behind its success, was the choice to elaborate a realism "within the new tangled co-ordinates of public knowledge about racism, criminal rights, civic corruption, reform and social determinants of poverty."[12] Engagement with social reality comes as no surprise, given the record of the main character's creator, Abby Mann. His work as screenwriter—including the Stanley Kramer movie *Judgment at Nuremberg* (1961) as well as the miniseries *King* (1978; Mann was personally acquainted with Martin Luther King Jr.)—was consistently committed to highlight social problems of the time.

The opening up of prime-time entertainment to social reality falls within the search for "relevance" which, between the late 1960s and the early 1970s, became a cornerstone for programming choices. In the wake of the long wave of protest and contestation that gripped the United States in that decade, network executives came to believe that, in order to gain a competitive edge, new products should reflect the concerns of ordinary citizens. In short, TV shows needed to incorporate those very items that the audience would find in the news. In this perspective, the turn toward relevance meant an attempt by network producers to reduce the gap between the world perceived through information outlets and the one represented in entertainment programs.

This belief was also supported by a crucial evolution in the perception of the TV audience. With a decisive change in perspective, the TV audience began to be understood not as homogeneous mass but as a stratified aggregate of different segments with different tastes and, crucially, different spending power. In particular, the most profitable viewers from the perspective of advertisers—those with bigger disposable income and in charge of spending choices—were found to be urban, between the ages of eighteen and forty-nine, and female.[13] Thus, in order to target these market segments, that included individuals aware of and possibly in tune with the social changes occurring at the time, networks invested in innovative projects that "subvert[ed] hegemonic ideology and criticize[d] established society" and "sacrifice[d] previous . . . idealization of American life."[14]

Innovation in police dramas meant primarily working against the blueprint provided by *Dragnet*, the show that had set the tone for this specific TV genre during the 1950s and early 1960s. In particular, *Dragnet*'s plotlines placed emphasis on procedures to solve the case and on evidence collected in the course of the investigation, while at the same time reducing the space of individual characters to the tasks required by their operative roles, with no mention of any personal life beyond the job. Together with a range of filmic and narrative choices, *Dragnet* projected the vision of a "fully functional apparatus of justice, able to react to crime as it happens," with a police force that "functions efficiently" and is part of a stable social order.[15] This show expressed faith in the system, with any cog in the law machine, from cops on the beat to state prosecutors, endowed with the power to administer justice and maintain social stability. With a system shaken such as the United States in the post–civil rights era, a show that promoted the optimistic ideology of *Dragnet* was no longer in tune with the times.

It is no accident that the early 1970s saw a proliferation of police dramas that took their title from the main character: *Kojak*, *Delvecchio*, *Petrocelli*, *Toma*, and *Ironside*, to name a few. One of the mainstays of new police dramas, in fact, was a return to the individual and a fresh interest in the private self. Also, the hero's relationship to the system became, at best, critical, when not antagonistic. The discovery of the My Lai massacre and the Watergate inquest, plus the political assassinations of the Kennedys and Martin Luther King, engendered "a new kind of political and social paranoia: a fear that the United States might be rotten from within."[16] Conspiracy fantasies centered on institutions plotting against innocent and helpless individuals best articulated this new mood. Figures like Joe Turner (played by Robert Redford) in Sidney Pollack's *Three Days of the Condor* (1975), embodied a new type of American hero that, as R. W. B. Lewis had predicted, resembled less an Adam than a Laocoon, "a figure struggling to stand upright amid the most violent cross-currents."[17] What saved Turner from the conspiracy was his anticonformism and his moral principles, as well as his identification with the counterculture, which granted him power to discard standard rules and succeed using "unconventional, highly individualistic methods."[18]

The early 1970s ethnic cop fits perfectly within this new liminal space of the hero epitomized by Turner: thanks to the implied connection with an immigrant past, suggesting tradition and community, ethnicity "represented a haven of authenticity that existed at a remove from the bloodless, homogenizing forces" of the system.[19] Further, as Savalas remarked in an interview, Kojak was the type of cop who "grew up on the same kind of block" as most of the criminals he arrested.[20] His "ghetto" upbringing gave him access to the practical knowledge essential to navigate the labyrinthine metropolis, with an insider ability to read the forest of signs which inhabit its streets. In particular, the ethnic cop is able to empathize with those who break the law and to see not just the criminal but also the human being behind the criminal;

he is aware that, more often than not, delinquency is the product of unfavorable social circumstances.

The cultural background of the hero, however, wasn't the only element that ensured identification with the audience. In line with the drive toward intimacy that constituted one of the stylistic trademarks of the show, the writers endowed the lieutenant with a personality that would make him stand out against other lead characters of the small screen. In that, it is quite safe to assume that they received help from Savalas himself. As director Bernard Gordon, who had worked with the Greek American actor in the years just before *Kojak*, recalls in his memoir, Savalas had a reputation of always trying to "make his own creative contribution to the scenes, especially if that meant stealing the scene from everyone else."[21] Having him on the show, therefore, made the addition of personal touches on the character very likely. In fact, the actor "only agreed to take the role if he could give his character a Greek dimension."[22] The lieutenant came to be identified by his lollipops, the catchphrase "Who loves you, baby?" as well as his ethnicity, which came to the surface in one-liners such as "Greeks, they don't threaten, they utter prophecies," or "Don't tell me about democracy, my ancestors invented it." Moreover, Savalas's "tight-fitting suits and piercing gaze," as well as his frequent kissing of women's hands were "geared to melt his feminine audience,"[23] which, as stated earlier, represented one of the major demographics in TV audience. When in July 1974, *Kojak* topped the Nielsen rankings, *People* magazine featured a bare-chested Savalas on its cover: the issue went on to sell more than a million copies, the first time in the magazine's history, and firmly established the actor's reputation as national star and sex symbol.

Beside focusing on the Savalas persona, another major strategy to connect with the public was to underline the family dimension of the workplace. The squad led by the main hero gradually constructed an atmosphere of intimacy with the viewer: Stavros, Saperstein, McNeil, Crocker, Rizzo, joined frequently by Gomez and African American Gil Weaver, gradually developed a kinship "more familial than occupational in nature."[24] With Crocker, the young, inexperienced and often naïve cop who considers Kojak a sort of father figure; Stavros, a lovable oddball with a green thumb; and McNeil, the captain who makes sure the hero doesn't get carried away in his frenzy to obtain justice, the South Manhattan squad meets the audience's fantasy of a workplace endowed with "community and collective solidarity."[25] Kojak's team comes across as a "protective, peer-oriented enclave."[26] Also, the presence of Greek, Irish, Italian, Jewish, Hispanic and African American cops created a multicultural platoon that mirrors New York City's ethnic fabric. In this perspective, the series followed in the footsteps of a line uttered by Kojack at the end of *The Marcus-Nelson Murders*, where the character says that "the police force is the community." The squad, in this light, expresses a utopia where Americans of different origins come together united in a common cause, the improvement of society and the hunt for whatever threatens its stability.

Thus, the production of *Kojak* was geared toward rousing the audience's interest: by turning upside down the worn conventions of police shows like *Dragnet*, the series pursued a double-edged strategy to capture a public. On the one hand, viewers were aware of living in a complex society that didn't lend itself to easy readings in black and white; on the other, they were eager to identify with the values and histories of fictional characters as an antidote to an anonymous working life. The languages of relevance and intimacy, then, became the shaping forces of the show, and would influence its major narrative choices.

Kojak: *The Ethnic as Representative Self*

The Kojak character first appears in the TV movie *The Marcus-Nelson Murders* (1973).[27] Written by Abby Mann, the movie is inspired by a real case that occurred ten years earlier, when detectives of the New York Police Department coerced an innocent African American into confessing the murder of two young women.[28] The truth would slowly surface thanks to the stubborn work of detectives and lawyers who questioned the consistency of the confession. The case would later feature in a book, *Justice in the Back Room*, written by journalist Selwyn Raab,[29] and it was also mentioned in a Supreme Court hearing as an example of police misconduct: the court as a result would promote the so-called Miranda warning, whereby every individual arrested had to be informed about the right to remain silent and to receive legal counseling.[30]

The link between the film and the momentous Supreme Court decision is established in a voiceover that introduces the first scene and will be reaffirmed by the main character himself, Lieutenant Kojack, at the end. Therefore, Mann's script makes explicit its purpose to project "relevance," dramatizing a real case when individual action within the system (the work of detectives and lawyers unconvinced of the veracity of the confession) could lead to the improvement of the system itself (by promoting a measure meant to inform unaware individuals of their rights in case of arrest). *The Marcus-Nelson Murders* thus explicitly supports the liberalism of the civil rights movement by promoting wider access, especially for people of color, to the benefits of equal citizenship. The connection with the movement is established by showing Martin Luther King himself in the opening scene: in the apartment where Jo Ann Marcus and Kathy Nelson are about to be killed, a TV screen is showing the now iconic images of King delivering his "I have a dream" speech. As the plot unfolds, however, the audience is made aware of the gap between the hopes voiced by King and a system plagued by social injustice where African Americans are still the major victims of discrimination. Lewis Humes, the young man wrongly accused of being the killer, is shown as a disempowered and emasculated character: he stammers, is nearsighted (he is given glasses only after the trial begins), and he is unemployed, thus suggesting his lack of discursive power, inability to grasp reality, and failure to support himself financially, his status being representative of the general condition of African Americans in the country at the time. From the moment he is taken to the police station for questioning, Humes is depicted as a puppet in the hands of white cops who physically surround him and symbolically erode his defenses. Starved and powerless, in the end the young man yields to the mounting pressure and confesses the murder.

If visual choices highlight the white/black power relations, more explicit connections with social injustice are pursued as the film proceeds. Humes, realizing he has been charged with a murder he didn't commit, complains that "the cops are trying to lynch me"—thus hinting that discrimination is very much alive even in the cosmopolitan metropolis, and not just a faded memory from the Jim Crow South. Later, during the trial, his lawyer, Jake Weinhaus, addresses the court, saying that "law and order in this country is used as a catchphrase for 'Stop the nigger.'" Finally, in a heated conversation between prosecutor Mario Portello and the press, one of the journalists underlines the similarities between the Humes case and the Sacco and Vanzetti trial—once again hinting at the flimsy evidence on which the case was built, and anticipating a miscarriage of justice.

Within a police department brimming with enthusiasm for the successful conclusion of the investigation, Kojack is alone in his skepticism about the confession: he conducts parallel research to find out inconsistencies and puts every piece of evidence under scrutiny. Despite his success, however, he is unable to convince colleagues to reconsider accusations. Like other heroes of the era, he clashes against a system that seems to work against and not for the citizen: the Police Department and City Hall are too interested in having a guilty party, and not enough in pursuing justice. The only thing left for the lieutenant to do is show reserved information to Weinhaus in the hope of persuading him to defend the young man in court. The charges against Humes will be dropped only after the real murderer, the burglar Teddy Hopper, is found. Humes's acquittal, however, will not usher in a happy ending: instead, Portello insists on having him tried for an attempted rape, another crime the African American didn't commit, which will result in a five- to ten-year sentence. This bleak ending is mainly due to Portello's desire to secure a personal victory to counterbalance the humiliating defeat in the previous case.

The screenplay presents the ethnic cop Kojack as the positive hero of the story. The script was written before any actor was considered for the part, and its name, Kojack, sounding vaguely Eastern European, must have been chosen to inspire foreignness.[31] Kojack's past gets only passing reference as, in one of the first scenes, he explains the reason for his penchant for elegant Italian suits—a promise he made himself as a child to "stop wearing my brother's hand-me-downs," hinting at a poor childhood that fits within the "Ellis Island epic." His ethnicity in the movie is functional to his positive role: the immigrant past gives him the ability to empathize with African Americans and to be aware of the discrimination they face. At the same time, however, his choice to join the police testifies to a firm belief in working inside the system.

The story presented in the TV movie creates for Kojack what Frye Jakobson has termed the "breakthrough moment," when "the lead character crosses from the ethnic periphery into the wider, more cosmopolitan, world"[32]—in this case, the ethnic cop takes upon himself the responsibility to free the American space from the negative interference of those who prefer to bend the founding ideals of the nation to personal interest. Kojack is framed as an American Adam whose duty is to protect society from the hostile forces that threaten to divide it. His reflections at the end of the movie, where he expresses disappointment for the unsatisfactory outcome of the case, at the same time reassures the audience that he will stick to his role as guardian angel of the community. Borrowing from Sacvan Bercovitch, we can say that Kojack becomes a representative self, as his private acts are "part of a communal venture,"[33] the establishment of a "New Israel"—the individual choice to occasionally disregard official procedure motivated by the pursuit of justice. Thus, Kojack performs his normality and acceptability as a white ethnic in front of an American public. Although his faith in the system is shaken by the unjust sentencing of Humes, Kojack doesn't let his own personal anger get the upper hand. He doesn't resign from the police, despite having a strong impulse to do so; instead, he carries on with his work trying to improve society little by little. The purpose of the series, which started six months after the movie, therefore, will be to chronicle, episode after episode, Kojak's "errand into the wilderness" of the metropolis, and his unwavering dedication to the promise to protect the community, to be part of the community.

The sequence when Hopper is finally apprehended and then makes his confession is revealing. Angered by the burglar's hesitation, Kojack attacks him physically, grabbing his neck as though to choke him. Other cops surround the lieutenant and make him realize he was using the same violent methods his colleagues employed to extort the confession from Humes. Immediately after, we see a close-up of Hopper in a room at the police station. He is quietly telling the whole story and then the camera frames Kojack, now cool and composed, listening to the confession and asking for details. Thus, the lead character on the one hand is shown as rightly angered in front of a man who killed two young women, but on the other being able to keep himself in check. He comes out as different from other cops because he has the strength to control his outrage and realize that, in order to be valid, a confession must be given out of free will. He shows the audience two sides

FIGURE 1. A frame from the opening credits of *Kojak*.

of himself: he is physically able to defend the citizen, but at the same time he shows how personal anger or ambition will not obscure his real duty, to serve society, and he will achieve more by having a real murderer convicted and an innocent man released. The public understands he is not an uncivilized, violent, and animalistic immigrant, but a rational American ethnic who has learned the rules of civil society. His "guardian angel" credentials will be reaffirmed in the opening theme of the series: one small part of the screen features a picture of the lead character, while the remaining black part is gradually covered by geometrical lines that reconstruct an image of New York City (Figure 1). The effect is to suggest Kojak's attentive gaze on what happens in the city surrounding him.

If the ethnic hero thus becomes a representative American, the same seems not to apply to other descendants of European immigrants. An integral part of the perverted system that oppresses African Americans are Irish and Italian cops. Detectives Black, Corrigan, and Jaccarino, to different degrees, embody the narrow-minded, insensible, racist cops who are willing to bend the rules in order to have the case solved, little caring whether their accusations are founded. The real villain, though, is prosecutor Mario Portello: despite holding public office, thus being more educated than ordinary cops as well as more detached from the life on the streets that often results in conflicts with African Americans, Portello is gripped by the same unwavering urge to put Humes behind bars. The prosecutor is only moved by desire to advance his career, and in fact we learn at the end of the movie that Portello would later become an assemblyman. Thus, he appears as the typical villain of the Watergate era, the "Bad Man against the Good System,"[34] the character who is willing to damage society for personal gain. His Italian name implies a back story of immigration: in his case, however, we have not an "Ellis Island epic," but a "farce." Portello has overassimilated, has forgotten his immigrant past, and is thus blinded to the plight of other marginal communities. Further, he is assimilated to the point of embodying the worst vices that public opinion was imputing to the system.

Six months after the airing of *The Marcus-Nelson Murders*, the first episode of the *Kojak* series would appear. A major development between the prequel and the series was a clear move to emphasize Kojak's ethnicity. With Savalas now the focus of the project, his personal history was easily made to fit into the show. However, along with the emergence of Kojak's Greekness, the series witnesses an effort to rebalance its focus. The white/black scenario would be expanded to offer a vision recalling Glazer and Moynihan's perception of the metropolis as a multiethnic milieu. One of the innovations in the show would be, in fact, the decision to surround Kojak with a multiethnic squad. Also, besides Rizzo, many other Italian detectives and cops are granted minor roles. Consequently, the portraits of Italian Americans, despite several stereotypical figures, gain a more positive treatment.

"What Kind of a Greek Guy Are You?"

In May 1976, Telly Savalas marched at the head of the annual Greek Independence Day Parade in New York City.[35] In just a few years, thanks to the popularity of *Kojak*, the actor had become a national celebrity, and his immigrant origins featured as core traits of his star persona. Profiles and interviews, printed on publications as different as the *New York Times* and *People*, never failed to mention Savalas's ethnicity and refer to bits of his humble childhood as son of immigrants. The tale of success in the conflated Savalas/Kojak persona took on the form of an Ellis Island epic. Thus, Savalas had accomplished what he had suggested in an interview to the *Times* on the eve of the first episode of the series: getting "more" out of the character handed down by the prequel, and making him a representative of the struggle and hard work that led millions of Americans from the margins to the center of society.

Television in the United States had been particularly oblivious to Greek Americans. According to Marina Hassapopoulou, "over the years ... Greek representations remain outdated or simply nonexistent."[36] One of the few pre-*Kojak* series with a Greek leading character, *Arnie*, which aired on CBS between 1970 and 1972, despite a pilot conceived otherwise, played down the hero's ethnicity.[37] Thus, writers were unencumbered by established representations and images of Greekness. Prompted by Savalas's widely publicized ethnic self, they managed to accommodate within some of the episodes confrontations with fellow Greeks. In these cases, storylines were made to fit within a field of tensions that replicates the "family-versus-society"[38] contrast that was instrumental in shaping the series itself.

In "A Question of Answers,"[39] the first episode of the third season, Kojak deals with an old acquaintance, Lee Curtin, a small-time criminal of Greek origin who anglicized his name after having left the old neighborhood. In exchange for a reduction of the charges against him in a forthcoming trial, Curtin agrees to help the police collect evidence to incriminate a notorious loan shark. In conversation with Kojak he confesses he hasn't been back to Ditmars Boulevard, one of the main thoroughfares in the Greek enclave of Astoria, in three years. He had put off going back until he could do it "in style"—by this meaning he intended to come back only after he could afford the expensive goods, such as clothes or a sports car, that indicate affluence. Curtin, therefore, comes across as a parody of the adjusted and assimilated ethnic: not only has he denied his heritage and severed the connection with his background, but he also upholds a mistaken vision of the American dream as self-indulging conspicuous consumption. Within the family-versus-society scenario, Curtin falls in the latter because he has been blinded by a false idea of America as a land of hedonism. Further, to pursue affluence, he has forsaken his origins as well as the ethic of hard work and steady economic improvement of the immigrant.

Curtin is also in danger of losing the connection with his son, Tony. The latter, who lives with Curtin's ex-wife, rejects the father after learning about his criminal activity. Tony tells Curtin that, although he will abide by the separation arrangement to spend time with his father one day a week, he doesn't have to "know" him, thus implying a distancing that would grow into indifference and estrangement once he becomes an adult. The very continuity between generations, therefore, is at stake, although it is Curtin's detour from the "Ellis Island epic" narrative that is mostly responsible for the fracture. Tony's rejection is based on the realization that his father is "dirt," a thief who has disavowed the immigrants' ethos of hard and honest work. Curtin's decision to help Kojak and the police is thus an attempt to make amends for a life of crime but also to recover the respect of his son and at the same time retrieve his own family past. In the end, Curtin is killed during the undercover operation that allows the police to arrest the criminal: his sacrifice is a testimony to his attempt to redeem himself—a sacrifice that will encourage Tony to relate with his Greek ethnicity in adult life.

The same contrast between the family sphere and the larger world is found in the episode "Sweeter Than Life."[40] This time, though, it is the young offspring of the ethnic who is in danger of straying from the connection with roots. Kojak finds out that his nephew Tony has become a drug addict. In the episode addiction is constructed as a disavowal of the family and its traditional values. The sequence at the beginning of the episode, where the family is gathered to celebrate Kojak's birthday, displays the conflict between competing loyalties: Tony is persuaded by his friend Donnie Collins to leave the party and go somewhere to find a dose. To get the money for the drug, Donnie has stolen a camera belonging to Kojak and that the lieutenant was using to take pictures: when Tony finds out, Donnie asks his friend if he prefers "to get high or get dumb family pictures," once again pitting the community against a larger world of individual gratification. By leaving the party and selling the camera, with its precious film containing pictures that would provide memories for future times, Tony symbolically rejects his own past. Like Curtin, Kojak's nephew follows a misconception of Americanism identified with hedonism and selfish gratification.

It is significant that in these two episodes the alternative to a bond with one's own roots is set in opposition to practices censured by society, theft and drug addiction: ethnicity's connection with collective values and a meaningful past is thus contrasted to a way of being American built on an exasperated individualism that leads to loneliness, while the denial of the ethic associated to the "Ellis Island epic" ends in personal ruin. To make Tony quit his addiction, Kojak takes him to a dilapidated building full of young addicts who have reached the final stage of their habit and now look like zombies—the inability to value ethnicity in constructing one's American identity, the episode seems to suggest, turns the individual into a being deprived of will and strength. Shaken by the vision of his "future self," Tony agrees to undergo a shock treatment that will clean his body from the poisonous substances.

The third episode dealing with Greek content, "The Forgotten Room,"[41] presents again the ethnic subject with a choice between immigrant roots and the larger American scene, but this time it is the former which threatens to steer the individual away from the right course. The body of a prostitute is found in an area where many Greek immigrants live. One of them, Nikos Triforos, is included in the list of suspects, although several people vouch for his innocence and, most of all, his moral integrity. One woman in particular, the widow Katerina, comes forward to Triforos's defense: she is the owner of the bakery where the suspect works and is also a personal friend of Kojak's.

The lieutenant finds himself in an awkward position: recognizing in Triforos a fellow immigrant, Kojak is willing to blindly grant him those traits, such as honesty and hard work, associated to the Ellis Island epic. Consequently, the cop assumes the immigrant's innocence. The detective is nonetheless bound to go through the routine police procedures, to question him and check his alibi. He owes society at large scrutiny of Triforos equally thorough to that which he routinely performs on any other suspect. In the meantime, perceiving the pressure of the community, Kojak betrays an unusual eagerness to pursue Andy Cooper, another suspect, and pin the case on him. As the evidence collected makes the immigrant's position worse, the detective confesses he was "kind of hoping that Triforos was off the suspect list." Reluctantly, Kojak proceeds with the investigation of the immigrant, thus provoking a clash with Katerina, who, feeling betrayed by the lieutenant's lack of trust in his own people, bans him from her shop—a gesture that suggests Kojak's exclusion from the community.

In the end Triforos confesses the murder, and while Kojak hugs a brokenhearted Katerina, a sad tune sung in both English and Greek is heard. The audience feels that Kojak has passed one of his most difficult tests: despite the pressures and the personal feelings involved, he has once again shown his loyalty to his job and the larger community he serves. The lieutenant has proved he was willing to alienate his kin in order to comply with the obligation he owes to society at large.

These three episodes, then, dramatize the ethnic character as caught between the family—be it the nuclear one or the larger ethnic community—and America. The plots revolve around a lack of balance between the two polarities. The Ellis Island epic suggests instead a wholesome compromise: if, on the one hand, connection with family life is a source of positive values that will make the individual a good American citizen, on the other the risk of falling victim of tribalism must be avoided. As for the other polarity, the larger society, America is the land that offers marginal people the opportunity to be assimilated and achieve a modicum of prosperity, but once again the success story shouldn't be confused with affluence and consumption, two evils that are likely to lead the individual on the wrong path.

The "Other" Ethnics: Cold-Blooded Italians

As previously mentioned, Italians come out of *The Marcus-Nelson Murders* as villains, the negative foil to the true valuable ethnic American, the lieutenant played by Savalas. Mario Portello in particular stands for the rogue ethnic, more concerned with his individual interest than that of society. The contrast with Kojack couldn't be starker, as the Italian prosecutor performs what we might consider an "Ellis Island farce," a trajectory into the mainstream that, by bending the system to personal interest, corrupts it from within.

The portrayal of Portello as villain falls within a media ecosystem that, in the early 1970s, was geared toward negative perceptions of Italians. Since the 1930s, in fact, "there ha[d] been regular association between the gangster figure and the Italian-American male."[42] The growing presence of the Mafia in public discourse, with spectacular investigations and murders, as well as the appearance of *The Godfather* movie, conspired to ossify the unflattering connection between Italian Americans and organized crime in accepted stereotypes. Worse still, some observers noticed how when eventually law-abiding Italian characters came to the screens in the early 1970s, they displayed the traits of what had been identified as "Italian machismo": they were "cocky, arrogant, and quick with . . . fists."[43]

The series *Kojak* is mostly in line with public perception associating Italians and crime—and many are the gangsters or small criminals with Italian names. However, within this fictional ecosystem geared against Italians, writers tried to introduce Italian males who, thanks to prominent roles in the economy of an episode, are the subject of more in-depth characterization. Detectives Nick Ferro and Benny Fiore, together with the ex-convict Ben Giordino as well as delivery driver Danny Zucco, are examples of Italian Americans who don't fit into the usual macho stereotypes. In an effort to present also Italian Americans in a positive way, writers resorted to the same field of force created within the contrast between family and the larger post-Watergate world. These Italians, even when they commit a crime, act in response to the breaking up of family harmony. The audience, therefore, in judging these characters, negotiates between a private sympathy with their individual plight and a social censure of the unlawful act they committed, a tension that shuts off the easy interpretative short circuits made available by stereotypes.

Nick Ferro, the villain in the episode "Web of Death,"[44] for instance, elaborates a murder plan that testifies to his being a calculating, cold-blooded, meticulous antihero. A detective with an impressive record, Ferro devises a complex plan to kill Quincy Forsyth, a Wall Street lawyer who had started an affair with his wife. While driving a semiconscious drug addict to the police station, Ferro makes a quick stop at the rear of the building where Forsyth lives, enters the apartment, and shoots him dead. At the police station, a composed Ferro coldly goes through the arrest procedure for the drug addict while receiving praise from colleagues.

Ferro acts with the same sangfroid toward his unfaithful wife, only once shouting his disapproval of her conduct. The woman is visually identified as antithetic to a model wife: she is mostly seen in languid poses on an armchair, wearing a negligee and with a drink in her hand, so that viewers can easily associate her to a femme fatale who has a peculiar understanding of family loyalty. It is also significant that the woman's lover is connected with that corporate world which Americans criticized at the time. This way, Ferro's revenge plan can be seen in terms of a conflict between the values of the average family and that of the elite, with the latter threatening the stability of the former. Therefore, even if not to the point of condoning murder, the audience is made to sympathize with Ferro.

Danny Zucco, the bomber in the episode "Therapy in Dynamite,"[45] is another unusual Italian villain. Brought up in a violent family, Zucco has developed low tolerance for relationship conflicts; whenever differences arise between members of a group, he feels uncomfortable and edgy. Danny attends group therapy at a psychiatric clinic, and the participants become his new "perfect" family. In one therapy session, where two women argue with animosity, Danny interrupts the exchange, asking them to stop: as the doctor leading the group underlines, Danny takes upon himself the burden of creating solidarity between the participants. In fact, the audience discovers that Danny's bombing targets are carefully chosen, each victim in some way responsible for causing distress to one of the patients. His criminal activity, then, can be seen as an extension of the duty Danny has forced upon himself, a distorted desire to do good. In the episode, Danny wants to help fellow patient Louise by killing her husband's mistress, who in his eyes is guilty of "breaking up" Louise's family. The attempt to avoid stereotypes of Italian Americans is also evident with Lou Giordino, the character at the center of "Down a Long and Lonely River."[46] As soon as he is released from prison, Giordino wastes no time in tracking down his ex-wife and a former business associate whom he believes were implicated in the scheme that sent him to jail. The narrative line, therefore, delineates a typical revenge plot, a structure that could easily result in a violent end. However, Giordino does not conform to the image of the stereotypical "impetuous" Italian, as Kojak himself describes him. In fact, before the decisive confrontation with the man who betrayed him, Giordino indicates he is neither hasty nor driven by impulse. His intention is not to kill but to obtain a confession from the traitor, who then will be handed over to the police. Thus, revenge would not be taken by murder, but by bringing the real guilty party to court. In so doing, Giordino replicates the modus operandi of the ethnic cop who bends the rules only in pursuit of a superior and collective good: to get the real criminals behind bars.

This overview of Italians ends with "Dead on His Feet."[47] Benny Fiore, a detective, is terminally ill but nevertheless decides to find the killer of his longtime partner, Eddie Ryan. The episode brings together the job and the private life of the detective, and in both Fiore emerges as a reliable man who shuns the spotlight and prefers to stay behind the scenes. In fact, throughout his life, Fiore has been attempting to fill the gaps that Ryan had created in his pursuit of success and front-page fame. It is Kojak himself who tells Fiore how he had tolerated Ryan's initiatives for the good publicity they brought to the department, but he personally considers Fiore a more valuable cop because he had done all the dirty work, collecting the evidence that would "hold up in court," while Ryan was presumably too concerned with the spectacular arrests and the photo opportunities involved. Thus, the lieutenant recognizes in Fiore a mirror of himself, one fellow ethnic who works for the good of society: like himself, he hasn't been misled by an understanding of American achievement as fame, but thinks that "real" success is the possibility to contribute to the improvement of the country. Fiore had played the same backup role in his partner's family life: being secretly in love with Ryan's wife Helen, Fiore had always stayed by her side, never forgetting a birthday or an anniversary, providing the support that the husband was sometimes unable to offer and demanding nothing in exchange. Thus, Fiore has made sure that Helen could, at least in part, enjoy the pleasures of intimacy and self-realization associated to the family, acting as her guardian angel.

Conclusion

Stereotypes play an important role in television. Helping the audience to situate a character inside a back story with no effort, they are a "shortcut to what might be otherwise long, complicated ... character development."[48] They are, therefore, a precious tool for writers who must fit complex narratives into the twenty-three- or forty-five-minute format of sitcoms or dramas. *Kojak* makes use of stereotypes, too. In "Dead on His Feet," Fiore confronts a character, Solly DeCicco, who fits the stereotype of the Italian mobster perfectly, wearing an expensive suit and even emphatically performing the gesticulation traditionally associated with members of the ethnic group; in another episode, Kojak himself is seen performing a traditional dance with his family, in a sequence that suggests a connection with the then iconic character of Zorba from the eponymous 1964 movie, which associates Greekness with exoticism and a Dionysian spirit.

Despite examples such as these, the series all the same pursues a conscious ethnic project which attempted to reshape TV perception of ethnic groups. This was done primarily by granting ethnic characters the "long, complicated character development" denied by stereotypes. Italians and Greeks are given prominent roles in single episodes, which allowed for complex portrayals. In particular, these ethnic characters display preoccupations shared by the audience: a desire for the intimacy and safety of a family nest, and a skeptical attitude, even conflict, with the larger social environment. The values related to these two dimensions are often in contrast with the ones connected to the family, always in danger of being corrupted or shattered by those of the larger world. This dynamic was very much in tune with public mood at the time, when lack of confidence in institutions was common.

However, the ethnic project of the series went beyond a humanization of the offspring of immigrants and their homologation to the mainstream. In fact, *Kojak* relied on the increasing popularity of Savalas, and on his personal tale of success, to legitimize the ethnic as a new form of representative American. The trajectory from humble beginnings to assimilation that marginals like Savalas and Kojak had accomplished became the fairytale that the public needed to reconnect with America. A poor childhood, the drive to improve one's own condition, the hard work and final assimilation became the signposts of a narrative which updated the American tale of success, the Ellis Island epic, and at the same time reaffirmed the role of the nation as "land of opportunity," an identification that had been overshadowed by the political and international scandals of the 1960s and early 1970s. Children of immigrants, thus, not only started to be considered legitimate Americans: they came to embody the very essence of being American.

To this end, the active role played by Savalas himself cannot be underestimated. The actor, by demanding to remodel the Kojak character into a Greek American and to make his Greekness visible, presented to the general public the image of an adjusted, dependable, self-assured ethnic whose very marginality in US society became appealing. The implied narrative of Kojak's ascent from humble beginnings to valuable citizen fit within the American tale of success and transformed the character into a pop-culture icon who expressed the very meaning of the American experience itself. What's more, the centrality granted to ethnicity in the lead character's personality by extension affected the series itself, which was filled with hyphenated Americans who, presented not as exotic "other" but as individuals not much different from the audience, shared in Kojak's implied tale. In the context of early 1970s TV entertainment, then, *Kojak* crucially contributed to the dissemination of that new perception about the ethnic which brought about the "new syntax of nationality and belonging" and put Ellis Island at the core of American identity.

NOTES

1. Glazer and Moynihan, *Beyond the Melting Pot*, 20.
2. Jacobson, *Roots Too*, 6.
3. Novak, *Unmeltable Ethnics*, 35.
4. Taylor, *Prime-Time Families*, 44.
5. Ibid., 14.
6. Ibid., 55.
7. After the first season, *Kojak* was among the top-rated series in the Nielsen ranking, reaching eight place with 23,3 per cent of TVs tuning on each week. See table 2 in ibid., 48.
8. Ibid., 5.
9. Ibid., 14.
10. Laird, "Web of Death."
11. This conflict replicates Novak's distinction between the elite Americans as "atomistic people" who "know no neighborhood" and "move a great deal," and the white ethnics as "network people," with family, in-laws, relatives, friends, streets, and stores entering "into their definition of themselves" (81).
12. Cobley, *The American Thriller*, 119.
13. Taylor, *Prime-Time Families*, 49.

14. Kellner, "Network Television and American Society," 41–42.
15. Mittell, *Genre and Television*, 139.
16. Patzig, "Crisis of Americanism," 33.
17. Lewis, *The American Adam*, 197.
18. Patzig, "Crisis of Americanism," 60.
19. Jacobson, *Roots Too*, 23.
20. "The Two Sides of Terrible Telly Savalas."
21. Gordon, *Hollywood Exile*, 276.
22. Georgakas, "Remembering Telly Savalas."
23. Conway-Marmo, "Fundamental Mythology of Television," 31.
24. Taylor, *Prime-Time Families*, 51.
25. Ibid., 2.
26. Ibid., 13.
27. *The Marcus-Nelson Murders*.
28. Emily Hoffert, a schoolteacher, and Janice Wylie, a researcher at *Newsweek*, were killed in their Upper East Side apartment on August 28, 1963. The homicide featured prominently in the media, under the designation "The Career Girls Murder," identifying in the victims a new type of New York residents, young single women looking for opportunity and a career in the service sector. The police extorted a confession from George Whitmore, a nineteen-year-old African American, who then spent more than three years in jail despite repeated pleas of innocence. Whitmore was released after the real murderer, Richard Robles, a burglar and drug addict, was found guilty of the crime.
29. Raab, *Justice in The Back Room*.
30. In March 1963, Ernesto Miranda was arrested in Phoenix for the kidnapping and rape of a young woman. After a long interrogation, which took place with mention of his right neither to legal counsel nor to remain silent, Miranda confessed to the charges. During the trial, the defense argued that the confession couldn't be used as evidence because Miranda wasn't in full knowledge of his rights. Three years later the case came to the US Supreme Court (*Miranda v. Arizona*), which, in a 5–4 decision, overturned the conviction. In his majority opinion, Chief Justice Earl Warren maintained that the confession was not admissible in court because the defendant, not being aware of his rights under the Fifth Amendment, could not waive them.
31. In a footnote in *The American Thriller*, Cobley writes that Savalas's character was "originally envisaged as a Pole" (215). One of the people involved in the original investigation and mentioned in Raab's book was named Kostes. This might have been the source for inspiration for the name Kojack.

32. Jacobson, *Roots Too*, 90.
33. Bercovitch, *The Rites of Assent*, 33.
34. Kellner, "Network Television and American Society," 47.
35. Breasted, "It's All Greek as Marchers Mark Independence."
36. Hassapopoulou, "It's All Greek to Me," 65.
37. Lisanti, *Drive-In Dream Girls*, 85. Lisanti quotes actress Sue Ann Langdon, who played the hero's wife in the show.
38. In the previous pages, the dichotomy at the heart of the new sensibility of relevance employed the terms "family" and "corporate world." This same dichotomy frames the analysis of characters that follows. However, the label "family" includes not just the domestic nucleus but also the larger ethnic group, whereas it has seemed appropriate to group the negative connotations of the "corporate world"—soullessness, anonymity, corruption, hostility to the individual freedom—under the different labels of "society," "larger world," and so on.
39. Ruben, "A Question of Answers."
40. Armus, "Sweeter Than Life."
41. Bonnet, "The Forgotten Room."
42. Gardaphé, *From Wiseguys to Wise Men*, xiii.
43. Greeley, "TV's Italian Cops."
44. Laird, "Web of Death."
45. Kearney, "Therapy in Dynamite."
46. Foster, "Down a Long and Lonely River."
47. Laird, "Dead on His Feet."
48. Brizzolara, "The Image of Italian Americans on U.S. Television," 162.

Bibliography

Armus, Burton, writer. *Kojak*. Season 3, episode 3, "Sweeter Than Life." Aired September 28, 1975, CBS.

Bercovitch, Sacvan. *The Rites of Assent: Transformations in the Symbolic Construction of America*. London: Routledge, 1993.

Bonnet, James, writer. *Kojak*. Season 3, episode 15, "The Forgotten Room." Aired January 4, 1976, CBS.

Breasted, Mary. "It's All Greek as Marchers Mark Independence." *New York Times*, May 17, 1976.

Brizzolara, Andrew. "The Image of Italian Americans on U.S. Television." *Italian Americana* 6, no. 2 (1980): 160–67.

Cobley, Paul. *The American Thriller: Generic Innovation and Social Change in the 1970s*. London: Palgrave, 2000.

Conway-Marmo, Kathryn. "Fundamental Mythology of Television." *Canadian Journal of Communication* 5, no. 1 (1978): 23–33.

Foster, Robert, writer. *Kojak*. Season 1, episode 19, "Down a Long and Lonely River." Aired March 20, 1974. CBS.

Gardaphé, Fred. *From Wiseguys to Wise Men: The Gangster and Italian American Masculinities*. New York: Routledge, 2006.

Georgakas, Dan. "Remembering Telly Savalas." *The Greek American*, February 6, 1994.

Glazer, Nathan, and Daniel Patrick Moynihan. *Beyond The Melting Pot: The Negroes, Puerto Ricans, Jews, Italian, and Irish of New York City*. Cambridge, MA: The MIT Press and Harvard University Press, 1964.

Gordon, Bernard. *Hollywood Exile, or How I Learned to Love the Blacklist*. Austin: University of Texas Press, 2013.

Greeley, Andrew. "TV's Italian Cops—Trapped in Old Stereotypes." *New York Times*, July 27, 1975.

Hassapopoulou, Marina. "It's All Greek to Me: Misappropriations of Greekness in American Mass Media." *Journal of the Hellenic Diaspora* 33, no. 1–2 (2007): 59–80.

Kearney, Gene R., writer. *Kojak*. Season 1, episode 21, "Therapy in Dynamite." Aired April 10, 1974, CBS.

Kellner, Douglas. "Network Television and American Society: Introduction to a Critical Theory of Television." *Theory and Society* 10, no. 1 (1981): 31–62.

Jacobson, Matthew Frye. *Roots Too: White Ethnic Revival in Post-Civil Rights America*. Cambridge, MA: Harvard University Press, 2006.

Laird, Jack, writer. *Kojak*. Season 1, episode 2, "Web of Death." Aired October 31, 1973, CBS.

———. *Kojak*. Season 1, episode 18, "Dead on His Feet." Aired March 6, 1974, CBS.

Lewis, Richard Warrington Baldwin. *The American Adam*. Chicago: University of Chicago Press, 1955.

Lisanti, Tom. *Drive-In Dream Girls: A Galaxy of B-Movie Starlets from the Sixties*. Jefferson, NC: McFarland & Company, 2003.

Mann, Abbie, writer. *The Marcus-Nelson Murders*. Aired March 8, 1973, Universal.

Mittell, Jason. *Genre and Television: From Cop Shows to Cartoons in American Culture*. New York: Routledge, 2004.

Novak, Michael. *Unmeltable Ethnics: Politics and Culture in American Life.* New Brunswick, NJ: Transaction Publishers, 1996.

Patzig, Johannes. "Crisis of Americanism in Hollywood's Paranoia Films of the 1970s: *The Conversation, Chinatown* and *Three Days of the Condor.*" *PhiN -Philologie im Netz* 40 (2007): 32–66.

Raab, Selwyn. *Justice in the Back Room.* New York: World Publishing, 1967.

Ruben, Albert, writer. *Kojak.* Season 3, episode 1, "A Question of Answers." Aired September 14, 1975. CBS.

Taylor, Ella. *Prime-Time Families: Television Culture in Postwar America.* Berkeley: University of California Press, 1989.

"The Two Sides of Terrible Telly Savalas." *New York Times*, October 7, 1973.

Irrevocable or Irreversible?

Authenticating Identities in Italian and Greek Immigration Documentaries

Yiorgos Kalogeras

Italian and Greek immigrants constituted part of the Second Great Migration to the United States (1880–1924); the two groups also had an important history of political and cultural contact long before their migration.[1] It was to be expected then that both Italian and Greek immigrants would interact on their way to the United States as well as after their arrival at their new home.[2] Certainly, widespread popular stereotypes in the United States negatively categorized both Italian and Greek immigrants; however, Greeks did not suffer the type of racial and social categorization that the Italians did.[3] Greek immigrants also escaped the continuing ambivalent projection of images of heroes/villains by the popular press, Hollywood films, and later television shows throughout the twentieth century. Certainly, in popular US culture, Greeks have been exoticized but never massively criminalized the way the Italians have been.[4] That said, both groups have responded to what they perceive as popular stereotypical oversimplifications of what they had been as immigrants and what they have been subjected to as US citizens.

Numerous documentaries look back to the Second Great Migration and place Italians and Greeks and their financial and social histories within the history of that massive movement of people and their various adaptations. The first category of documentaries usually begins with the immigrant arrival during the Second Great Migration, the struggle to find work and spaces of belonging within the US society, the immigrants' upward social movement, and finally, their social and political legitimation as US citizens. This has been primarily a straightforward and mostly celebratory approach of many documentaries produced in the United States. Such an approach to the Italian and Greek presence has been complemented but also complicated by the contribution of the second category of documentaries produced in Greece and Italy on the same topic. A question is whether these films from the homeland promote a similar agenda as the US-produced ones.[5]

One could question the rationale of feature films such as Gianni Amelio's *Lamerica* (1994), Pantelis Voulgaris's *Nyfes/Brides* (2004), and Emmanuele Crealese's *Nuovomondo* (2006) from the homeland's point of view on a wave of immigration that took place at the end of the nineteenth and the beginning of the twentieth century. Is this an overdue tribute to a historical event that was not perceived in a positive light by state officials in Italy and Greece at that moment in history? After all, at the time the two countries were in the process of political, economic, and territorial reorganization and needed the young men who instead were opting to move to the Americas. Are these European documentaries belated attempts by Italy and Greece to claim diasporas across the Atlantic, and if so, to what purpose? Significantly, the Greek example in my discussion is part of a cycle of similar documentaries produced by the Greek State channel that involve brief histories of other Greek diasporas around the world. However, it could also be claimed that these and others have been produced to allay fears of "the immigrant other" by reproducing it as oneself.

I suggest that we can understand the ideological underpinnings of a film only when we place it in its time frame, its local, its political, and certainly its global context. Then, a partial answer to the broader question "Why the

European documentaries now?" would involve contextualizing them within the humanitarian crisis and the controversies surrounding such a crisis throughout Europe. The two countries, Italy and Greece, but also the EU as a totality, face an important crisis as recipients of an overwhelming influx of refugees and immigrants from the East and across the Mediterranean.[6] The reality of these European documentaries is that they implicitly point to the prevailing argument among many European countries for and against the concept and the realities of "fortress Europe." These Italian and Greek documentaries reflect on the theme of immigration *qua* immigration as a communal trauma and they dramatize each, in its own way, the consequences of such traumas on a political, communal, and personal level.[7]

Similar issues concerning the migration of southern Europeans at the turn of the twentieth century are viewed as relevant in the twenty-first century from the perspective and with the experience of the migration of people from the Middle East and Africa to the EU and more specifically to Italy and Greece. At first glance, the European documentaries indicate a recent renaissance of Greek and Italian interest in immigration and diaspora communities. But given the time frame of their production, one could argue that they go beyond a search for diasporas or a celebration of the financial and social progress of the former immigrants. The two European films to be discussed are chronologically, Tassos Rigopoulos's *Defteri Patridha* (*Second Motherland*, 2001), and Gianfranco Norelli's *Pane Amaro* (*Bitter Bread*, 2009). In order to contextualize the discussion of the two European films, I will also refer to two US documentaries, Gia Amella's *And They Came to Chicago: The Italian American Legacy* (2007) and Maria Iliou's *The Journey: The Greek American Dream* (2007).[8]

These four films share common themes, such as emigration, settlement, and integration into US society. They focus on the issues of displacement, homelessness, transculturalism, transnationalism, and eventually postethnicity, among others. Their point of view is hegemonic; these four films are not minority/diasporic/migrant articulations of a population movement that was once a minority. They describe migrant groups and diasporic populations which are no longer minority or migrant. Their articulations are enunciated from the perspective of social legitimation, and a secure position within US society.[9]

The two films produced in the United States can be characterized as celebratory articulations of a community's postethnic status; the fleeting references of some of the interviewees to an ethnic background that can prove a source of creativity or an emotional investment are enunciated from the point of view of the subjects' secure position within US society. These references to ethnicity are present but are totally peripheral, they do not interfere socially with the US identity of the subject/interviewee. On the other hand, the two European films introduce analysis and arguments that qualify significantly that type of celebratory mood. In other words, the European films, acknowledging the realities and the social and political fallout from the twenty-first-century migrant and refugee crisis, have realigned their focus on issues that are politically and academically relevant to the older migration as well but are still under discussion and yet to be resolved.

Most particularly, the European documentaries avoid the use of the pre-American history of both groups seen in much popular media as problematic; they also problematize the uncritical connection of the immigrant to US popular mythology such as the United States as the promised land, the frontier as the touchstone of American character, or Manifest Destiny as the major motivational idea behind the nation's westward expansion. Instead, they predicate a rereading of home and homeland experiences. They place such experiences in the context of racial, class, and social politics; they perceive them as most important in the collective memory of the two groups. Furthermore, the in-depth study of individual cases of immigration introduces a reconsideration of the psychic forces at play in the individual's sense of identity formation. At least one documentary, Tassos Rigopoulos's *Defteri Patridha*, presents cases where postethnicity cannot be separated from racial and ethnic performativity.

An Italian American Proposition: Gia Amella's And They Came to Chicago

The modes by which the interviewees in *And They Came to Chicago* are represented and represent themselves are indicative of a paradox at the root of the revived ethnicity described in the US-produced films. On the one hand, such documentaries are produced in order to counter the discourse of negative stereotypes circulating through the popular media regarding the Italians and the Greeks in the United States.[10] On the other hand, they also aim to construct a community-sanctioned narrative of the historical presence of these groups in the United States as well as their distinctive contribution to US culture. Yet what appears to motivate these films is the desire to promote a postethnic identity for the group.[11]

As David Hollinger has proposed, "post-ethnicity prefers voluntary to prescribed affiliations, appreciates multiple identities, pushes for communities of wide scope, recognizes the constructed character of ethno-racial groups, and accepts the formation of new groups as a part of the normal life of a democratic society."[12] Following a similar argument, the documentaries under discussion, through the testimonials they record and the foundational US national narratives these testimonials refer to, prioritize an uninterrupted narrative that postulates the following sequence: immigrant, ethnic, US citizen. A common reference point of self-definition in both Gia Amella's and Maria Iliou's documentaries is developed through the stories of an older immigrant/migrant generation. Such stories predicate, on the one hand, the immigrants' Americanization before the move to their new home. On the other, they emphasize their wish to belong to a wider community, a community beyond the prescribed affiliation of ethnic belonging. In other words, postethnicity is an already emerging identity in the horizon of the prospective immigrant.

For instance, a woman's voice at the beginning of Amella's film claims, "My father was born to be an American." Eventually that voice says, "I'm my father's dream." The voice repeats two immigrant venerable ideas: America as a completion of Italy, and immigration as an antiparental and a profilial act.[13] In other words, the voice valorizes the move from a preindustrial to a highly industrialized country, the move to modernity; the voice also alludes to the prevalent immigrant idea that migration is meant to provide a better future for the second generation. At the same time, however, it states the crucial idea of a new beginning in America, a spiritual and national rebirth.

Similarly, the Columbian Exhibition of Chicago in 1893 provides a narrative comment about the Italians having been the harbingers of Western civilization in America through Christopher Columbus. Consequently, a very problematic allusion to European colonialism emerges; in the face of massive evidence for the consequences of the encounter between native populations and European colonialist Empires, bypassing the issue of slavery, the narrator valorizes the celebration as a source of ethnic pride for the new immigrants. The underlining emphasis remains that the Italians are participants in the great project of Manifest Destiny, as movers of Western civilization from east to west.

Furthermore, Chicago is ideologically construed as a frontier city; according to this documentary, it is the starting point for the Italian immigrants' search for a better future and for their encounter with modernity and therefore postethnicity. In Amella's film, the descendants of immigrants validate the pioneering spirit of their parents to transform themselves into members of a wider totality and assist in the transformation of the city of Chicago into a metropolis; the descendants accept that as their own legacy. Such acceptance conceives turn-of-the-century migration as part of the idea of American westward expansion and Manifest Destiny, a strongly politicized view, and suggests endorsing internal colonialism and racial politics. The whole is perceived in the context of the Industrial Age.

A Greek American View of Postethnicity

Maria Iliou has called her documentary *The Journey*. The title is intentionally ambiguous, meant to allude to the voyages of the Greek colonizers in antiquity who spread across the Mediterranean and along the Black Sea coastline, famously creating Magna Grecia in southern Italy and Sicily; it also alludes to the diasporic experience of the Greeks over the centuries as well as their migration to the Americas.[14] It creates, in other words, a historical and illustrious pedigree for the economic immigrants of the Second Great Migration. Furthermore, such a pedigree is mythologized when the documentary's talking heads refer to the archetypal journey of Odysseus; one of them, in fact, is careful to point out that Odysseus's journey involves both his departure for a foreign land, but also his nostalgia and eventual return to his homeland. He thus reinforces the relevance of the myth for the immigrants and their progeny, but he also introduces a paradox that prevails among the interviewees in the documentary. Identity is presented in this case as both postethnic and in flux.[15]

In an uncanny instance reminiscent of and parallel to Amella's opening sequence in his documentary, former US Senator Paul Sarbanes proclaims that there was never a conflict between Greek and American culture, "since Greek culture is the fountainhead of Western democracy." For the sake of the documentary, Sarbanes chooses to sanitize the immigrant experience and the plight of the new immigrants in the United States The actual historical and sociological facts militate against his pronouncement.[16] There certainly has been conflict, and the Greeks, like the Italians, have experienced marginalization and prejudice.

However, what is striking about such a comment is the attempt to connect the twentieth-century Greek immigrant with Western democracy and consequently with Western culture. Sarbanes pronounces, in spite of himself, a sociological fact about the Greek immigrant's project of working toward a postethnic state. The incompatibility of the folk culture that the immigrant brought from his native village to the United States remained marked when transplanted to industrial America; then, the immigrant had to focus on the ancient/classical heritage that the nineteenth-century "rediscovery" of Greece by Western travelers and intellectuals foregrounded in the consciousness of the immigrant. Here, then, was an all but tenuous connection with Western traditions and institutions, and especially democratic traditions and institutions. Sarbanes implies that the formation of a "new group" beyond ethnic affiliations is to be founded on the democratic traditions that the United States has inherited from classical Greece. However tenuous, in the United States such a view became a usable past which would guarantee, in the immigrant's view, a way into American culture and eventual acceptance. Hence the paradox of arriving at postethnicity via a usable past.[17]

Nevertheless, Sarbanes's pronouncement is not the only suggestion of similarity between the two documentaries. There seems to be an unavoidable foundation on US official mythologies in this narrative of white Greek presence in the United States. In film footage that openly predicates America as "the promised land," the narrator foregrounds the arrival of post–

World War II Greek immigrants who kiss the ground and cross themselves. Later, poet Olga Broumas explains how her personal destiny was fulfilled in America. She construes a totally preindustrial, simplistic view of the homeland when she "reveals" to the interviewer that in Greece during her youth there were no books for her to read! That statement is made in the face of the interviewer's awareness of Broumas's Greek upper-middle-class background and education in elite institutions.

Fiction writer George Pelecanos asserts his self-fulfillment in the United States as well, and also that of the second generation: "From the labor of the hands to the great leap forward, *artists*," he proclaims emphatically. Unlike Broumas, Pelecanos, who is the grandson of immigrants, differentiates between the working-class status of the immigrant generation and the upward social move of their progeny. However, as in Broumas's case, the vision of America he entertains and promotes is that America is a completion of Greece, the necessary step the individual has to take toward self-fulfillment and modernity.

The emplotment of such narratives in both films places the themes of homelessness and displacement that immigration inevitably recalls to mind within the firm ground of US history. The not so implicit arguments of these narratives integrate homelessness and displacement as simply midway stations on the road to embourgeoisement and Americanization. The plots of these narratives are future-oriented and comply with popular, state-sanctioned mythologies of immigrant progress in the United States and Darwinian selection.

A View of Immigration from the "Other Side"

Pane Amaro and *Defteri Patridha*, the two documentaries produced in Italy and Greece, respectively, offer a more complex approach to identity formation and postethnicity. They underline not so much the inevitability as the irreversibility of the move from Europe to the United States. The voyage to the new home, the United States, for these two documentaries is not necessarily meant to signify the immigrant's contact with modernity and modernization; once it is undertaken, though, it creates a trauma that cannot be healed. Furthermore, these two documentaries also assert what David MacDougall reminds us of, that "cultural difference is a fragile concept, often undone by perceptions that create sudden affinities between the self and others apparently different from us."[18] In such a context and in an unexpected narrative move, unlike the previously discussed films, these two documentaries involve issues of race in their plotting of the US identity of the former immigrant. These two films predicate along with Hollinger that "a post-ethnic perspective is not an all purpose formula for solving policy problems, but it is a distinctive frame within which issues in education and politics can be debated."[19]

PANE AMARO

Pane Amaro's Italian immigration story to the United States does not begin on the frontier but in New Orleans, where Italian immigrants replace Blacks in the workforce, move into their neighborhoods, and suffer the kind of violence that Blacks have experienced. In a somber moment, the film provides actual numbers and statistics regarding lynching activities in the United States in the first part of the twentieth century.

This documentary begins by underlining the racial ambiguity that Italians and other southern Europeans in general faced upon their arrival in the United States. It also emphasizes the racial criteria of American businesses who hired these new immigrants and who categorized them in similar terms as the African Americans: "they are better niggers than niggers," which, according to the narrative of the film, was a popular saying among employers. *Pane Amaro* presses such identifications upon the audience. Reminding the viewers of the 1891 murder of the chief of police in New Orleans, it narrates the grim story. Italian immigrant workers are apprehended as the alleged culprits; when the case collapses because of lack of evidence, a mob enraged by the acquittal of the alleged murderers storms the prison and lynches them. This case provides the documentary with an opportunity of parallel accounts of turn-of-the-twentieth-century lynching of southern European immigrants and African Americans.

Pane Amaro promotes and sustains throughout, with either narrative commentary or images, the idea of a social affinity between Italian new immigrants and African Americans. The issue of how different European groups "became" white has already been addressed by several researchers, including David Roediger and Matthew Frye Jacobson. In Roediger's analytical terms, "color-races" and "nation-races" had to compete for the same jobs. As these scholars have stated the issue, "whiteness" was achieved at the expense of the Blacks, or, in Toni Morrison's phrase "on the backs of Blacks." The documentary does not argue against such facts but modifies and qualifies them,[20] insisting that cultural difference is a fragile concept. It argues that different situations and different historical moments force us to form alliances with those who appear to be different from us. And without idealizing or romanticizing such alliances, it presses upon the viewer that all the same they can be found. *Pane Amaro* refers to Fiorello La Guardia, the three-term mayor of New York City (1934–1945) who transformed the metropolis. The narrator points out that La Guardia's mother was an Italian Jew, while his father an Italian Catholic.

The film throughout insists on such cross-ethnic and cross-racial allegiances. It focuses, for example, on Italian Harlem and especially on the church of Our Lady of Mount Carmel. As the film informs us, the church was built by the labor of Italian workers/parishioners. This is taken as a proof of the communal ethos of the parishioners, who experienced life in those days before World War II in Italian Harlem as if they still lived in their villages. However, the film gives particular attention to the multiracial makeup of the parishioners today as compared to the past, when the church was exclusively Italian Catholic.

Benjamin Franklin High School, founded by Italian American educator Leonardo Covello, is another Harlem institution that argues for multiethnic and multiracial encounters and is also featured in the documentary. The multiracial status of the school today is promoted in the film as well. The film focuses on Italian American politicians such as Fiorello La Guardia and Vito Marcantonio. Marcantonio brought together Italians, Blacks, and Puerto Ricans as a political coalition and initiated legislation to stop lynching.

In terms of coalition politics, *Pane Amaro* does not shy away from more radical activities that questioned the entire discourse of the immigrant's American Dream. It prioritizes the unionizing activities of the Italians; it gives emphasis to the New York garment industry, where many immigrant women worked at the beginning of the twentieth century. It discusses and depicts the 1909 women's strike, which was called "The Uprising of the 20,000" and was supported by middle-class American women. The tragedy that went down in American labor history as the Triangle Shirtwaist Company disaster on March 26, 1911, is also described; 146 immigrant women workers were killed. The film emphasizes that March 26 has become a transethnic memorial day celebrating the struggles of workers.

The film goes so far as to represent anarchism and political radicalism among the Italian immigrants. It narrates the history of the Galleanisti, Sacco and Vanzetti, and the September 16, 1920, Wall Street explosion when thirty-nine people were killed by an anarchist bomb. Finally, the connection of the Italians with the Industrial Workers of the World (IWW) is established. *Pane Amaro* also recalls Paterson, New Jersey, "The World Center of Anarchy," and both its silk factories and strikes by 2,500 self-proclaimed anarchists. Union organizer Carlo Tresca is mentioned as a man who opposed both Mussolini and Stalin and who was eventually assassinated by the Mafia in 1943.

All in all, the film does not bypass modes of representation that argue for the embourgeoisement and Americanization of the Italian Americans. However, it argues that the change undergone in the community involves not only the subjects' transition from Italian to Italian American to American, from immigrant to ethnic to American. It also includes the crossing of racial, economic, political, religious, and class boundaries and insists on the importance of including such crossings in the makeup of the identity of the Americans of Italian descent.

The film modifies the entire discussion of postethnic identity by specifying that it addresses and does not bypass issues of race and class. It focuses not on which collective memory is particularizing, as was the case for much of Italian American history in film, but rather which collective memory can be universal.

DEFTERI PATRIDHA

Whereas *Pane Amaro* indicates personal as well as communal/labor struggles that sometimes end in bitter victories, the title of the Greek documen-

Authenticating Identities in Italian and Greek 309

tary *Defteri Patridha* foregrounds filiation.[21] This is not to claim that affiliation is not an issue in this film. It is actually strongly connected with postethnicity, very much like the other films surveyed in this chapter. As I will point out, like the other films under consideration in this chapter, *Defteri Patridha* insists that affiliation is not necessarily a straightforward process but differs from the other films considered by pointing out that such a process does not conclude necessarily in a happy ending. In fact, this documentary insists, albeit quite ambiguously, on the meaning of the postethnicization of the former immigrant on a personal level.

In terms of plotting the narrative, director Tassos Rigopoulos uses archival material, reconstructed images, and finally interviews, much as do the previously discussed films. However, in his selection of the film's talking heads, Rigopoulos does not prioritize celebrity figures, academics, or politicians; for his interviews, he selects four first-generation immigrants and one second-generation ethnic who autobiographically focus on different types of immigration, ethnicization, and postethnicization. One of them, John Kallas, was at the time a recognizable figure in the New York Greek artistic community, and another, Sano Halo, had become a celebrity in the same community and in Greece because her life story had been written down and published by her daughter Thea. Sam Chekwas, on the other hand, was an entrepreneur whose business was located in the heart of Astoria, New York. In structuring these testimonials, the director employs a palimpsest-like mode of presentation where the stories narrated intermingle so that each one obliquely sheds light on the others in a relationship of intimacy and separation.[22]

The film begins conventionally and linearly. It begins, that is, chronologically with a brief mention of sixteenth-century sailors of Greek origin who arrived on Spanish ships in what today is the United States, primarily in the South and most particularly Florida; the film then takes us briefly to the Greek Revolution (1821–27), the American philhellenic response to it, and the war orphans who were eventually brought to the United States to be educated and sent back to Greece and Anatolia as Protestant missionaries. Subsequently, the well-known nineteenth-century scholars and educators Michael Anagnos and Evangelinos Apostolides/Sophocles are mentioned.[23] A chronological leap forward takes the audience briefly from the beginning of the nineteenth century to the years of the Second Great Migration. Finally, we are introduced to the stories of three twentieth-century immigrants (one recent, Gabriel Panayosoulis, and two older, Sano Halo and Elizabeth Poulos), a second-generation ethnic (John Kallas), and a diasporic affiliate of Greek culture (Sam Checkwas). When the interviewees are introduced, the documentary abandons its linear narrative movement.

At this point the film assumes a palimpsest-like structure and interweaves the interviewees' storylines. The viewer is presented with such a structure as a result of the process of layering, and the subsequent reappearance of the underlining scripts, that is the different layered stories of the interviewees.[24] Their stories intermingle and produce alternative narratives of immigration: however, all these individual stories have as a narrative starting point, the trauma of the rupture of filiation.[25]

Such trauma that this documentary presents has been caused, according to the testimonials, by certain determining factors. The point remains, however, that the subjects cannot anticipate the consequences and cannot reverse the processes which these factors have set in motion. The move to the new/second country or homeland, *"defteri patridha,"* albeit not inevitable as the previous documentaries present it, remains irreversible. As *Defteri Patridha* develops, its plotline weaves in and out of the five subjects' stories; the narrators posit as the reason for their or their families' migration, a crime committed (John Kallas), political sedition (Gabriel Panayosoulis), marriage through the institution of "mail order brides" (Poulos and Halo), and a diasporic search for cultural affiliation (Chekwas).

It is noticeable that economic necessity is not included among these factors; the director perhaps meant to emphasize the embodied and emotional quality of the factors he chose, perhaps randomly, to include. The documentary, after all, focuses on the melancholy quality of the stories narrated, a quality that radiates from each and every story, a melancholy that mourns and comes to terms with a loss.[26] Such losses include generational continuity, community ties, family, culture, language.

Second-generation Greek American engineer and writer John Kallas narrates the story of his father and his father's brothers' illegal entry to the United States after the father and the father's brothers took over the ship where they were working; he continues by recounting his father's move to Maine and eventually his marriage to another immigrant there, underscoring the father's determination to raise a family in the United States. The son, John Kallas, was introduced to the English language at the age of six. He regrets the loss of the Greek language and culture in the third and fourth generation in his family. Elizabeth Poulos reminisces, from a home for the elderly, her family's uprooting from a Black Sea coastal town in 1922, her immigration to the United States as a mail-order bride, and her childless marriage to a Greek immigrant. She refers to her loneliness after her husband's death and her final years in a home for the elderly. Gabriel Panayosoulis, a relatively recent immigrant, narrates his decision to move to America after World War II for political reasons. His marriage to a Latin American woman and his new family imply his further removal from the language and the culture in which he was raised.

Sano Halo, a ninety-two-year-old woman at the time of the documentary, presents a special case in the documentary. In fact, her story spreads throughout the fifty-two minutes of the film and is developed with many details; the film concludes with her. Finally, Sam Checkwas is a Nigerian national who lived and studied in Greece before he moved to Astoria, where he owned at the time the only Greek-language bookstore in the New York area and perhaps on the entire East Coast.

These stories emphasize multiple identifications for the five interviewees. Such identifications complicate ethnicity/ethnicization and do not present it as the straightforward process the other documentaries in this chapter claim. Furthermore, *Defteri Patridha* does not insist on the inevitability of immigration as fulfillment and success that other similar films do. It does not seek to make connections between Greek and American cultures resorting to popular American myths. All in all, it does not treat immigration to the United States as a teleological event. And neither does it treat Greek American ethnic identity as well-defined and unproblematic.

In fact, it is the melancholia of being asked to declare one's "true" ethnicity that informs the narrating subjects who have to deal with the reality of the loss very poignantly. Kallas's heartfelt sigh that his grandchildren could perhaps learn to use at least one Greek word, "*pappou*/grandpa," as a vestige of a lost culture; Poulos's lonely recollections of a life and a place she cannot go back to because neither one of them any longer exists: these experiences characterize the trauma of the rupture of filiation. However, it is Sano Halo's dramatic story narrated through almost the entire film that introduces the dazzling series of routes taken by her; and it is also Sam Checkwas's voice and presence that characterize the film's view of diaspora, filiation, and affiliation. As a whole, these aspects make *Defteri Patridha* different from the typically celebratory history of immigration and achievement in the other films discussed here.

Sano Halo was born and raised to the age of ten in a Pontic/Black Sea area village whose name she remembers but whose location she has forgotten.[27] Sent on a death march with the women and children of her family in 1922 by the Turkish authorities, Sano Halo lost everyone on the way. A lone survivor, she was originally taken in as a servant by a Kurdish farming family who mistreated her and changed her name to Sano; she consequently ran away and worked for an Armenian family in Diyarbakir. As a mail-order bride, she married an Assyrian American Christian, moved to and lived in New York, had ten children, and emerged to tell her story in the final years of her life, first on paper through her daughter, then through film.[28] By then, she was already a carrier of several dimly remembered cultural traditions and partially forgotten languages: Pontic Greek, Ottoman Turkish, Kurdish, Armenian, and Assyrian. And yet in the film she is the only one interviewed exclusively in English. Unlike Poulos, Panayosoulis, Checkwas, and even Kallas, Sano Halo does not use any Modern Greek or even the Pontic variety of the language. However, when pressured by her interviewer to speak Greek, perhaps Pontic Greek, her response concludes the documentary as follows: Sano Halo sits up as if to pay her respects to what she is about to do and then she recites the Christian creed of faith in impeccable *koine* Greek.

What are we to make of Halo's testifying to a language that to all practical purposes she has lost but can still remember in texts of its *koine* form, because of her early Greek Orthodox indoctrination? It seems that filiation in her case represents her turning not to an originary native language and culture but to an institution, that of the Orthodox Church. Such an institution implemented a program of Hellenization and ethnonationalism throughout the nineteenth and the beginning of the twentieth centuries in

Ottoman Turkey; it left its marks on young members of the minority communities as the last scene of the documentary proclaims. In the case of Sano Halo, her shattering, often tragic, but sometimes also semicomic diasporic experiences, the forced routes she has taken, have established the irreversibility of the rupture of filiation more so than in the case of the other interviewees.

The last among these interviewees to appear in the film is Sam Checkwas. His introduction in the documentary provides a dynamic confluence of questions that have been circulating in the interviews, which in his explanations peak and acquire their complex substance. The director presents Chekwas to the viewers first by voice. The camera takes us around Greek Astoria and stops in front of the Greek bookstore as we hear but do not see its owner explaining in perfect Demotic Greek the reason why the store is there. Then, the camera focuses on Chekwas's smiling face. Such an introduction carries a mild shock value for an audience who associates a Greek voice and language with a white man's face. The reversal of such expectations opens an imperceptible crack in this film for the consideration of race among Greek Americans and Greeks. The move from voice to face also indicates a complexity that informs the structure of this documentary as far as the other interviews are concerned as well. We are presented with a Greek speaker, a self-proclaimed affiliate of Greek culture whose ethnicization is a consequence of a series of diasporic relocations: from Nigeria to Greece and then to the United States, from Nigerian to Nigerian Greek to Nigerian Greek American. This is a complex collocation and confluence of identities that competes with those in the case of Sano Halo and in that of Elizabeth Poulos.

As he narrates his story, Checkwas is also a self-proclaimed Nigerian-born representative of the new immigration to Europe; he lived, studied, and married in Thessaloniki, Greece, but eventually emigrated to the United States. Checkwas is certainly not a typical immigrant from Africa to Greece and the European Union; he moved to Greece as a university student. But considering himself an affiliate of Greek culture and moved by an enterprising spirit, he founded a Greek-language bookstore in the New York area. His decision was motivated by his desire to promote primarily Greek vernacular culture. His anxiety as revealed in the film is that Greek culture and language are becoming defunct in the United States. His joy becomes apparent when young people who enter the bookstore look for modern and contemporary Greek writers.

Sam Chekwas's and Sano Halo's narratives introduce what the other immigration stories surveyed here lack: the idea of performativity in the context of ethnicity and race. Here we have an alternative to racial and ethnic categorization; instead we witness a blurring of ethnicity and race in the construction of a postethnic identity. Sam Chekwas and Sano Halo are American citizens who perform in the film their identities as affiliates of Greek society; in the case of Sam, we also have a proponent of Greek vernacular culture, one who openly proclaims himself a Nigerian.

Sam Chekwas's and Sano Halo's stories problematize the idea of postethnicity. *Where* exactly is the crossing point these two traverse to become Americans? And furthermore, *what is* this crossing point? How many lines did they have to cross? And what happens to the confluence and contiguity of all the identities they bring with them? Doesn't their contiguity point to the fact that cultural difference is a fragile concept undone by perceptions that create affinities? And aren't their stories more proof that what we call assimilation is simply an idealistic construct, an empty letter? How do these voices compare with the celebratory tenor of the voices we heard in the other documentaries discussed in this chapter? Finally, and most important, can we accept that race and by extension ethnicity is socially "constructed" and at the same time can we simply change what we want race and ethnicity to mean? And is it not true that "the meanings of race and [ethnicity] are socially created through interaction between and within individuals and groups?"[29]

What persists throughout *Defteri Patridha*'s testimonials is a wistfulness and a melancholia. Could it be that melancholia in this film is a structure of feeling which allows the interviewees to come to terms with the rupture of filiation? Is it not the distancing procedure that argues for the subjects' move into a state of postethnicity? Such questions suggest how *Defteri Patridha* differs from the other documentaries discussed in this chapter. The five interviewees cross that psychic line from wistfulness to melancholia to become Americans.

Conclusion

Pane Amaro and *Defteri Patridha* emphasize that immigration and postethnicity involve more than the amelioration of the economic status of the immigrants and their descendants. They do not suggest that the immigrants' aspirations to become US citizens involve a transformation for which presumably they come prepared; postethnicity is not inevitable or predictable. Having absorbed myths such as America as the promised land, the Manifest Destiny of the white colonizers, and so forth while still in their homelands, the immigrants are not necessarily already Americanized before immigration. However, such seems to be the argument of *The Journey* as well as *They Came to Chicago*.

Pane Amaro and *Defteri Patridha* analyze the experience of the immigrant assuming a new identity. The immigrant crossing of economic, political, religious, linguistic, and class boundaries takes priority in these two films and complicates the easily defended assumptions of the interviewees of the two US documentaries. The interviewees in *The Journey* as well as *They Came to Chicago* speak, however emotionally, about their ethnic background from a self-aggrandizing position of postethnicity. What is lacking from their words and worlds is any reference to the trauma of a loss, as well as the inevitable dilemmas of the necessity of racial, class, and religious affiliations. In so many words, what is lacking in *The Journey* as well as *They Came to Chicago* is the narrative recognition of what is left behind, but also what needs to be transcended when the immigrant assumes a postethnic identity.

Furthermore, and in such a context, it is my claim that the differences among the four documentaries are motivated by the humanitarian crisis resulting from the dogma of "fortress Europe" that has involved Italy and Greece in the past decades. *Pane Amaro* and *Defteri Patridha* function as mirrors that forcefully reflect and introduce issues of political radicalization, racial and religious affiliations, identity collocations, ethnic performativity, and most important, psychic traumas. These issues are presented and analyzed vis-à-vis the history of the older immigration to the Americas, but they are also relevant to the new wave of immigration. These issues are all but missing from *The Journey* and *They Came to Chicago*. Certainly, the two documentaries, primarily albeit not exclusively, address a US audience, whereas *Pane Amaro* and *Defteri Patridha* address a Greek and Italian one. My reading suggests that although all four films reconstruct the immigrant presence in the United States, *The Journey* and *They Came to Chicago* are past-oriented narratives whereas *Pane Amaro* and *Defteri Patridha* are future-oriented ones.

All four documentaries read and reconstruct the history of immigration of the two groups starting at different narrative points but focusing exclusively on the Second Great Migration; they look back at immigration to the Americas as a historical event connected with modernity and modernization; in retrospect, they evaluate this historical move of people in positive terms. However, it is *Pane Amaro* and *Defteri Patridha* that take the discussion of this historical event into the present. For example, the insistence of the former on racism in "the promised land" or the emphasis of the latter on ethnic performativity in the construction of a postethnic identity underline that such issues are still open to discussion and theorization. Such a problematic transcends the boundaries of US immigration history and connects the past with the present—and most urgently with the future. It certainly has its bearings on the refugee crisis facing "the new promised land," Europe.

NOTES

1. Byzantine rule of parts of the Italian Peninsula lasted until 1071. The Venetian rule of Crete (1665) and other areas of the Byzantine/Greek world lasted well until 1715. The medieval and modern intellectual exchanges between the Greeks and Italians had always been very strong; the long list of Greek graduates of the University of Padua attests to such an exchange.

2. See Georgakas, *Greek America at Work*; Papanikolas, *Toil and Rage in a New Land*; Ottanelli, *Italian Workers of the World*.

3. Perhaps the reason was the natives' reaction to the overwhelming numbers of the Italian immigrants entering the country; in contrast, the Greeks immigrated in more modest numbers. The negative image associated with the Italians had to do with the criminal organizations that they allegedly imported to the United States from southern Italy and Sicily. Furthermore, the Italians were associated with anarchism and terrorism.

4. The controversy that erupted around the popular TV serial *The Sopranos* (1999–2007) is indicative of the reactions to negative stereotyping of

the Italian Americans. Hollywood has been kinder to the Greeks than it has been to the Italians. The representation of the immigrant as an innocuous albeit inarticulate outsider in films like *The Juke Girl* (1942) or *Thieves Highway* (1948), the misunderstood Greek soldiers in *The Glory Brigade* (1952), and the heroic defender of democracy in *Guerilla Girl* (1951) are some early examples. The 1950s witnessed a discovery of an exotic Greece by Hollywood, and primarily Fox, with films like *The Boy on a Dolphin* (1957), *The Angry Hills* (1959), *The 300 Spartans* (1962), among others. In the 1960s, extremely popular films like *Never on Sunday* (1960) and *Zorba the Greek* (1964) continued to exoticize but still would not demonize the Greeks.

5. The crossing of boundaries between Greek and Italian immigration studies examined in this chapter introduces the idea of how US ethnic studies could benefit, enrich, and understand their content. The editors and the authors of volumes such as the present one certainly bring their expertise from different fields in the humanities, but most important, they represent both home and homeland. Furthermore, their work reflects an important aspect of their national, ethnic, and diasporic identities brought to bear on their research. See, for example, Anagnostou, "Model Americans, Quintessential Greeks"; Patrona, *Return Narratives*; Kalogeras, "Entering through the Golden Door."

6. Donna Gabaccia and Frazer Ottonelli have pointed out the threat that nation-states believe that they face, due to the influx of immigrants and refugees, the cultural diversity caused by international migrations and the globalization of capital. Gabaccia and Ottonelli, "Diaspora or International Proletariat?" 61.

7. Greece and Italy have been more immediately and dramatically affected by the migration of refugees than other EU countries, and they experience far more intimately the crisis in the European identity, which they had believed in enthusiastically with the emergence of "New Europe" after World War II and the subsequent formation of the EU. Consequently, both countries have struggled to come to grips with the new reality of the influx of refugees and immigrants in terms of a past experience. In other words, these films objectify immigration *qua* immigration as an intimate and yet distant historical phenomenon for Greece and Italy today; they describe and analyze it as an experience of their own people at the turn of the twentieth century when both Greece and Italy were countries of immigrants. They posit this perception face-to-face with the humanitarian crisis that concerns both countries as well as with the counterforces (racism, xenophobia, ultranationalism) engendered by the presence of the refugees and the immigrants; such counterforces have spread across the EU countries in general and constitute a threat to its cohesion. See Loshitzky, *Screening Strangers*, for filmic treatments.

8. The production of *The Journey* was primarily financed by Greek American funds. The National Bank of Greece and the Greek Parliament TV Channel also supported the production. The director, Maria Iliou, is a very accomplished, award-winning transnational artist who studied in Italy and Greece and lives and works, according to her CV, between Athens and New York. Greek American financial supporters of its production, US political figures, and academics appear and speak in the documentary, investing the narrative with an official tone. This documentary was screened on the Greek Public TV Channel and the Benaki Museum in Athens.

My discussion of these four documentaries is not meant to categorize the European-produced ones as "good" and the US ones as "bad." I simply meant to underline the different ideological points of departure of the narratives of the two sets of films. My interest in all of them was kindled by the realization that the US-produced ones "spoke" from within the community and in vindication of the place of that community within the history of the United States (hence my comment that they seem to be past-oriented); the two European-produced ones, on the other hand, viewed immigration to the United States as part of the global movement of populations. In the latter case, the ideological, political, and humanitarian issues relevant to such movements do not belong to the past; they need to be constantly updated and are in need of constant reevaluation. Hence my comment that the two European ones are more future-oriented.

9. Two PBS documentaries produced and directed by George Veras on the Greek Americans in the late 1990s introduced a discussion on the community's self-representation. The interviews focused exclusively on high profile figures such as actors, politicians, athletes who uttered stereotypical narratives of family cohesion, ambition, struggle, and success much like *The Journey*. The strong ties between modern Greek Americans and the ancient Greeks were also part of the stories of the interviewees. The jackets of the videocassettes even declared that "our accomplishments in the arts, politics and education ... echo the glorious past of ancient Greece." Such a line of argument expurgates any kind of conflict or negativity the community or the individual immigrants and ethnics might have encountered. Furthermore, Yiorgos Anagnostou mentions that the version shown on PBS differs from the version reproduced on the videocassettes and DVDs, even though both include Olympia Dukakis's memories of a problematic childhood as a Greek American. Anagnostou, "When 'Second Generation' Narratives and Hollywood Meet."

10. If *The Sopranos* raised the fury of the Italian Americans, the response to the fantastically successful Greek American comedy *My Big Fat Greek*

Wedding revealed the sensitivity to ethnic stereotyping still prevalent among the Greek Americans. For a cogent analysis, see ibid.

11. A postethnic identity predicates that ethnicity is no longer important in the self-identification of the subject socially, culturally, or existentially. Such a stage sounds suspiciously like a stage of complete assimilation. And yet, could postethnicity or even assimilation be conceived as nothing more than still another identity assumed by the immigrant, the ethnic, the diasporic in an effort to belong? Could home permanently erase the memory and the influence of homeland?

12. Hollinger, *Post-Ethnic America*, 116.

13. Antiparental and profilial symbolize the turning away from the past, leaving behind the parents, and espousing the future represented by the children, who are to be born or raised Americans.

14. This is not new in the lore of the Second Great Migration. At the beginning of the twentieth century, the popular press in Greece employed this connection between the ancient and the new migration and suggested that the Greek immigrants were to strive to emulate their ancient predecessors in colonizing culturally their new home (Lykoudes). In Iliou's film, labor historian Dan Georgakas complicates this view by pointing out that the journey refers both to the outward thrust of the Greek colonization but also to the nostalgic tendencies of the immigrants.

15. The interview with Martha Klironomos of San Francisco State University drew a lot of attention when the film was screened on Greek TV. I suggest that Professor Klironomos's emotional response during the interview reflects this interpretation of Odysseus's journey, which labor historian Dan Georgakas described earlier in the film. It also exemplifies the theme prioritized in Rigopoulos's documentary *Defteri patridha*. For once in Iliou's film, mourning/loss and melancholia provide a different tenor to the largely celebratory accounts of most of the other interviews.

16. Reading through Henry Pratt Fairchild's Yale University dissertation *The Greeks in the USA* (1911) could cure any fantasies that the US intellectuals at the time (1880–1924) entertained the thought that such a connection could be true.

17. An interesting film on this subject is *The Glory Brigade* (1952). It was filmed as part of a series of propaganda films in the early 1950s, when the Cold War was at its peak. In the 1950s and in the flurry of films on World War II, *The Glory Brigade* remains something of an anomaly; it looks at US involvement in the Korean War and the Cold War. The democratic values of the Greek society are indisputably proven, according to the film, when Greece sends a brigade to fight Chinese communism. Furthermore, the plot of the film,

without much ceremony, connects common Greek and American political and cultural interests. For a more thorough analysis of this film's ending see Kalogeras, "Working with and against Conventions."

18. MacDougal, *Transcultural Cinema*, 245.

19. Hollinger, *Post-Ethnic America*, 3.

20. See also Marianna de Marco Torgovnick's personal narratives in *Crossing Ocean Parkway* and Fred Gardaphé's edited volume *Anti-Italianism*. Racial politics are viewed as central in the experience of the Italian ethnics. Gardaphé concludes that "ignorance of Italian American history invites us to regenerate a racist mentality that insures us that white will dominate" (2). Torgovnick, on the other hand, underscores the uncomfortable transformation of formerly exclusively Catholic neighborhoods (24).

21. Filiation relates to generational continuity and natural bonds and "natural forms of authority—involving obedience, fear, love, respect, and instinctual conflict [whereas] the new affiliative relationship changes these bonds into what seem to be transpersonal forms—such as guild consciousness, consensus, collegiality . . . and the hegemony of dominant culture. The filiative scheme belongs to the realms of nature and of 'life', whereas affiliation belongs exclusively to culture and society." Said, *The World, the Text, and the Critic*, 20.

22. Rigopoulos's approach to *Defteri Patridha* reflects David McDougal's idea of a documentary: "For me the commitment to documentary has always been a commitment to the possibilities of discovery and testimony—that is, to the proposition that ways can be found to document experiences actually happening to people that have never before been given public expression." McDougal, *Transcultural Cinema*, 225.

23. Michael Anagnos (1837–1906) became director of the Perkins Institute for the Blind in Boston in 1876. Evangelinos Apostolides/Sophocles (1804–1883) was professor of classics at Harvard University.

24. Dillon, *The Palimpsest*, 3.

25. "A trauma is an event in the subject's life defined by the intensity, by the subject's incapacity to respond adequately to it, and by the upheaval and long-lasting effects that it brings about in the psychical organization." Laplanche and Pontalis, *The Language of Psychoanalysis*, 465.

26. Melancholia is an "intrapsychic process, occurring after the loss of a loved object, whereby the subject gradually manages to detach himself from this object." Ibid., 485.

27. Elizabeth Cowie suggests that "remembering is not simply the recall of past events; it is also the reencountering of emotions attached to those past events and their losses, and in this, it is work of memorializing that can

become a process of mourning in which pastness is commemorated as the having been, which the subject is able to mourn rather than remember traumatically." Cowie, *Recording Reality*, 156.

28. Halo, *Not Even My Name*.

29. I follow here the work of Kimberly DaCosta and Rebecca King, who argue, "Most people realize that race is socially constructed, which means that although they know that race is not 'real' in a biological sense, they cannot just refuse to use race as analytical category, cannot simply individually change what they want race to mean, nor can they ignore that race has very real consequences." DaCosta and King, "Changing Face, Changing Race," 229.

Bibliography

FILMOGRAPHY

Amella, Gia. *And They Came to Chicago*. 2007.
Iliou, Maria. *The Journey: The Greek American Experience*. 2007.
Norelli, Gianfanco. *Pane Amaro* [*Bitter Bread*]. 2009.
Rigopoulos, Tassos. *Ellines kai Amerikanoi: Defteri Patridha* [*Greeks and Americans: Second Motherland*]. 2001.
Veras, George. *The Greek Americans*. 1998.
———. *The Greek Americans: Passing the Torch*. 1999.

PRINTED SOURCES

Anagnostou, Yiorgos. "Model Americans, Quintessential Greeks: Ethnic Success and Assimilation in Diaspora." *Diaspora* 12, no. 3 (2003): 279–327.
———. "When 'Second Generation' Narratives and Hollywood Meet: Making Ethnicity in *My Big Fat Greek Wedding*." *MELUS* 37, no. 4 (2012): 139–63.
Connell, William J., and Fred Gardaphé. *Anti-Italianism: Essays on a Prejudice*. London: Palgrave Macmillan, 2010.
Cowie, Elizabeth. *Recording Reality: Desiring the Real*. Minneapolis: University of Minnesota Press, 2011.
DaCosta, Kimberly, and Rebecca King. "Changing Face, Changing Race: The Remaking of Race in Japanese American and African American Communities." In *The Multiracial Experience*, edited by Maria P. P. Root, 227–44. Thousand Oaks, CA: Sage Publications, 1996.

Dillon, Sarah. *The Palimpsest: Literature, Criticism, Theory.* New York: Bloomsbury, 2013.

Fairchild, Henry Pratt. *The Greeks in the USA.* New Haven, CT: Yale University Press, 1911.

Gabaccia, Donna R., and Frazer Ottanelli. "Diaspora or International Proletariat? Italian Labor Migration, and the Making of Multiethnic States, 1815–1939." *Diaspora* 6, no. 1 (1997): 61–84.

Georgakas, Dan. *Greek America at Work.* New York: Greek American Labor Council, 1992.

Halo, Thea. *Not Even My Name.* New York: Picador, 2001.

Hollinger, David A. *Post-Ethnic America: Beyond Multiculturalism.* New York: Basic Books, 2000.

Kalogeras, Yiorgos. "Entering through the Golden Door: Cinematic Representations of a Mythical Moment." *Journal of Mediterranean Studies* 21, no. 1 (2012): 77–99.

———. "Working with and against Conventions: The Hollywood Career of A. I. Bezzerides." *Journal of Modern Hellenism* 32 (2016): 66–81.

Laplanche, J., and J. B. Pontalis. *The Language of Psychoanalysis.* New York: Norton, 1973.

Loshitzky, Yosefa. *Screening Strangers: Migration and Diaspora in Contemporary European Cinema.* Bloomington: Indiana University Press, 2010.

Lykoudes, Emmanuel. *The Immigrants.* Athens: n.p., 1903.

MacDougal, David. *Transcultural Cinema.* Princeton, NJ: Princeton University Press, 1999.

Ottanelli, Frazer M. *Italian Workers of the World: Labor Migration and the Formation of the Multiethnic States.* Urbana: University of Illinois Press, 2001.

Papanikolas, Helen. *Toil and Rage in a New Land: The Greek Immigrants in Utah.* Salt Lake City: Utah State Historical Society, 1974.

Patrona, Theodora D. *Return Narratives: Ethnic Space in Late-Twentieth-Century Greek American and Italian American Literature.* Madison, NJ: Fairleigh Dickinson University Press, 2017.

Peck, Gunther. *Reinventing Free Labor: Padrones and Immigrant Workers in the North American West, 1880–1930.* Cambridge: Cambridge University Press, 2000.

Said, Edward W. *The World, the Text, and the Critic.* Cambridge, MA: Harvard University Press, 1983.

Torgovnick, Marianna de Marco. *Crossing Ocean Parkway: Readings by an Italian American Daughter.* Chicago: University of Chicago Press, 1994.

American(ish) Rebels

Class, Gender, and Ethnicity in Moonstruck and My Big Fat Greek Wedding

Michail C. Markodimitrakis

The representation of the ethnic American subject in popular culture, especially film and television, often reinforces stereotypical understandings of ethnic identities. Non-WASP characters have been portrayed simplistically as distorted or otherwise inappropriate ethnic tokens; contemporary examples include the mobster trope and related depictions of inner city crime, as well as overachieving progenies who strive relentlessly for upward mobility, often with the benevolent help of a white savior (e.g., *Gran Torino*, 2007). This storytelling practice leads to one-dimensional plots based on cultural prejudices, perpetuating the image of ethnic Americans who strive to assimilate to mainstream models of American identity.[1] The casual depiction of boisterous Mediterranean characters with strong ties to Orthodox and Catholic Christianity and extended families glosses over the development of hybrid identities in younger generations of immigrants and/or ethnic Americans. For Italian American and Greek American characters onscreen, the portrayal of their journey to assimilation into the "melting pot" of American society—a journey during which the characters maintain segments of their ethnic cultures—is often connected to class aspirations and social mobility. However, the process of merging with an idolized America also includes performances of ethnicity in which ethnic subjects cross class and gender roles in public and private spaces. The post-immigrant generations of Italian Americans and Greek Americans, while representing a socioeconomic status that differs from that of their ancestors, explore their American identity through cultural anxieties related to their personalized, more nuanced pursuit of happiness.

The ethnic American family, the subject of various film genres, is foregrounded in two of the most widely acclaimed contemporary romantic comedies: the Italian American–themed *Moonstruck* (1987) and its Greek American counterpart *My Big Fat Greek Wedding* (2002).[2] Set in New York and Chicago respectively, the storylines follow Loretta Castorini and Toula Portokalos in their journeys of self-discovery and empowerment. Having each been raised in close-knit immigrant families, the two female characters navigate multiple aspects of their identities and social spaces, such as the workplace and the church, with their own codes and languages informed by American and ethnic culture. Producing and resolving personal crises, Italian American and Greek American men and women negotiate their ethnic and class identities in public as well as private settings. As both fathers and partners, Greek American and Italian American men demand respect and obedience from the women in their lives, often inciting conflicts as their patriarchal roles are challenged by their mothers, daughters, or partners. While the Italian American and Greek American women characters in both films undermine the authority of their male counterparts without the males' having fully understood the challenge to their patriarchal model of the family, the women are still limited by prescribed cultural, gender, and societal roles. As conflicts occur both inside and outside of the domestic sphere, the differing sociocultural settings call for varied performances of ethnic and class anxieties and elicit rebellious actions and cultural compromises.

Comedy and humor have often provided fruitful ground for the examination of stereotypes and cultural practices among ethnic groups in America. Scholars and comedic artists discuss ethnicity in their work as performative, open to cultural interpretations and influences on a communal and personal level.³ Ethnic comedians and comedic productions, whether stand-up performances or television shows and films, modified their themes and approaches throughout the twentieth century under the influence of the civil rights movement and multiculturalism. The approaches of the creators toward their ethnic characters greatly vary, reflecting the different historical moments and the corresponding political climate in the United States. Such varied depictions can be also attributed to the ethnic identities of directors and writers: on the one hand, Norman Jewison, a much-awarded WASP directing *Moonstruck*, a film about Italian Americans, was positioned outside the ethnicity in question; on the other hand, Nia Vardalos, a Greek American artist, wrote *My Big Fat Greek Wedding*. Ultimately, both movies use satire and humor to represent ethnic identities. However, satirical representations of characters' responses to their ethnic legacy and habits transcend what Laura Ruberto (2007) describes as "exaggerated ethnicity" (88),⁴ a simplistic exaggeration of ethnic identity that reproduces and sustains cultural and gender misconceptions.

The comedic genre allows for a closer examination of stereotypes by reflecting what is typically assumed in public discourse, and can thus prompt an understanding of individual and group identities as complex and dynamic. In his discussion of ethnic comedies, David Gillota posits multiculturalism as a central influence on the narrative structure and plot of the works he studies. He defines multiculturalism as an ideology that "promotes the active celebration and embracing" of ethnic characteristics in American context.⁵ For the films compared in this chapter, multiculturalism shapes the central narratives through the directors' exploration of what it means to be "ethnic American." The directors project an understanding of multiculturalism as group enactment of common cultural metaphors, such as the "melting pot" or "tossed salad" ideologies, such that members can still retain their respective in-group characteristics. Thus, they are not completely American, but instead are moving toward assimilation toward American cultural models. What makes the particular comedies distinct, perhaps *Moonstruck* more so than *My Big Fat Greek Wedding*, is the creators' attempt to subvert the expected treatment of ethnic characters in various roles. More conventional ethnic films with similar themes typically underline the characters' singular relationship to and interaction with the dominant white culture. In contrast, *Moonstruck* and *My Big Fat Greek Wedding* both show their main characters attempting to redefine themselves in terms of gender, class, and ethnic categories. Despite the exaggerated elements of their respective films, Jewison and Vardalos construct comedic situations where ethnicity is not the defining element of the characters' behavior. Instead, they each depict processes of ethnic belonging that are influenced by personal desires and interpersonal interactions, and therefore avoid an essentialized view of ethnic differences. The families in the two films have dynamic relationships to the world around them; they each interact with the dominant culture through the lens of their cultural inheritance and social expectations. Ethnic identities in the two films are fluid, and the characters' desires transcend rigid confines of crystallized stereotypes, which Ruberto refers to as the "whitewash" of assimilation to the dominant American culture.[6] The two films, both critically acclaimed, show how two models of popular culture, each immersed in a particular historical context, address the issue of happiness and belonging, thereby foregrounding two ethnic American communities with strong intrafamilial relations and close connections to both a religious identity and a historical homeland.

The Italian American and Greek American families feature members of different generations who are constantly negotiating their identity with members of their family, ethnic culture, and mainstream culture, asking more broadly what it means to be an American at home and in the public domain. Gender identities are contested through domestic and external influences, pulling the Castorini and Portokalos families between stable, inherited roles on the one hand and socially and politically innovative identities on the other hand, particularly those related to the expression of feminism in public and private domains. The gendering of space, as Doreen Massey observes, reflects and affects how gender is constructed and understood, creating expectations and perpetuating stereotypes about ethnic and gender performances—even generating false memories of gender relations within the discussed ethnicities.[7] Until fairly recently, the humorous representation of gender interactions was largely controlled by men;[8] thus, Vardalos's film, an independent production, should be credited for the agency it assigns to its protagonist. This enables Toula to tell her story from her perspective, offering the audience an opportunity to follow her thoughts with a first-person narrative. Complementing the role of perspective in the narrative of the film, both public and private settings shape the viewers' understanding of ethnicity, class, and sexuality, particularly in spaces marked by gender and class performance: the kitchen, the opera, the restaurant, and the workspace.

My Big Fat Greek Wedding and *Moonstruck* foreground complexities of identity-making among immigrants and ethnic Americans as they strive to find their place in American society. The comparison of the two films allows for a close reading of ethnic Americans' expectations to participate fully in modern-day American society, and the resulting departure from ethnic cultures and practices. While some of the practices are often viewed as antiquated, the main characters' crises echo internal conflicts of many ethnic communities as they witnessed a transformation of model citizenship and the creation of new paths towards the American Dream. A careful analysis of two films from different eras can reveal how changes in American society in the twentieth and early twenty-first century were expressed externally, as seen through the characters' persistent attempts to accumulate financial and social capital.

Protagonists in the two movies face various difficulties, depending on their generation as ethnic Americans. Toula's parents are first-generation and Loretta's second, yet both the Portokalos and Castorini families perform their ethnic anxieties through social, economic, and personally motivated actions, attempting to redefine themselves as members of American society, while also struggling to retain their distinct cultural identities.

Masters of the House, Anxious Performers

The male characters in both films follow the action from the sidelines. Often unaware of the plans and desires of their female counterparts, the males from the Castorini and Cammaneri families in *Moonstruck* and the Portokalos family in *My Big Fat Greek Wedding* are often trapped in archetypal patriarchal roles. Thus, fathers and sons from the main families, as well as business owners, boyfriends, and prospective husbands perform their social and ethnic identities by attempting to establish dominance, inciting conflict whenever possible. Set in the 1980s, *Moonstruck* takes place in the heart of New York City in neighborhoods where Italian American culture prevails. The plot introduces several Italian American men whose behavior is at times caricatured.[9] Johnny, Loretta's fiancé, exemplifies the complex of social and ethnic identities that Italian American men enact in Hollywood films. His reluctance to set a date for the wedding, citing his mother's death as a reason, subverts the expectation of the strong ethnic patriarch. However, Johnny's reverence for his mother also illustrates another cultural stereotype, described in a study by Penelope Morris and Perry Wilson, that mother figures in American families of Italian (and often Greek) descent exert considerable power over their sons' futures.[10] On the other hand, Gus and Cosmo, Toula's and Loretta's fathers, while representing two different periods of immigration, behave similarly as traditional patriarchs during family crises, thereby maintaining the stability of their identities and surroundings.[11] Reminiscent of Harry J. Elam Jr.'s depiction of race as performance,[12] the fathers of the Greek American and Italian American families perform their ethnicity and social position in the form of dress code, material possessions, and customary obligations, such as paying for a daughter's wedding or providing for the newlywed's future.

The masters of the ethnic household find their domains and social roles in transition. In urban New York of the 1980s, Cosmo provides for his family as a successful plumber, a profitable (in his case) blue-collar occupation. However, unlike the stereotypical representation of the working-class ethnic American, Cosmo is self-employed, well-dressed, extremely articulate when explaining the cost and quality of his work, and, according to his wife, "rich as Roosevelt." Distancing himself from the working-class stereotypes of immigrant, blue-collar professions, Cosmo's class performance follows prevalent depictions of Italian Americans in postwar perceptions and Hollywood representations of Italian American culture, as demonstrated in Gardaphé's seminal work.[13] Cosmo has lavish taste: he dresses well, owns a luxury car, and buys expensive jewelry for his mistress, which he gives to her in posh restaurants. He also takes her to the opera, a public space, as Marcia Citron argues, typically associated with social status and closely connected with Italian culture.[14]

The opera is also a location in which the intersection of class, gender, and ethnicity becomes apparent. Aside from its personal significance to Cosmo himself, the opera as a public space provides for the performance of middle-class aspirations. Positing a diachronic connection between space and gender, Natalie Fullwood describes these as "interlinked social structures with real impact on lived realities," emphasizing the processes through which space and gender are renegotiated and maintained as a unity.[15] When Cosmo and Loretta meet at the opera, each accompanied by their own extramarital partners, Cosmo reluctantly speaks with his daughter in order to maintain his facade as a member of a professional educated class. Donna Peberdy, in her discussion of Butler and Modleski, argues that in social encounters—and their cinematic representations—masculinity is performed to eliminate the threat posed by women, so that male dominance is reaffirmed.[16] In this case, the confrontation between father and daughter is enacted as an aggressive low-tone conversation that ends with each turning away from the other, deescalating their fight; both leave with knowledge of each other's infidelity while simultaneously hiding their private affairs from outsiders present (*fare la brutta figura*).[17]

In contrast to his smoothly scripted behavior in the public domain, in domestic scenarios Cosmo has difficulty negotiating his intersecting identities. The Castorini patriarch owns a large old house that he refuses to sell, and he listens to opera and classical music in his free time. However, he is reluctant to pay for anything else, especially Loretta's wedding; his attitude is oppositional to traditional Italian culture and custom, as his father points out. His body language, which is more controlled in public as compared to private domains, also reflects his attempt to adopt unmarked white American behavior: as Gardaphé notes, "being [white] American means talking without using hands."[18] Throughout the film Cosmo always tries to be less kinetic in social settings, saving his intensity for the privacy of domestic settings. For example, his extramarital affair represents a personal identity crisis for Cosmo, and it affects his domestic performance as paterfamilias. Yet the household setting allows Cosmo's gender and ethnic identities to be reaffirmed. As opposed to Peberdy's description of the "average white male" in his discussion of Michael Douglas's erratic public performance of midlife crisis,[19] Cosmo's character ultimately deals with identity crisis within the family institution, discussing his problems openly at the family dinner table. Cosmo repents with the help of his family, who remind him of his domestic role and duties, and he returns to his role as Italian American patriarch. Ultimately, his development from a distant, negligent, and adulterous patriarch to a vulnerable and apologetic husband and father foreshadows the concern for white middle-class masculine identity that emerged in the 1990s.[20]

In the Greek American family of the new millennium, a blend of an anachronistic representation of familiar relations and a modern middle-class lifestyle, Gus Portokalos is more comfortable with the performance of his ethnicity and the ties to his class and masculinity, although his presence is positioned within the intimate social space of family and community. Belonging to a first generation of immigrants who came to the United States in the 1960s, Gus owns both a large house in the suburbs of Chicago and a Greek restaurant, Dancing Zorba's, which reflects his desire to display publicly his Greek heritage.

American suburbia, as a primarily middle-class white space, challenges Gus's sense of Greek identity, which relies on the patriarchal structure of his household. He responds by modeling his home as a kitsch imitation of an ancient Greek temple, a public display of his cultural capital and his economic status, which according to Rodanthi Tzanelli ironically undermines his claim to being middle-class.[21] Gus's ethnic anxiety is also expressed symbolically in his language: he often traces the roots of English words, often incorrectly, to some stage of the Greek language. In this way he resists assimilation to the American middle class, to which he economically aspires to belong. Gus recognizes language as a cultural artifact that can protect his legacy and memories, as well as provide a medium to express ethnic pride. The continuous effort to reinforce linear cultural links to ancient Greek civilization also takes the form of an inclusion/exclusion (*dhikos/xenos*) dialectic in the case of Ian, his future son-in-law. Toula's marriage to Ian could be considered an instance of upward social mobility, since he is white and his family is visibly affluent; however, for Gus, Ian is a *xenos*, a member of the dominant ethnic group that the Greek patriarch opposes culturally. Gus strongly refuses to accept Ian in the Greek American family unit until he has ascertained that Ian is not a cultural threat.

While Gus resists some aspects of white middle-class male identity, he performs other components that he finds acceptable. His behavior echoes Monica McDermott's discussion of white identity as a "set of dynamic yet patterned social experiences and interactions."[22] Gus's ethnicity has not always been part of mainstream whiteness, being an Orthodox Greek immigrant in the United States: he, nevertheless, expresses and unconsciously reproduces a white, middle-class anxiety, as Michael Teitz and Karen Chapple discuss it,[23] about Toula attending college in the center of Chicago, concerned about her being influenced by others, including the liberal college culture or the more visible criminal elements. The drug-dealing scenario that Gus berates, other than revealing his blatant sexism and misogyny, shows his perception of the city center as a magnet for illegal activity and echoes the long-standing effects of racial targeting of the 1980s war on drugs, as Michael Tonry points out.[24] Gus perceives his daughter as a young innocent in danger of inadvertent involvement in criminal activities, and he fails to understand her need for personal and professional growth. His prejudiced perception of the racially inflicted demonization of cities places him within a performative aspect of the same white identity he so adamantly resists. Complicating Gus's construction of white identity, Gus's frustration with the Millers at the extended family dinner celebration, according to Anagnostou, stems from the Millers' lack of general expressiveness and their bewildered gazes toward the Portokaloses.[25] The Millers' behavior is perceived as antagonistic to the role of the Portokalos patriarch and the Greek customs of participatory festivity. The Millers' middle-class propriety, rooted in their lavish household, lifestyle, formal interactions with Toula and her parents, as well as their horrified reactions to the Portokalos' drinking and eating customs, is met with resistance by Gus. The Greek patriarch calls the Millers "dry toast" to underline their Anglo-Saxon reserved manners.[26] Anagnostou elaborates on the use of micropractices (drinking, pranks, and name-calling) as techniques the film uses to depict how the "culturally subordinate appropriate [them] to exercise power and experience its effects."[27] Those practices, especially in the case of Nick and Ian's interaction, showcase a performative aspect of antagonism between representatives of two worlds. The cultural and social gap between the two families is thus reinforced by their different economic classes,[28] even if the Portokaloses otherwise aspire to become part of the Millers' world. The families passively engage in a cultural conflict fueled by intercultural anxieties and class decorum during public interactions, creating several situationally comedic instances.

The patriarchs of the Castorini and Portokalos families aspire to join America's middle class, trying to assimilate cultural traits of their respective ethnicities to their new identity or abandoning others altogether. For Cosmo the movement upward on the social ladder, into mainstream masculinity, is interrupted when his daughter and wife confront him in culturally marked public and private spaces (the opera and the kitchen). Finding fulfillment in the intimate space of the family and reaffirming his masculinity through his role as a father and husband, Cosmo leaves behind a focus on performance of material prosperity; as Edvige Giunta argues, *la famiglia* and its space have triumphed, as the Castorini family manufactures old dreams in the new country, protecting the domestic haven of the ethnic family.[29] Gus, who sees his patriarchal role as protector of the Greek family, its traditions and values undermined by the emancipatory choices of his daughter, accepts Toula's marriage only when it becomes apparent that the newlyweds, while moving upward in terms of social mobility, affirm their Greek past. The cultural connections are both symbolic (the gifts Toula receives from her grandmother) as well as material (the new house next to the Portokaloses); thus, Toula and Ian re-create a modern Greek American identity and rely upon the close geographical and cultural proximity to the extended Greek family.

"A Woman Knows . . ."

The Castorini and Portokalos women also negotiate and challenge performative aspects of their ethnicity and class in domestic and public spaces. Rose Castorini and Maria Portokalos, the mothers of their respective families, are often seen in their domestic domain, arguing with their husbands and children, functioning as peacemakers who resolve antagonisms. Rose embodies the role of *la mamma*, a stereotype that Morris and Wilson read as widely associated with Italian national characters in their own country and abroad.[30] As Anna Bravo describes the stereotype, *la mamma* is the loving servant and owner of her children; she is often emotionally manipulative in order to keep the family in order. *La mamma* also has a strong maternal relationship with her husband or sons.[31] The stereotype, reinforced by the Catholic Church's impossible ideal of the chaste Madonna, is equally prevalent in the New World and Italy.[32] The maternal role of Rose, a reference to the literary and onscreen history of motherhood in Italian American culture,[33] is complicated by her dissatisfaction with her marriage. Rose is trapped between her conventional inferior role in the household and her personal desires. She is expected to endure all hardship, much like many other heroines in Italian American women's narratives, as Mary Jo Bona argues.[34] Aware of her husband's extramarital affair, Rose avoids confrontation in order to spare the family, protecting its sacred character;[35] resolution will come only in the last scene of the film, set in the intimate sphere of the kitchen, away from public exposure.

While introducing herself in a public setting, Rose chooses to be frank about her occupation, playfully deflecting questions that reproduce the Italian American mother stereotype. Defying the sociocultural expectations of a married woman confined in her household, Rose flirts in public and sets the boundaries of her night out:

> *"What do you do?"*
> "I'm a housewife."
> *"How come you're eating alone?"*
> "I'm not eating alone."

Rose ponders the role of family and social relations during the course of her impromptu dinner date and walk with Perry, a WASP English professor. The encounter presents a moment for Rose to reflect on her inevitable confinement within her ethnic and class boundaries. Rose's philosophical questioning of love and her own place in both the Italian American household and American society in general echoes the resistance of Italian American women to traditions that define them exclusively within the domestic imagination.[36]

More recently, Theodora Patrona investigates selfless motherly love and family cohesion as two of the most prominent values perpetuated by southern Italian women.[37] While Rose's family origins are not specified in the movie, her cultural, gender (*mamma* and wife), and class identity are prescribed by familiar stereotypical models, impeding her expression of sexuality outside the boundaries of a failing marriage. Rose's hesitation to fulfill her desires outside the suffocating constraints of her family can be understood as part of a more general pattern explored in a study by Nancy Caronia and Edvige Giunta,[38] in which Louise DeSalvo comments on Italian American women who defy their domestic roles, and, thus run the danger of being considered "whores" or "prostitutes."[39] Unlike Cosmo, who flaunts his stylish clothes and extramarital affair publicly at the opera, Rose is reserved and self-contained, unable to fulfill her desires independently.[40]

Rosa's behavior is shaped by prescribed ethnic, gender, and cultural expectations that function as corrective measures at the exact moment when she is thinking of breaching them: she is abruptly reminded of her place in the Castorini household when, during her walk with Perry, they encounter her father-in-law. The presence and surprised stare of the elder male of the family disciplines Rose silently. The encounter exemplifies how a family crisis should not be resolved in the public sphere: Italian culture values the preservation of family status in the public domain, which takes precedence over any intrafamily conflicts. Rose, enduring the silent accusing look of her father-in-law, experiences what Morris and Wilson (2018) describe as the "close, protective unit, one that is both supportive and suffocating."[41] In the end, despite every opportunity Rosa has to develop a meaningful relationship with another male, her role as the faithful *mamma* of the family and her desire to save her marriage and the cohesion of the Castorinis prevail.

As opposed to Rose Castorini, Maria Portokalos maintains a more active role in her household, in spite of her confinement to an extended domestic space which includes the house and the family business. First introduced at the Portokaloses' restaurant, Maria perpetuates the social pressure focused on Toula, with the aim of convincing Toula to get married and bear children. Maria's sexuality is not explicitly explored in the film, nor does she face the same dilemmas and challenges as Rose. However, in the Greek American Portokalos household, Maria acts as a mediator across generations. Toula describes her mother as a person who simultaneously offered wisdom and guilt, following the same life path that she herself is encouraged to pursue: early marriage, child-bearing, and family nurturing. Unlike Toula, Toula's mother and sister both represent the "nice Greek girl" stereotype, as the audience discovers in the first sequences of the film. Yet Maria is also the "neck" of the Portokalos family, in one of the most often quoted lines of the movie that describes the gender dynamics of the immigrant household: "The man may be the head of the household. But the woman is the neck, and she can turn the head whichever way she pleases." The metaphor Maria uses is not dissimilar to Massey's argument of how the "home" is most often constructed as a "woman's place," according to Massey, home functions not only as a "source of stability, reliability and authenticity" but also represents the nostalgic and the "female."[42] The idea that the traditional model of Greek womanhood,[43] personified by Maria and her older daughter, would not be Toula's chosen lifestyle is incomprehensible to the rest of the family.

Maria staunchly defends and takes pride in her role as a mainstay in the family's economic success, even if her role is unrecognized by her immediate social circle. Women's labor, whether paid or unpaid, is typically represented through stereotypical oversimplifications in films that foreground ethnic families.[44] In *Moonstruck*, for example, there is very little, if any, recognition of Rose's labor, even inside the Castorini household. Exploring this issue in the context of Italian American community life, Ruberto argues that narratives which gloss over the paid/unpaid dimension of women's labor contribute significantly to the process of assimilation to the American middle class and create false nostalgia for a past that never existed.[45] A similar narrative in the Greek American context is analyzed in Vardalos's work: when Gus denigrates Toula's, and generally women's, intelligence, Maria vehemently challenges her husband, sternly reminding him of her role in developing the family's prosperity with her managerial skills. With the ethnic comedy maintaining a precarious balance between collapsing and reinforcing stereotypes,[46] Gus's patriarchal role is undermined in several cases; such sequences reveal the complexity of power structures within the immigrant household. Gus's naiveté is foregrounded when Maria and Aunt Voula trick him into sending Toula to a job that guarantees her autonomy and distance from the suffocating intimacy of the Greek family. The power play within the Greek American family separates the public from the domestic sphere, preferring the latter as a space for confrontation: Maria challenges her husband's intelligence and managerial skills in their own bedroom, away from public observation. The Portokalos family dynamics, with Maria asserting control in a private domestic space, echoes Ernestine Friedl's claims about kinship structure in rural Greek families. Friedl identifies the domestic space as a center where real attribution of power takes place, thereby allowing women rather than men to control the family.[47] Maria skillfully manipulates her role as wife in the privacy of her marriage to maintain a false appearance of the performative power of patriarchy over the family, to her own advantage. As a team, Maria and Aunt Voula subversively challenge patriarchy at the family restaurant, within the intimate sphere of the family business. However, the confrontation is still situated outside the household, playing out with well-placed silences and a great composure that creates the illusion in Gus's mind that "his idea" releases Toula from her restaurant duties. The Greek father retains the performative aspect of masculinity as defined by his ethnicity and maintains the illusion of patriarchal control.

Assimilation and Happiness

Despite their differences in age and lifestyle, the protagonists of both films each experience a similar process of self-discovery. Likewise, audiences in both cases are introduced to the respective protagonist's life trajectory in the setting of an ethnic restaurant. As a narrative choice, Toula's monologues in *My Big Fat Greek Wedding* provide ample information about her life, while in Loretta's case analogous information is conveyed in the first two scenes of the film. Loretta thrives independently as a highly skilled professional, working as an accountant who serves the Italian American community of New York; Toula, on the other hand, works at her family's restaurant as hostess, while also taking on a number of additional responsibilities that leave little time for herself. Both storylines define happiness as a primary goal for the protagonists, connecting this goal to aspects of gender, class, and ethnic identity. Toula candidly explains that "[nice] Greek girls that don't find a husband work in the family restaurant," describing herself as "thirty and way past my expiration date." Toula compares herself to her sister, who embodies the ideal of Greek American womanhood and, according to their mother, married early to become a "Greek baby making machine." Loretta, on the other hand, is a widow. She blames herself and her secular choices that not only drew her away from Catholicism and her Italian roots but also contributed in part to her husband's fatal accident. Loretta associates happiness with an adherence to her cultural identity. The pursuit of self-fulfillment, seen as a partial departure from tradition and the domestic space, clashes with the cultural policing of ethnic cultures and foregrounds the ambivalent relationship of Italian American (and Greek American) women to their ethnicity.[48] In an early discussion with Ronny, Loretta questions her departure from the stereotypical Italian model of the married woman who prioritizes child-bearing and child-rearing. Any approach to self-fulfillment which lies outside of domestic space and minimizes the role of motherhood is viewed in opposition to the Italian American ideal of woman as mother, particularly because such connotations of motherhood can be traced to religious prescriptions.[49]

Italian tradition and superstition further complicate Loretta's arranged marriage to Johnny and her prospective class mobility. Although Loretta's future mother-in-law proves to be extremely resilient, Johnny's random encounter at the airport with another elderly Italian American woman wearing black results in the latter putting a curse on Johnny's flight to Sicily because of an old family feud.[50] With superstition and faith holding such important positions in Italian cultural belief, Loretta's arranged marriage seems doomed from the start.[51] In a cogent discussion of mystical connections to an ancestral homeland, Maddalena Tirabassi notes that popular culture has contributed to widespread stereotypical representations of Italian Americans, including that of the Italian *mamma* of southern origins, which reflects enduring "archaic practices and traditions."[52] Such a strong cultural connection can further explain Loretta's fears and her insistence that her second marriage follows Italian American norms. However, Rose and Loretta's ambivalent relationship to southern Italian archaic practice, the prototype of numerous Italian American traditional practices, is contested. Loretta's happiness depends on Johnny's dying mother in Sicily, and her miraculous recovery underlines the battleground between the Old and the

New World: "This is modern times! There ain't supposed to be miracles no more!" proclaims Loretta, to which her mother responds thus, "I guess it ain't modern times in Sicily." The *mamma* therefore introduces a cultural crisis, soon to be resolved, following the formulaic structure of romantic comedies as outlined by Leger Grindon.[53] Rose, in turn, as an Italian American *mamma*, attempts to save the arranged marriage while also expressing disapproval of her daughter's behavior, only to conclude that Loretta's ideal of happiness opposes her own beliefs about nontraditional married life.

Throughout *My Big Fat Greek Wedding*, Toula also associates her unhappiness with her ethnic identity as a Greek American. Since childhood, Toula's exoticized ethnic body type and her typical diet have been construed in mainstream society as a clear departure from the American "normal."[54] The comic scene during opening sequences set in the family restaurant features a sarcastic exchange regarding her body type, which supposedly bears no similarity to the archetypical classical Greek artistic standards.[55] This interaction confirms how Greek identity for Toula contributes to a "matrix of domination," borrowing Patricia Hill-Collins's term,[56] based on highly circumscribed social and gender roles that undermine both her self-esteem and happiness. She opposes her family's plans to send her to Greece to get married, much to the frustration of the Portokaloses, who cannot understand that for Toula, her mainstream American identity is precisely that which secures both her social and individual position in American society. The role her family has defined for their daughter, by comparison, offers no space for professional and personal growth outside the boundaries of the Greek American household.

Toula and Loretta each undergo physical and behavioral transformations that visibly depart from their respective onscreen introductions. They both leave behind a conservative appearance associated with social position within their communities, Loretta as a widow and Toula as a single woman, both of whom are beyond the appropriate age for marriage established by cultural norms. Their changes in hairstyle and clothing are prompted by encounters with their romantic interests and dating rituals. For Toula, the metamorphosis comes as a result of her emancipation from her father's direct influence in the workplace, which leads her to enroll in computer classes at a downtown college and get a job at her aunt's travel agency. Her journey from suffering in the family restaurant to experiencing women's agency echoes Claire Mortimer's identification of suffering as part of the narrative process toward self-discovery that characterizes the genre of romantic comedy.[57] The suffering in these cases stems from cultural roots and close familial relations, and the solution presented is for ethnic characters to distance themselves from cultural practice and assimilate in part to the dominant cultural paradigm. Toula's liberation from the expectations of premarital purity, which conditions Greek women to seek sexual intimacy only within the institution of marriage, is set against her intimate and sexually charged dates with Ian. As she performs the role of obedient Greek daughter during the sequences that show parallel arranged dates, Toula comes to realize that her happiness is attainable through her relationship with Ian, following the rom-com convention of lovers professing they were made for each other,[58] as well as through rejecting the possibility of love within the Greek community. The Greek men stereotypically represented in the movie are caricatures that are constructed as both funny and inferior to the appearance and composed demeanor of Ian, a white middle-class history teacher who is financially comfortable, soft-spoken, and willing to immerse himself in Greek culture to win the approval of Toula's parents. Toula is happier when she does not follow Greek customs as her parents wish, yet she returns to family traditions, such as dance and Greek lessons for her daughter, only after ascertaining that they would not interfere with her emancipatory journey to self-fulfillment.

Accordingly, Loretta's transformation from a conservative widow who cares little about her appearance to a modern woman who attracts the gaze of all male bystanders as she moves past them is showcased vividly in the sequence outside the hairdresser's salon, which represents a visible shift in the protagonist's mindset. The scene can be read as a departure from the cultural confines of the Italian American ethnicity toward a more acceptable onscreen proximity to an ideal of unmarked whiteness. The blend of Loretta's onscreen Italian and white ethnicities, performed as visual changes, is also a characteristic of what Diane Negra calls a mode of ethnic selfhood.[59] The so-called blended ethnicity of Cher, who portrays Loretta, is seen on screen as the combination of two or more ethnic backgrounds and later signaled a common marketing strategy among movie celebrities and pop icons.⁶⁰ While the stereotypical representation of passionate Italian lovers in Loretta's scenes with Ronny is discernible, Loretta's change of behavior also estranges her from her family members and creates distance from them. Loretta's first rebellion against the culture of her upbringing was her marriage of love; in her second rebellion, she undergoes a physical transformation. Loretta has a sexual encounter with her future husband's brother at his house, prioritizing her own needs over family bonds, a cornerstone of Italian and Italian American culture. "Leave nothing left for him to marry, nothing but the skin left over my bones," she passionately proclaims, acting outside cultural and social boundaries, embracing a self-centered fulfillment of her desires. From the subversion of kinship expectations to her appearance and private moments, Loretta's search for happiness leads her partially outside of the constrictions of the parental ethnic household.⁶¹

Searching for happiness outside the boundaries of their inherited cultures, Loretta and Toula seek personal fulfillment without necessarily abandoning their cultural backgrounds, as each attempts to participate actively within the socioeconomic communities to which she belongs. Drawing on Natasha Warikoo and Donald Tricarico's discussion of assimilation models, I read the contested relationship Loretta and Toula have with their respective ethnicities and their pursuit of happiness as examples of the segmented assimilation model, a theory of immigrant and ethnic group incorporation in the United States.⁶²

According to the theory, ethnic groups exhibit variable patterns in their assimilation to a highly stratified social roles, as defined by markers of education, consumption, residence, and employment. In this context, the immigrant lived experience and its relationship to social institutions and cultures are not examined as sole quests for acceptance, but rather as markers of overlapping and continuous processes of preserving ethnicity while simultaneously pursuing assimilation to dominant cultures. Both Loretta and Toula see tradition as antagonistic to their happiness, yet each reaffirms her identity by returning to tradition. Toula, for example, accepts a gift from her mother and grandmother that signifies her Greek ethnicity. Soon afterward the audience discovers the motive that prompted the Portokalos family to migrate to America was a better life for their children. By providing the newlywed couple with a deed to their own home, the

Portokalos parents offer their daughter the experience of the American Dream while at the same time encouraging her adherence to Greek cultural traditions.

The material conceptualization of happiness has a long history in American culture. Thomas Jefferson's famous phrase in the "original rough draught" of the Declaration of Independence (1776), which calls the "pursuit of happiness" an "inalienable Right," is often associated with Locke's philosophical connection of the term to property and ownership. Nevertheless, according to Robert Darnton, pursuing happiness has often become the central argument of commercial, medical, and entertainment legal cases, expanding the meaning of the word, gradually associating the concept of happiness with that of personal fulfillment.[63] For immigrants of the nineteenth and early twentieth centuries, the pursuit of happiness did not involve conquering the frontier, but rather owning the land; acquiring a house in the suburbs is the late twentieth-century enactment of the American Dream for former immigrants.

Property as a constitutive component of the American Dream is also connected to Toula's happiness. Gus offers the newlyweds a house very close to his own in the Chicago suburbs. His gift symbolizes segmented assimilation; the American Dream, as John Archer observes, is based on cherishing personal possession (also an ideal for the Greek peasant); acquiring personal property, on the other hand, also reflects "the good life," the "height of civilization."[64] Toula and Ian end up living in the suburbs in close proximity to her parents, and they have a child who partakes in both WASP and Greek American culture: the new nuclear family is "Americanish," combining elements and practices, a self-invented version of their ethnicities. The "apples and oranges" metaphor of Gus's wedding speech, as well as the gift to his daughter and his son-in-law, signifies what Tricarico describes as a common process most ethnic groups willfully undergo; they compromise their ethnicity in order to acquire economic and cultural capital, escape social and economic boundaries but also gain respect from the people in the same economic and social class.[65] The Millers' participation in the Greek festivities and Ian's immersion into Greek culture and the Orthodox religion is how far a mainstream American could go when it comes to negotiate with the ethnic "other." Conversely, Toula's economic, professional, educational, and personal transformation marks the aspects of US culture she, with the help of her family, is willing to accept and adapt to.

Likewise, Loretta's domestic crises are resolved comically at the family table. The nuclear family is the core unit, a catalyst for the diffusion of crises and a primary agent of happiness, in tandem with a reaffirmation of the Italian American family values and roles. Loretta will marry the person she loves, in accordance with Catholic traditions, realizing the social incorporation of herself and Ronny to mainstream America.[66] Loretta thus functions as a cultural and class intermediary. Cher's interpretation of Loretta embodies the best of both worlds: Cher portrays Loretta as an independent woman. Her portrayal of Loretta blends, on the one hand, ethnic attitudes viewed as positive by the Italian American community but also the United States;[67] on the other hand, Cher's portrayal combines these ethnic attitudes with proof of her compliance with the social and economic norms of the cultures she moves between, that is, the mainstream American and the Italian American.

Conclusion

The conclusion of both films finds the protagonists in close proximity to their cultural roots, near their parents, and free from the crises they face at the beginning of the respective storylines. Loretta boldly proclaims, "Everything's different!" when her mother comments on her hair, from her feelings to her attitude toward life and her pursuit of personal fulfillment. Toula, on the other hand, realizes her middle-class aspiration of having a house in the suburbs, close to her parents. The elders in the two families firmly reestablish their nuclear and extended families and challenge popular representations of ethnic Americans as single-dimensional, working-class, or criminally inspired. The transformation of gender relations and class performance is not only a result of the characters' efforts to assimilate but also a reflection of the elements that constitute their ethnicity, both present in the context of an ethnic romantic comedy. While exaggerated ethnic stereotypes are inevitably reproduced, the viewers see the characters struggling with gender and class roles, while frequently challenging preconceptions.

The Italian American and Greek American families reshape their ethnic American identity, finding solace in each other, seeking happiness in the intimate domestic space. The nuclear family remains the key point of reference for the aspiring middle-class household, yet the films each present a critical view of its suffocating qualities and deconstruction of gender roles in the public sphere.

Loretta, and to a greater extent Toula, each considers ethnicity as part of her identity, but also view it as an obstacle to happiness. Loretta's and Toula's happiness always comes in the form of partially letting go of their ethnic identity as females in favor of a more commodified, "liberal" form of womanhood. The paths Loretta and Toula choose to pursue happiness show how onscreen performance of ethnicity in the United States is closely linked to personal fulfillment. The protagonists' happy endings lie outside the rigid confines of their ethnic identity, to a more mainstream public and private American(ish) cultural becoming. Loretta and Toula are ethnically flexible, balancing their respective cultural backgrounds with the so-called normalcy of dominant middle-class values. Recent romantic comedies with predominantly nonwhite casts such as *Crazy Rich Asians* (2018) also examine the contested relationship between happiness and ethnic identities. As Hollywood shifts toward films that better represent the ethnic makeup of the United States, the question that persists is how happiness is related to the assimilation of socioeconomically successful ethnic groups to a dominant culture. The comparative approach to analyzing films that foreground American ethnic families allows for a close examination of the changes in cultural expectations from non-mainstream Americans and the cultural exchange that takes place, superficial as it might seem for those willing to search beneath stereotypical end scenes of tolerance and pluralism. After all, perhaps Ian Miller does look Greek by the end of the *My Big Fat Greek Wedding*, suggesting that all ethnic identities are acceptable in the big US melting pot, so long as they reaffirm the core values of the elusive American Dream and its derived happiness.

NOTES

1. Movies that reinforce the mobster trope include *Goodfellas* (1990, dir. Martin Scorsese) and *The Godfather* (1972, dir. Francis Ford Coppola). In

regard to "inner city" crime, some examples include *Candyman* (1992, dir. Bernard Rose) and *Dangerous Minds* (1995, dir. John N. Smith). Finally, concerning the overachieving story of upward mobility, often with the benevolent help of a white savior, a commercially and critically successful movie often discussed as a controversial example has been *Gran Torino* (2007, dir. Clint Eastwood).

    2. *Moonstruck* (1987, dir. Norman Jewison) won three Oscars in 1988, for best actress in a leading role (Cher), best actress in a supporting role (Olympia Dukakis), and best writing/screenplay (John Patrick Shanley); two Golden Globes (Cher, Dukakis); a Silver Berlin Bear (Jewison); and a Writers' Guild of America Award (Jewison). *My Big Fat Greek Wedding* (2002) is the most successful independent comedy to date, grossing over $368 million worldwide. Stephen Holden, in a 2002 review article in the *New York Times*, calls *My Big Fat Greek Wedding* the "Greek-American answer to *Moonstruck*."

    3. David Gillota, in the introduction and the first chapters of *Ethnic Humor*, provides an overview of humor theory and describes how academics and comedians have dealt with ethnic humor in the United States, particularly in the Black and Jewish communities. At the heart of his book, Gillota explores how humorists use humor to defend, redraw, or challenge the traditional boundaries diachronically used to separate and define various ethnic groups (6).

    4. Ruberto, *Gramsci and Women's Work*, 88.

    5. Gillota, *Ethnic Humor*, 3.

    6. Ruberto, *Gramsci and Women's Work*, 89.

    7. Massey, *Space, Place and Gender*, 186.

    8. Gillota, *Ethnic Humor*, 8.

    9. Johnny and Ronny are constructed as caricatures of Italian American stereotypes in the beginning of the film. On the one hand, Johnny cannot make any important decision about his life, especially marrying Loretta, without the explicit blessing of his mother and his estranged brother, and he has a supernatural fear of bad luck. Ronny, on the other hand, is extremely emotional to the point where he maimed himself in a rage of anger over a quarrel with his brother, having rage fits (targeting Loretta in a few of them) and completely surrendering to his passion for Loretta.

    10. Morris and Wilson, *La Mamma*.

    11. Joseph Roach's definition of performance as a "particular class or subset of restored behavior in which one or more persons assume responsibility to an audience and to a tradition as they understand it" sheds light on the crisis the two patriarchs face. Trapped between the expectations of their role in the ethnic household towards the members of the family and their own

desires, Gus and Cosmo are assertive and protective of their public face, even if in practice they are rarely aware of what their daughters and wives do behind their back.

12. Elam, "We Wear the Mask."
13. Gardaphé, *Leaving Little Italy*, 16.
14. Citron, "Opera and Desire in 'Moonstruck.'"
15. Fullwood, *Cinema, Gender, and Everyday Space*, 27.
16. Peberdy, *Masculinity and Film Performance*.
17. Margaux Fragoso analyzes Louise DeSalvo's discussion of the *bella figura* cultural stereotype in *Crazy in the Kitchen*. Much like Cosmo, Fragoso argues that the "regality" that a formal attire gives the male subject often entails the possibility to "disown a family member who manifests abject behavior," often against personal desires, to save public face.
18. Gardaphé, 16.
19. Peberdy, *Masculinity and Film Performance*, 49.
20. Peberdy's work discusses in length the fragility of masculinity in society and films, with a special focus on post-1980s filmography.
21. Tzanelli, "Europe Within and Without," 44.
22. McDermott, "Ways of Being White," 436.
23. Teitz and Chapple. "The Causes of Inner-City Poverty."
24. Tonry, "Race and the War on Drugs," 27.
25. Anagnostou, "Making Ethnicity," 150–51.
26. Tzanelli, "Europe Within and Without," 50.
27. Anagnostou, "Making Ethnicity," 150–51.
28. Ibid, 142.
29. Giunta, "The Quest for True Love," 262.
30. Morris and Wilson, *La Mamma*, 2.
31. Ibid., 2.
32. Ibid.
33. Some examples of academic explorations into the representation of the Italian American mother in relation to other stereotypes in literature and onscreen are Szczepanski, "The Scalding Pot"; Negra, *Off-White*; Gardaphé, *Leaving Little Italy*; Morris and Wilson, *La Mamma*; and Tricarico, *Guido Culture*.
34. Bona, *Claiming a Tradition*, 11.
35. Ibid., 8.
36. Giunta, "The Quest for True Love," 259.
37. Patrona, "Women Knocking on the *Golden Door*," 268.
38. Caronia and Giunta, *Personal Effects*, 11.
39. DeSalvo, "A Portrait of the Puttana," 35–54.

40. Tirabassi discusses sociological studies in the 1970s and 1980s that showcase the multiple responsibilities Italian women had toward the elderly members of their families as well as their children. Citing sociological studies of the time, she mentions that in Italian families the priority of family over individual interests had been maintained in relation to the past, emphasizing that "faithfulness to the family had outranked all other allegiances and all personal preferences."

41. Morris and Wilson, *La Mamma*, 6.

42. Massey, *Space, Place and Gender*, 180.

43. Tzanelli, "Europe Within and Without," 42.

44. Ruberto, *Gramsci and Women's Work*, 82.

45. Ibid.

46. Gillota, *Ethnic Humor*, 9.

47. Friedl, "The Position of Women," 97.

48. Giunta, *The Quest for True Love*, 259; Caronia and Giunta, *Personal Effects*, 11.

49. Morris and Wilson (2018) discuss extensively the relationship between the *mamma* stereotype in Italian and Italian American culture and the role of Catholicism.

50. The woman at the airport, in clothes and black colors, recognizable in Mediterranean cultures as usually worn by widows, curses the plane because the sister "stole" from her the man she loved. The woman in black, based on her account, is a first-generation immigrant.

51. Patrona, "Women Knocking on the *Golden Door*," 268.

52. Tirabassi, "*Mammas*," 178.

53. Grindon, *The Hollywood Romantic Comedy*.

54. Anagnostou, "Making Ethnicity," 144.

55. Ibid., 145.

56. Hill-Collins, *Black Feminist Thought*.

57. Mortimer, *Romantic Comedy*, 4.

58. Ibid., 10.

59. Negra, *Off-White*, 167.

60. Ibid., 166.

61. Loretta is seen alone, pondering after a meeting with Ronny, as she prepares for her date. The intimacy of the scene, as she is in her nightgown and looking at the clothes, underwear, and shoes she bought, presents an interesting case on how consumerism and privacy are transformative forces immediately connected to her femininity. This depicted version of femininity is only attainable through consuming. Only after the "transformation" does the audience see Loretta as a woman in love.

62. Warikoo, *Balancing Acts*.
63. Darnton, "The Pursuit of Happiness."
64. Archer, "The Resilience of Myth," 9.
65. Tricarico, *Guido Culture*, 285.
66. Negra, *Off-White*, 171.
67. Ibid., 167.

Bibliography

Anagnostou, Yiorgos. "When 'Second Generation' Narratives and Hollywood Meet: Making Ethnicity in *My Big Fat Greek Wedding*." *MELUS* 37, no. 4 (Winter 2012): 139–63.

Archer, John. "The Resilience of Myth: The Politics of the American Dream." *Traditional Dwellings and Settlements Review* 25, no. 2 (Spring 2014): 7–21.

Bona, Mary Jo. *Claiming a Tradition: Italian American Women Writers*. Carbondale: Southern Illinois University Press, 1999.

Caronia, Nancy, and Edvige Giunta, eds. *Personal Effects: Essays on Memoir, Teaching, and Culture in the Work of Louise DeSalvo*. New York: Fordham University Press, 2015.

Citron, Marcia J. "'An Honest Contrivance': Opera and Desire in 'Moonstruck.'" *Music & Letters* 89, no. 1 (2008): 56–83.

Darnton, Robert. "The Pursuit of Happiness." *Wilson Quarterly* (Fall 1995): 42–52.

DeSalvo, Louise. "A Portrait of the Puttana as a Middle-Aged Woolf Scholar." In *Between Women: Biographers, Novelists, Critics, Teachers and Artists Write about Their Work on Women*, edited by Carol Ascher, Louise DeSalvo, Sara Ruddick, 35–54. New York: Routledge, 1993.

Elam, Harry J., Jr. "We Wear the Mask: Performance, Social Dramas, and Race." In *Doing Race: 21 Essays for the 21st Century*, edited by Hazel Rose Markus and Paula M. L. Moya, 545–61. New York: Norton, 2010.

Fragoso, Margaux. "Louise DeSalvo's 'Even in Death, La Bella Figura': A Meditation on Honor, Respect, and the Silences That Bind." In *Personal Effects: Essays on Memoir, Teaching and Culture in the Work of Louise DeSalvo*, edited by Nancy Caronia and Edvige Giunta, 37–49. New York: Fordham University Press, 2015.

Friedl, Ernestine. "The Position of Women: Appearance and Reality." *Anthropological Quarterly* 40, no. 3 (1967): 97–108.

Fullwood, Natalie. *Cinema, Gender, and Everyday Space: Comedy, Italian Style.* London: Palgrave Macmillan, 2016.

Gardaphé, Fred. *Leaving Little Italy: Essaying Italian American Culture.* Albany: SUNY Press, 2004.

Gillota, David. *Ethnic Humor in Multiethnic America.* New Brunswick, NJ: Rutgers University Press, 2013.

Giunta, Edvige. "The Quest for True Love: Ethnicity in Nancy Savoca's Domestic Film Comedy." In *Screening Ethnicity: Cinematographic Representations of Italian Americans in the United States,* edited by Anna Camaiti Hostert and Anthony Julian Tamburri, 259–75. Boca Raton, FL: Bordighera Press, 2002.

Grindon, Leger. *The Hollywood Romantic Comedy: Conventions, History, Controversies.* London: Wiley-Blackwell, 2011.

Hill-Collins, Patricia. *Black Feminist Thought: Knowledge, Consciousness, and the Politics of Empowerment.* Boston: Unwin Hyman, 1990.

Holden, Stephen. "Quality Films Brush Away The Fluff." *New York Times,* August 30, 2002.

Massey, Doreen B. *Space, Place and Gender.* Cambridge: Polity Press, 1994.

McDermott, Monica. "Ways of Being White: Privilege, Perceived Stigma, and Transcendence." In *Doing Race: 21 Essays for the 21st Century,* edited by Hazel Rose Markus and Paula M. L. Moya, 415–38. New York: Norton, 2010.

Moonstruck. Directed by Norman Jewison. Metro-Goldwyn-Mayer, 1987.

Morris, Penelope, and Perry Wilson. "La Mamma: Italian Mothers Past and Present." In *La Mamma: Interrogating a National Stereotype,* edited by Penelope Morris and Perry Wilson, 1–27. New York: Palgrave Macmillan, 2018.

Mortimer, Claire. *Romantic Comedy.* New York: Routledge, 2010.

My Big Fat Greek Wedding. Directed by Joel Zwick. IFC Films, 2002.

Negra, Diane. *Off-White Hollywood: American Culture and Ethnic Female Stardom.* New York: Routledge, 2001.

Patrona, Theodora. "Women Knocking on the *Golden Door* (2006): Female Migrants and Cultural History Through Film." In *Racial and Ethnic Identities in the Media,* edited by Eleftheria Arapoglou, Yiorgos Kalogeras, and Jopi Nyman, 263–76. London: Palgrave Macmillan, 2016.

Peberdy, Donna. *Masculinity and Film Performance: Male Angst in Contemporary American Cinema.* Basingstoke, UK: Palgrave Macmillan, 2011.

Roach, Joseph. "Kinship, Intelligence and Memory as Improvisation: Culture and Performance in New Orleans." In *Performance and Cultural Politics,* edited by Elin Diamond, 219–38. New York: Routledge, 1996.

Ruberto, Laura E. *Gramsci, Migration, and the Representation of Women's Work in Italy and the U.S.* Malden, MA: Lexington Books, 2007.
Szczepanski, Karen. "The Scalding Pot: Stereotyping of Italian-American Males in Hollywood Films." *Italian Americana* 5, no. 2 (Spring 1979): 196–204.
Teitz, Michael B., and Karen Chapple. "The Causes of Inner-City Poverty: Eight Hypotheses in Search of Reality." *Cityscape: A Journal of Policy Development and Research* 3, no. 3 (1998): 33–70.
Tirabassi, Maddalena. "*Mammas* in Italian Migrant Families: The Anglophone Countries." Translated by Stuart Oglethorpe. In *La Mamma: Interrogating a National Stereotype*, edited by Penelope Morris and Perry Wilson, 161–84. New York: Palgrave Macmillan, 2018.
Tonry, Michael. "Race and the War on Drugs." *University of Chicago Legal Forum* 1994, no. 1 (1994): 25–81.
Tricarico, Donald. *Guido Culture and Italian American Youth: From Bensonhurst to Jersey Shore.* New York: Palgrave Macmillan, 2019.
Tzanelli, Rodanthi. "Europe Within and Without: Narratives of American Cultural Belonging in and through *My Big Fat Greek Wedding* (2002)." *Comparative American Studies* 2, no. 1 (2004): 42.
Warikoo, Natasha. *Balancing Acts: Youth Culture in the Global City.* Berkeley: University of California Press, 2010.

AFTERWORD

Beyond Methodological Singularity

Donna R. Gabaccia

In March 1972, I boarded a cut-rate Icelandic flight and began what my mother termed "Donna's European adventure." In the ten months since I had graduated from Mount Holyoke College, at age twenty-one, I had crashed (so we said in those days) with friends in Boston, and I had endured bouts of boring, low-paid work as a temporary secretary in order to finance a series of long hitchhiking and backpacking trips around the United States. These were meditative journeys devoted more to contemplation than to adventure; retrospectively, I recognize them as constituting a highly idiosyncratic strategy that made mobility a route to settlement on a life's plan. On one of those trips, I met the young man who would become my husband, and I was going to Europe to begin an extended and grand, if also low-cost, tour with him—one that would also be marked by considerable time standing, thumbs out, at the side of European roads. But while most of my English-speaking North American counterparts chose to ease into the foreignness of their own foreign adventures among other English speakers in London or in hip, dependably bilingual Amsterdam, I planned to board a train in Luxembourg, headed for Athens, where I would visit *poste restante*, learn of my final destination, and—three days after my arrival in Europe—climb the gangplank onto a ferry taking me to the Cycladic island of Naxos. To my surprise, I quickly made several big decisions about my future while traveling in the Mediterranean. Before crossing the Alps again, three months later, I had decided to apply to graduate school, to move to Ann Arbor, Michigan (where I would also marry), and to begin graduate study of a topic that—in those days, a half-century ago—was uniformly understood to be immigration history.

My initial dissertation thoughts did not sound much like a study in immigration, however—even to me. In Greece, I repeatedly met older English-speaking men who had returned home to live on American savings or social security checks. These men were as eager to tell their stories as I was intrigued to understand their lives. Although I watched my boyfriend (a classicist, at the time) learning modern Greek, I acquired only the rudiments of everyday speech during my sojourn in Greece because I was instead learning German and Italian in preparation for longer visits there. Not to worry, reported the future husband: in Ann Arbor I would find a lively Greek community (today, it numbers roughly 150,000), and I could learn Greek, if I wanted, at St. Nicholas Greek Orthodox Church on Main Street. Once he and I committed to a joint future, I decided to abandon my earlier study of sociology and to apply to the history doctoral program at the University of Michigan, which at that time was home to a well-known immigration historian.

In Ann Arbor in the 1970s, my intellectual life took new directions. My personal identity as an Italian American and my head start in learning the Italian language certainly influenced my choices. So did my graduate school realization that there already existed a good study of repatriated Greeks.[1] Furthermore, new publications by Virginia Yans-McLaughlin, Rudi Vecoli, and many others were making studies of Italian immigration into a kind of scholarly "cutting edge" in the 1970s. From 1974 onward, I traveled less frequently to Greece and more often to Italy. The dissertation I ultimately wrote compared Sicilians living in Sicily to Sicilian immigrants resident along Elizabeth Street on New York's Lower East Side.

Despite my shift toward migration research on, about, and in Italy, the themes developed during my Greek sojourn have remained with me throughout my life. Those elderly Greek men had left me with analytical questions and research sensibilities centered on the shape and experience of ongoing connections (today we call them transnational, transcultural, or diasporic) between migrants and their homelands and among kin and friends in other countries. When in the 1990s I began writing about Italy's migrations around the world and about migrants' ongoing connections to their village homelands and to each other, I was acutely aware the word diaspora had Greek roots, meanings, and scholarly uses. The long-ago decisions I had made in Naxos, Apiranthos, and Athens and on visits to a vast array of Greek temples in Greece, southern Italy, and Sicily transformed me into the somewhat idiosyncratic Italianist I became. By accepting the kind invitation of editors Yiorgos Anagnostou, Yiorgos Kalogeras, and Theodora Patrona to prepare this afterword, I have been able to enjoy the satisfaction of closing an autobiographical circle and to do so by thinking through some of the thematic strands that held its circumference together.

This autobiographical introduction clearly establishes that I have no particular scholarly expertise on Greek immigrants in the United States. Neither, I must confess, am I a specialist on the kinds of cultural representations—architectural, literary, filmic, or linguistic—that are the focus of so many of this collection's individual chapters. As someone who does write on interdisciplinarity and methodology, I will thus focus my remarks on some of the critically important editorial choices that shaped this volume. These choices were both conceptual and methodological, of course, and not merely editorial. Social scientists might say my focus here is on research design, but I am fully aware that few scholars in the humanities think in quite that way when they contemplate future research.

The chapters you have just read examine life, culture, and experience among migrants who were born or who lived in Greece and Italy and among their descendants. The editors consciously recruited contributors from across scholarly disciplines. Although individual chapters in the collection refer to life and culture in Europe, Italy, or Greece, or in Australia or Canada, Greek and Italian immigrants in the United States provide the spatial referent for most authors. Chronologically, too, most chapters concentrate on a span of years stretching from the late nineteenth to the early twenty-first century, with a decided weighting toward the years after World War II. These choices generated a collection that, in the editors' words, privileges "encounters, comparisons, and identities" among two groups. By focusing on choices made by editors and authors, readers have an opportunity to ponder both the choices made and alternatives rejected. I believe that a reflective exercise of this sort generates ample space for readers to think about their own choices as they plan future research.

The editors make clear in their introduction that one of the most foundational choices made in planning this collection was their decision to find ways to move beyond what I would call a methodology of singularity: the study of an individual immigrant group or migration from a single modern nation. Their decision deserves wide emulation. I regard their editorial commitment to be one of this collection's most important contributions and salient features. I concur with the editors that methodological singularity continues to characterize most scholarship on migration and that finding ways to move beyond that singularity is essential if research is to generate new knowledge. Nevertheless, others in the past have made similar commitments without, apparently, reorienting scholarship in migration studies away from methodological singularity. So I begin with a question to readers: How might one formulate one's own research in order to change the direction of migration studies in future generations?

To answer that question, I believe that, first, it helps to ponder the origins of methodological singularity. Its origins are easy enough to discern, especially in American immigration studies and especially in my own discipline of history. Until the 1970s, studies of American immigrants often depended exclusively on English-language sources; in theory this provided an opportunity to write about multiple immigrant groups, and indeed, some of the earliest works in immigration history did just that.[2] Early works written by immigrants' children instead accessed sources in a single immigrant language, and the choice of methodological singularity became even more common after 1970, as a new, much larger generation of social historians recognized the importance of doing research in archives of immigrant language sources. Clearly all members of the current scholarly community did not have native fluency in an immigrant language (as my own story suggests). Facility with more than one immigrant language remains uncommon among American scholars, given the investment of time language studies requires of graduate students. (I suspect that Greek scholars educated in Greece are more likely to be multilingual, since their native language is not hegemonic in scholarly work the way English clearly is.) A desire to document immigrants in their own voices and in their languages has also long encouraged the creation of group-specific historical societies and archival collections, while repositories that collect in multiple languages (such as the University of Minnesota's Immigration History Research Center Archives, IHRCA: www.lib.umn.edu/ihrca) often struggle to survive. Finally, as the work of Benedict Anderson reminds us, the writing of history has historically been closely associated with group formation, and, especially, with the formation of national or ethnonational groups. The consolidation and reproduction of group identities among immigrants—whether they generated studies of immigrant contributions, immigrant assimilation, or studies of persistent immigrant ethnicities or cultures—have all powerfully pushed scholarship toward analysis of single groups. In some but not all cases, authors of immigration histories have been aware of studying an ethnic group the author identifies with or aspires to build or to reproduce.

It helps to understand the development of resistance that such hegemonic methodologies also inspired. The editors of this volume are scarcely the first to call on scholars to move beyond single-group studies. Readers will want to understand earlier efforts, if only to gain insight into their failures. Within American immigration studies, historians of American pluralism such as Gary Gerstle are by no means marginal; on the contrary, theirs may be the only books on immigration that nonspecialists read. Gerstle has continued an older tradition, dating back to Randolph Bourne and Horace Kallen, Arthur Schlesinger, Marcus Hansen, and Oscar Handlin in considering immigrants, collectively, in relationship to other American social groupings, whether based on race, indigeneity, or class position.[3] (In Canada, official multiculturalism also encourages the juxtaposition and analysis of immigrants of diverse backgrounds.) For the purpose of analysis such studies tend to collapse immigrants into pan-ethnic groupings—Asian American, Euro-American, "new" or "old immigrants," or "white"—that obscure sizable cultural variations within each category. Among earlier studies, Ron Takaki's work provides a model for acknowledging cultural differences among immigrants while focusing on immigrants' place in the dynamics of American pluralism.[4]

Comparative and connective methods for moving beyond methodological singularity have been extensive but also less successful in altering the mainstream of American immigration studies. For example, one needs no high level of diligence to identify earlier scholarship that studied two or more American immigrant groups together, almost all of it undertaken by social historians. In the 1970s, for example, Italian immigrants in the United States were compared to Jewish immigrants or Polish immigrants, and occasionally to other groups such as Romanians.[5]

More general methodologically focused arguments for comparative or connected or interactive (sometimes called interethnic or intercultural) methodologies emerged somewhat later in the 1990s. In 1992, James Barrett sought the origins of the Americanization of newer immigrants in their encounters with older immigrants.[6] A year later, Rudolph J. Vecoli published a plea for an interethnic perspective.[7] Then, in 1994, Nancy L. Green advocated for a "comparative method" and for "poststructural structuralism" in migration studies.[8] Still, it is impossible to argue these alternative approaches became hegemonic. A recent literature search for twenty-first-century studies of Italians and other immigrants or of Greeks and other immigrants returned no more than a handful of titles. And while anthropologist Caroline Brettell has made powerful arguments for the importance of comparative methods in the study of culture,[9] publications using comparative methods for the study of migrants or immigrants have remained unusual in cultural studies, too.[10] Given the research focus of its contributing authors, this volume holds special promise for influencing other scholars in cultural studies. What can readers do to guarantee that this discouraging pattern is not repeated in future research?

It helps, I believe, to become ever more conscious of the choices one makes among alternatives to methodological singularity. Although a number of methods—comparative, intercultural—present alternatives for the scholar seeking to move beyond methodological singularity, they do not resolve the choice of which migrations or which migrants to compare or connect. Most obvious among the foundational choices made by the editors of this volume was the decision to include comparative and intercultural work on migrants from Greece and Italy. The choice rests on the assumption, scarcely unfounded, that Greeks and Italians can be compared because they share something in common and that those commonalities can draw them into encounters or interactions. After all, even common sense warns us not to compare apples and oranges in everyday life. This is a reminder that the nature of the commonality chosen needs to be articulated clearly. If a researcher's main analytical interest is in tree fruits or in how tree fruits differ as seed-bearers from tomatoes or pumpkins, then it is certainly possible to justify a comparison of apples and oranges. Remembering the choices made in earlier comparative studies may make this point even more clearly. Scholars in the 1970s compared Italians to Jews because of the groups' shared positions as the two largest urban and industrial immigrant groups between 1890 and 1920 or because of their shared centrality to New York's garment industry. It was their similarities that made them comparable and that generated new insights into the way the two groups differed in other respects—educational achievement, for example, or rates of social mobility or home ownership. Italians and Poles were also compared because both were simultaneously Catholic, industrial workers, and disparaged as inferior southern and eastern Europeans (categorized somewhat defensively in the early work of Michael Novak as PIGS—Poles, Italians, Greeks, Slavs).[11] In this volume, comparisons and connections of Greeks and Italians allow scholars to begin to deconstruct overarching axes of similarity such as whiteness, European, Euro-American, and especially, I believe, Mediterranean. I am hopeful that the recent renaissance in Mediterranean studies will reinforce the work of this volume and encourage more scholars to explore more fully the cultural influences of the Mediterranean as a diverse and interconnected region on the dynamics of migration and immigrant life in the United States, Europe, Africa, and the Middle East. That approach seems especially important for those interested in the development into the twenty-first century of civilizational variations in religion, kinship, and culture, broadly defined, and their consequences.[12] It is especially important, also, for those who wish to explore intercultural interactions and not just straightforward comparison.

Straightforward? Well, perhaps not: it is also worthwhile for readers of this volume to reflect on the kinds of comparison they will choose to undertake. It is important to do this because different types of comparison often yield somewhat different analytical insights. Nancy Green distinguished between three types of comparisons in migration studies—convergent, divergent, and linear. Convergent studies compare migrants from differing origins who arrive and live, and sometimes also interact, in the same destination, whether that is a single city or one country, such as the United States. Divergent studies (much like diaspora studies) instead follow groups of migrants outward from a shared origin to differing destinations and compare their lives across destinations. According to Green, convergent comparisons focus our attention on cultural and national differences. (It is worth noting that most of the comparisons on offer in this volume are convergent comparisons.) Divergent comparisons instead show how culture changes with migration as migrants in differing diasporic locations interact with diverse settings and diverse populations.[13] I attempted what Green calls a linear comparison in my own work on Sicilians; in *From Sicily to Elizabeth Street* and again in *Militants and Migrants*, I compared Sicilians abroad to Sicilians in their homeland in order to gain a more precise sense of the kinds of changes accompanying migration and life in the United States.[14]

Precisely because both Italian and Greek migrations produced rather far-ranging scatterings, diaspora studies can be simultaneously divergent, convergent, and linear in their perspectives. I could also imagine an engaging collaborative study that compared Greek and Italian diasporas. Such a study would include at least two parts: a section that focused on diaspora/ homeland connections in both groups and a second that compared their interactions in a select group of cities in Latin America, Australia, Europe, and North America. As this suggests, I continue to believe that the metaphor of diaspora offers a flexible array of methodologies for researchers seeking to escape the tyranny of methodological singularity.

Finally, scholars adopting any alternative to methodological singularity will also want to ponder the analytical consequences of authorial positionality, if any, on scholarly production. According to Wendy Rowe's entry in the *Sage Encyclopedia of Action Research*, positionality "refers to the stance or positioning of the researcher in relation to the social and political context of the study—the community, the organization or the participant group. The position adopted by a researcher affects every phase of the research process."[15] Although we tend to think of positionality as a concatenation of personalistic and individual traits, disciplinarity may well constitute the most important dimension of positionality in structuring research since disciplinarity very much drives the kind of knowledge scholars can produce. In the case of this collection, the editors very consciously chose to recruit contributors who could compare and connect Greek and Italian migrants from a variety of disciplinary perspectives. The collection's individual chapters have been written by specialists trained in or teaching in the fields of history, art history/archaeology, education, and cultural studies (including, film, television, music, language, and literature studies). The result is in fact a thoroughly interdisciplinary collection, albeit one that will be of most interest to scholars who, like most of the authors, work from within the humanities or within traditions of humanistic scholarship. It thus challenges migration studies, which remains a field dominated to a considerable degree by scholarly production in the disciplines of sociology, history, and anthropology in their more social scientific variations.[16] Because work in the humanities and cultural studies has too often been either excluded, marginalized, or simply ignored within migration studies, I regard the distinctive interdisciplinarity of this collection as especially welcome. That interdisciplinarity might be highlighted more forcefully by authorial reflections on their disciplinary training as a key dimension of their own biography or positionality within migration studies.

A second consideration sometimes overlooked in discussions of authorial positionality is the institutional, and thus also the national, location of contributors. Almost anyone working in transnational, transcultural, postcolonial, or diasporic studies of single groups soon becomes aware of how scholarly production is shaped by institutional location and national scholarly cultures and publication genres (an *essai* in French is most decidedly not a research monograph as Anglo-Saxon speakers of English understand either genre). Scholars in scattered locations often find ways to remain in dialogue with scholars elsewhere, but institutional location can shape both the extent of their interactions, their access to diverse readerships, and even their research assumptions and questions. One straightforward influence of institutional location on scholarship is whether scholars publish their work in English-, Italian-, or Greek-language publications.

The importance of institutional location also reaches beyond language choices. For example, I argue elsewhere that the distinctively American school of immigration studies—one in which history and sociology have dominated and assimilation has provided the central analytical perspective—has been challenged since the 1990s by a more presentist and more social science–oriented European school of migration studies that has chosen instead to study incorporation or integration or mobility itself.[17] At times, too,

I have personally observed competition in diaspora studies between scholars who live and work in the homeland (while also publishing in homeland languages) and scholars living and working in diaspora (where English- and to a lesser extent French-language publication predominates). In this collection, biographical notes allow readers to observe that contributors in Canada, Australia, and (especially) the United States outnumber those in Europe. Even those contributors who are institutionally located in Europe often received at least some portion of their educations in English-speaking countries with significant diaspora populations. One has to suspect that had the editors chosen to publish their contributions in a Greek, Italian, or even a bilingual Greek-Italian collection with a European publisher, the institutional positionality of contributors recruited might have been quite different.

The final, yet also most widely assumed as significant, dimension of authorial positionality is also the most difficult for readers to discern or to assess in this volume, like many others. That dimension is defined by authors' cultural identifications and identities. Published biographical notes rarely include statements of authorial identifications, although these could easily be signaled through statements about the native or scholarly languages authors use for their research or through their inclusion in authors' bios of some lines on personal genealogies of migration, ethnicity, class, or culture. Whether or not to include such reflexive elements in any given chapter remains a choice left entirely to individual authors. In this collection a few contributors do write reflexively in ways that signal identity positions. Still, as this afterword suggests, an older or more secure scholar like me may feel considerably more comfortable in raising issues of personal biography or identification than would younger, more precarious scholars.

Readers are of course always free to speculate about authorial identifications—certainly, I have watched generations of graduate students do this, at least privately—and when they do so they usually base their speculations on authors' surnames. However, surnames can be quite misleading given the way patronymics, intermarriage, and mobility intersect. It would appear, however, that those of Greek and Greek diasporic identifications predominate among editors and chapter authors in this volume, while two self-identified Italian Americans write the preface and afterword. There appear to be fewer Italian or diasporic Italian authors of chapters represented in the volume.

Does this dimension of positionality matter analytically? My own belief is that Italian-speaking Greeks, or for that matter a German or Jewish Argentine with Greek and Italian language skills (real life examples could be named!), can produce absolutely worthwhile scholarship on the two migrations. But I am not convinced this means that disciplinary, institutional, or national locations or cultural identifications of authors are completely irrelevant or that they should be ignored in the biographical paragraphs that establish the bona fides of editors and contributing authors. Scholarly interest in authorial positionality has been powerful enough in recent years that editors and publishers might want to continue to find appropriate ways to include even modest reflections on authorial identifications, especially in collections, like this one, that feature identity and cultural identification as central analytical themes. Even if we leave it to readers to draw their own conclusions about the intellectual and analytical consequences of positionality (and I believe we should), more reflexive author biographies would be a welcome feature of future collections.

NOTES

1. Theodore Saloutos, *They Remember America: The Story of the Repatriated Greek Americans* (Berkeley: University of California Press, 1956).

2. George M. Stephenson, *A History of American Immigration, 1820–1924* (Boston: Ginn, 1926).

3. Oscar Handlin, *The Uprooted: The Epic of the Great Migrations That Made the American People* (Boston: Little, Brown, 1951); Gary Gerstle, *American Crucible: Race and Nation in the Twentieth Century* (Princeton, NJ: Princeton University Press, 2001); Paul Spickard, *Almost All Aliens: Immigration, Race and Colonialism in American History and Identity* (New York: Routledge, 2007).

4. Ronald Takaki, *From Different Shores: Perspectives on Race and Ethnicity: Perspectives on Race and Ethnicity in America* (New York: Oxford University Press, 1988).

5. For obvious reasons, I cannot provide an exhaustive bibliography here. For a few earlier examples of comparative immigration studies, see Josef Barton, *Peasants and Strangers: Italians, Rumanians, and Slovaks in an American City, 1890–1950* (Cambridge, MA: Harvard University Press, 1976); Thomas Kessner, *The Golden Door: Italian and Jewish Mobility in New York City* (New York: Oxford University Press, 1977); John Bodnar, Roger Simon, and

Michael Weber, *Lives of Their Own: Blacks, Italians, and Poles in Pittsburgh, 1900–1960* (Urbana: University of Illinois Press, 1982).

6. James R. Barrett, "Americanization from the Bottom Up: Immigration and the Remaking of the Working Class in the United States, 1880–1930," *Journal of American History* 79, no. 3 (December 1992): 996–1020.

7. Rudolph J. Vecoli, "An Inter-Ethnic Perspective on American Immigration History," *Mid-America* 75 (April–July 1993): 223–35.

8. Nancy L. Green, "The Comparative Method and Poststructural Structuralism: New Perspectives for Migration Studies," *Journal of American Ethnic History* 13, no. 4 (Summer 1994): 3–22.

9. Caroline B. Brettell, "Theorizing Migration in Anthropology," in *Migration Theory: Talking across Disciplines*, 3rd ed., ed. Caroline B. Brettell and James F. Hollifield (New York: Routledge, 2014), 148–197.

10. Rachel Buff, *Immigration and the Political Economy of Home: West Indian Brooklyn and American Indian Minneapolis, 1945–1992* (Berkeley: University of California Press, 2001).

11. Michael Novak, *The Rise of the Unmeltable Ethnics* (New York: Macmillan, 1972).

12. Claudio Fogu, "From *Mare Nostrum* to *Mare Aliorum*: Mediterranean Theory and Mediterraneism in Contemporary Italian Thought," *California Italian Studies* 1, no. 1 (2010): 1–23.

13. This was the approach my coauthors and I took in the "Italians Everywhere" project of the 1990s; see, as one example, Donna R. Gabaccia and Franca Iacovetta, eds., *Women, Gender and Transnational Lives: Italian Workers of the World* (Toronto: University of Toronto Press, 2002).

14. Donna R. Gabaccia, *From Sicily to Elizabeth Street: Housing and Social Change Among Italian Immigrants, 1880–1930* (Albany: SUNY Press, 1984); Donna R. Gabaccia, *Militants and Migrants: Rural Sicilians Become American Workers* (New Brunswick, NJ: Rutgers University Press, 1988). This type of comparison has roots at the University of Chicago Anthropology Department, where both Robert Redfield and Charlotte Gower (Chapman) first undertook, respectively, studies of rural Mexico and Sicily in order to establish a kind of baseline for measuring social cultural change among immigrants in the urban United States.

15. Wendy Rowe, "Positionality," in *The Sage Encyclopedia of Action Research*, ed. David Coghlan and Mary Brydon-Miller (London: Sage, 2014), 62.

16. Donna R. Gabaccia, "Historical Migration Studies: Temporality and Theory," in *Migration Theory: Talking across Disciplines*, 4th ed., ed. Caroline Brettell and James Hollifield (forthcoming).

17. Ibid.

Bibliography

Barrett, James R. "Americanization from the Bottom Up: Immigration and the Remaking of the Working Class in the United States, 1880–1930." *Journal of American History* 79, no. 3 (December 1992): 996–1020.

Barton, Josef. *Peasants and Strangers: Italians, Rumanians, and Slovaks in an American City, 1890–1950*. Cambridge, MA: Harvard University Press, 1976.

Bodnar, John, Roger Simon, and Michael Weber. *Lives of Their Own: Blacks, Italians, and Poles in Pittsburgh, 1900–1960*. Urbana: University of Illinois Press, 1982.

Brettell, Caroline B. "Theorizing Migration in Anthropology." In *Migration Theory: Talking Across Disciplines*, 3rd ed., edited by Caroline B. Brettell and James F. Hollifield. New York: Routledge, 2014.

Buff, Rachel. *Immigration and the Political Economy of Home: West Indian Brooklyn and American Indian Minneapolis, 1945–1992*. Berkeley: University of California Press, 2001.

Fogu, Claudio. "From *Mare Nostrum* to *Mare Aliorum*: Mediterranean Theory and Mediterraneism in Contemporary Italian Thought." *California Italian Studies* 1, no. 1 (2010): 1–23.

Gabaccia, Donna R. *From Sicily to Elizabeth Street: Housing and Social Change Among Italian Immigrants, 1880–1930*. Albany: SUNY Press, 1984.

———. "Historical Migration Studies: Temporality and Theory." In *Migration Theory: Talking across Disciplines*, 4th ed., edited by Caroline Brettell and James Hollifield (forthcoming).

———. *Militants and Migrants: Rural Sicilians Become American Workers*. New Brunswick, NJ: Rutgers University Press, 1988.

Gabaccia, Donna R., and Franca Iacovetta, eds. *Women, Gender and Transnational Lives: Italian Workers of the World*. Toronto: University of Toronto Press, 2002.

Gerstle, Gary. *American Crucible: Race and Nation in the Twentieth Century*. Princeton, NJ: Princeton University Press, 2001.

Green, Nancy L. "The Comparative Method and Poststructural Structuralism: New Perspectives for Migration Studies." *Journal of American Ethnic History* 13, no. 4 (Summer 1994): 3–22.

Handlin, Oscar. *The Uprooted: The Epic of the Great Migrations That Made the American People*. Boston: Little, Brown, 1951.

Kessner, Thomas. *The Golden Door: Italian and Jewish Mobility in New York City*. New York: Oxford University Press, 1977.

Novak, Michael. *The Rise of the Unmeltable Ethnics*. New York: Macmillan, 1972.

Rowe, Wendy. "Positionality." In *The Sage Encyclopedia of Action Research*, edited by David Coghlan and Mary Brydon-Miller. London: Sage, 2014.

Saloutos, Theodore. *They Remember America: The Story of the Repatriated Greek Americans.* Berkeley: University of California Press, 1956.

Spickard, Paul. *Almost All Aliens: Immigration, Race and Colonialism in American History and Identity.* New York: Routledge, 2007.

Stephenson, George M. *A History of American Immigration, 1820–1924.* Boston: Ginn, 1926.

Takaki, Ronald. *From Different Shores: Perspectives on Race and Ethnicity in America.* New York: Oxford University Press, 1988.

Vecoli, Rudolph J. "An Inter-Ethnic Perspective on American Immigration History." *Mid-America* 75 (April–July 1993): 223–35.

ACKNOWLEDGMENTS

We express our appreciation to the editors of the Critical Studies in Italian America series, Nancy Carnevale and Laura Ruberto, who embraced the project from the start. We would like to thank the two anonymous reviewers for their careful reading of the manuscript and valuable insights, from which we have benefited greatly. Special thanks go to the editorial board for their generous support.

CONTRIBUTORS

YIORGOS ANAGNOSTOU is the Miltiadis Marinakis Professor of Modern Greek Language and Culture at Ohio State University. His research interests include modern Greek studies and American ethnic studies, with a focus on Greek America. His published research covers a broad range of subjects, including film, documentary, ethnography, folklore, literature, history, sociology, and public humanities. His work has appeared in *Melus, Diaspora, Ethnicities, Italian American Review, Journal of American Folklore, Journal of Modern Greek Studies*, and *The Classical Bulletin*, among other publications. He is the author of *Contours of White Ethnicity: Popular Ethnography and the Making of Usable Pasts in Greek America* (Ohio University Press, 2009), whose translation in Greek is forthcoming from Nisos Publishers. He is the editor of the online journal *Ergon: Greek/American Arts and Letters* (http://ergon.scienzine.com/). He writes regularly for the Greek and Greek American media.

ELEFTHERIA ARAPOGLOU has been teaching in the American Studies department at UC Davis since 2012. Before that she taught at Aristotle University and Anatolia College in Greece. She has received several fellowships and scholarships from the Fulbright Program, the Friends of the Princeton University Library, and the Greek State Scholarship Foundation, among others. She has coedited six volumes and has contributed as an assistant editor to two special issues of the journal *GRAMMA*. Her monograph *A Bridge over the Balkans: Demetra Vaka Brown and the Tradition of "Women's Orients"* was published by Gorgias Press in 2011, while her most recent publications are *Mobile Narratives: Travel, Migration, and Transculturation* (Routledge, 2013) and *Racial and Ethnic Identities in the Media* (Palgrave Macmillan, 2016).

ANGELYN BALODIMAS-BARTOLOMEI is a professor in the School of Education at North Park University–Chicago and coordinator of the ESL/Bilingual Teachers Endorsement and MALLC programs. In both Greece and America, she earned degrees in Greek studies and social work; Greek pedagogy; linguistics/ESL; and comparative international education and policy studies. Having received numerous grants, Angie has performed extensive studies on Greek Americans and Italian Americans, southern Italian Griki, Greek Romaniote Jews, and the endangered Colognoro dialect of Tuscany. She has also examined Holocaust education in Greece, anti-Mafia education, Italian images in foreign language textbooks, and Italian American statue makers. Her latest work focuses on the Greek communities of Europe.

JIM COCOLA is an associate professor in the Department of Humanities and Arts at Worcester Polytechnic Institute. He is the author of *Places in the Making: A Cultural Geography of American Poetry* (University of Iowa Press, 2016). A past chair of the Modern Language Association's Forum on Italian American Language, Literature, and Culture, he has published related work in journals including *Italian Americana*, *Studies in American Jewish Literature*, and *VIA: Voices in Italian Americana*.

FRANCESCA DE LUCIA taught at Minzu University in Beijing from 2016 to 2020 and previously worked as associate professor at Zhejiang Normal University of China in Jinhua. Her book *Italian American Cultural Fictions: From Diaspora to Globalization* was published by Peter Lang in 2017. Her research focuses on ethnicity and American identity in literature, with a particular concentration on the work of Italian American and Chinese American authors.

DONNA R. GABACCIA is professor of history emerita at the University of Toronto. She previously served as director of the Immigration History Research Center at the University of Minnesota. She is the author of many books and articles on class, gender, and ethnicity in American immigration history, on migration in global history, and on Italian emigration around the world. She is a past president of the Social Science History Association and writes often about interdisciplinarity in migration studies. She is a descendant of Italian migrants and the first person in her family to obtain a higher education.

FRED L. GARDAPHÉ is distinguished professor of English and Italian/American studies at Queens College/CUNY and the John D. Calandra Italian American Institute. He is a Fulbright fellow (University of Salerno, 2011) and past president of the Italian American Studies Association (formerly AIHA), MELUS, and the Working Class Studies Association. His books include *Italian Signs, American Streets* (Duke University Press, 1996), *From Wiseguys to Wise Men* (Routledge, 2006), *The Art of Reading Italian Americana* (Bordighera, 2011), and *Read 'Em and Reap* (Bordighera, 2017). He is cofounder and coeditor of *VIA: Voices in Italian Americana*, editor of the Italian American Culture Series of SUNY Press, and associate editor of the *Fra Noi*.

YIORGOS D. KALOGERAS is professor emeritus of American ethnic and minority literature at Aristotle University in Thessaloniki, Greece. He is the author, coauthor, or editor of twelve books, and he has produced numerous articles in Greek and English, primarily in the field of Greek American studies. *Ethnic Resonances in Performance, Literature and Identity*, coedited with Cathy Waegner (Taylor and Francis, 2020), and *Palimpsests in Ethnic and Postcolonial Literatures and Cultures: Surfacing Histories*, coedited with Jopi Nyman (Palgrave Macmillan, 2021), are his latest publications. He is the founder of HELAAS (The Hellenic Association of American Studies). He also founded and edited *GRAMMA: Journal of Theory and Criticism* (1993–2014). Since 2012, he has been the president of MESEA, the Society for Multi-Ethnic Studies: Europe and the Americas.

KOSTIS KOURELIS is an architectural historian who specializes in the archaeology of the Mediterranean and how it shapes modern notions of identity, space, and aesthetics. His recent fieldwork focuses on the archaeology of labor, housing, and modern immigration. He directs archaeological surveys of deserted villages and refugee camps in Greece, as well as ethnic slums, temporary housing, and internment camps in the United States. He is associate professor of art history at Franklin & Marshall College.

PANAYOTIS LEAGUE is assistant professor of ethnomusicology at Florida State University and director of the Center for Music of the Americas. His research has appeared in *Ethnomusicology*, the *Journal of Modern Greek Studies*, *Journal of Greek Media and Culture*, and *The Harvard Review of Latin America*. His monograph *Echoes of the Great Catastrophe: Re-Sounding Anatolian Greekness in Diaspora* was published in 2021.

STEFANO LUCONI teaches US history at the University of Padua in Italy. His research interests focus on immigration to the United States, with specific attention to Italian Americans' voting behavior and transformation of ethnic identity. His publications include *From Paesani to White Ethnics: The Italian Experience in Philadelphia* (SUNY Press, 2001) and *The Italian-American Vote in Providence, Rhode Island, 1916–1948* (Fairleigh Dickinson University Press, 2004). His most recent book is *L'anima nera degli Stati Uniti: Quattrocento anni di presenza afro-americana* (CLEUP, 2020).

MICHAIL C. MARKODIMITRAKIS is an associate liaison expert for the UNHCR in Greece. His ethnographic field research focuses on host countries, policies on migration, and the experiences of displaced populations in host communities, along with representations of ethnicity, nationality, and racism in digital media and archives. He has published book chapters and articles on popular culture, with an ongoing interest in intermedial representations of the Other, abject fear, horror, and embodiments of evil. He has taught modules on academic research and writing, ethnic studies, Anglophone literature, and Greek/English for speakers of other languages.

THEODORA PATRONA is affiliated with the School of English of Aristotle University in Thessaloniki, Greece, as Special Teaching Fellow (EDIP). She previously taught at the Hellenic Mediterranean University (ELMEPA) in Heraklion, Crete. She holds the 2010 American Italian Historical Association (AIHA) Memorial Fellowship and the 2012 Tsakopoulos Hellenic Collection Fellowship. She has numerous articles and chapters on Italian American and Greek American literature and film and regularly reviews for American and European journals. She is the author of *Return Narratives: Ethnic Space in Late-Twentieth Century Greek American and Italian American Literature* (Fairleigh Dickinson University Press, 2017).

ANDONIS PIPEROGLOU is an adjunct research fellow at the Griffith Centre for Social and Cultural Research, Griffith University, Australia. He is a cultural historian who examines the interrelationship between migration, race, and ethnicity across settler-colonial worlds and is interested in bringing Mediterranean and Pacific histories into conversation. He has published widely in various scholarly outputs, including the *Journal of Modern Greek Studies*, the *Journal of Australian Studies, History Australia, Ergon: Greek/American Arts and Letters, Australian Historical Studies,* and the *Australian Journal of Politics and History.* He currently serves on the Executive of the International Australian Studies Association and was recently awarded an Australian National University Herbert and Valmae Freilich Early Career Research Grant. Andonis is also a cofounder of the Australian Migration History Network, Australia's chief national body for migration history.

FEVRONIA K. SOUMAKIS taught in the history and education program at Teachers College, Columbia University, until 2019. She is currently an adjunct assistant professor in the European Languages and Literatures Department at Queens College, City University of New York. Her academic research interests include the history of education, immigration and ethnicity, and religion and education. She has recently completed a coedited volume titled *Educating Greek Americans: Historical Perspectives and Contemporary Pathways* (Palgrave Macmillan, 2020) and was past Program Chair for Division F, History and Historiography, of the American Educational Research Association.

SOSTENE MASSIMO ZANGARI specializes in US ethnic writing between the wars. He has published articles on Herman Melville, Richard Wright, Michael Gold, and John Fante. He has coauthored two studies on American culture and literature, *Americana: Storie e culture degli Stati Uniti dalla A alla Z* (Il Saggiatore, 2012), and *Guida alla letteratura degli Stati Uniti* (Odoya, 2014).

INDEX

Abbot, Megan, 212, 217, 225, 232, 234–36
Addonizio, Hugh J., 48
Afentakis, Sofronios, 123
affiliation/filiation, 11, 188, 309, 312, 320n
affirmative action, 46–47, 58–59
African Americans, 272, 275, 279–81, 283–84
Agnew, Spiro T., 48–51, 53–61, 73
Ahmed, Leila, 92
Albanians, 126–27
Aldrich, Robert, 226
Alex, Gus, x
Alioto, Joseph, 54
American cultural studies, 186
American Dream, 16–17, 274, 285
American Independent Party, 55
American Italian Historical Association, vii
American Studies Association, 185
Americanism, 287
Americanization, ix, 16
Anagnostou, Yiorgos, viii, 186, 206, 213, 214, 216, 234, 236
Anderson, Benedict, 355
Anglo American identity, 73–76, 81, 94n
Ann Arbor, Michigan, 351–52
Arapoglou, Eleftheria, 13
Armenians, 126
Asia Minor, 14, 253–55
Asian American identity, 73–74, 77, 91–93

Asian Americans, 91–92, 355; Chinese, 73, 84, 91; Filipinos, 73, 91; Japanese, 73, 91; Koreans, 91; Turks, 77; Vietnamese, 91
assimilation, 1, 16–17, 324–26, 330, 335–36, 340–41, 343; segmented assimilation, 340–41
Astoria, NY, 285
Athens, Maria, 234, 236
Atlanta, 133
Atlas, Charles, 73
Australia, 10–11, 23–27

Bakhtinian dialogism, 188
Bal, Mieke, 243
Balodimas-Bartolomei, Angelyn, 12
Baltimore, 125
Balzano, Michael P., Jr., 61
Bard, Frederick, 119
Baroni, Geno, 61–62
Barre, Vermont, 116
Barrett, James, 356
Batuman, Elif, 92
Bellotti, Francis X., 51
belonging, 326
Bezzerides, A. I., 226, 235–36; *Thieves' Market*, 228, 235
bilingual education, 142–43, 156–57, 162–63, 166, 169, 173–74, 175, 177, 180
Black Power, 46, 48, 51

373

Index

Bona, Mary Jo, 186
Boston, 123, 130, 238–64
Boston Globe, 52
Bourne, Randolph, 185, 205, 355
Braudel, Fernand, 74
Brettell, Caroline, 18n, 356
British Empire, 72
Brookline, Massachusetts, 133
Brown, H. Rap, 51
Bryant, Dorothy Calvetti, 21, 236
Buffalo, 105
Bulgarians, 127
Burton, Howard William, 117
Bush, George H. W., 62
busing, 47–48, 58, 61

Cain, James M., 211, 231
Calotychos, Vangelis, 186
Cambridge Companion to Transnational American Literature, 186
Canadians, 118
Capiello, Rosa, 75, 95n
capital, 327, 330, 341
Caravacos, Emmanuel, 125
Carmichael, Stokely, 51
Cassavetes, John, 94n
Catholic archdioceses, 105–6, 112, 115, 122, 126, 130–31
Catholic Church, 149–50, 156–57, 179, 181
Catholic identity, 77, 83, 85, 88
Catina's Haircut: A Novel in Stories, 188, 191–94, 197–98, 201–5
Cavafy, C. P., 96n
censorship, 88. *See also* Motion Picture Production Code
Chandler, Raymond, 210, 212, 217, 222, 226, 231, 234, 236; *The Long Goodbye*, 218; "The Simple Art of Murder," 211, 234, 236
Chapin, Geracimos Helen, 17n
Cher, 339, 342
Chesterton, G. K., 210
Chiang, Kai-shek, 222
Chicago, 105, 107, 115, 120, 123, 125, 128

Christie, Agatha, 210–11
Ciardi, John, 73, 77–78, 82
Cleveland, Ohio, 105, 119
Cocola, Jim, 11
collective memory, 189
Collins, Wilkie, 210
comedy, 324, 339, 344; ethnic, 335, 342
commonalities (between Italian Americans and Greek Americans), 5–8, 14, 16
comparative approach (comparison), 3–9; methods, 355–58
Conzen, Kathleen, 17n
Corso, Gregory, 11, 73, 76, 78–82, 91–92, 95n, 96n, 99
Corso, Paola, 13, 188
cultural: criticism, 201; heritage, 189; studies, 353, 356, 359
Cuomo, Mario, 73
Cutter, Weston, 234–36

Dagit, Henry, 116
Dago, 10, 23, 25–26, 28–31, 35, 37–39
D'Alessandro, Thomas, III, 58
Damaskinos, Bishop, 132
dance, 238–64
D'Angelo, Pascal, 75
D'Ascenzo, Nicola, 123, 125
Davis, J. Madison, 212, 234, 236
DeLillo, Don, 78
De Lucia, Francesca, 14, 236
democratic party, 53–54, 61
demographics, 6
DeSalvo, Louise, 186
Detroit, 105
dialogic: microethnography, 15, 242; transculturalism, 188
diaspora, 186, 353, 357–61
Dinwiddie, Emily, 108
di Prima, Diane, 73, 77–78, 82
disciplinarity, 358–59
discursive narrative practices, 188, 196
dissimilarities (between Italian Americans and Greek Americans), 6–8, 16

documentaries, 16
Dokos, Nikolaos, 116
domestic, 324, 326, 329, 330, 332–37, 342
Doyle, Arthur Conan, 210–11
Dukakis, Michael, 62, 73
Durang, Edwin Forrest, 116

educational institutions, 12
Eisenhower, Dwight D., 61
emigration, 45, 72–73, 75–77, 82, 369. *See also* immigration
English, George Brooks, 234, 236
Epic of Gilgamesh, 80–81
ethnic: culture, 324, 326–27; education, 12; family, 13; gender roles, 13, 17; kinship, 13; literature, 13–14; music, 13–15; whiteness, 263
ethnicity, 11, 62, 66, 73–78, 84, 86, 88, 90–94, 98n, 324–32, 336–37, 339–43
ethnoracial Otherness (of Italian Americans and Greek Americans), 3
Eugenides, Jeffrey, 76, 78

family, 192, 324, 326–28, 330–33, 335–40, 342–43
Fante, John, 215
Farrant Bevilacqua, Winifred, 219, 234, 236
father, 324, 327–29, 330, 332, 336, 338
feminism, 326
feminist resistance, 192
Ferraro, Geraldine, 62
filmic representations (of Italian Americans and Greek Americans), 11, 16, 17
Firmani, B. G., 92
Fisher Fishkin, Shelley, 185–86
food, 106, 110
Fortress Europe, 300, 315n
Franciosa, Anthony, 83
Frangos, 18n
Fra Noi (Chicago), 60
Frears, Stephen, 212
French, 116, 118, 126

Gans, Herbert, 214
García, Carmen Mendez, 212, 232, 234–36
Gardaphé, Fred, 186
Gary, Indiana, 133
Gazzara, Ben, 94n
Germans, 106, 116, 121–22, 126
Gerstle, Gary, 355
Giallelis, Stathis, 83
Gibson, Kenneth A., 48
Gifford, Barry, 234, 236
Giunta, Edvige, 186–87
Glazer, Nathan, 271, 284
The Godfather, 289
Gordon, Bernard, 278
Goyal, Yogita, 186
Greece (regions of), 79–81; Aegean, 79; Athens, 79, 81; Crete, 79
Greek: government, 147, 151, 158, 160–61, 164, 167–68; language instruction, 151, 159, 163, 167–68, 173; schools, 147, 155, 157, 160, 168
Greek Americans in television, 285
Greek Orthodox: archdiocese, 105–6, 127, 131–32, 146, 151, 159, 167, 171, 174–77, 180; architecture, 12–13
Greek War of Independence, 110
Greekness, 275, 292
Green, Nancy, 356–58
Grillo, Giacomo, 55
Guarino, Philip A., 55
Guglielmo, Thomas, 213, 234

Hamilton, Cynthia, 211, 225, 234, 236
Hammett, Dashiell, 210–11, 215, 217–18, 222, 226, 231–32, 237; *The Maltese Falcon*, 212
Handlin, Oscar, 355
Hansen, Marcus, 355
Hansen, Theophilus, 120
happiness, 324, 326, 336–41, 343
hard-boiled detective novel, 14
Herman, Joanna Clapps, 78
Hicks, Louise Day, 48, 59
Himes, Chester, 212

historical experiences (of Italian Americans and Greek Americans), 3
Ho Chi Minh, 222
Homer, 78, 81
Humphrey, Hubert H., 54, 57
hybridity, 186

Iakovos, Archbishop, 127
identity constitution, 188; and identification, 352–53, 355, 360–61
Il Popolo Italiano (Philadelphia), 54, 56
Il Progresso Italo-Americano (New York City), 54, 56–58, 61
immigrant subjectivity, 192
immigrants, 323–24, 327–28, 330–31, 335, 340–41
immigration, 75–78, 93 (*see also* emigration); studies, 352, 354–55, 359–60
Immigration History Research Center, 355
institutional location, 359–60
intercultural contact zones, 186
interdisciplinarity, 353, 359
Irish, 106, 111–12, 116, 120–22, 126–28, 130, 134
Irish American identity, 77, 83, 94n
Iron Mountain, Michigan, 116
Irwin, John T., 210, 236
Italian: government, 148, 152–54, 162; language, 141–43, 149–50, 152–54, 161–62, 165–69; language instruction, 152–53, 161, 166–67
Italian Americans in television, 288–89
Italian American Studies Association, vii
Italy, 77–82, 352; regions of, 77–82; Basilicata, 78; Campania, 77, 82; Lazio, 82; Rome, 79–81

Jacobson, Matthew Frye, 3, 18n, 231, 237
Jewison, Norman, 325–26, 344
Jewish American identity, 82–84
Jews, 109, 111, 121, 132–33
Judgment at Nuremberg, 275
John D. Calandra Italian American Institute, viii

Johnson, Lyndon B., 50, 52, 54, 57–58
Johnson-Reed Act, 240

Kalamaras, Vasso, 75, 95n
Kallen, Horace, 355
Kalogeras, Yiorgos, viii, x, 16, 17n, 186, 226, 235, 237
Kanelos, George, vii
Karanikas, Alexander, 235, 237
Karas, Paul, x
Kausokalyves painters, 123
Kazan, Elia, 11, 73, 75, 82–84, 87–92, 94n, 96n–98n, 99
Kennedy, John F., 52, 57
Kessler, David, 207
King, 276
King, Martin Luther, Jr., 50, 58, 105, 276–77, 280
kinoitis, ix
Klironomos, Martha, 186
Kojak, 15
Kontoglou, Photis, 123–24
Kourelis, Kostis, 12–13
Kramer, Stanley, 275
Kübler-Ross, Elisabeth, 207
Ku Klux Klan, 77

labor, viii
Lady Gaga, 92
La Farge, John, 123
LaGumina, Salvatore, 221
Lalami, Laila, 92
Lamerica, 299
language retention, 12
La Parola del Popolo (Chicago), 61
Latin American Identity, 77, 91
League, Panayiotis, 13
Lebanese, 126
Lenz, Günter, 187, 206
Leontis, Artemis, 207
Let Me Explain You, 188–91, 194–201, 204–5
Lincoln, Bruce, 8–9, 18n
Liontas, Annie, 13, 188–89

literary representations (of Italian Americans and Greek Americans), 13–14
Lombardo, Maria, 18n
Londos, Jim, 73
Loukakis, Angelo, 75, 95n
Lovatt, George I., 116
Lowell, 118
Luconi, Stefano, 11, 18n
lynching, 84, 89–90

Madonna, 92
Mafia, 16, 289
Magna Grecia, vii–viii
Mahoney, George P., 48
Maisano, Anthony A., 55
mamma, 332–34, 337–38
Mangione, Jerre, 221
Mann, Abby, 275–76, 279
Mao Zedong, 221–22
Marcus, Stephen, 211, 234, 237
The Marcus-Nelson Murders, 274, 279–80, 288
Markodimitrakis, Michail C., 16–17
marriage, 330, 332–40
masculinity, 330, 332, 336
McCormick, Edward, 51
Mediterranean (European) American(s), 1–2, 4–5, 9, 11, 91–93, 94n; Albanian, 92, 94; Anatolian, 82–83, 91; Balkan, 81; Calabrian, 73, 82, 91; Croatian, 94; Egyptian, 81, 91; family dynamics of, 73, 77–78; identity, 72–74, 76–78, 82–83, 87–92, 94, 97n; Levantine, 81; Maghrebi, 75, 80–81, 93; Mashriqi, 75, 91, 93; Mesopotamian, 81; Near Eastern, 78, 81, 92; North African, 77, 80, 91, 93; racialization of, 76–77, 86, 97n; Romanian, 94; Serbian, 94; Sicilian, 73, 77, 82–85, 87–91, 97n; studies, 357; Syrian, 77, 90, 92, 94; Turkish, 77, 90, 92
Mediterranean Australian identity, 75–76, 95n

melting pot, 185
MELUS, viii
MESEA, viii
methodology, 354–58
Meyer, Lily, 234, 237
middle class, 330–31, 335, 339, 342–43
Miller, Arthur, 96n
Milwaukee, 105, 115, 133
Minneapolis, 105
miscegenation, 87–88, 97n
monolingualism, 354
Moonstruck, 17, 323–28, 335, 344–45, 348
Morley, Christopher, 107–9, 134
Moss, Richard, 17n
Motion Picture Production Code, 87–90, 97n. *See also* censorship
Moynihan, Daniel, 271, 284
multiculturalism, 325–26, 355
multilingual identity, 244–48
multilingualism, 354–55
multivocality (and the immigrant experience), 190, 197
Muskie, Edmund, 54
Mussolini, Benito, 219–22
My Big Fat Greek Wedding, 17, 325–27, 336, 338, 343

narrative polymorphy, 188–89
Native American identity, 94n
Naxos, 351, 353
network (and the immigration experience), 197, 207
Neumann, John Bishop, 128
Newark, 130
New England, 14
New Orleans, 106
New York, 105, 107, 123, 125, 127, 271, 275, 279, 283–84
New York Times, 50, 52
Nixon, Richard M., 11, 49–51, 53–57, 59–62
Northern United States, 78, 83, 88, 95n; Connecticut, 78; Massachusetts, 83; New Jersey, 78; New York, 78, 83, 95n

Novak, Michael, x, 49, 75, 98n, 213, 272, 357
Nuovomondo, 299
Nyfes, 299

oliveface, 82–83
Onassis Foundation, viii
On Grief and Grieving, 207
Ottoman Empire, 72, 75

palimpsest, 309, 310
panethnicity, 355
Panunzio, Constantine, 221
Papadaki, Kallia, 18n, 78
Papanikolas, Helen, 77
Pappas, Thomas A., 53
paraethnicity, x, 11, 76, 78
patriarchy, 324, 327, 330, 332, 335–36
Patrona, Theodora, viii, 17n, 18n
Peabody, Endicott, 51
Pearson, Drew, 54
peasants, 7–8
Peckinpah, Sam, 212
Pelecanos, George, 14, 210–12, 214–16, 224, 226, 229, 231, 234–36; *The Cut*, 225, 228, 230, 234–35; *A Firing Offense*, 225–27, 230, 235, 237
Perates, John W., 125
performativity, 73, 301, 314–16, 331, 336
"Persephone's Daughters," 187
Philadelphia, 107, 112–14, 116, 123, 125, 128, 130–31
PIGS (Polish, Italians, Greeks, and Slavs), 49
Piperoglou, Andonis, 10
Pirrone, Gino M., 56
Pittsburgh, 115
Pituková, Veronica, 218, 234, 237
pluralism, 355
Plymouth Rock, 271
Poe, Edgar Allan, 210
Polish, 109, 111, 115, 120, 129
Pollack, Sidney, 277
polymorphy, x

polyvocal (narrative) organization, 198
population exchange, 240
Porter, Dennis, 211, 237
Portland, Maine, 125
positionality, 358–61
postethnicity, x, 15–16, 301–5, 309, 314–15, 319
Post-Gazette (Boston), 53, 60
presidential elections, 11
Priestman, Martin, 234, 237
probationary whites, 3, 5
Protestant, 106, 110–12, 120–22, 126, 132
public school language instruction, 141–42, 151–53, 156–57, 159, 161–63, 165

racial slur, 23, 25, 37
racialization, 27, 38, 75–77, 86, 92, 97n
Raphael, Amy, 235, 237
Reagan, Ronald, 62
reflexivity, 360
regional variations (of Italian Americans and Greek Americans), 3, 7–8
relational models of subjectivity, 198–99
religious affiliations, 7
religious architecture, 12–13
repatriation, 352
Republican Party, 56, 60
research design, 353
Rexha, Bebe, 92
Riis, Jacob, 108
The Rise of the Unmeltable Ethnics, 206
Risorgimento, 110
Rizopoulos, Perry Giuseppe, 17n
Rizzo, Frank, 48, 73
Rockefeller, Nelson A., 52, 60
Romanians, 126–27
Roosevelt, Franklin Delano, 220, 234
rootedness, 198, 201, 205
Rourke, Henry L, 118
Ruskin, John, 111
Russians, 106, 119, 122, 126–27
Russoniello, Luigi, 115
Ryan, Patrick Archbishop, 114–15

Sacco and Vanzetti, 281
Said, Edward, 92
Saint Paul, Minnesota, 130
Salt Lake City, 117–18
San Francisco, 127
Savalas, Telly, 15, 273, 277–78, 284–85, 288, 292–93; Greekness of, 275, 293
Sayers, Dorothy, 211
Scambray, Kenneth, 215, 234, 237
Schlesinger, Arthur, 355
Scranton, 115, 116
Second Vatican Council, 111
self-representation (of Italian Americans and Greek Americans), 6, 9
Serbians, 126–27
settler colonial, 25, 371
settlers, 29
sexuality, 327, 334
Sicilians, 352, 358
Sikelianos, Eleni, 78
Sim, Stuart, 226, 235, 237
similarities (between the Italian and Greek ethnic groups), 7–8
"single group" approach, 4–6
skin privilege, 72. *See also* whiteness
Smith, Joanna M., 218, 234, 237
Società del Mutuo Succorso, ix
solidarity, 75, 78, 91–92, 94, 105, 236
Southern United States, 77, 83–84, 88, 90, 97n; Alabama, 77, 83, 97n; Mississippi, 84, 88, 90
Soumakis, Fevronia, 12
Spanish, 120, 126; Empire, 72
Spillane, Mickey, 226
Springfield Republican, 52
Stamford, Connecticut, 133
Stansberry, Domenic, 14, 210–12, 214–16, 219–21, 224–25, 230, 234; *Chasing the Dragon*, 222–23, 232, 235, 237; *The Last Days of Il Duce*, 217–18, 221–23, 226, 231–35, 237; *Manifesto for the Dead*, 212; "Noir Manifesto," 212
stereotypes, 16, 273–74, 289–90, 291–92
subjectivity, 194

Supreme Court, 279–80
symbolic ethnicity, 73
symbolic ethnics, 6
Syrians, 126

Takaki, Ron, 355
Talese, Gay, 73, 77
Tarpon Springs, 238
television; 15, audience, 275–76; "intimacy," 273, 278–79, 292; "relevance," 272–73, 276, 279
territorialization, 186
Thompson, Jim, 212, 226, 236
Thompson, W. Stuart, 133
Three Days of the Condor, 277
Tiffany, Louis Comfort, 123
Till, Emmett, 84, 90
transcultural, 200, 204; affiliations, 192; American studies, 185, 187; negotiation, 203
transnational, 23, 30; American Studies, 185, 187; Mediterraneans, 5
Triantaphillou, Constantine, 125
Trump, Donald J., 49
Tsavalas, Theodore, 125
Turkey, 72, 75, 90, 119

Ukrainians, 126–27
US Southeastern Europeans, 5, 9, 11

Valentino, Rudolph, 88
Vardalos, Nia, 325–26, 335
Vecoli, Rudolph J., 214, 234, 237, 352, 356
Viscusi, Robert, 75–76, 221, 235, 237
visual culture, 15
Volpe, John A., 49–57, 59–62
voting patterns, 11

Wallace, George C., 50, 55, 58–59
Ward, Joseph D., 51
Washington, DC, 112
Washington Post, 54
Watergate, 272, 277, 284
Waters, Mary, 214

weak comparisons, 8–9
wedding, 328–29, 341
Western United States, 77, 83; California, 83; Utah, 77
White, Kevin H., 59–60
white ethnicity, 3, 5, 272, 282, 331, 339; savior, 323, 344
whiteness, 31, 40, 75, 84, 86, 92–93. *See also* skin privilege
Whitman, Christine Todd, 57
Williams, Tennessee, 82, 84–87, 89–90, 96n–98n
Winterbottom, Michael, 212
wop (slur), 84–86
Wright, Frank Lloyd, 133

Yans-McLauglin, Virginia, 352

Zangari, Sostene Massimo, 15
Zorba, 292

Critical Studies in Italian America

Nancy C. Carnevale and Laura E. Ruberto, *series editors*

Joseph Sciorra, ed., *Italian Folk: Vernacular Culture in Italian-American Lives*
Loretta Baldassar and Donna R. Gabaccia, eds., *Intimacy and Italian Migration: Gender and Domestic Lives in a Mobile World*
Simone Cinotto, ed., *Making Italian America: Consumer Culture and the Production of Ethnic Identities*
Luisa Del Giudice, ed., *Sabato Rodia's Towers in Watts: Art, Migrations, Development*
Nancy Caronia and Edvige Giunta. eds., *Personal Effects: Essays on Memoir, Teaching, and Culture in the Work of Louise DeSalvo*
Teresa Fiore, *Pre-Occupied Spaces: Remapping Italy's Emigration, Immigration, and (Post-)Colonialism*
Giuliana Muscio, *Napoli/New York/Hollywood: Film between Italy and the United States*
Danielle Battisti, *Whom We Shall Welcome: Italian Americans and Immigration Reform, 1945–1965*
Yiorgos Anagnostou, Yiorgos Kalogeras, and Theodora Patrona, eds., *Redirecting Ethnic Singularity: Italian Americans and Greek Americans in Conversation*

www.ingramcontent.com/pod-product-compliance
Lightning Source LLC
Chambersburg PA
CBHW032024290426
44110CB00012B/658